NOT TO BE
TAKEN AWAY

British – and European – Social Attitudes

the
15th report

Social and Community Planning Research (SCPR) is an independent, non-profit social research institute. It has a large professional staff together with its own interviewing and coding resources. Some of SCPR's work - such as the survey reported in this book - is initiated by the institute itself and grant-funded by research councils or foundations. Other work is initiated by government departments, local authorities or quasi-government organisations to provide information on aspects of social or economic policy. SCPR also works frequently with other institutes and academics. Founded in 1969 and now Britain's largest social research institute, SCPR has a high reputation for the standard of its work in both qualitative and quantitative research. SCPR has a Survey Methods Centre and, with Nuffield College Oxford, houses the Centre for Research into Elections and Social Trends (CREST), which is an ESRC Research Centre. It also houses, with Southampton University, the Centre for Applied Social Surveys (CASS), an ESRC Resource Centre, two main functions of which are to run courses in survey methods and to establish and administer an electronic social survey question bank.

The contributors

Duane Alwin
Professor and Chair of Sociology and Program Director, the Institute for Social Research, University of Michigan, Ann Arbor, USA

Michael Braun
Senior Project Director, German General Social Survey (ALLBUS), ZUMA, Germany

Lindsay Brook
Research Director at SCPR and Co-director of the *British Social Attitudes* survey series

Caroline Bryson
Research Director at SCPR and Co-director of the *British Social Attitudes* survey series

John Curtice
Professor of Politics and Director of the Social Statistics Laboratory, University of Strathclyde

Russell Dalton
Professor, University of California

Geoffrey Evans
Faculty Fellow, Nuffield College, Oxford

Roger Jowell
Director of SCPR and Co-director of the *British Social Attitudes* survey series; Visiting Professor at the London School of Economics and Political Science

Max Kaase
Research Professor, Wissenshaftszentrum, Berlin

David McCrone
Professor of Sociology, University of Edinburgh, and Convenor of the Unit for the Study of Government in Scotland

Kenneth Newton
Professor of Government, University of Essex; Executive Director of the European Consortium for Political Research

Alison Park
Research Director at SCPR and Co-director of the *British Social Attitudes* survey series

Alan Renwick
PhD student, Department of Political Science, Central European University, Budapest

Robert Rohrschneider
Associate Professor, Indiana University

Helen Russell
Research Officer, The Economic and Social Research Institute, Ireland

Jacqueline Scott
Assistant Director of Research and Fellow of Queens' College, University of Cambridge

Paula Surridge
Lecturer in Sociology, University of Aberdeen

Peter Taylor-Gooby
Professor of Social Policy, University of Kent

Katarina Thomson
Research Director at SCPR and Co-director of the *British Social Attitudes* survey series

Gábor Tóka
Assistant Professor, Department of Political Science, Central European University, Budapest

British – and European – Social Attitudes
the 15th report

How Britain Differs

Edited by
Roger Jowell
John Curtice
Alison Park
Lindsay Brook
Katarina Thomson
& Caroline Bryson

Ashgate

Aldershot • Brookfield USA • Singapore • Sydney

Published by
Ashgate Publishing Limited
Gower House
Croft Road
Aldershot
Hants GU11 3HR
England

Ashgate Publishing Company
Old Post Road
Brookfield
Vermont 05036
USA

ISSN 0267 6869
ISBN 1 84014 046 1

Printed and bound by Athenaeum Press, Ltd., Gateshead, Tyne & Wear.

Contents

CHAPTER 3.   WHAT PEOPLE EXPECT FROM THE STATE: PLUS ÇA CHANGE ...

by Max Kaase and Kenneth Newton **39**

CHAPTER 4.   COMMITMENT TO THE WELFARE STATE

by Peter Taylor-Gooby **57**

Introduction

This volume describes and interprets the social, moral, political and economic attitudes held not only by people in Britain, but also by people in a number of other European countries, mainly fellow-members of the European Union. Recent events in Britain and Europe make this an especially important time to take stock of how people in the EU think and feel about their world and themselves.

The change in government in Britain on May 1 1997 brought about a perceptibly warmer relationship between Britain and the EU. Now Britain was prepared to sign up to the long-resisted Social Chapter, to endorse the Amsterdam Treaty and to embrace the European Convention on Human Rights. True, there remains a measure of British reserve in respect of a common currency and a 'passport-free' EU, but at least some old frontiers have been breached and others are looking less impregnable than before.

With government attitudes towards the EU changing, what then has become of British public attitudes? We know that during the 1980s, when Mrs. Thatcher's government was becoming more and more openly Eurosceptic, so public attitudes seemed not only to resist the trend but to become increasingly sympathetic to a stronger relationship with the EU. What now? As Geoffrey Evans reports in Chapter 9, with a government that is now more sympathetic towards the EU, public opposition or suspicion seems perversely to have been on the rise. His chapter charts the recent cooling in British public sympathy for the EU - through BSE and beyond - but stresses nonetheless the very small proportion of people nowadays who advocate actual British withdrawal from the EU.

The British public may feel ambivalent about the EU, but is there anything in particular that sets them apart from their counterparts in mainland Europe?

Do they feel differently about family life, or work, or social *mores*? Is Britain distinctive from the rest of the EU in its attitudes - more insular perhaps? Or is it more the case that *all* nations differ profoundly from one another in different ways? These questions are at the heart of this book.

As David McCrone and Paula Surridge report in Chapter 1, the British certainly stand out in the degree of pride they attach to their country's history, scoring relatively highly on other aspects of national pride too. The Germans in contrast, with their twentieth century history still clearly in their minds, steadfastly resist expressing too much pride in Germany and its achievements. In general, however, notwithstanding their different histories, economies and political climates, most nations do have quite similar levels of patriotism and nationalism, as well as shared views on what counts in defining their national identity. Moreover, feelings of national pride are by no means all positive. In every country, individuals with high levels of national pride also tended to have negative attitudes towards 'outsiders', particularly immigrants and other 'outgroups'.

Relative consensus between nations is reported by Max Kaase and Kenneth Newton in Chapter 3, who examine public attitudes towards the role and the scope of the state in Britain and western Germany. They find no evidence of support either for a 'rolling back' of the frontiers of the state or for any extension of its scope. While the British are a little more supportive of state intervention than are the west Germans, neither deviate much from a remarkable cross-national consensus within the EU.

In Chapter 4, Peter Taylor-Gooby examines public attitudes towards the welfare state more closely, examining how much support there is in various countries for different types of welfare provision. Although he too finds many similarities in western Europe, he also discovers some unexpected national differences - in particular that the German public's commitment to its welfare state is now less strong than elsewhere, including Britain. Despite evidence of a slight decline over time in several different countries in public support for a strong welfare state, Taylor-Gooby assembles persuasive evidence against the notion that a wave of cross-national anti-welfare attitudes has been sweeping over Europe in recent years.

During the 1980s the welfare state attracted much of the blame for undermining the work ethic and creating a 'dependency culture'. More recently, the spread of unemployment has been said to have generated a similar effect. In Chapter 5, however, Helen Russell examines such claims within a number of countries and finds them wanting. Neither the level of welfare provision, on the one hand, nor unemployment, on the other, seem independently to reduce work commitment in a country. However, job insecurity - which may of course be a product of rising levels of unemployment - does appear to have a detrimental effect on work commitment, and its impact is particularly evident in Britain. Although EU countries vary in their measured levels of work commitment, Russell anticipates a reduction in such variation in response to growing labour market flexibility throughout the EU.

In Chapter 2, Jacqueline Scott, Michael Braun and Duane Alwin, examine attitudes towards family life and gender roles within the EU, and in particular the impact on 'family values' of continuing rises in divorce and premarital cohabitation. Despite a common movement towards more 'liberal' attitudes throughout the EU, they show that there is considerable variation between countries and that 'traditional' views about the role of women in family life are resilient. Even so, they find evidence that the more liberal views of the young more or less everywhere are gradually replacing the more traditional views of their elders.

Chapter 6, by Russell Dalton and Robert Rohrschneider, examines national variation in attitudes towards the most prominent of the 'new' political issues - the environment - discovering not only that British levels of environmental concern lag behind those in most other countries, but also that the values associated with such concerns are palpably less widespread in Britain. So, despite sustaining a remarkably active environmental lobby, Britain remains more resistant than are other countries to the introduction of assertively 'green' policies.

In any case, as Caroline Bryson and John Curtice reveal in Chapter 7, the emergence of a 'new politics' in western Europe is actually less in evidence than some commentators have suggested. They dispute in particular the theory that, relatively free from war and financial insecurity for over fifty years, the people of western Europe have now adopted a coherent and distinctive cluster of 'postmaterialist' and 'postmodern' values, comprising a rejection of economic and security concerns in favour of libertarian and environmental ones. This change, say the authors, has, at best, been exaggerated and hardly appears to be the new driving force of politics and social attitudes. Their persuasive evidence that no massive culture shift has actually taken place comes from five quite different countries.

Discussions are well under way to recruit several ex-communist states to the EU and, in Chapter 8 by Alan Renwick and Gábor Tóka, the possible impact of such enlargement is investigated. They find in particular that public attitudes in the ex-communist 'applicant' countries are more conservative on moral matters and more left-wing on economic matters than are their counterparts in the existing EU. This is in large part a function of their different socio-economic and religious patterns, both of which pre-date communism. Although the authors concede that these differences between east and west are probably not large enough to have a very sizeable impact on overall EU attitudes or policies, they show clearly what the likely political direction of their joining the EU is likely to be.

In general then, the chapters in this book - all based on high quality survey evidence from a number of EU and other countries - tend to dispute or at least modify much conventional wisdom about national differences and similarities. In particular, it appears that neither globalisation nor cross-national groupings of nations lead inexorably to a convergence in which national differences and cultural diversity diminish. On the contrary, national variations in social and political attitudes seem perversely to persist in the face of all those academic theories about 'convergence'. Similarly, reports of the death of materialism are exaggerated. In short, it appears that those who seek heroic 'laws' of international attitudinal or cultural change are always likely to be disappointed. Some national variations in values stem from deep-seated historical and cultural factors, others from more short-term political or economic circumstances, but - whatever their source - they frequently prove to be remarkably resilient, and all the more interesting for that. However, those who argue that Britain is quintessentially different from its EU neighbours will also be disappointed, as the national differences we uncover do not conform to any clear pattern.

Almost all the data in this book come from sets of questions (or 'modules') fielded by member-countries of the *International Social Survey Programme* (ISSP), a voluntary grouping of teams from research institutes and universities in all parts of the world.[1] Each undertakes to field the same module of questions each year among a nationwide, probability-based sample of adults.[2] There are currently 31 member nations:

Australia	Czech Republic	Japan	Russia
Austria	Denmark	Latvia	Slovakia
Bangladesh	France	The Netherlands	Slovenia
Britain[3]	Germany	New Zealand	South Africa
Bulgaria	Hungary	Norway	Spain
Canada	Irish Republic	The Philippines	Sweden
Chile	Israel	Poland	USA
Cyprus	Italy	Portugal	

A working group of representatives from a small number of the participating countries has the task of drafting each year's module. It is then finalised at a plenary conference to which all ISSP national teams are present. There, new applications for membership are considered and the programme of future modules is decided. Eight topics have been covered to date, each being repeated periodically in order to build up time-series data. In order to refresh the series, and ensure that each module remains up-to-date, only around two-thirds of a module is repeated each time, the balance being filled with new questions.

The topics covered to date and planned for the future are:

1985	Role of government
1986	Family networks and support systems
1987	Social inequality
1988	Family and changing gender roles
1989	Work orientations
1990	Role of government II
1991	Religious beliefs and observance
1992	Social inequality II
1993	Environment
1994	Family and changing gender roles II
1995	National identity
1996	Role of government III
1997	Work orientations II

1998	Religious beliefs and observance II
1999	*Social inequality III*
2000	*Environment II*
2001	*Family networks and support systems II*

This means that we are now able to examine and interpret not only cross-national differences (and similarities) at one point in time, but also the pace and nature of changes in attitudes over more than a decade.

The editors and authors owe an immense debt of gratitude to the staff of the *ZentralArchiv* in Köln, Germany. With meticulous care, they assemble the annual datasets from all *ISSP* member countries, transform them into a single dataset that analysts can use with confidence, and document the results in an annual codebook. Had the *ZentralArchiv* foreseen back in 1985 how the *Programme* would grow, from its then only four founder-members, they might well have been warier about taking on such a commitment. We are profoundly grateful that they did. Now, we are glad to report that they will be supported in this role by *Analisis Sociologicos, Economicos Y Politicos* (ASEP) in Madrid, Spain.

Our annual volumes usually present and interpret findings from the previous year's *British Social Attitudes* survey rather than from the *International Social Survey Programme*. However, in election years - 1997, as well as 1992 and 1987 - our core funders (the Gatsby Charitable Foundation) allow us to deploy their grant towards the study of political attitudes and behaviour via the *British Election Study* series. For reasons of continuity, however, we wished also to field a scaled-down *BSA* in 1997, interviewing only 1,400 or so respondents instead of the usual 3,500, and using only one instead of the usual three versions of the questionnaire. Thanks to the ESRC,[4] the Countryside Commission, the Charities Aid Foundation and the Departments of the Environment and Transport - now joined together within the DETR - and a further grant from the Gatsby Charitable Foundation, we were able to do so. This enabled us to field easily the most comprehensive module of questions on attitudes to the EU ever asked in the series, which we devised in collaboration with colleagues at the Royal Institute of International Affairs (1997). Further interpretations of the findings are included by Geoffrey Evans in Chapter 9 of this Report, and the technical details of the 1997 survey are contained in the BSA Technical Report (Bryson *et al.*, 1999 forthcoming). Meanwhile, the dataset join its predecessors in the ESRC Data Archive at the University of Essex.

Our deepest thanks, as always, go to those who help to fund this series. The annual participation of the *British Social Attitudes* survey in the ISSP is made possible by the Economic and Social Research Council (ESRC). Among the long term funders of the BSA are the Departments of Health, Social Security, Environment Transport and the Regions, Education and Employment, and Trade and Industry, as well as the Countryside Commission. This year, the Nuffield Foundation, together with the Robert Gavron Charitable Trust, has supported an ambitious new module of questions on the role of grandparents in family life, which we have designed in collaboration with Michael Young and Geoff Dench of the Institute of Community Studies. Meanwhile, the Wellcome Trust is supporting a new module this year on public attitudes to genetic research and its applications, which we have designed in collaboration with Theresa Marteau at Guy's Hospital and Martin Bobrow at Cambridge University. And the Leverhulme Trust is supporting a new module on civic engagement and disengagement, on which we are collaborating with Michael Johnston of Colgate University, New York.

Our most steadfast funder, however, without whose support the series would never have taken root, remains the Gatsby Charitable Foundation, one of the Sainsbury Family Charitable Trusts. Having core-funded the series continuously since 1984, they have now placed their support on a 'rolling' basis, giving us the ability (so rare enough in social research) to plan up to three years ahead.

One of the aims of the series from the outset has been to make its findings as widely accessible as possible. With this in mind, we have been working closely with Richard Topf of London Guildhall University on the creation of a new *British Social Attitudes* Information System, containing the complete text of every question asked in the series since its inception in 1983, together with the distribution of its answers, all displayed in a set of tables with topic and free text search facilities. The test copy of this database is now available and the final version will soon be available on CD-ROM and later on a special web-site (see the SCPR web-site for further details in due course).

This year we are also running a new *Young People's Social Attitudes* (YPSA) survey, covering the attitudes of 12-19 year olds. The first such survey was carried out in 1994 in collaboration with Barnardo's.[5] Now, four years later, many of the questions on topics such as education and housing are being repeated, while others on civic engagement and family relationships have been added. We are grateful to the ESRC,[6] the Nuffield Foundation, the Leverhulme Trust and the DETR for funding this add-on to the main survey, comprising young people in the same households as our adult BSA sample members, enabling comparisons not only between generations but also between parents and their own children. In addition, of course, we shall now also be able to chart any changes in the attitudes of young people during the last few years.

With renewed Research Centre funding from the ESRC[7] for the *Centre for Research into Elections and Social Trends* (CREST) - directed jointly by SCPR and Nuffield College Oxford - the *British Social Attitudes* series remains closely linked to the *British Election Studies*. Joint development of questions and - in election years - a two-pronged approach to the measurement of certain elusive subjects, has thus enabled the BSA series to play an important role over the years not only in the monitoring and explanation of social attitudes but of political attitudes and voting behaviour too.

This year, appropriately perhaps, we have parted company with the *Northern Ireland Social Attitudes* (NISA) survey. Started in 1989 with funding from the Nuffield Foundation and the Central Community Relations Unit (CCRU) in Belfast, this annual survey was run during the early 1990s by the SCPR team in collaboration with colleagues in Queen's University Belfast and in the Northern Ireland Statistics and Research Agency (NISRA). It was latterly funded on the same basis by all the Northern Ireland Government Departments. Now colleagues at Queen's University and the University of Ulster have succeeded in raising new local funding and, against the background of the new political arrangements in Northern Ireland, we have all agreed that the new *Northern Ireland Life and Times Survey* would be better served by cutting its formal links with its British counterpart. The two teams will, of course, continue to co-operate closely and intend to carry many questions in common each year for purposes of comparison. So our warm wishes go to Lizanne Dowds, Gillian Robinson and their colleagues for the success and longevity of their new independent sister survey.

The *British Social Attitudes* survey series is, *par excellence*, a large team effort between researchers who control the overall design of the study and are responsible for devising the questions and analysing the data, programmers who translate the questions into a computer-assisted questionnaire and later clean the data for analysis, clerical teams who implement the sampling strategy and data processing, fieldwork controllers, area managers and interviewers who organise and carry out all the interviewing, and administrative staff who organise the printing and distribution of documents and, of course, the finances of the whole operation (incoming and outgoing). A special mention goes to the secretarial staff - in this case almost a lone and sterling contribution by Sheila Vioche - who produce countless documents, not least the camera-ready copy for this volume. All the skills and co-operation of these different groups continue to make this complicated and multifaceted project such a joy to work on.

Outside SCPR we owe an immense debt to Ann Mair of the Social Statistics Laboratory at the University of Strathclyde for her annual efforts in producing a meticulous SPSS system file for use initially by the authors, but also later by the whole research community through the Data Archive at the University of Essex and the *ZentralArchiv* in Germany.

We wish to pay a special tribute to our colleague, Lindsay Brook, who retires this year. As a Co-director of the series since 1985, a co-editor of twelve of the fifteen books in the series to date and a frequent chapter author, his exacting standards have contributed greatly to the series' survival and success. His overall contribution to the project's coherence, its visibility and its longevity have all been incalculable.

Our heartfelt thanks also go out to literally hundreds of thousands of respondents, not only in Europe but all over the world, who have patiently answered the questions put to them over the years as part of the *International Social Survey Programme* on which this book is based.

The Editors

Notes

1. SCPR was a founder-member of the ISSP, along with the National Opinion Research Center, University of Chicago, the Institute of Advanced Studies, Australian National University and the *Zentrum für Umfragen, Methoden und Analysen*, University of Mannheim. We are grateful to the Nuffield Foundation for providing the seed-funding that ensured SCPR's early participation in the enterprise.
2. For details see Davis and Jowell (1989), Taylor and Thomson (1996), pp.9-10 and 214-15, and Appendix I of this book.
3. Between 1989 and 1991, and 1993 and 1996, the ISSP modules were also fielded as part of the *Northern Ireland Social Attitudes* survey (described later).
4. Under Grant no. M 543 285 001 to the *Centre for Research into Elections and Social Trends* (CREST). Half of this grant was used (at the ESRC's request) to fund a module of questions prior to the 1997 general election, on attitudes to the political parties, for which there had been no space in the *British Election Study* (BES) cross-sectional questionnaire.
5. See *inter alia* Jowell and Park, 1998; Park, 1997; and Roberts and Sachdev, 1996.
6. Under Grant no. R 000237765.
7. Under Grant no. M 543 285 001.

References

Royal Institute of International Affairs (1997), *An Equal Partner: Britain's role in a changing Europe*, London: Royal Institute of International Affairs.

Bryson, C., Jarvis, L., Park, A. and Thomson, K. (1999 forthcoming), *British Social Attitudes 1997 survey: Technical report*, London: SCPR.

Davis, J. and Jowell, R. (1989), 'Measuring National Differences', in Jowell, R., Witherspoon, S. and Brook, L. (eds.) *British Social Attitudes: special international report*, Aldershot: Gower.

Evans, G. and Norris, P. (eds.) (1999 forthcoming), *A Critical Election? The 1997 British Election in Long-term perspective*, London: Sage.

Jowell, R. and Park, A. (1998), 'Young People, Politics and Citizenship - a Disengaged Generation?', London: The Citizenship Foundation. (Reprint of a lecture delivered at the Foundation's Annual Colloquium, The Royal Society, London, December 9th 1997.)

Park, A. (1995), 'Teenagers and their politics', in Jowell, R., Curtice, J., Park, A., Brook, L. and Thomson, K. (eds.) *British Social Attitudes: the 12th Report*, Aldershot: Dartmouth.

Roberts, H. and Sachdev, D. (1996), *Having their Say: the views of 12 to 19 year olds*, Barkingside: Barnardo's.

Taylor, B. and Thomson, K. (eds.) (1996), *Understanding Change in Social Attitudes*, Aldershot: Dartmouth.

1 National identity and national pride

David McCrone and Paula Surridge [*]

National identity is one of the most discussed but least understood concepts of the late 20th century. It is of considerable relevance, with allegiance to state identity, citizenship or 'nationality' under threat not only from the rise of different national identities within states, but also by the growth of systems (such as the European Union) that seek to encompass a plurality of states (McCrone, 1998).

Social scientists are aware of the challenges posed by national identity, but struggle to find ways of tapping how people make sense of it. This is largely because it is part of what we can call the 'furniture of everyday life'. We may be aware that new pieces have been added to the room, or that the existing furniture has been moved around - but rarely do we question why it is there in the first place. This taken-for-granted quality of national identity has been termed 'banal nationalism' (Billig, 1995). Take the example of a national flag flying in a garage forecourt - rarely acknowledged as having anything to do with national identity, but having a subtle capacity to reinforce it. The modern state requires us to be 'nationals', not simply because it issues us with passports when we want to travel outside state boundaries, but more because it is the fundamental political identity that we have. Ernest Gellner (1983) pointed out in his classic study of nationalism that we are 'nationals' not because we want to be (although we usually do) but because we have no choice. The modern state requires us to obey it willingly, to give it legitimacy through the political system, and to die for it if and when the moment arises.

[*] David McCrone is Professor of Sociology at the University of Edinburgh, and Convener of the Unit for the Study of Government in Scotland. Paula Surridge is a Lecturer in Sociology at the University of Aberdeen.

It is a mark of the moral power of the state that people usually do precisely that.

At the same time, we do not often think of ourselves as having a 'national identity'. Most are only likely to affirm their national identity explicitly when there is political conflict, most obviously in wartime, or during that peaceful and surrogate form of modern warfare, the sporting contest. Think of the salience of national emotion at the time of the 1998 football World Cup, and especially of the political spin-off for victorious countries such as France in 1998 and England in 1966. That said, it does not take war alone, real or surrogate, to bring national identity to the fore. Where identities are problematic, where people believe they have a choice as regards who they want to be in national terms, we find a debate about national identity. In these islands, for example, we are more likely to find that the Scots, the Welsh and Northern Irish (of whichever persuasion) are better able than the English to articulate the ways in which their *state* identity (being British) differs from their *national* identity (being Scottish, Welsh and so on). The English, the majority within these islands, are less able to make this sort of distinction precisely because they are the majority, and to them being British and English appear synonyms.

National identity entails a notion of an 'other' (Anderson, 1996). We know who we are, because we know, or think we know, who we are *not*. This is not, however, a sufficient condition of national (and, indeed, social) identity. There must be some substance to who we think we are, some shared set of values or beliefs. And, in this sense, the construction of national identity is a gradual process, taking place over a long period of time. It is fragmented, constructed out of a variety of symbolic resources which can be recovered, interpreted and mobilised as needs be. 'Britishness', for instance, is constructed out of a series of fragments of history: imperial wars, the Industrial Revolution, the building of democracy, the welfare state, and so on. Most of the time this is fairly inert material, but it can be mobilised without much difficulty in times of conflict and struggle during which the British people need to be reminded who they 'really are'. Of course, there are also different, often competing, tales to be told out of the raw materials offered by history: an elite history, and a workers' history; a Scottish history, and an English one; a men's history and a women's history; a black history and a white one, and so on. It is this fragmented quality that makes Britishness 'fuzzy' - with a boundary that is 'historically changing, often vague, and, to a degree, malleable' (Cohen, 1994: 35).

We are still at a fairly early stage when it comes to understanding national identity, even though the concept has existed as long as the modern state. Its implicit and 'taken for granted' nature makes it a difficult subject to research, with argument still existing as to whether 'national identity' is more than merely a concept generated by analysts to aid their understanding of human behaviour. However, surveys such as that reported on here, represent a start to this process.

In this chapter we use data from a survey focusing on attitudes towards national identity, fielded in 1995 as part of the *International Social Survey Programme* (ISSP).[*] We use this to address national differences and similarities in three key issues: national identity; national pride; and attitudes towards 'others'.

Four countries are examined here: Britain, western Germany,[**] Sweden and Spain. Why these four? Largely because they encompass a range of factors likely to be of relevance to national identity. Germany, for instance, is usually taken by writers on nationalism (Brubaker, 1992) as the exemplar of a national identity that is based on ethnicity rather than residence. In other words, you can claim German nationality if you can show that you have German ancestors (*jus sanguinis* - the law of blood). This is in contrast with most other western countries in which *jus soli* - the law of the soil - is the key. Further, the German case is a good one to include because we have the ability to divide the sample into two, western and eastern Germany. Given the very different and quite recent histories of these territories, as well as their political unification of less than one decade, we can assess the extent to which there has been a unification of identity within Germany, or whether they remain culturally distinct parts of the German state.

What of Sweden and Spain? Both were chosen as representing 'outliers' with quite different historical and cultural experiences: Sweden, as a small and homogeneous northern European state with a strong social democratic welfare state; and Spain, as a southern European state whose experience of democratic and industrial development has been relatively recent. Spain also has the analytical merit of containing, like Britain, significant minority identities - Catalans, Basques and Galicians.

The four countries considered also differ in their history as regards the EU, as do the attitudes of their populations towards it. This is of significance. In Britain, for instance, 'Euroscepticism' is often treated as a reflection of British or English nationalism. According to 1998 Eurobarometer figures, Spain (who joined in 1986) has the most pro-European population, with just over half (53 per cent) saying that membership was 'a good thing for Spain'. Germany (who were founder-members) and Britain (who joined in 1973) show similar levels of support to each other, with 38 per cent and 36 per cent respectively taking the view that membership is good for the country. The lowest level of support is found in Sweden (which joined in 1997), where 31 per cent think that membership is 'a good thing', nearly half (48 per cent) taking the opposite view.

---

[*] See the Introduction and Appendices to this Report for further details about ISSP.
[**] By western Germany we mean the geographical area known until unification as the Federal Republic of Germany. By eastern Germany we mean the area formerly known as the German Democratic Republic.

National identity

Attachment to place

How does national identity relate to other forms of territorial identity? Are those who are highly attached to smaller areas within their nation (such as a particular neighbourhood or region) more likely than average to be strongly attached to their nation as well? Or does attachment to one's country - national identity - occur only when other territorial attachments are weak?

To assess this we asked respondents to say how close they felt to a number of different territorial areas. As the next table shows, with the exception of Spain, the area to which the highest proportion feel 'close' is the country within which they live, followed either by their neighbourhood, town or city. Compared with other countries, British attachment to all the areas mentioned is relatively weak. Although nearly seven in ten report feeling close to their country, this compares with around eight in ten Germans and Swedes, and nine in ten Spaniards.

Feelings of attachment to different areas

% feel 'very' or 'fairly' close to:	Western Germany	Base	Eastern Germany	Base	Britain	Base	Sweden	Base	Spain	Base
Neighbourhood	73	1180	76	562	64	999	65	1253	88	1216
Town or city	71	701	76	368	55	956	67	1132	93	1217
County	65	1149	74	550	50	942	67	1195	91	1217
Country [i]	79	1187	82	573	69	947	83	1217	90	1216
Europe	59	1097	59	507	22	907	39	1126	63	1191

[i] The country was specified in each case as follows: Germany; Britain; Sweden; Spain.

In all cases, the lowest level of attachment is felt for the largest geographical entity - Europe. That said, majorities in Germany (59 per cent) and Spain (63 per cent) feel close to Europe. By contrast, in Sweden and Britain this only applies to a minority - in Britain, for instance, only 22 per cent take this view. The European continent is not a key feature of identification for the British on their offshore island. Of course, geographical proximity is likely to be a factor here, but both Sweden and Spain also belong to the European periphery.

We also asked respondents how willing or unwilling they would be to move to a number of different places if, by doing so, 'you could improve your work or living conditions'. Although majorities in each country (again, with the exception of Spain) would be willing to move from their current neighbourhood for work, far fewer would contemplate moving to another town or city, and fewer still to another country or continent. In this respect, the British do not differ particularly from those in other countries, with around a quarter (26 per cent) being willing to move country to improve their work or living conditions. It is worth noting in passing, however, that the Spanish and those in eastern Germany are the least likely to be willing to move to another country.

Willingness to move to different areas in order to improve work or living conditions

% 'very' or 'fairly' willing to move:	Western Germany	Base	Eastern Germany	Base	Britain	Base	Sweden	Base	Spain	Base
Neighbourhood	61	1179	51	568	58	937	54	1244	47	1208
Town or city	45	1131	37	548	49	906	37	1228	44	1206
County	36	1135	31	549	40	898	32	1228	36	1208
Country	22	1145	12	556	26	892	30	1211	20	1204
Continent	16	1124	9	552	23	874	24	1207	19	1200

Certainly within the nations considered here, the primary geographical unit to which people feel attached is their country, although those in Britain report comparatively low levels of 'closeness' in this respect. It is perhaps because of this relatively low attachment to Britain that the British are among the more likely to say they would consider moving to another country or continent in the pursuit of better work or living conditions. The majority, however, would not.

The basis of national identity

On what sort of grounds do people base national identity? There are some obvious criteria (such as birth, citizenship, residence, cultural criteria like language and religion, respects for laws and institutions and so on) as well as more diffuse ones such as the feeling of 'belonging' to a particular nation. But which matter most? And are there national differences in the importance assigned to particular facets of identity? To assess this, we asked, for a range of different criteria, how important or unimportant each was for being 'truly' British, or German, or Spanish and so on. The next table shows the proportion of people in each country who said that a particular attribute was important in this respect.

The importance of different factors in being 'truly' British/German/Swedish/Spanish

% 'very' or 'fairly' important	Western Germany	Base	Eastern Germany	Base	Britain	Base	Sweden	Base	Spain	Base
Born in country	51	1243	56	598	79	1025	51	1269	79	1211
Have citizenship	78	1231	81	592	86	1016	84	1270	83	1201
Lived most of life there	64	1224	68	580	76	1003	63	1254	73	1206
Able to speak language	90	1245	88	595	88	1023	96	1278	82	1207
Religion	34	1213	22	561	34	997	18	1223	47	1198
Respect political institutions and laws	93	1230	88	574	87	1000	98	1277	88	1198
Feels 'British' etc.	76	1223	75	579	78	1000	88	1236	89	1203

We look first at the rank order of the different characteristics. It is notable that Britain, Germany and Sweden are alike in stressing the importance of being able to speak the national language and having respect for the political institutions and laws of the land. They differ, however, in the degree of importance they see language as having. Around two-thirds of the Swedish (71 per cent) and British (65 per cent) see being able to speak the national language as being 'very important', compared to around half of the Germans.

Spain is as likely as the other countries here to see having respect for political institutions and the law as being important factors underpinning national identity. However, it gives them the same weight as 'feeling' Spanish (and downplays the importance of speaking Spanish, presumably reflecting the fact that Spain is a more multilingual society than any of the others considered here). In all countries, having citizenship is also granted considerable importance, with around eight people in ten saying that this is an important aspect of national identity.

Britain and Spain place the greatest weight on having been born in the country, around eight in ten saying that this is important. This is substantially higher than the comparable proportion in Germany or Sweden. Similarly, both the British and Spanish also place more weight on having lived in the particular country for most of one's life, with around three-quarters thinking that this is an important factor in being 'truly' British or Spanish (41 per cent of the British take the view that this factor is 'very important'). This gives some support to the view, explored earlier, that Germans are less likely to have a national identity based upon residence - although it should be noted that Swedes are even less likely to see residence as important.

The importance granted to religion as a source of national identity varies considerably. In all the countries considered, it is the characteristic seen as having the *lowest* degree of importance. Although in Spain it is a significant marker of national identity, less than half (47 per cent) actually think that it is important in being 'truly' Spanish. Perhaps more surprising, is that a significant minority - around a third - of the British attach some importance to religion. This is interesting, particularly given that the levels of religiosity there (as measured by church attendance) are much lower than in virtually every other western industrial country (Bruce, 1995). We can only speculate as to the reason why a third of Britons see religion as being important to being 'truly' British, but it may indicate that in this context religion is marking *cultural* nationality, rather than *religious* practice. After all, in England the links between religion and nationality are historically strong, given that the monarch is *ex officio* head of the state church. The importance granted to religion may also reflect a desire by some to exclude certain groups (such as post-war immigrants from the Asian sub-continent) from being 'British'.

The weakest attachment to religion as an indicator of national identity is found in Sweden (where only 18 per cent attach importance to it) closely followed by eastern Germany. There 22 per cent think religion is important in being 'German', compared with 34 per cent taking this view in the area comprising western Germany.

We have seen that some national differences exist in the importance given to different attributes in determining national identity. More striking, however, is the relative similarity between countries in the emphasis that their populations place upon these attributes. Birth, citizenship, residence, institutional respect, language and a 'feeling' of national identity are seen as important by clear majorities in all countries. Only religion is not a key identifier of nationality, even in Spain. The end product - being 'British' or 'German', 'Spanish' or 'Swedish' - may differ, but considerable cross-national consensus exists with regard to the importance of the basic building blocks that make up national identity.

Looking inwards - national pride

If the criteria used to construct individual national identities are shared, do nations differ in their levels of national pride? Are the British more proud of Britain than are Germans of Germany, or the Spanish of Spain? How much variation exists in *what* countries feel most proud of, and how can this sort of variation be explained?

We start by considering responses to the statement:

> *I would rather be a citizen of [Britain/Germany/Sweden/Spain] than of any other country in the world*

Broadly similar percentages in each of our countries (around 70 per cent) agree with this statement. However, this pride in one's country is not uncritical.   Three-quarters of the British, for instance, agree with the statement 'there are some things about Britain today that make me ashamed of Britain' - a figure broadly comparable with Sweden (76 per cent), and western Germany (71 per cent). Even higher levels of agreement are found in eastern Germany (85 per cent). The Spanish stand in marked contrast - there only around a third (36 per cent) feel ashamed of certain aspects of modern Spain. Spain is also unusual in the relatively high level of support it gives to the notion of 'my country, right or wrong'. We asked people whether they agreed or disagreed with the following statement:

People should support their country even if the country is in the wrong

Nearly half the Spanish (47 per cent) agreed with this view, over double the proportion in the other countries considered here. Thus, in Britain only 24 per cent agreed, as did 17 per cent of those in western Germany, 25 per cent of those in eastern Germany and 26 per cent of the Swedish.

National bombast is largely conspicuous by its absence. Only a (bare) majority of the British agree with the view that Britain 'is a better country than most other countries' (55 per cent), followed by Sweden (48 per cent) and Germany and Spain (at around 36 per cent).

When considering a concept as complex and multi-faceted as national identity, it is clearly dangerous to rely upon responses to single questions. For this reason, we asked a series of statements about national identity and national pride, which can be summarised to form an additive index or 'scale, where a high score indicates a high level of national pride, and a lower score, a lower level. As the next table shows, the highest levels of national pride are found in Britain and Spain, and the lowest in Germany (particularly in the area that was western Germany). This suggests that fears about excessive nationalism in Germany may well be ill-founded.

Mean scores on national pride scale

Britain	Spain	Sweden	Eastern Germany	Western Germany
20.6	20.4	19.8	17.9	17.2
Base 912	1021	1004	455	997

National pride varies within each country, as well as varying between countries. Higher levels of national pride are displayed by the over 55s than are by younger people, and those with lower levels of education have higher national pride than the more educated (see the appendix to this chapter for further details). Men and women do not vary in their national pride (with the exception of western Germany, where men have significantly higher levels of national pride than women).

Not surprisingly, national pride is related to attachment to one's country. In general, those who feel 'close' to their country display higher levels of national pride that those who do not feel as close. However, attachment to place is not the only factor at work. We saw earlier that the British are less likely than those in other EU countries to feel 'close' to their country. Their score on the national pride scale is, however, the highest considered here. We turn now, therefore, towards the things about which people might feel proud. To assess this, we asked people how proud they were of a variety of different national achievements and institutions, ranging from 'its scientific and technological achievements' to 'its history'.

Pride in national achievements and institutions

% 'very' or 'somewhat' proud	Western Germany	Base	Eastern Germany	Base	Britain	Base	Sweden	Base	Spain	Base
Way democracy works	68	1185	34	573	66	949	64	1230	54	1181
Political influence in world	60	1152	63	534	54	931	42	1119	41	1081
Economic achievements	83	1182	83	571	43	935	17	1191	42	1126
Social security system	72	1215	39	573	48	974	65	1241	53	1176
Scientific achievements	82	1156	88	533	88	942	87	1114	71	1102
Sports achievements	68	1139	82	559	76	974	85	1221	90	1152
Arts and literature	69	1060	81	520	80	912	73	1049	88	1126
Armed forces	31	1059	28	491	88	974	33	1035	50	1130
History	34	1145	31	554	89	990	69	1115	83	1162
Fair and equal treatment of groups in society	37	1078	25	503	53	942	43	1185	61	1149

The highest levels of pride in Germany are reserved for the country's economic and scientific achievements. The latter is also important in Sweden, alongside its sporting achievements - while in Spain sporting prowess ranks alongside achievements in arts and literature. By contrast, in Britain, the highest levels of national pride are associated with 'its history' and 'its armed forces', reflecting perhaps the emphasis placed on the past in the construction of British national identity. By contrast, in Germany only a minority express any pride in their history or armed forces, a reflection perhaps of the way that Germany's recent past has been rejected as having any role in the construction of a modern Germany national identity. Of note too, is that this rejection is equally spread across the German state, varying little between east and west.

The British are not entirely fixated on their past. They also take pride in their scientific and technological achievements, as well as those within the arts and literature, and within sport. In all these areas over three-quarters said they felt proud of Britain in these respects. Like those within western Germany and in Sweden, around two-thirds also said that they felt proud of the way democracy works within their country. A lower proportion, just over a half, felt proud of Britain's 'political influence in the world', lower than the proportion of Germans who felt proud of Germany's influence. This possibly reflects the way the world, especially Europe, has changed over the last few decades. The British also fall behind Germans in the level of pride they express in Britain's economic achievements (although the Swedes are the most gloomy in this respect), and in the British social security system.

We might sum up the national assessments of each country as follows. The British take most pride in their history, their armed forces, and scientific and technological achievements - and the least pride in Britain's economic performance. Those living in western Germany are most proud of their economic achievements, their social security system, and achievements in science and technology. They are least proud of their armed forces. Their east German counterparts are most proud of their achievements in sport, in the arts and literature, and in science and technology, and again are least proud of Germany's armed forces as well its record as regards the fair and equal treatment of citizens. Swedes take greatest pride in sport, science and technology, and their history, and least pride in Sweden's economic performance. Finally, Spaniards are most proud of their history, sporting achievements, and their arts and literature, and express the least pride in Spain's political influence in the world.

Looking outwards...

An important aspect of national identity and national pride lies in perceived relations with other countries. Like all forms of identity, one's nationality is essentially a relational attribute. How open or closed, then, are different countries to external influences? And how does this relate to national identity and feelings of national pride?

Attitudes towards protectionism and independence

We begin by examining attitudes towards economic and political independence. We asked respondents whether they agreed or disagreed with a number of statements, as follows:

> *[Britain/Germany/Spain/Sweden] should limit the import of foreign products in order to protect its national economy*
> *[Britain/Germany/Spain/Sweden] should follow its own interests, even if this leads to conflict with other nations*
> *For certain problems, like environmental pollution, international bodies should have the right to enforce solutions*

As the next table shows, the Spanish are the most protectionist, with over three-quarters thinking that Spain should limit foreign imports. They are also the most likely to feel that their country should pursue its own interests, even if this might lead to conflict. The Spanish are followed, albeit some way behind, by the British, nearly two-thirds of whom think that Britain should impose some limits on foreign imports. Those living in western Germany, and the Swedes, are the least likely to advocate economic protectionism. People in both western and eastern Germany are the least likely to advocate their country following its own interests irrespective of the conflicts this might cause, this again, perhaps, reflecting German history. Despite substantial proportions in all countries bar Germany feeling that their nations should pursue their own interests, there is an acceptance of the need for external constraints (for instance, to control environmental pollution). Around three-quarters take this view in Britain, and higher proportions in Sweden, Spain and western Germany.

Economic protectionism and political independence

% agree:	Western Germany		Eastern Germany		Britain		Sweden		Spain	
		Base		Base		Base		Base		Base
Economic protectionism	41	1201	59	584	64	1012	45	1214	77	1130
Follow interests even if conflict	31	1194	27	571	50	1003	45	1197	60	1120
International enforcement	86	1218	73	584	74	998	81	1206	80	1085

Economic protectionism is favoured more than cultural protectionism. Only in Spain do more than half think that 'Spanish television should give preference to Spanish films and programmes', only around a third in Britain taking this view about British television. The Swedes are the least likely to hold this view, just over one in five (22 per cent) doing so. There is also low support for the view that 'foreigners should not be allowed to buy land' in the respondent's country (although it must be said that around a third of the British, Swedish and those in the area formally covered by eastern Germany do think that such sales should not be allowed). And high levels of support exist for teaching foreign languages, with around eight in ten agreeing with the statement:

> [British/German/Spanish/Swedish] schools should make much more effort to teach foreign languages properly

In this respect Sweden stands out, with a far lower proportion (54 per cent) agreeing that schools should make more effort. Of course, this may well reflect a high degree of satisfaction with the state of language teaching in Sweden, rather than a disapproval of such teaching in principle.

Cultural protectionism and attitudes towards others

% agree:	Western Germany		Eastern Germany		Britain		Sweden		Spain	
		Base		*Base*		*Base*		*Base*		*Base*
Ban foreign land purchase	15	*1179*	35	*547*	32	*1012*	36	*1218*	29	*1106*
Preference to domestic TV/film	30	*1220*	45	*591*	36	*1021*	22	*1259*	56	*1182*
More effort in language teaching	82	*1196*	81	*562*	81	*1034*	54	*1224*	83	*1174*

In summary, therefore, some national differences exist in support for economic protectionism and political independence, with Spain and Britain at the more independent end of the scale. However, all countries largely recognise the need for some form of external restraint, and appear relatively liberal when it comes to cultural protectionism and land-ownership.

Attitudes towards immigration

We cannot, of course, divorce issues of national identity from attitudes towards immigration. In Britain, for one, the politics of race and immigration over the last forty years have been intimately tied up with who the British believe themselves to be. The 'fuzziness' of 'British' national identity reflects not only the complex patterns of nationality and citizenship among the English, Scots, Welsh and Irish, but also Britain's imperial legacy - both in terms of the settler societies of the old white Commonwealth, and more recent patterns of immigration since the 1950s (Cohen, 1994). 1998 saw the fiftieth anniversary of the arrival of the Empire Windrush from the West Indies, bringing the first wave of the post-war immigrants to Britain. In western Germany, large numbers of foreign or 'guest' workers were recruited in the 1960s and early 1970s to meet labour shortages. Many do not have formal citizenship - this applying, for instance, to nearly half a million second generation Turkish immigrants who were born and raised in Germany (Brubaker, 1992). On the other hand, ethnic Germans who migrated from eastern Europe immediately after the war and after the collapse of communism are possibly less likely to be seen as 'immigrants' by the native German population than other 'foreign' workers. Although Sweden has, by and large, a more homogeneous ethnic population, some immigration did take place during the 1960s, mainly from southern Europe and Finland. More recent immigration has largely been in the form of political and economic refugees, reflecting Sweden's liberal asylum laws. Finally, Spain has a relatively low immigration rate, the bulk of which takes the form of people retiring from other European countries (mainly northern). North African immigration into Spain runs at less than a third of that from the rest of Europe, with marginally less from Latin America.

We turn now to examine attitudes towards ethnic minorities, and particularly the relationship between these attitudes and feelings of national pride and identity. We start by considering responses to a series of positive and negative statements about immigration and ethnic minority groups.

When it comes to attitudes towards cultural assimilation, around half in each country (rising to 61 per cent in Sweden) think that 'it is impossible for people who do not share [country's] customs and traditions to become fully British/German/Spanish/Swedish'. This does not mean, however, that people think ethnic minorities should abandon their cultural heritage - high proportions in eastern Germany and in Spain think 'ethnic minorities should be given government assistance to help preserve their customs and traditions'. However, only one in five of the Swedish take this view, and only one in six of the British, these two nations thus appearing to have the most 'assimilationist' attitude towards immigration. Britain also shows a relatively low level of agreement with the view that 'immigrants make [country] more open to new ideas and cultures'. Only 55 per cent of Britons take this view, compared with around 70 per cent who take this view in Sweden and western Germany, and 60 per cent in eastern Germany and Spain.

What about the role of immigrants in the economy? Support for the notion that 'immigrants are generally good for [country's] economy' is relatively low - with the highest support for this view being expressed in the area covering western Germany (42 per cent), and the lowest in Britain (where only 18 per cent agree). The west Germans are also among the least likely to think that 'immigrants take jobs away from people who were born in [country]' (27 per cent doing so), with the British being among the most likely to take this view (nearly half doing so). People living in eastern Germany and Spain are also likely to express concern about immigrants 'taking jobs' from nationals.

Concern about the impact of immigration on crime levels is highest in Germany (and particularly in the area covered by eastern Germany) and Sweden, and lowest in Britain and Spain. Thus, nearly six in ten Swedes think that 'immigrants increase crime rates', double the comparable proportion in Britain.

Attitudes towards immigration and ethnic minorities

% agree:	Western Germany		Eastern Germany		Britain		Sweden		Spain	
		Base		*Base*		*Base*		*Base*		*Base*
Different cultures can't become fully 'national'	44	*1163*	48	*543*	52	*1014*	61	*1235*	46	*1129*
Government aid to preserve ethnic minority culture	41	*1161*	70	*567*	16	*1000*	20	*1179*	59	*1107*
Immigrants increase crime rates	54	*1168*	68	*564*	29	*996*	58	*1196*	28	*1154*
Immigrants good for economy	42	*1119*	32	*556*	18	*975*	27	*1138*	27	*1111*
Immigrants 'steal' jobs	27	*1185*	53	*568*	49	*1016*	17	*1194*	45	*1186*
Immigrants make culture more open	69	*1160*	58	*631*	55	*990*	71	*1221*	60	*1129*

What these data show is the complexity of people's attitudes to 'immigration'. There is no single and predictable set of responses. A majority of the British (albeit very small), for example, see immigrants as making Britain more 'open' to new ideas, but there is very little support for such immigrants maintaining their cultures and traditions. And the British are the least likely to have a positive view of the role that immigrants can play in the economy. They are, however, more likely to take a 'liberal' view when it comes to the relationship between immigrants and crime. A similar pattern exists in Spain. By contrast, in Germany there is considerable support for the view that immigrants commit crimes, but a greater acceptance of the role that they play within the German economy.

Considerable pressure exists within all the countries considered here to reduce immigration. Around two-thirds of the British, Swedes and Spanish take this view, as do over three-quarters of the Germans. However, when it comes to allowing those who have suffered political repression to remain within a country, majorities in all countries bar Britain agree they should be allowed to stay. Eight in ten Germans take this view, as do 67 per cent of Swedes and 60 per cent of the Spanish. Only in Britain do less than half (43 per cent) think that political refugees should be allowed to stay in the country.

Attitudes to immigration are associated with national pride. We have already seen that the highest levels of national pride are found in Britain and Spain, and the lowest in Germany. Levels of pride also vary within each country, and those who are most in favour of reducing immigration have higher scores than average on our national pride scale. The next table shows the scores of three different groups of people within each country, those who think that immigration should be increased (the overwhelming minority within each country), those who think the levels should remain as they are, and - the majority - those who think that immigration should be reduced.

Scores on the national pride scale, by attitudes to immigration

Immigration should be:	Western Germany	Base	Eastern Germany	Base	Britain	Base	Sweden	Base	Spain	Base
Increased	12.0	34	13.3	10	16.5	36	16.8	69	19.9	85
Remain the same	14.9	190	16.3	83	19.0	244	18.8	238	19.8	480
Reduced	18.5	695	18.7	329	21.7	586	20.6	640	21.3	369

A similar relationship exists between the belief that immigrants cause crime and national pride - with those scoring highest in terms of their national pride being the most likely to think that immigrants cause crime. It seems, therefore, that for many people in Europe, high levels of national pride go hand-in-hand with anti-immigrant feelings.

Conclusion

Perhaps our most striking finding relates to the *similarity* of attitudes within the four countries considered here. This is made all the more remarkable by the fact that they were deliberately selected because of their expected diversity. Germany, for instance, is seen to have at its core an ethnic rather than civic definition of nationality, and one might also have expected the areas that make up eastern and western Germany to be more divergent than proved the case, given their quite different histories over the last half-century and the relative recency of their unification. Spain is a relative newcomer to western democracy, as well as a country still undergoing rapid industrialisation, while Sweden - with its long history of social democracy and relative ethnic homogeneity - provided a marker against which to measure attitudes in Britain.

Overall, we generally find that the two Germanys have much more in common with one another than might have been expected, especially in terms of their agreement over the 'cultural markers' related to the German national identity. As we noted then, it is also evident that the German notion of national identity is not markedly different to that found in other countries. Swedes express key aspects of liberalism, but also some views about immigrants that are slightly at odds with this reputation. Spain, on the other hand, presents itself as a fairly tolerant and open society, proud of its history, but also open to external, especially European, influences.

What can we conclude, especially with respect to Britain? First of all, with a few exceptions, Britain is not dissimilar to the other nations. True, the British are the least committed to *any* level of territorial community (whether this be their specific neighbourhood, a city, or Britain as a whole). But, like all the other countries considered here (bar Spain), their highest level of attachment was reserved for the nation-state. Similarities also exist in terms of what people feel comprises being 'British' or 'German' and so on. A shared language, formal citizenship and having respect for national institutions and laws all figure highly. When it comes to national pride, the highest levels within countries are found among older generations, and among those with relatively low levels of education. Britain and Spain exhibit the highest levels of national pride, and Germany the lowest. A variety of achievements and institutions instil feelings of pride, Britain standing out in its emphasis on the pride it associates with its history and armed forces. Among all other countries, scientific, artistic and sporting achievements are likely to inspire the most pride. National pride is also linked to negative attitudes towards immigration and 'foreigners'.

Britain does clearly differ from the other nations considered here in one crucial respect, its attitudes towards separatism. We asked people to choose between two options:

> *It is essential that [Britan/Germany/Spain/Sweden] remains one nation/country*
> *Parts of [Britan/Germany/Spain/Sweden] should be allowed to become fully separate nations/countries if they choose to*

A much higher proportion of the British - 31 per cent - think that parts of the UK should be allowed to become fully separate nations, the allusion clearly being to the futures of Scotland, Wales and possibly Northern Ireland. In no other country - not even Spain (in which 16 per cent opt for separatism) - does acceptance of territorial secession approach the level found in Britain. Were this to occur, of course, British national identity would take on quite a different and intriguing meaning.

References

Anderson, B. (1996), *Imagined Communities: reflections on the origin and spread of nationalism*, London: Verso. Revised edition.
Billig, M. (1995), *Banal Nationalism*, London: Sage.
Brubaker, R. (1992), *Citizenship and Nationhood in France and Germany*, Harvard University Press.
Bruce, S. (1995), *Religion in Modern Britain*, Oxford University Press.
Cohen, R. (1994), *Frontiers of Identity: the British and others*, London: Longman.
Gellner, E. (1983), *Nations and Nationalism*, Oxford: Blackwell.
McCrone, D. (1998), *The Sociology of Nationalism: Tomorrow's Ancestors*, London: Routledge.

Appendix

National pride scale

The national pride scale is based upon responses to the following six statements:

I would rather be a citizen of [Britain/Germany/Spain/Sweden] than of any other country in the world

The world would be a better place if people from other countries were more like the [British/Germans/Spanish/Swedish]

Generally speaking [Britain/Germany/Spain/Sweden] is a better country than most other countries

People should support their country even if the country is in the wrong

When my country does well in international sports, it makes me proud to be [British/German/Spanish/Swedish]

[Britain/Germany/Spain/Sweden] should follow its own interests, even if this leads to conflicts with other nations

Average values on national pride scale*, by age, education and gender within each country

	Western Germany		Eastern Germany		Britain		Sweden		Spain	
		Base		*Base*		*Base*		*Base*		*Base*
All	17.2	*997*	17.9	*455*	20.6	*912*	19.8	*1004*	20.4	*1021*
Age										
16-34	15.2	*267*	15.8	*113*	19.2	*288*	19.6	*333*	19.5	*384*
35-54	16.7	*386*	17.5	*175*	20.5	*332*	18.8	*393*	20.3	*324*
55+	19.3	*339*	19.5	*165*	22.4	*290*	21.4	*278*	21.5	*313*
Education										
Primary	18.1	*699*	19.0	*288*	22.5	*336*	20.9	*520*	21.1	*704*
Secondary	15.1	*199*	16.1	*99*	20.0	*483*	19.1	*276*	18.8	*208*
University	14.9	*90*	15.1	*59*	17.9	*93*	17.9	*197*	18.7	*105*
Gender										
Male	17.5	*561*	18.0	*235*	20.8	*390*	20.0	*526*	20.4	*516*
Female	16.8	*433*	17.7	*218*	20.5	*522*	19.6	*478*	20.4	*505*

* low average values indicate strong national pride.

2 Partner, parent, worker: family and gender roles

Jacqueline Scott, Michael Braun and Duane Alwin [*]

Introduction

There seems no going back to the so-called 'traditional' family. In just one generation in Britain, the numbers marrying have halved, the numbers divorcing have trebled, and the proportion of children born outside marriage has quadrupled (Pullinger and Summerfield, 1997). People are marrying later than in previous generations and are having fewer children. A similar pattern is evident in most other EU countries, with the rapid increase in pre-marital cohabitation challenging the once privileged position held by marriage as the main route to adult independence.

Although the traditional nuclear family appears to be crumbling, many of the alternatives to it are by no means new. Working mothers and single parents have existed for some time. What have changed are the circumstances and structures within which family life is embedded. Families, like many other modern social institutions, exist in an increasingly global culture. New patterns of consumption and services have changed both the material circumstances and the moral fabric of family life. Increased choices are available in all aspects of daily life, throwing open to question beliefs and roles that were previously taken for granted. This is particularly the case when considering attitudes towards the family and gender roles. One stark

[*] Jacqueline Scott is an Assistant Director of Research and Fellow of Queens' College, University of Cambridge. Michael Braun is a Senior Project Director and was formerly Director of the German General Social Survey (ALLBUS), ZUMA, Germany. Duane Alwin is Professor and Chair of Sociology and Program Director at the Institute for Social Research, University of Michigan, Ann Arbor, USA.

example: only a few decades ago 'living together' would definitely be a shocking act. Love, sex, and marriage, if not exactly coupled like horse and carriage, were at least intrinsically linked. And, while cohabitation is often nowadays a prelude to marriage (rather than a replacement for it), it is becoming, at least in some parts of the EU, an alternative form of partnership. Many factors have served to promote more openness about sexual expression outside of marriage but among them are improved contraception, extended educational opportunities, greater feminist consciousness and women's expanding labour force participation.

Although equality between the sexes has proved an elusive goal, it is certainly no longer safe to predict that when a girl reaches adulthood she will be, first and foremost, a wife and mother. (Most women do, ultimately, opt for marriage and parenthood, but the changing nature of employment and family life has brought the traditional division of labour between the sexes into question.) Increasingly women, even those with small children, are in paid employment. Women are now expected to contribute to the family income - but are also expected to place family needs first. These sorts of contradictions regarding the importance of family and work, as well as the tensions that surround modern gender roles, are putting a new strain on the relationships that are at the centre of family life. As Ulrich Beck, in his consideration of the contradicting demands posed by marriage and the labour market, points out:

> This contradiction ... could only remain hidden so long as it was taken for granted that marriage meant renunciation of a career for women, responsibility for the children and 'comobility' according to the professional destiny of the husband. The contradiction bursts open when both spouses must or want to be free to earn a living as a salary earner (Beck, 1992:116).

In this chapter we use data from the 1994 *International Social Survey Programme* (ISSP)[*] module on Family and Changing Gender Roles to examine the ways in which attitudes towards family life, gender roles and employment vary across nations in the EU. The module repeated many questions used in an earlier ISSP module fielded in 1988 (Scott *et al.*, 1993). We concluded then that it would be premature to mourn the loss of traditional family values, but noted that there were certainly signs of strain. We found, for example, that women were not at all certain that marriage was a recipe for happiness. Moreover, there were clear signs of change. Support for traditional gender roles seemed to be eroding and, although there was widespread belief that mothers should stay at home when they have *young* children, there was also acceptance that women should work, both to maintain their independence and as a matter of economic necessity. We predicted that such a trend towards egalitarian values would continue to grow

---

[*] See the Introduction and Appendices to this Report for further details about ISSP.

over time.   In this chapter, we will see whether that prediction is substantiated.

Another goal of the chapter is to establish whether there has been greater convergence in attitudes across the EU, with some narrowing of the gap between the attitudes of more traditional and more liberal countries. To this end, we examine the attitudes of five nations: Britain, the Irish Republic, Sweden, western Germany[*] and the Netherlands.[1] There are clearly important political and institutional differences between these countries in their approaches to family life and employment - we expect these to influence both the way in which attitudes are structured and the degree to which traditional family values are being eroded.

The five countries we consider represent a broad spectrum. At one end we find the Irish Republic, with the Catholic Church providing considerable institutional support for traditional family values (by, for example, opposing contraception, abortion and divorce). It is a country marked by relatively high fertility levels, but also by very limited public provision of childcare for working parents. And, compared with the other EU countries we consider, the rate of labour force participation among mothers is low. This is in marked contrast to Britain, where a high proportion of mothers are in paid work. The Conservative administration, despite their pro-family rhetoric, did little in policy terms to promote the economic welfare of traditional families. New Labour has taken a different route and is actively encouraging all parents (including lone mothers) to work. By contrast, policy in Germany explicitly supports mothers who chose to stay at home to care for young children, this being achieved by way of a quite strong tax disincentive applicable to two-earner couples (Alwin *et al.*, 1992; Braun *et al.*, 1994). However, Germany does have relatively high levels of labour market participation among mothers (though not as high as those found in Britain or Sweden). In the Netherlands the traditional division of labour is still prevalent, although the participation of mothers in the labour market is increasing. Despite this, and the fact that fewer women are leaving the labour force when they have children, the trend, even among the young, is to stop working, or change from full-time to part-time work, following the birth of a child. Policy has also moved in a more egalitarian direction with, for example, the introduction in 1991 of parental leave for up to six months for either partner (Ditch *et al.*, 1995). However, it is Sweden that has gone furthest in terms of policy measures supporting gender equality, through, for example, radically extending the daycare system. And labour market participation among mothers is higher in Sweden than in any of the other EU countries considered here. Yet, even in Sweden, women's involvement in jobs is clearly shaped by family factors in a way that men's jobs are not (Hoem, 1995).

---

[*] By western Germany we mean the geographical area known until unification as the Federal Republic of Germany. By eastern Germany we mean the area formerly known as the German Democratic Republic.

Despite the many differences between the five countries considered here, all are marked by a high concentration of women in part-time work. In Britain, for instance, just over a quarter of women aged 20-64 were in part-time work in the early 1990s. In the Netherlands part-time work is even more common, especially among mothers. Part-time work allows women to maintain primary responsibility for the home and children, while at the same time contributing to the family income. However, whether women choose to work part-time in order to juggle family and work roles better, or whether they have little choice because they lack partners who are willing or able to share the parenting load is far from clear.

Countries clearly differ in the support they offer those attempting to reconcile work and family life. The policies of some encourage mothers to stay at home when children are young, while others adopt policies specifically geared to enable the mothers of young children to work. Childcare provision varies considerably from country to country, with the Netherlands and Sweden both having a far higher proportion of pre-school children in publicly funded childcare than is the case in either Britain or Ireland (European Commission on Childcare, 1994). In Germany, women's labour market participation is made more difficult because the school day ends at lunch-time and there is still a clear expectation that mothers of young children will not be in paid work.

Changes in family and work life are often discussed solely in terms of women's roles, as if those of men are not also subject to change. Yet the demise of traditional expectations about family life and gender roles is having a profound effect upon the roles of husbands and fathers, as well as upon those of wives and mothers. Yet, most questions about gender roles are posed in terms of the potential conflicts between work and *motherhood*. However, as we shall see, it is by no means straightforward to ask comparable questions about the impact of fatherhood, as such questions rarely involve challenging traditional gender role ideologies in a comparable way. For men, mixing fatherhood with a career, and economic independence with family life are not contradictions that have to be fought for, often in the face of unsupportive social conditions. Nevertheless, new contradictions may emerge as traditional gender role ideology is increasingly challenged.

This chapter addresses three main questions. First, how attitudes towards family and gender roles differ across the different countries; second, how attitudes have changed over time, and whether the *degree* of change has been similar across the countries we consider; and third, the extent to which any such change reflects *generational* differences in attitudes, with older cohorts retaining more traditional beliefs despite changing circumstances. We begin by examining attitudes towards family life in general - views about cohabitation and marriage, the benefits of children, and the rights and wrongs of divorce. We then turn to attitudes towards the basic division of labour between men and women, focusing upon beliefs about the participation of women - particularly mothers - in the labour market. We also examine attitudes towards the division of labour between men and women in the home, and assess the extent to which there is any perceived conflict between 'fatherhood' and the world of work.

Family choices

Cohabitation

It was not so long ago that cohabitation was widely regarded as 'living in sin'. Now, condemnation of premarital sex has all but disappeared and premarital cohabitation is becoming the norm in many countries. In this respect, Kiernan and Estaugh (1993) identify three main groupings of countries: those where cohabitation has been well-established for some years; those where it is still emerging as a significant pattern; and those where it remains relatively unknown. Among the five countries considered here, Sweden falls into the first category (over half the Swedish respondents had experience of cohabitation), Britain, the Netherlands and western Germany into the second (with around a third of respondents having cohabited), and Ireland into the latter (with ten per cent having cohabited). Given the huge increase in cohabitation since the 1970s, experience in some countries varies greatly by age. In Ireland, for example, a quarter of those in their early twenties have cohabited, compared to none of the over sixties. By contrast, in Sweden around a quarter of the oldest age groups report having cohabited at some point in their lives - and among younger cohorts cohabitation is the overwhelming norm.

We asked two questions in order to tap attitudes towards cohabitation. The first asks whether it is 'all right' for a couple to live together before marriage, and the second whether this is actually a good idea. The next table shows the proportion of people agreeing with each statement.

Views on cohabitation

	Western Germany	Britain	Irish Republic	Nether-lands	Sweden
% agreeing:					
It is all right for a couple to live together without intending to get married	64	64	50	82	82
It is a good idea for a couple who intend to get married to live together first	66	58	49	55	86
Base	*2324*	*984*	*938*	*1968*	*1272*

Acceptance of cohabitation varies considerably, with Sweden and the Netherlands the most likely to endorse it (82 per cent doing so), Britain and western Germany being somewhat less enthusiastic (64 per cent) and Ireland the least keen of all (50 per cent). It might seem that people would be more reluctant to endorse the idea that cohabitation is a 'good idea', but it is only the Dutch who clearly differentiate between the two questions, and who are far less likely to agree with the second, far more prescriptive, statement.

In all five countries, the young are much more likely than their elders to accept cohabitation. In Britain, for instance, 85 per cent of the under-25s think it all right for an unmarried couple to live together, compared with less than 30 per cent of the over-65s.

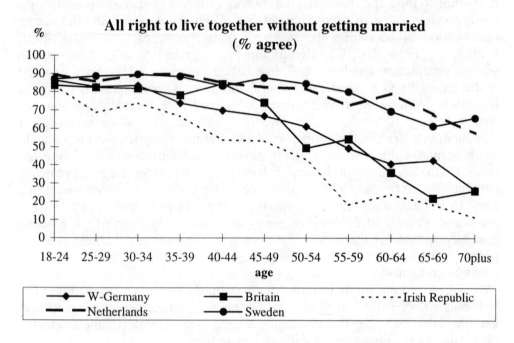

All right to live together without getting married (% agree)

We have seen that people in the Irish Republic hold the most conservative views about cohabitation. And, as the graph shows, Ireland also displays the most marked contrast between the views of young and old, implying that there has been a far more marked recent attitudinal change there than in other EU nations. By contrast, the 'gap' between young and old in Sweden and the Netherlands is relatively low, suggesting that little change in attitudes has taken place.

Marriage

Considerable changes have occurred recently in patterns of family life. Does this mean that the *meaning* attached to marriage has changed as well? The next table shows, for 1994, the proportion of people agreeing with a series of statements about marriage. The figures in brackets show the percentage point change since the question was first asked in 1994.

Views on marriage
1994, with change since 1988 shown in brackets

% agreeing:	Western Germany	Britain	Irish Republic	Nether-lands	Sweden*
People who want children ought to get married	62(-11)	57(-13)	71(-11)	31(-20)	38
The main purpose of marriage these days is to have children	23 (-5)	17 (-3)	28 (-4)	13 (-4)	12
Married people are generally happier than unmarried people	36 (-1)	24 (-9)	31(-15)	12 (-4)	16
Base	*2324*	*984*	*938*	*1968*	*1272*

* No data are available for Sweden in 1988.

When it comes to the link between marriage and children, the most 'traditional' view is clearly held in Ireland, and the least in Sweden and the Netherlands. Over seven in ten of the Irish feel that people who want children should get married beforehand, over double the proportion who take this view in the Netherlands. However, there is evidence of a marked change in attitudes in all countries over the last six years. In Britain, for instance, 57 per cent agree with the view that people who want children should get married first - a drop of 13 percentage points since this question was first asked in 1988. Similar changes have taken place in Ireland, western Germany, and the Netherlands. A corresponding, but far less pronounced, shift is apparent in the drop in the proportion viewing children as being the 'main purpose' of marriage. Although we cannot make confident predictions about change from just two readings, it does seem likely that the separation of marriage from parenthood will increase in the future. The least traditional ideas are held by the young and, as it is likely they will carry these views with them as they age, the gradual replacement of older cohorts by younger ones will result in an increasingly 'liberal' population.

In all our five countries only a minority, albeit a substantial one, take the view that married people are happier than unmarried ones. Those in western Germany are the most likely to agree with this view, just over a third doing so - and the Dutch are the least likely (around an eighth). In common with previous research findings, in all countries men take a more positive view of marriage than women (Scott *et al.*, 1993). In both Britain and the Irish Republic there has been a marked drop between 1988 and 1994 in the proportion feeling that married people are generally happier than their unmarried counterparts.

Children

We have seen evidence of a growing behavioural and attitudinal gap between childbirth and marriage. What, however, of attitudes towards children

themselves? Demographers have been warning for some time that existing
EU fertility rates are below those needed for population replacement.
Ireland's fertility rate was once an outlier in this respect but, as a result of an
extraordinary rapid decline in fertility, even it reached subreplacement
fertility in 1993 (Ditch *et al.*, 1995). In Scandinavia there has been evidence
of a recovery in fertility rates in recent years, but they have still not reached
replacement level.

When we asked about the *ideal* number of children in a family, western
Germany and Britain display a surprising uniformity, with almost everyone
opting for a relatively small family unit containing just two children. By
contrast, in Ireland there is much greater variation - with half opting for a
family comprising between two and four children and the rest divided
between either having *no* children whatsoever, only having one, or having as
many as six.

Of course, notions of ideal family size tell us little about the actual value
placed on having children. In all five countries this value is high, with over
three-quarters thinking that watching children grow up is 'life's greatest joy'.
And, in all but western Germany, a clear majority reject the notion that
children interfere too much with their parents' freedom. Intriguingly
however, west Germans are also by far the most likely to think that the
childless lead 'empty lives'.

Attitudes towards children
1994, with change since 1988 shown in brackets

	Western Germany	Britain	Irish Republic	Nether-lands	Sweden*
% taking 'pro-child' stance					
Watching children grow up is one of life's greatest joys (% agree)	83 (+7)	75 (-6)	84 (-3)	77 (+4)	86
Having children interferes too much with the freedom of parents (% disagree)	43 (0)	67 (-5)	78 (-5)	64 (-3)	71
People who have never had children lead empty lives (% agree)	42 (+8)	18 (-5)	21 (-8)	13 (-4)	17
Base	*2324*	*984*	*938*	*1968*	*1272*

* No data are available for Sweden in 1988.

In Britain and the Irish Republic, attitudes have certainly become less 'pro-
child' over time, particularly in respect to the notion that people without
children have 'empty' lives. In Britain, for instance, there has been a drop of
five points in the proportion of people taking this view, from an already low
23 per cent in 1988 to 18 per cent in 1994. In contrast, attitudes in western
Germany appear to have become more pro-child over time. Whether or not
these developments will be associated with any changes in fertility choices
remains to be seen.

Divorce

Divorce rates are a major indicator of the fact that long-term commitment within marriage can no longer be relied on. In just twenty years, the British divorce rate has doubled and for some years has been either the highest or one of the highest rates in the EU (Castells, 1996). A recent estimate, based on 1993-4 figures, predicts that four in ten British marriages will ultimately end in divorce (Haskey, 1996). Sweden's divorce rate is quite comparable with that in Britain, whereas those in the Netherlands and Germany are markedly lower. In the Irish Republic the legalisation of divorce was only endorsed in the 1995 referendum and so, at the time of our survey, was technically impossible.

We might expect attitudes towards divorce to be related to people's exposure to its consequences, both within their own families and within wider social networks. However, as the next table shows, there is little evidence of variation in this way. Indeed, in many respects it is the *similarities* between attitudes in different countries that are notable, given the quite different social contexts within which they exist.

Views on divorce

	Western Germany	Britain	Irish Republic	Nether- lands	Sweden
% taking 'pro-divorce' stance					
Divorce is usually the best solution when a couple can't seem to work out their marriage problems (% agree)	66	53	49	70	54
When there are children in the family, parents should stay together even if they don't get along (% disagree)	58	56	49	72	48
Even when there are no children, a married couple should stay together even if they don't get along (% disagree)	81	82	76	88	78
Base	*2324*	*984*	*938*	*1968*	*1272*

Ireland shows the lowest support for the notion of divorce as being 'usually the best solution', hardly surprising given the strong institutional support of the Catholic Church for the sanctity of marriage, as well as the very recent endorsement of divorce. However, the highest levels of support are found in western Germany and the Netherlands, despite their relatively low divorce rates. In Britain, there is an almost even split on whether divorce is usually the best solution but, like most other nations, the British are far more sanguine about marital separation when there are no children to consider. Far more contentious is whether couples *with* children should stay together. Here the Swedes, along with the Irish, are the most reluctant to see couples separating, although the Dutch retain their 'liberal' position by being far the least willing to concede that the presence of children should impede a couple's willingness to separate.

Within each country, older generations are considerably more opposed than younger ones to any notion of divorce when children are involved. However, unlike attitudes towards cohabitation, this is not leading to a convergence across nations. The difference between young people in our five countries is just as notable as those between their elders.

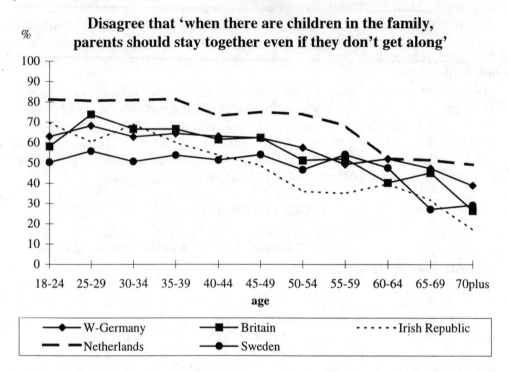

Disagree that 'when there are children in the family, parents should stay together even if they don't get along'

W-Germany   Britain   Irish Republic
Netherlands   Sweden

The gender division of labour

The benefits of women's paid employment

Family life has been deeply transformed in the last few decades by the influx of mothers into the labour market. But to what extent are public attitudes supportive of women combining family life and motherhood with the world of paid employment? We asked respondents to agree or disagree with three statements about the compatibility of work and family life for women. The next table shows the proportion taking what one might call the less traditional stance.

Views on combining work and family life
1994, with change since 1988 shown in brackets

	Western Germany	Britain	Irish Republic	Nether- lands	Sweden*
% taking less traditional stance					
A working mother can establish just as warm and secure a relationship with her children as a mother who does not work (% agree)	72 (+6)	63 (+5)	61 (+7)	70(+15)	64
A pre-school child is likely to suffer if his or her mother works (% disagree)	17 (+2)	42 (+7)	41 (+2)	34(+10)	46
All in all, family life suffers when the woman has a full-time job (% disagree)	23 (-2)	50(+10)	38 (+1)	36 (+4)	45
Base	*2324*	*984*	*938*	*1968*	*1272*

* No data are available for Sweden in 1988.

Clearly large majorities in all five countries support the notion that working women can establish good relationships with their children. However, when more precise circumstances are specified - the age of the child, for instance, or whether the job is full-time or part-time, differences between countries become more pronounced. Those in Sweden and Britain are the most likely to be supportive of working women and, in particular, working mothers. For instance, 42 per cent of the British and 46 per cent of the Swedish disagree with the view that pre-school children suffer if their mothers work. Ireland too, takes a similar stance, but is more likely to take a critical view of the impact that women working full-time has on family life. Attitudes in western Germany and the Netherlands are the least likely to be supportive of working mothers.

In all four countries which asked these questions in 1988 and 1994 there is evidence of a shift towards the view that work and motherhood are compatible (although a majority remain concerned that pre-school children may suffer if their mothers work).

To what extent do these findings reflect changing attitudes towards the roles of men and women in general? To assess this we asked three further questions about gender roles within the family, as shown in the next table.

Views on gender roles at home and work
1994, with change since 1988 shown in brackets

% taking less traditional stance	Western Germany	Britain	Irish Republic	Nether-lands	Sweden*
A man's job is to earn money; a woman's job is to look after the home and family (% disagree)	46(+12)	58 (+5)	52 (+7)	63(+10)	69
Being a housewife is just as fulfilling as working for pay (% disagree)	35 (+4)	33 (-1)	24 (+3)	31 (+1)	31
Both the man and the woman should contribute to the household income (% agree)	63(+16)	60 (+7)	76(+12)	28 (+5)	80
Base	2324	984	938	1968	1272

* No data are available for Sweden in 1988.

The pattern that emerges here is unclear. In response to perhaps the most unambiguous statement, the Swedish emerge as the most likely to disagree with the notion that a man's job is to earn money and a woman's is to look after the home and family. West Germans are the least likely to disagree with this view. The Swedes are also the most likely to think that both husband and wife should contribute to the household income, eight in ten taking this view.

When it comes to the desirability of both partners working, the country that emerges as unique is the Netherlands, where only one in four think that both partners should contribute to the household income. This perhaps mirrors differences in reality. In response to the statement 'most women have to work to support their families', the Dutch are again the least likely to agree.[2]

The most change over time has occurred in western Germany, with large shifts away from what we have called the 'traditional' stance. In 1988, for instance, around a third disagreed with the view that men should earn money and women should remain within the home. By 1994, the proportion disagreeing with this had risen to nearly a half, a rise of 12 points in only six years. A rise of a similar magnitude (16 points) has also taken place in the proportion of west Germans agreeing that both husbands and wives should contribute to their household's income.

Social commentators who argue that traditional roles have been overturned and that we live in an age of individualism with both men and women putting career interests first, should look closely at these indicators of public opinion. The British public are among the more liberal in their views on gender roles, but they can hardly be said to have abandoned traditional views. Moreover, although the trend is clearly one of increasing support for less traditional roles over time, attitudinal change is really quite slow (Scott et al., 1996; Scott, 1997).

Not surprisingly, there are marked generational differences in attitudes towards gender roles, as shown in the next figure. The British show the greatest difference in attitudes by age. While the oldest British are among the most traditional of the five nations, the youngest are among the most egalitarian. It is clear that 'age matters' on many of these attitudes, but the interesting question is *why* age matters. This question, however, goes beyond the scope of this chapter and it would require disentangling the life-cycle factors and socio-historical period effects that inhibit and propel social change (Alwin and Scott, 1996).

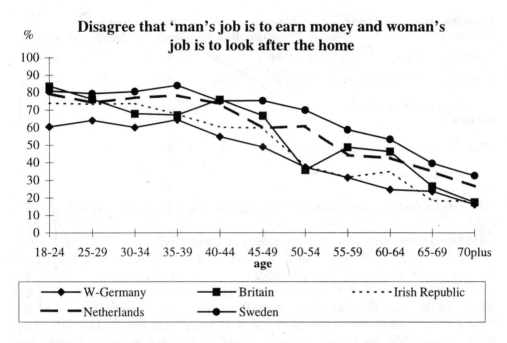

Organising domestic labour

In Britain there is little evidence that the increase of women in paid employment has been matched by a commensurate change in the way domestic tasks are divided within the households. Even when women are in full-time employment they appear to remain primarily responsible for both childcare and household chores (Witherspoon and Prior, 1991). To what extent is this true throughout the five countries considered here? Do men and women now share domestic tasks?

Traditional roles in this respect are fairly clear cut. Small repairs around the house are usually regarded as man's work, whereas doing the laundry is so much a female task that anyone unfamiliar with the power of socialisation might assume that there must be a 'whiter-than-white' gene! Caring for the sick is also traditionally regarded as lying within the female domain. To assess the extent to which such a traditional division of labour continues, we asked those living with a partner or spouse who did a variety of different household chores. For each, respondents could say that the chore was usually or always done by a woman, usually or always done by a man, done by both, or done by another person altogether.

  As the next table shows, those seeking to find evidence of 'new men' should probably read no further, if they want to preserve their dreams. The vast majority of households report that doing the laundry remains a predominantly female task, and that small repairs around the home remain largely male.

Household division of labour

% saying always or usually the woman -	Western Germany	Britain	Irish Republic	Nether-lands	Sweden*
Washing and ironing	88	79	85	87	80
Looking after sick family member	50	48	50	47	38
% saying always or usually the man -					
Makes small repairs around the house	80	75	69	78	82
Households with partners only *Base*	*1604*	*601*	*607*	*1255*	*883*

*For Sweden the base varies for the different tasks and this is the smallest unweighted base.

Of course, some might say that to expect an equal division of domestic labour is unfair as men usually contribute more than women to the household income, often by working longer hours. To explore this in more detail, we look now at two different categories of household within which *both* partners work. In the first, the man earns more than the woman and in the second the woman either earns the same as the man or more than him.[3] The following table shows, for both these groups, whether various household tasks are usually undertaken by the woman or the man. It demonstrates that, with one notable exception (the Irish Republic), households where the man earns more than his partner are more traditional than those where the woman earns the same or more than the man. This is not to say, however, that these latter households have firmly embraced a 'non-gendered' division of labour. Thus, of those British households where the woman earns the same or more than her partner, 63 per cent say that the laundry is usually done by the woman - compared with 83 per cent of those households where the man earns more than the woman. Similarly, the proportion of households where the woman usually cares for sick family members, drops from 48 per cent in households where the man earns more to 40 per cent in those where the woman earns the same or more than her partner. However, men's responsibility for small repair tasks is essentially unchanged by whether or not they are the dominant family breadwinner.

Household division of labour among dual-earning couples

	Western Germany	Britain	Irish Republic	Nether- lands	Sweden
% 'always' or 'usually' done by woman					
Washing and ironing					
Man earns more than woman	85	83	79	85	82
Woman earns more or same	78	63	80	70	72
Looking after sick family member					
Man earns more than woman	46	48	39	45	40
Woman earns more or same	35	40	37	17	30
% 'always' or 'usually' done by man					
Makes small repairs around the house					
Man earns more than woman	81	74	65	81	85
Woman earns more or same	81	79	70	78	74
Base: households where both partners work. Missing values excluded	*1586*	*577*	*602*	*1236*	*883**

*For Sweden the base varies for the different tasks and this is the smallest unweighted base.

Non-traditional gender roles

Traditional gender roles regarding the division of domestic tasks have shown great resilience. We might expect, then, minimal support for complete role reversal - as illustrated by what have been called 'house-husbands', men who stay at home to look after the children while their partner goes out to work. To assess this, we asked people to agree or disagree with the following statement:

> *It is not good if the man stays at home and cares for the children and the woman goes out to work*

Somewhat surprisingly, disapproval of these sorts of arrangements is actually quite rare. Nearly three-quarters of the Dutch (72 per cent) *disagree* with the traditional view put forward in the statement, as do half or more of those in Britain, Ireland and Sweden. It is west Germans who are the *least* likely to oppose the statement - 42 per cent doing so. In all countries, younger cohorts (and women) are more favourable than average of non-traditional roles.

What then of the potential conflict between the male role of 'breadwinner' and family life? We asked respondents to agree or disagree with the following statement:

Family life often suffers because men concentrate too much on their work

Substantial majorities agree with this statement - ranging from 58 per cent in the Netherlands to 73 per cent in Ireland. The *least* likely to agree that family life often suffers because men focus too much on work are those in Sweden, perhaps reflecting the more 'family-friendly' policies regarding men that exist there.

Earlier in this chapter we suggested that the young hold much less traditional gender role attitudes than their elders. This includes their being less likely to feel that family life suffers when women work full-time. However, when it comes to the impact on family life of *men* working there is much less variation between different age groups. It seems likely that a statement about the possibly detrimental consequences for family life of men's commitment to work does not trigger the same ideological response as a similar question regarding a woman's job. For men, work and family life are not deemed as being in conflict in the same way that they are for women. By devoting themselves to paid work, men are seen to fulfil their familial obligations, and increased hours, promotion, and greater income is regarded as beneficial for the family. For women, the situation is quite different. Consequently, the decision for a woman to enter paid employment may be seen, especially by older generations, as sacrificing family responsibilities for the selfish pursuit of self-fulfilment.

Summary and conclusions

Throughout the EU there have been dramatic changes in family life, resulting in an increasing diversity of family forms and a corresponding decline in the so-called traditional nuclear family. And, as this chapter has shown, attitudes towards family life have also changed.

There has been much debate about whether attitudes and behaviour within the EU are converging with one another or whether national differences will persist despite closer political union. The data we examine here suggest that there is no simple answer to this question. On some issues, traditional views appear very resilient. There is still, for instance, widespread concern about mothers of young children taking up paid work. On the other hand, however, with respect to other aspects of family life (such as the acceptability of cohabitation) traditional values are rapidly being overturned.

Many of the key national differences we have uncovered correspond broadly to the different religious and political contexts within the five countries considered. Thus, attitudes in the Irish Republic are among the more traditional and those in the Netherlands and Sweden among the more liberal, with Britain and western Germany somewhere in between. Nevertheless, there are sufficient exceptions to defy any simple generalisations. The Dutch, for example, are very liberal with respect to individuals' freedom to choose not to marry even if they want children, but are remarkably traditional when it comes to beliefs about whether or not mothers should work.   Similarly, although the Swedes are very supportive of egalitarian gender roles, they are relatively traditional in their reluctance to endorse divorce.

Variations in social policy are obviously very important when interpreting national differences in attitudes.   Thus, in many respects Sweden has gone the farthest towards adopting policies that are explicitly conducive to modern family forms.   There is, for example, a generous system of childcare benefits that reduces the problems that can be faced by working mothers, and there are few legal distinctions between cohabitation and marriage.   In fact, it may well be that because marriage and children are seen as optional and families are well supported, the Swedes hold such relatively restrictive attitudes towards divorce.

In the Irish Republic, public attitudes are clearly affected by the Church's stance on reproduction and divorce.   The Irish, along with their reluctance to approve of divorce, strongly endorse marriage and oppose cohabitation, and place considerable value on high fertility.   The Irish are also among the least likely to support the notion of the mothers of young children working, an attitudinal stance that both reflects and re-enforces the low rates of female labour force participation and the limited state provision of childcare. Nevertheless, it seems that the Catholic Church is losing its battle to preserve traditional family values, and that modern attitudes are gaining support, especially among younger generations.

In practice, traditional gender roles seem remarkably resilient.   In all five countries, it remains overwhelmingly women who do the laundry and men who do small household repairs. The clear segregation of gender roles across all five nations suggests that claims that men and women can create their own lifestyles are often exaggerated.   Men and women are still constrained by traditional roles, and gender remains a powerful factor in shaping opinion and belief.

Within all the countries examined, there are clear and systematic attitudinal differences linked to age. This is hardly surprising. Younger generations are more likely to have experienced cohabitation, less likely to have got married, less likely to have had children within marriage, and (with the exception of Ireland) are more likely to have experienced divorce, either themselves or through their parents. And, in most of the countries considered, the more recent cohorts of women are more likely to have worked. These experiences have helped create more individualistic and less traditional beliefs. Further, there are some interesting variations across countries in these generational differences. For example, on many issues the gap between young and old is most marked in Ireland.   There, until very recently, traditional family structures and fertility policies have proved remarkably resilient to change. However, younger cohorts of the Irish are coming into line with the rest of the EU in their endorsement of cohabitation and even the acceptance of divorce.

The relationship between age and attitudes towards family and gender roles is strong enough to suggest a 'generational' effect.   This occurs when successive generations of people hold distinctive attitudes that adhere to them over time, resulting in subsequent changes in the balance of attitudes held within society as a whole. However, we are unable here to assess the exact extent to which the patterns we uncover reflect such generational differences or, alternatively, whether they simply reflect the stages that different age groups have reached in the life-cycle.

What remains clear, however, is that attitudes and beliefs about family life and gender roles differ markedly throughout the EU. We have seen that some of these differences are likely to reflect the social and political circumstances within each country. This explanation is not, however, likely to be sufficient. Are, for instance, attitudes in Sweden different from those in Ireland because there are more working women in Sweden (and working women tend to have more egalitarian attitudes than those who are not at work)? Or, conversely, are attitudes simply more liberal in Sweden, irrespective of the labour market position of women? In short, does public policy create or reflect a broader social climate that is not simply the result of differences in social composition? This is a difficult question to disentangle, but earlier research has suggested that differences in the rate of women's labour market participation do not account for much of the observed variation in attitudes between countries. This is the case even when it comes to attitudes particularly related to issues concerned with working women, such as whether a mother of pre-school children should work (Alwin *et al.*, 1992).

To make much progress in understanding national differences, future research will need to address the ways political, institutional and cultural differences help shape how people think about the everyday life choices concerned with their roles as partner, parent, or worker. Certainly, this chapter has shown that, in a comparative perspective, Britain is relatively liberal when it comes to family values and gender roles. However, it is also clear that, along with other countries within the EU, British attitudes are often contradictory, perhaps reflecting the tensions involved in reconciling the individual ethos required by the labour market with the responsibilities of family life.

Notes

1. For the sake of comparability with the 1988 ISSP data on women and the family, it was decided to use only the 1994 data for western Germany, and to exclude eastern Germany from the analysis.
2. Agreement with the statement 'most women have to work to support their families' was 91 per cent in Sweden, 84 per cent in Ireland, 75 per cent in western Germany and Britain, and 26 per cent in the Netherlands.
3. The country containing the highest proportion of households where the woman earns the same or more than the man is the Irish Republic (30 per cent), followed by Britain, Sweden and Germany come next (around 20 per cent in each), and then the Netherlands (18 per cent).

References

Alwin, D. and Scott, J. (1996), 'Attitude Change - Its Measurement and Interpretation Using Longitudinal Surveys' in Taylor, B. and Thomson, K. (eds.) *Understanding Change in Social Attitudes*, Aldershot: Dartmouth.

Alwin, D., Braun, M. and Scott, J. (1992), 'The Separation of Work and Family: Attitudes Towards Women's Labour Participation in Germany, Great Britain and the United States', *European Sociological Review*, **8**, 13-37.

Beck, U. (1992), *Risk Society: Towards A New Modernity*, London: Sage.

Braun, M., Scott, J. and Alwin, D. (1994), 'Economic Necessity or Self-Actualization? Attitudes toward Women's Labour-Force Participation in East and West Germany', *European Sociological Review*, **10**, 29-47.

Castells, M. (1996), *The Power of Identity*, Oxford: Blackwell.

Commission of Social Justice (1994), *Social Justice, Strategies for National Renewal*, London: Vintage.

Ditch, J., Barnes, H., Bradshaw, J., Commaille, J. and Eardley, T. (1996*), National Family Policies in 1994*, European Observatory, York: Social Policy Research Unit.

European Commission Network on Childcare (1994), *Monitoring Childcare Services and Their Use*, Brussels: European Commission.

Hantrais, L. and Letablier, M. (1996), *Families and Family Policies in Europe*, London: Longman.

Haskey, J. (1996), 'The Proportion of Married Couples Who Divorce: Past Patterns and Current Prospects', *Population Trends*, **83**, 25-36.

Hoem, B. (1995), 'The Way to the Gender-Segregated Swedish Labour Market', in Mason, K. and Jenson, A-M. (eds.) *Gender and Family Change in Industrialized Countries*, Oxford: Clarendon Press.

Kiernan, K. and Estaugh, V. (1993), *Cohabitation: Extra-Marital Childbearing and Social Policy*, Occasional Paper 17, London: Family Policy Studies Centre.

Pullinger, J. and Summerfield, C. (eds.) (1997), *Social Focus on Families*, London: Office for National Statistics.

Scott, J. (1997), 'Changing Gender Roles' in Dench, G. (ed.) *Re-negotiating the Sexual Contract*, London: Institute of Community Studies.

Scott, J., Braun, M. and Alwin, D. (1993), 'The Family Way' in Jowell, R., Brook, L. and Dowds, L. (eds.) *International Social Attitudes: the 10th BSA Report*, Aldershot: Dartmouth.

Scott, J., Alwin, D. and Braun, M. (1996), 'Generational Changes in Gender Role Attitudes: Britain in a Cross-National Perspective', *Sociology*, **30**, 3: 471-492.

Witherspoon, S. and Prior, G. (1991), 'Working Mothers: Free to Choose?' in Jowell, R., Brook, L. and Taylor, B. (eds.) *British Social Attitudes: the 8th Report*, Aldershot: Dartmouth.

Acknowledgements

The support of the Economic and Social Research Council is gratefully acknowledged. This work is a continuation of research done under the ESRC's Population and Household Change Initiative (#L315253024). Duane Alwin's work on this project was supported by funding from the National Institute on Ageing (AG04743-07).

3 What people expect from the state: plus ça change …

Max Kaase and Kenneth Newton [*]

The scope and functions of the state have expanded in most western nations during the course of the twentieth century, not just in the core provisions of health and welfare but also in other aspects of social, economic, and political life. Now, in most EU nations the public sector touches most facets of life in one form or another - from the economy, public order and foreign relations to health, welfare, education, the family, and even the arts and sport.

By the 1970s the expanding role of the state was thought by some commentators to have gone too far, leading them to anticipate both a popular backlash against government regulations, taxes and services, and a 'fiscal crisis of the state' (O'Connor, 1973; Offe, 1984[1]). As a result of the state's having over-reached itself, there would, they predicted, be a widespread loss of confidence in government and increasing political challenges to its legitimacy in various spheres of life. Harold Wilensky (1975), anticipated a similar backlash in the USA among the growing 'middle mass' of American citizens. They would, he predicted, rebel against rising taxation and welfare payments and begin instead to reassert the value of individualism, hard work, and self-sufficiency. The anti-welfare mood of middle America, argued Wilensky, would then spill over into a broader attack on the state and its entire range of operations.

Since then, the western world has certainly seen many examples of political attacks on the state, including demands to roll back its frontiers, to liberalise

[*] Max Kaase is Research Professor at the Wissenshaftszentrum, Berlin and Kenneth Newton is Professor of Government at the University of Essex and Executive Director of the European Consortium for Political Research.

it, to privatise and de-regulate its functions, and generally to 'get it off the backs' of its citizens. New party groupings have been formed designed to curb state functions or power, such as the Glistrup anti-tax party in Denmark or the Referendum Party in Britain. Attempts have been made in the USA to peg tax levels, while demonstrations and even riots against new forms of local taxes have taken place in Britain. The elections during the 1970s and 1980s of Reagan, Thatcher, Kohl, and Schlüter (Denmark) were all said to symbolise this mood which represented more than a narrow reaction against taxes and welfare. It was widely described as a fundamental switch towards a mood of anti-politics, anti-party, and anti-state.

Yet, despite the swings in voting towards the right in some countries during the period, the widespread claims about a popular backlash against the modern state did not seem to materialise. Empirical research has found only very slight and very qualified evidence of any sea change in mass opinion. As Coughlin concluded from his analysis of comparative survey evidence in the USA and Europe almost twenty years ago:

> ...despite the presumed fiscal crisis of the welfare state, the taxpayers' revolt, runaway inflation and other scenarios of doom and gloom..., some types of social welfare are deeply entrenched in popular attitudes and are likely to survive whatever the developments over the next few years (1980: 153-154).

In the late 1980s further survey research came up with pretty much the same conclusion. Writing in an earlier *British Social Attitudes* Report, using data from Britain, the USA, Australia, western Germany,[*] Austria, and Italy, Taylor-Gooby concluded that:

> ...the pattern of attitudes charted by our survey conforms more to the post-war democratic welfare capitalist tradition than to the radical proposals from right or left. Public opinion in all the countries seems opposed to 'rolling back the state', or to 'a free economy and strong state', or to a highly interventionist 'democratic centralism', or to a large extension of civil liberties. Social circumstances have recently undergone fundamental change, and new theories may be developing as to the proper role of government. But reformers, whether of the left or of the right, seem to have some way to go before they win over the majority of citizens (1989: 51).

The most recent and most comprehensive review of mass opinion in Western Europe on the role and functions of the state (Borre and Scarbrough, 1995) also arrives at a similar conclusion, arguing that although the policy agenda of

---

[*] By western Germany we mean the geographical area known until unification as the Federal Republic of Germany. By eastern Germany we mean the area formerly known as the German Democratic Republic.

the general public in most Western European countries is shifting somewhat, it seems to be doing so only slowly and selectively. They conclude that public opinion almost universally regards the core services of the welfare state, including provision for health, education, housing, old age and unemployment as proper responsibilities of government. As many as around nine in every ten citizens in most Western European countries take this view, and around two in every three also hold that the state should be responsible for minority rights, gender equality, economic redistribution, and assistance for industry. True, they also find evidence of increasing support for a degree of deregulation of the economy, but this is counter-balanced somewhat by growing support for more government action on environmental issues.

Even so, as worldwide economic competition continues to become fiercer, capital becomes more mobile, unemployment still rises in many countries of Western Europe, changing family patterns lead to growing numbers of single parents, and work patterns produce more part-time, casual, and short-term jobs, the role and function of the state is bound to be called into continuous question. If, as the argument goes, the price of world labour is set in South China and nation states are no longer masters of their own fate, then a great deal of attention in many countries will be devoted to questions such as:

- whether the Keynesian demand management policy of trying to create the conditions of economic stability and growth can be sustained
- whether further de-regulation and privatisation is required
- whether cuts in public expenditure and taxation can be afforded (or avoided)
- whether an overhaul of the welfare state is inevitable, involving a re-think of policies to do with redistribution, minimum standards and universal welfare benefits.

Naturally, by no means all of the pressures arising from global changes are for a reduction in state services and activities. As noted, some of the calls are for more action by governments in relation to issues that are international in cause or likely effect. Examples include environmental matters, crime, drugs, terrorism, as well as military interventions into certain local or regional wars, and disaster or famine relief.

In short, while the proper role of the state has always been a contentious issue in western politics, it is now likely to take on a new complexion and to be injected with new vigour. In particular, the political and ideological battles will increasingly be joined not just between the traditional left and right, but also between liberals and authoritarians and a range of other competing single-issue pressure groups.

We ask in this chapter whether there are any new signs in Britain and Germany of a shift in mass attitudes towards the role and functions of the state.

Britain and Germany

Probably no western state has done more to change and reform the role of the state than Britain did between 1979 and 1997. Four successive Conservative administrations, led respectively by Margaret Thatcher and John Major, made a concerted (though not entirely successful) effort to reduce state activity across a wide spectrum of activities, to cut income taxes and public expenditure, to privatise various public services and de-regulate other services, and generally to reduce and reform the apparatus of the state. Throughout this whole period, however, successive *British Social Attitudes* surveys and other survey material showed that all this activity and the considerable rhetoric accompanying it had almost no apparent impact on public opinion towards the state and its role. Rather, in relation to issues such as tax-cutting, public opinion moved steadfastly in the opposite direction from that of the government (see, for instance, Jowell *et al.*, 1997).

Meanwhile, in Germany, debates about the proper social role of the state have been occasioned by the policies of the Kohl government - ideologically similar in certain respects to the 1979-1997 Conservative government in Britain. But two particular developments have helped to bring the debate to the fore. First, Germany contributes heavily to EU funds and has had to impose strict financial disciplines in order to meet the financial conditions for entry into the EMU. These costs have take their toll on public expenditure. Secondly, unification with eastern Germany has itself imposed very high costs, bringing about a further reassessment of the expenses of the welfare state in an era of high unemployment and relatively sluggish economic growth. On the other hand, the fall of the Berlin Wall might also have reinforced west German beliefs in the virtues of its own powerful state and strong economy.

So, if shifts in mass attitudes towards the role of the state are to be found anywhere in the EU, we might well expect them to appear in Britain and western Germany.[2] The data we use are from the *International Social Survey Programme* (ISSP)[*] surveys on the role of government in 1985, 1990 and 1996. For 1990 and 1996, we use data from western Germany in preference to reunified Germany in order to keep the comparison with 1985 valid. We confine our attention to 23 questions that were asked in all three surveys in both countries. But in order both to make the data more manageable and also to smooth out biases that might arise from single items, we have grouped responses by means of factor analysis - a statistical technique that groups sets of answers which are linked by the same underlying belief (see the appendix to this chapter). Where the factor analysis allows us to do so, we combine certain answers to form an additive measure or index.

---

[*] See the Introduction and appendices to this Report for further details about ISSP.

Our simple question then is whether and in what ways public opinion about the role of government has changed in Britain and western Germany since 1985.

The breadth of government responsibilities

All respondents in all ISSP countries were asked in 1985, 1990 and 1996 whether they thought it was or was not the government's responsibility to:

> ... *provide a job for everyone who wants one*
> ... *keep prices under control*
> ... *provide health care for the sick*
> ... *provide a decent standard of living for the old*
> ... *provide industry with the help it needs to grow*
> ... *provide a decent standard of living for the unemployed*
> ... *reduce income differences between the rich and the poor.*

These questions are used by Peter Taylor-Gooby in this volume to dissect attitudes to aspects of the welfare state. We use them differently as an indication of the *breadth* of responsibility that people think the state should have. Following the results of the factor analysis, we were able to divide the answers into three separate indices, on each of which we allocated respondents a score depending on how many of the responsibilities in that index they believed should be the responsibility of government.

Social and economic intervention

The first index refers to support for government responsibility in the spheres of social and economic intervention - such as for providing jobs, helping industry, providing decent standards of living for the unemployed and reducing income differences. Thus, if a respondent thought that the state should (definitely or probably) have responsibility for all of these roles, they would obtain a score of four points and, if none of them, a score of zero.

In general, support for social and economic intervention by the state is rather strong in both countries. In the latest surveys, for instance, almost two in three west Germans (64 per cent) and almost three in four British respondents (72 per cent) thought the government should definitely or probably be responsible for at least three of the four roles. The comparable figures in 1985 were 70 per cent in western Germany and 79 per cent in Britain, so there is some evidence of a slight decline, but nothing dramatic.

Index of government responsibility for
social and economic intervention

	Western Germany			Britain		
	1985	1990	1996	1985	1990	1996
Number of govern-						
ment responsibilities	%	%	%	%	%	%
None	5	5	4	1	2	2
One	17	21	20	13	15	16
Two	9	13	12	7	9	9
Three	34	30	30	21	26	26
Four	36	31	34	58	49	48
Average	2.89	2.69	2.78	3.28	3.13	3.11
Base	*908*	*2469*	*1811*	*1323*	*1053*	*840*

Note: the index runs from 0 (not in favour of government responsibility in any area) to 4 (in favour of state responsibility in all four areas).

Health care and pensions

The second index (scoring from 0 to 2) combines the responses to the questions on health care and minimum standards for the old, again referring here to those who felt the government should definitely or probably be responsible.

Index of government responsibility for health care and pensions

	Western Germany			Britain		
	1985	1990	1996	1985	1990	1996
Number of govern-						
ment responsibilities	%	%	%	%	%	%
None	2	5	3	1	1	1
One	*	*	*	*	*	*
Two	98	95	97	99	100	99
Average	1.96	1.90	1.94	1.98	2.00	1.98
Base	*1028*	*2746*	*2098*	*1509*	*1176*	*973*

* = less than 0.5%

Note: the index runs from 0 (not in favour of government responsibility in either area) to 2 (in favour of state responsibility both areas).

This table shows as near universal agreement as there is ever likely to be in a sample survey that health care and basic old age pensions should be the responsibility of the state. Over 95 per cent of people in both countries in all three survey periods take this consensual view.

State intervention in general

The next table (with a possible scoring range of 0 to 7) shows a combined index containing a single measure of how broadly or narrowly people in both countries define the boundaries around the role of the state.

Index of state intervention in general

	Western Germany			Britain		
	1985	1990	1996	1985	1990	1996
Number of govern-ment responsibilities	%	%	%	%	%	%
0-4	20	29	26	11	15	15
Five	18	20	19	12	15	15
Six	30	24	25	19	24	25
Seven	33	27	30	58	47	45
Average	5.41	4.91	5.07	6.02	5.78	5.76
Base	887	2427	1763	1310	1034	824

Note: the index runs from 0 (not in favour of government responsibility in any area) to 7 (in favour of state responsibility in all four areas).

Like Peter Taylor-Gooby in the chapter about the welfare state, we find that support for an active role for the state in general is higher in Britain than it is in western Germany. This has been the case for at least the last ten years. But different patterns of change *within* each country appear to have occurred. In western Germany, public sympathy for a large role for the state was at its lowest in the 1990 reading, having recovered somewhat more recently. In Britain, however, the decline (from a much higher starting point) between 1985 and 1990 has not been reversed. Nonetheless, most people in both countries still see a substantial role for the state in these seven areas. Even after the decline over the last decade, well over two-thirds of the British (70 per cent) and over one half of the west Germans (55 per cent) still think that the government should be responsible for at least six of the seven areas of state activity we asked about.

Economic policy

Other ISSP questions ask more directly whether people are in favour or against government intervention in various areas of the economy. Our factor analysis identified a selection of these to create three separate measures - one on wage and price control, one on job creation and protection, and one on less government.

Wage and price control

The scoring here is different from that in the previous indices. Here we divide our sample into three groups - those in favour of both wage and price control, those neutral or ambivalent, and those against both measures.

Attitudes to wage and price control

	Western Germany			Britain		
	1985	**1990**	**1996**	**1985**	**1990**	**1996**
	%	%	%	%	%	%
In favour of both	42	42	39	45	37	48
Neutral or ambivalent	23	29	29	33	33	27
Against both	34	29	33	22	30	25
% pro minus anti	+8	+13	+6	+23	+7	+23
Base	*1030*	*2750*	*2125*	*1478*	*1159*	*943*

Wage and price controls are issues on which the population in both countries is somewhat polarised, but with the balance of opinion (especially in Britain) in favour of state intervention. Both countries have, however, experienced fluctuations in opinion over time on these issues, probably in response to their different economic cycles - so much so that, in 1990, west Germans were more in favour of state action on prices and wages than were the British. By 1996, the 1985 pattern had re-established itself.

Job creation and protection

The second economic policy measure combines attitudes towards government intervention to finance "projects to create new jobs" and "support for declining industries to protect jobs".

Attitudes to job creation and protection

	Western Germany			Britain		
	1985	**1990**	**1996**	**1985**	**1990**	**1996**
	%	%	%	%	%	%
In favour	67	73	77	73	75	83
Neutral or ambivalent	23	22	19	24	23	16
Against	1	5	5	3	3	2
% pro minus anti	+66	+68	+72	+70	+72	+81
Base	*1028*	*2744*	*2124*	*1487*	*1170*	*955*

Opinions on government intervention to protect jobs are rather similar in Britain and western Germany, but once again the British are consistently slightly more in favour. More important, however, is the preponderance of support for this type of state intervention in both countries (at least two-thirds in all three years and most recently up to 77 per cent and 83 per cent respectively).

Less government

The third economic policy measure combines answers to two questions, which the factor analysis identified as a separate underlying dimension. The first asked respondents how much they favoured or rejected less government regulation of business, and the other how much they favoured or opposed a reduction in government spending. The next table shows those in favour of or against less government.

Attitudes to less government

	Western Germany			Britain		
	1985	**1990**	**1996**	**1985**	**1990**	**1996**
	%	%	%	%	%	%
Favour	67	67	82	49	48	53
Neutral or ambivalent	29	28	16	42	44	38
Against	5	4	2	9	8	9
% pro minus anti	+62	+63	+80	+40	+40	+44
Base	*1022*	*2727*	*2119*	*1460*	*1149*	*936*

As usual, west Germans are rather less sympathetic to state intervention than are the British, favouring less regulation. Moreover, the differences here have become more marked in the last decade largely because British attitudes have remained fairly stable while German support for government intervention in these spheres of business activity has declined in the 1990s from a low base.

The frontiers of the state

The first conclusion to have emerged from the data so far is that most people do not have any consistent ideology that is either pro- or anti- state activity or intervention in general. Rather, they tend to distinguish between different kinds of state services and responsibilities and react to them differently, supporting some and not others, favouring expansion on some fronts and contraction on others.

The second conclusion to emerge so far from the measures we have produced suggest that, despite differences of emphasis between the two countries stemming largely from their rather divergent histories and economic performance in recent decades, the similarities between them are more striking than the differences.   For instance, in both countries there is:

- overwhelming support for the public provision of health care and pensions
- a slight overall preference in favour of the control of wages and prices
- a strong disposition towards government action and money to create jobs and to support declining industries
- a strong disinclination towards government regulation of business
- a similar average number of roles that people believe should be government responsibilities.

In this respect, British and west German citizens conform quite closely to a larger Western European pattern (see for example Borre and Scarbrough, 1995; Kaase and Newton, 1995).   There is, it seems, a sort of consensus across the populations of the EU nations about what the state should and should not do, and about where the approximate boundaries of public activity ought properly to be drawn. As long as such a consensus remains, it will be one of the EU's greatest assets in enabling it to hammer out a common framework for social and economic policy in the future.

The third conclusion to emerge so far is that movements in public opinion over time on these issues have not been very large. Despite major changes in economic and political circumstances over the last decade or so and a decline in political trust, at least in Britain (Curtice and Jowell, 1997), we are unable to produce any heroic generalisations about changes in public opinion in that period with respect to the scope and functions of the modern state. Public opinion appears instead to be more subtle and discriminating than this, steadfastly resisting the ebbs and flows of ideological debates, party shifts and political fashions, or at any rate of those which advocate either a blanket expansion or a radical contraction of state activities.

Most, though not all of the figures are thus pretty much the same in 1996 as they were in 1990 and 1985, after taking into account the normal ranges of sampling variance. In any event, there are no marked shifts towards more regulation or de-regulation of wages and prices, no discernible movement away from the more or less universal belief that the state is responsible for maintaining our health and our standard of living in old age, and no large changes (though such change as there is is upward) in the proportion who favour government action to create and protect our jobs. In view of the globalisation of economic competition and increasing unemployment, we might wonder why there has not been any greater shifts in favour of more state intervention on economic matters. Perhaps the answer lies in the public's awareness that there is little that individual nation states can do about these global trends.

Has *anything* changed?

There are three rather significant and interesting exceptions to this general *plus ça change* conclusion. One notable movement, especially in western Germany, is towards decreasing public sympathy for government regulation of industry, wages and prices. In this respect, it seems that public opinion has adopted a more economically 'liberal' position than before. On the other hand, the changes are modest, or at least somewhat tentative, and might thus not be robust in the face of, say, a well-publicised instance of a failure of deregulation. Suppose, for instance, that the spread of BSE (mad cow disease) in Britain was seen to be partly a result of the lifting of government regulations, public sympathy for deregulation in general would almost bound to be affected.

Two other notable changes emerge from another set of measures we compiled on taxation and public spending, based on a set of ISSP questions where respondents are asked whether they want more or less government spending on seven broad areas. To avoid easy options, the questions include the warning that "if you say 'much more' [government spending], it might require a tax increase to pay for it". Our factor analysis uncovered three separate attitudinal dimensions from the answers to these questions - attitudes towards social spending, spending on law enforcement and defence and spending on the environment. As the next table shows, there was only a small movement over the period in attitudes towards social spending (that is on health, pensions and unemployment benefits). The British start off overwhelmingly more in favour of increases in social spending than do west Germans and they end the period even more so. But - apart from fluctuations - the change within each country is not as appreciable as might have been expected during such a turbulent period.

Attitudes to social spending

	Western Germany			Britain		
	1985	1990	1996	1985	1990	1996
	%	%	%	%	%	%
Spend more	25	39	25	49	50	52
About the same	41	39	35	37	40	38
Spend less	34	22	41	14	10	11
% more minus less	-9	+17	-16	+35	+40	+41
Base	*979*	*2671*	*2034*	*1440*	*1131*	*920*

The more interesting changes occur in the other two dimensions, law enforcement and the environment.

Law and defence

The next measure is based on two questions about spending on "the police and law enforcement" and "the military and defence".

Attitudes to law and defence spending

	Western Germany			Britain		
	1985	1990	1996	1985	1990	1996
	%	%	%	%	%	%
Spend more	18	14	30	36	34	58
About the same	55	50	54	51	56	37
Spend less	26	35	17	12	10	5
% more minus less	-8	-21	+13	+24	+24	+54
Base	979	2664	2032	1436	1128	913

Here we see a shift in western Germany away from support for increases in such spending between 1985 to 1990, followed by a bigger shift (in Britain as well as western Germany) in the other direction between 1990 and 1996. On further examination, we discover that this overall trend actually hides two separate and rather different trends. In both Britain and western Germany there has been a growth in support, dating back to 1985, for more spending on domestic law and order. Crime is increasingly seen as too serious a problem in both countries to avoid devoting extra public expenditure on trying to curb it. Although part of the same attitudinal dimension, public attitudes towards defence expenditure followed a different and less decisive pattern. In this case, support dropped between 1985 and 1990 and then rose between 1990 and 1996. It seems that neither the British nor German publics were persuaded of the certainty of any peace dividend resulting from the breakdown of the balance of power between two major power blocs in the early 1990s. Naturally, the wars in Bosnia and Iraq may also have had an effect here. At any rate, domestic and international order now seems to be a rather more urgent problem in the minds of the general public than it was a decade ago, and one that merits higher public spending.

The environment

As the next table shows, divergent trends hold true as far as public spending on the environment is concerned.

Attitudes to environment spending

	Western Germany			Britain		
	1985	**1990**	**1996**	**1985**	**1990**	**1996**
	%	%	%	%	%	%
Spend more	83	90	58	37	63	45
About the same	16	9	36	58	34	50
Spend less	2	1	7	6	3	6
% more minus less	+81	+89	+51	+32	+60	+39
Base	*1020*	*2752*	*2098*	*1382*	*1119*	*924*

When our first reading on this issue took place in 1985, the British were overwhelmingly less concerned about environmental issues than were the west Germans or, for that matter the citizens of many other EU countries. Now, it seems they are catching up, though it is more a case of a dramatic drop in concern in Germany during the 1990s than any startling rise in British concern.

It seems that German economic problems in the 1990s, occasioned partly by the costs of unification and resulting in higher taxes, may have begun eroding the longstanding sense of affluence there. A consequence of this might be less public concern than before about the environment and more about economic matters - as our measure on economic action and job creation certainly suggests. To the extent that this represents a major shift in emphasis rather than a temporary fluctuation, it could have important implications for broader academic theories about postwar culture change exemplified in countries such as Germany.

In particular, Inglehart (1997) has argued that the relatively peaceful and prosperous fifty years that Europe has enjoyed since the second world war has caused a fundamental shift away from material concerns such as prices, wages and security, towards *postmaterial* concerns such as the quality of life, individual self expression and the environment. Could it be the case instead that the 'culture shift' identified by Inglehart in countries such as Germany was not really a fundamental value change at all, merely a concomitant of steady economic growth. Thus, as economic circumstances deteriorate, perhaps, some people will become more materialist, and *vice versa*. The time period covered by the ISSP so far is, of course, too short to allow us to draw conclusions about fundamental shifts or sea-changes in mass attitudes, but further readings on this issue will be critical.

Conclusions

In spite of profound changes in political and economic circumstances between 1985 and 1996, public attitudes in both Germany and Britain towards the roles and functions of the state appear to have changed only modestly. There is certainly no evidence to suggest appreciable public support in either country for the political rhetoric that encourages a 'rolling back of the frontiers of the state'. On the other hand, neither is there evidence of any widespread wish to extend the boundaries of the state. In this respect our latest readings confirm earlier survey results (Coughlin, 1980; Taylor-Gooby, 1989; Borre and Scarbrough, 1995) which suggest that the public's core beliefs about the proper role and functions of the state are remarkably robust. In apparent defiance of those politicians and ideologists who have argued for a contraction of state activity on the grounds that big government has already gone too far, the public mood is broadly for more of the same. Certainly, we find no signs of any incipient tax revolt or welfare backlash in either country.

On the other hand, there does appear to have been a rise in support for the deregulation of business and a fall in support (western Germany) during the 1990s for public spending on the environment. In both countries there is now a greater willingness than before to spend public money on law and order. Even so, the overall picture is one of continuity rather than change, of gradual shifts in emphasis rather than any radical or wholesale transformation. The political agenda in both countries in the mid-1990s is barely different from what it was in the mid-1980s.

Moreover, there has been no discernible change in values or ideology within either country. Public opinion continues to resist the rhetoric of both left and right about the near-universal virtues or dangers of state involvement, choosing instead to discriminate between policy areas in which the state should or should not intervene. Thus, there is on the one hand near-unanimity in both countries that the state should maintain or increase its spending on health and pensions, but considerable diffidence about the state's proper role in the regulation of business and industry. No welfare backlash or tax revolts seem remotely in view.

As these observations suggest, there is surprisingly little to distinguish British from west German opinion on most of these matters. True, there are differences of emphasis and shading, but in most respects there is a close family resemblance of attitudes and values, with the British a little more supportive of state involvement than the Germans. Both nations are, however, close enough to a general EU consensus in respect of attitudes to the scope of government for their differences to be matters of detail rather than great substance (Borre and Scarbrough, 1985; Kaase and Newton, 1985).

Notes

1. Offe's first writing in German was published in Germany in 1973 but it was not published in English until 1984.
2. Both Britain and western Germany fitted the general Western European pattern of mass attitudes towards the scope and functions of the state in the 1970s and 1980s, and there is no reason to expect that their recent political histories make them any different in the 1990s.

References

Borre, O. and Scarbrough, E. (eds.) (1995), *Beliefs in Government Volume 3: The scope of government*, Oxford: Oxford University Press.

Coughlin, R. M. (1980), *Ideology, Public Opinion, and Welfare Policy*, Berkeley, California: Institute of International Studies, University of California.

Curtice, J. and Jowell, R. (1997), 'Trust in the political system' in Jowell, R., Curtice, J., Park, A., Brook, L., Thomson, K. and Bryson, C. (eds.) (1997), *British Social Attitudes the 14th Report: The end of Conservative values?*, Aldershot: Ashgate.

Inglehart, R. (1997), *Modernization and Postmodernization*, Princeton: Princeton University Press.

Kaase, M. and Newton, K. (1995), *Beliefs in Government Volume 5: Beliefs in government*, Oxford: Oxford University Press.

O'Connor, J. (1973), *The Fiscal Crisis of the State*, New York: St. Martin's Press.

Offe, C. (1984), *Contradictions of the Welfare State*, London: Hutchinson.

Taylor-Gooby, P (1989), 'The role of the state' in Jowell, R., Witherspoon, S. and Brook, L. (eds.) *British Social Attitudes: Special International Report*, Aldershot: Gower.

Wilensky, H. (1975), *The Welfare State and Equality*, Berkeley and Los Angeles: University of California Press.

Appendix

The factor analysis

The factor analysis was performed on three batteries of questions:

The economy

Here are some of the things the government might do for the economy. Please show which actions you are in favour of and which you are against:

a. *Control of wages by law*
b. *Control of prices by law*
c. *Cuts in government spending*
d. *Government financing of projects to create new jobs*
e. *Less government regulation of business*
f. *Support for industry to develop new products and technology*
g. *Support for declining industries to protect jobs*
h. *Reducing the working week to create more jobs.*

Responses were scored on a five point scale: (1) Strongly in favour, (2) in favour, (3) neither in favour nor against, (4) against, and (5) strongly against.

Taxes and Spending

Listed below are various areas of government spending. Please show whether you would like to see more or less government spending in each area. Remember that if you say 'much more', it might require a tax increase to pay for it.

a. *The environment*
b. *Health*
c. *The police and law enforcement*
d. *Education*
e. *The military and defence*
f. *Old age pensions*
g. *Unemployment benefits*
h. *Culture and the arts.*

Responses were scored on a five point scale: (1) spend much more, (2) spend more, (3) spend the same as now, (4) spend less, and (5) spend much less.

Government responsibilities

On the whole, do you think it should be or should not be the government's responsibility to...

a. *provide a job for everyone who wants one*
b. *keep prices under control*
c. *provide health care for the sick*
d. *provide a decent standard of living for the old*
e. *provide industry with the help it needs to grow*
f. *provide a decent standard of living for the unemployed*
g. *reduce income differences between the rich and the poor.*

Responses were scored on a four point scale: (1) Definitely should be, (2) probably should be, (3) probably should not be, and (4) definitely should not be.

The factor loadings are shown in the table below. The analysis picked out a number of distinct underlying dimensions. For example, those who favour the control of wages by law also generally favour the control of prices by law. Similarly, those who do not favour one are likely to reject the other as well. In the same way, in both countries and in all years, those who favour government funds for projects to create new jobs also generally favour public support for industry to develop new products and technology. Conversely, those who reject one of these are highly likely to reject the other as well. The result of this analysis was used to inform the construction of the indices reported in the chapter.

Western Germany

Factor	1985			1990			1996		
	1	2	3	1	2	3	1	2	3
The economy									
Control wages	.746			.878			.838		
Control prices	.780			.845			.842		
Cuts in spending	.624				.475				.624
Projects for jobs		.748			.759			.710	
Deregulation of bus.			.727			.701			.693
Support new products			.706			.697			.656
Support decl. indust.		.643			.600			.701	
Reduce working time		.698			.701			.641	
Tax and spend									
Environment		.678			.522			.632	
Health	.695			.683			.704		
Police			.784			.766			.767
Education		.649			.812			.759	
Defence			.807			.764			.807
Pensions	.835			.810			.804		
Unemployed	.680			.753			.752		
Culture		.798			.776			.774	
Government responsibilities									
Job for everyone	.725			.713			.745		
Prices under control	.693			.672			.687		
Health care	.650			.700			.689		
Provide for the old	.683			.699			.701		
Help to industry	.542			.495			.541		
Help unemployed	.679			.670			.608		
Reduce income diffs	.668			.685			.623		

Notes:
1. Varimax rotation was used except where only one factor was extracted by Principal Components Analysis.
2. Factor loadings below .400 are not shown.

	Britain								
	1985			**1990**			**1996**		
Factor	1	2	3	1	2	3	1	2	3
The economy									
Control wages		.853		.797			.837		
Control prices		.781		.813			.844		
Cuts in spending	-.548					.643			.745
Projects for jobs	.581			.795			.696		
Deregulation of bus.			.761			.800			.745
Support new products			.699	.762			.801		
Support decl. indust.	.704			.440	.543		.402	.578	
Reduce working time	.509								
Tax and spend									
Environment			.616		.689			.629	
Health	.787			.775			.838		
Police		.822				.705			.651
Education	.639			.602	.423		.732		
Defence		.804				.832			.892
Pensions	.739			.745			.611		
Unemployed	.619			.615			.482	.455	
Culture			.890		.780			.858	
Government responsibilities									
Jobs for everyone	.821			.779			.726		
Prices under control	.638			.645			.652		
Health care		.864			.872		.600		
Provide for the old		.842			.833		.711		
Help to industry	.473			.402			.564		
Help unemployed	.635			.624			.662		
Reduce income diffs.	.793			.768			.714		

Notes:
1.   Varimax rotation was used except where only one factor was extracted by Principal Components Analysis.
2.   Factor loadings below .400 are not shown.

4 Commitment to the welfare state

Peter Taylor-Gooby [*]

The political traditions of all western European nations agree that governments should take the primary responsibility for the welfare of their citizens within an otherwise market-orientated society. This distinctive characteristic of European capitalism contrasts sharply with the more *laissez-faire*, non-interventionist systems of the major liberal democracies (notably the USA and Australia) and with the 'Confucian' systems of family and community obligation of the Far East.

However, European welfare states are now under greater pressure than ever before. In the short-term, the fiscal demands of monetary union have required EU member states to restrain state spending in order to reduce budget deficits. Meanwhile, longer term trends have been chipping away at the fabric of state welfare capitalism. In particular, the ageing of the populations in most developed countries will mean rising costs in pension provision and health care. Technological changes, combined with the concentration of industry and enhanced competition from outside Europe, generate rising levels of unemployment. In addition, politicians in many developed countries are increasingly coming to the conclusion that the taxes necessary to finance expansive welfare systems are no longer electorally sustainable (see also Kaase and Newton in this volume).

This chapter looks at developments in public attitudes towards the welfare state in four countries (Britain, Germany, Italy and Sweden) and considers how governments might deal with the challenges they face. It asks whether public attitudes may press European welfare states to converge on lower levels of state provision, targeting only certain closely-defined 'needy'

[*] Peter Taylor-Gooby is Professor of Social Policy at the University of Kent.

groups, or whether welfare systems in different countries will instead begin to diverge, each nation adopting its own distinctive solutions.

Looked at from the perspective of public attitudes and their impact on policy, we ask whether or not the welfare state - a European invention that rapidly spread to other countries principally through the influence of Europe's ex-colonial nations - is now beginning to lose some of its near-universal appeal within Europe itself.

These issues are particularly important in Britain, which spends relatively less on its welfare provision and is generally more market-orientated than most other nations in the EU. Indeed, according to OECD figures, the proportion of the GDP allocated by government to welfare is lower in Britain than in any other EU state (OECD, 1994). Moreover, the emphasis of current British policy on the creation of an 'opportunity society' as successor to the more traditional welfare state signals a possible shift from a social democratic to a more liberal democratic approach to policy-making.

Already somewhat adrift in its welfare policies from the dominant tradition in the rest of the EU, it may be that Britain will move still further out of step. How much and at what speed will, of course, depend on the ways in which other nations move - hence this examination of cross-national differences and similarities.

Patterns of state welfare

Commentators generally distinguish three different types of welfare state within Europe, each having been influenced by different historical circumstances, political frameworks and social values (see Castles and Mitchell, 1990; Esping-Andersen, 1990; 1996; Leibfried, 1990). These are:

- The *corporatist* welfare systems of most of mainland EU - for instance those in Germany, France, Austria and the Benelux countries. The central feature of their welfare provision is social insurance. Benefit entitlements tend to be closely linked to the contributions made by individuals during their working lives. Similar systems finance access to health and social care. These arrangements tend to produce a strong sense of benefits as a right because of the direct link between an individual's contributions and a particular package of entitlements. Nonetheless, these state-backed insurance systems are also typically designed to pay benefits on an earnings-related basis, thus replicating the inequalities of working life in the benefit levels available to the unemployed or pensioners. Moreover, those who have had only intermittent employment are also likely to have inadequate insurance, eroding their entitlements. By the same token, contribution credits for those (mostly women) who spend periods on child care outside the formal labour market tend to be limited. Thus, at a time when working lives are becoming more flexible and family break-ups more frequent, the risk in these countries is that a two-tier system of entitlement may develop in which those with continuous and secure employment opportunities are relatively well provided for while those without such opportunities may have to rely on stigmatic and low levels of social assistance.

- The *social democratic* welfare systems of Scandinavia, whose welfare provision is characterised by a strong concern to promote social equality pursued through high standards of universal state benefits and strong programmes to spread equal opportunities in education and employment. Initially the state benefits in these countries were financed mainly through direct taxation, weakening the link between one's work record and one's entitlement and strengthening a system of universal provision. In recent years, however, earnings-related provision has begun to develop mainly for additional pensions and similar benefits, resulting in greater differentiation of outcomes. Even so, the Scandinavian countries retain their commitment to universality and continue to provide the most generous entitlements in the EU to the unemployed, lone parents and pensioners. They also continue to pursue 'active labour market' policies and equal opportunities legislation which has resulted in advances by women and other groups traditionally at a disadvantage in the occupational hierarchy. Such systems are highly expensive and require continued political endorsement, and there is growing concern that they cannot survive in the context of an EU in which most states organise welfare provision on different lines. These concerns have been prominent in the campaigns against EU membership in these countries.

- The *liberal-leaning* systems of the Western fringe (Ireland and Britain), which tend to target state help towards the demonstrably needy and have substantial private welfare sectors in, for instance, pension provision. These nations do not have purely liberal welfare systems (which would imply the restriction of state provision solely to the poorest sections of society who could not otherwise meet their needs through the market). On the contrary, the British model includes, for instance, a tax-financed and virtually universal National Health Service, as well as universal child benefits. Even so, the British national insurance system is not based on the sorts of entitlement contracts typical of continental social insurance. It is in fact little more than welfare provision mainly financed through a specific tax on employment and always vulnerable to variation - both in benefit levels and in contribution levels - by immediate decisions of the government of the day. In any event, entitlement to many welfare services in Britain and Ireland (particularly cash benefits) tends to be more restricted and at a lower level than in most other European countries.

Such a broad-brush categorisation inevitably obscures important distinctions. For instance, France and Germany have particular traditions of citizenship based on a territorial or a blood relationship that influences rules of welfare entitlement. In addition, German re-unification has had a strong impact on its welfare regime, having linked the leading corporatist system with the highly inclusive model of a former communist state which provided secure employment and other welfare services - such as child care for both men and women - but with relatively low levels of benefits and wages. Meanwhile, the Dutch system, though often described as corporatist, is in many respects close to the social democratic Scandinavian models.

Some commentators (Ferrera, 1993) also identify a fourth model of welfare provision - the *Mediterranean* model - as represented by Italy, for instance, which is characterised by low spending on the needs of those of working age, accompanied by an emphasis on promoting universal health care and education and on social insurance for pensions.

Responses to pressures on welfare

How might the various EU welfare systems respond to the pressures they are experiencing? Several studies of the way pension systems respond to the pressures of an ageing population (which demands more spending at a time when there are fewer people in work to provide the revenue) has concluded that the trend is for different countries to diverge (Myles and Quadagno, 1996; CEC, 1995; Daly, 1997). In the past provision has tended to converge slowly, especially during the 1950s, 1960s and early 1970s, as social insurance systems moved away from strict insurance rules, and tax-financed systems slackened means-tests. However, when a nation experiences pressure on its expenditure, there is a tendency to retreat to its core principles of provision. Since it is always difficult to take away entitlements 'bought' by contribution under the social insurance systems, their rules become stricter and the division between those in and out of stable employment grows sharper. Conversely, the tax-financed systems tend to target more narrowly and introduce stricter means-tests. The result, according to these analysts, is that pressures will operate differently on the different systems and lead them to diverge more than they have done to date.

An alternative view is that common pressures will lead to greater similarity in provision. Concerns have been expressed that differences in welfare entitlements will lead to inefficiencies within the single European market. Thus, while workers in the best-served countries will seek to protect their privileges, big business will respond by shifting operations to countries with less expensive welfare provision and lower labour costs. This process has already led the Commission of the EU to press for wider powers to enforce uniformity in tax regimes, health and safety and training (Glennerster, 1993). Meanwhile the Maastricht Treaty has led to more uniform enactment of equal opportunity and equal entitlement provisions by gender, race and religion.

In addition to these pressures, the EU has to deal with the problems of economic globalisation, often thought to demand a 'levelling down' of provision within developed countries in order to reduce labour costs and beat off competition from more recently industrialised nations, particularly in South-East Asia. Meanwhile, international agencies such as the OECD have advocated the need for restraint in welfare spending by European countries, as well as greater flexibility in employment practices and a wider role for non-state provision, if they are to continue producing high quality products at acceptable prices (Oxley and Martin, 1991; OECD, 1995).

The research questions

In this chapter we use the data provided by the *International Social Survey Programme* (ISSP)[*] to examine two issues. First, we ask whether trends in the patterns of public support for welfare provision are different in different EU countries and, in particular, whether they are converging or diverging. Secondly, we ask whether public attitudes tend to reflect the distinctive corporatist, social democratic and liberal-leaning frameworks that are supposed to characterise the governance of different countries.

We shall also use the material to examine an important issue in relation to current welfare debates - closely associated with new Labour's approach to the issue - which emphasises opportunities for education and work rather than the passive provision of benefits. Encapsulated in a slogan in Tony Blair's foreword to a wide-ranging welfare Green Paper, the policy is to modernise the welfare state so that it is designed to provide "work for those who can, security for those who cannot" (DSS, 1998). We ask whether an approach which seeks to redirect effort towards jobs rather than benefits is likely to find favour not only in Britain but elsewhere in Europe too.

Trends in support for the welfare state

The data

The data in this section are drawn from the ISSP modules asked in 1985, 1990 and 1996, all of which concentrated on aspects of 'the role of government'. We look first at a series of questions designed to elicit how much the political culture in the countries differs in its support for government intervention in various spheres of life and, if so, how closely these differences match actual patterns of intervention in those countries. In each of the years, the questionnaires included a number of questions asking whether, on the whole, it should or should not be the government's responsibility to ...

 ...provide a job for everyone who wants one

---

[*] See the Introduction and Appendices to this Report for further details about ISSP.

...provide health care for the sick

...provide a decent standard of living for the old

...provide a decent standard of living for the unemployed

...reduce income differences between the rich and the poor

The answers thus allow us to compare, within and between countries, public attitudes towards the government's role in different aspects of welfare provision. The five examples include the core elements of welfare provision (health care and pensions) which involve the greatest amounts of state spending everywhere; the element which has provoked the most strident debates about the interface between welfare and the market (unemployment benefit); and other pillars of state welfare in the post-war years (full employment and progressive taxation).

Unfortunately, since countries joined the ISSP at different times and deposit their data at different rates, we do not have all three rounds of data for each of the four countries we examine here. For Britain and western Germany[*], we have all three rounds; for Italy we have only two rounds (1985 and 1990); and for Sweden only one round (1996).[1] Although this produces some discontinuities in time periods, it does allow us to compare the largest representatives of the corporatist tradition (western Germany), the liberal-leaning tradition (Britain), the social democratic tradition (Sweden), and the Mediterranean tradition (Italy).

Not surprisingly for European nations (unlike the US, for instance, where answers are very different), we found a good deal of public support everywhere for the notion that governments should assume some responsibility for all of these aspects of life. To distinguish general sympathy for these policies from reasonably unequivocal support for them, we confine the distributions in the following tables to those who said it was ***definitely*** the government's responsibility to provide each service.[2]

Patterns of support

Given the different models of welfare state provision we have referred to, we might have expected large national differences in public attitudes to how far their governments should involve themselves in these different areas of life. In particular, if the different styles of welfare provision were echoed in public attitudes, we would expect the public in western Germany to be supportive of welfare provision as a central state responsibility, although only to the extent

---

[*] We confine our attention here to the responses from western Germany rather than to those from the whole of Germany, as our benchmark figures in 1985 applied only to what was then the Federal Republic of Germany. The inclusion of eastern Germany, the area formerly known as the German Democratic Republic, with its very different systems and the legacy of a different political ideology would otherwise have confounded our comparisons.

that state intervention does not conflict with the operation of the market economy. Public attitudes in Sweden would show even more marked support for the welfare state, with less concern for the costs. Italians would tend to support government intervention in health care and pensions, but less so in other areas, while the British would tend to give all these services a lower priority than elsewhere. As the tables show, however, the reality is rather different.

Health care for the sick

% saying government should definitely be responsible	Western Germany		Britain		Italy		Sweden	
		Base		Base		Base		Base
1985	54	1028	85	1509	87	1569	n.a.	
1990	57	2746	85	1176	88	979	n.a.	
1996	51	2293	82	973	n.a.		71	1189

n.a. = not available

A decent standard of living for the old

% saying government should definitely be responsible	Western Germany		Britain		Italy		Sweden	
		Base		Base		Base		Base
1985	56	1028	78	1503	82	1564	n.a.	
1990	54	2749	79	1178	82	982	n.a.	
1996	48	2296	73	969	n.a.		69	1200

n.a. = not available

A decent standard of living for the unemployed

% saying government should definitely be responsible	Western Germany		Britain		Italy		Sweden	
		Base		Base		Base		Base
1985	24	1006	44	1448	39	1528	n.a.	
1990	19	2667	32	1139	32	964	n.a.	
1996	17	2199	29	924	n.a.		39	1175

n.a. = not available

Providing a job for everyone who wants one

% saying government should definitely be responsible	Western Germany		Britain		Italy		Sweden	
		Base		Base		Base		Base
1985	36	1020	38	1441	51	1553	n.a.	
1990	30	2702	24	1136	38	974	n.a.	
1996	28	2238	29	935	n.a.		35	1163

n.a. = not available

Reducing income differences between the rich and the poor

% saying government should definitely be responsible	Western Germany		Britain		Italy		Sweden	
		Base		Base		Base		Base
1985	28	968	48	1419	47	1508	n.a.	
1990	22	2623	42	1137	38	969	n.a.	
1996	25	2180	36	913	n.a.		43	1163

n.a. = not available

The preceding tables show a clear and substantial commitment in all four countries, regardless of their welfare state traditions, to the state's responsibility for services of mass need, such as health care and old age pensions.[3]   However, although substantial minorities in all these countries also support government action on job creation, benefits for the unemployed and redistribution of income, there is much less enthusiasm for these options. So, in these respects at least, a common pattern emerges that transcends the different models of welfare state provision and runs counter to the proposition that public attitudes will tend to reflect these varying traditions of welfare governance.

   To the extent that there are consistent *national* differences, by far the most marked, running through all aspects of welfare state provision, is a division between corporatist western Germany on the one hand, and Mediterranean Italy, liberal-leaning Britain, and social democratic Sweden on the other. Public support for a strong interventionist role by government in welfare provision is weaker in Germany than in any of the other three countries (the single exception being the British public's relative hostility to job creation). Once again, if we had anticipated different models of actual welfare policy to be reflected in public attitudes, we would be disabused by these findings. That approach implies that liberal-leaning Britain rather than corporatist western Germany would lead the opposition to wide state responsibility for welfare goals. It turns out to be the other way around. Moreover, there is more within-nation variation in attitudes to different service areas and policies than there is between-nation variation in overall public values.

Convergence or divergence?

The findings above reveal a slight common cross-national tendency over time against the view that health care, pensions and unemployment benefits should be the responsibility of government. The same pattern applies to redistribution, except in Germany. As for job creation, public support declines sharply in the late 1980s - possibly in response to the somewhat improved employment situation after the economic crisis of the early 1980s - but the decline is much less marked in Germany and reversed in Britain in the 1990s.

Since these changes over time are similar in each of the countries, the effect is that differences between the countries persist over time, particularly the markedly lower level of support for welfare policies in western Germany. Therefore, the anticipated *convergence* of European public attitudes has not taken place. For that to have happened, the pressures on welfare provision throughout the EU would have had to operate in different directions or at different speeds in different countries, which does not seem to be the case.[4] Indeed, even in Britain, where government attention has been sharply focused on the need for retrenchment, public attitudes have grown no more distinctive than they were.

The foundations of attitudes to welfare

Much academic discussion of European welfare states has centred on the argument that the differences between them are sustained by different patterns of public support. Although this view seems to be partially contradicted by our finding that countries with very different models of welfare nonetheless seem to have similar public attitudes, these national averages may hide underlying differences in the sources of support.

It has been argued that the corporatist model exemplified by Germany owes much to the Bismarckian strategy of pacifying the working classes in order to defuse the threat of class-struggle. However, as a strategy geared towards labour market participation it tends to reflect the preferences and interests of those in formal employment. People (mostly women) who have interrupted work records through unemployment or child-rearing or home-making receive lower levels of support. Thus Germany has been defined as a 'strong bread-winner welfare state', embodying not only a strict division between the domestic sphere and the labour market, but also valuing the latter much more highly (Lewis, 1992; see also Shola Orloff, 1993).

In contrast, the Scandinavian model owes much to the political struggles of small farmers and industrial workers, which led to more or less stable social democratic government in favour of an inclusive, egalitarian system. This model generated strong opportunities for women to enter the labour market with an impressive degree of equal opportunity and good support services for parents in full-time paid employment. Even so, most of the jobs held by women, particularly at a senior level, are within the state sector (Esping-Andersen, 1990).   The welfare cleavages in Scandinavian countries lie between state and non-state sector workers rather than between the social classes to a greater extent than elsewhere.

The liberal-leaning welfare system is exemplified in Europe by Britain, but is seen in its purest forms in countries such as the USA and Australia. It developed in societies where capitalism was particularly self-confident. In these systems, welfare tends to be more subject to market principles, so that state benefits are relatively low and there is a particular aversion to redistribution or to benefits which might strengthen the position of unemployed people. Equal opportunity legislation for women also tends to be relatively weak in these countries.

If these national differences have indeed become entrenched in public attitudes, then:

- in relation to *income inequality*, we should expect that Britain, the most liberal-leaning society, should display stronger conflict over state responsibility than either Germany, where conflict is contained through a corporatist tradition, or Sweden, where the objective is greater equality and social inclusion;

- in relation to *gender inequality*, we should expect Germany with its 'strong breadwinner' model to produce stronger conflict over state responsibility than either Britain, where welfare has always been less concerned with household roles, or Sweden, where the welfare state seeks to provide services which will underpin gender equality;

- in relation to *employment status*, we should expect the division in attitudes between those working in the large state sector (which is seen as an integral part of the welfare state) and the private sector to be greater in Sweden than elsewhere;

- in relation to *labour market position*, we should expect the cleavage in support for welfare provision between those in full-time work in Germany, where entitlement is clearly related to employment record, to be more marked than in Sweden with its universalist ethos, with Britain occupying an intermediate position;

- in relation to *different kinds of welfare provision*, we should expect variation *within* as well as between countries. For instance, we should expect provisions that meet basic health needs and pensions to provoke less conflict or dissent than would more interventionist activities such as providing benefits or jobs for the unemployed, or redistributing income.

We shall use data from the 1996 ISSP survey to test these predictions.

In order to simplify the analysis, we focus from now on upon reunified Germany, Sweden and Britain as exemplars of the three main welfare regimes. We are able to switch at this point from western Germany to reunified Germany, because our focus now moves away from trends (where the base has to be kept constant) to pressures operating on governments at one point in time. We also focus on only three key aspects of the welfare state: pensions, unemployment benefits and income distribution.

Providing a decent standard of living for the old

% saying government should definitely be responsible	Germany	Base	Sweden	Base	Britain	Base
Gender						
Men	49	1673	65	610	68	396
Women	57	1715	74	590	76	573
Income						
High income	39	508	65	225	59	180
Middle income	57	1068	70	584	67	431
Low income	59	589	77	391	85	243
Economic status						
Full-time employed	50	1657	62	606	63	414
Other economic status	56	1731	76	698	74	579
Employed						
State sector	46	420	71	390	75	254
Private sector	53	1124	73	105	72	532

Notes: High income = top quartile; middle income = middle two quartiles; low income = lowest quartile.

Other economic status includes those working part-time, the unemployed and the economically inactive.

Providing a decent standard of living for the unemployed

% saying government should definitely be responsible	Germany	Base	Sweden	Base	Britain	Base
Gender						
Men	21	1632	31	598	24	386
Women	26	1638	46	577	32	538
Income						
High income	12	493	34	383	18	177
Middle income	24	1028	39	568	24	411
Low income	36	576	46	224	42	228
Economic status						
Full-time employed	19	1619	28	588	19	415
Other economic status	29	1651	48	688	32	579
Employed						
State sector	16	410	40	483	32	240
Private sector	21	1088	36	481	28	510

Notes: High income = top quartile; middle income = middle two quartiles; low income = lowest quartile.

Other economic status includes those working part-time, the unemployed and the economically inactive.

Reducing income differences between the rich and the poor

% saying government should definitely be responsible	Germany	Base	Sweden	Base	Britain	Base
Gender						
Men	29	471	37	599	34	378
Women	36	575	50	564	38	535
Income						
High income	15	496	32	372	14	172
Middle income	34	1016	46	572	30	412
Low income	45	566	54	219	55	228
Economic status						
Full-time employed	28	1598	34	591	24	414
Other economic status	37	1632	51	675	38	578
Employed						
State sector	30	401	48	481	35	236
Private sector	30	1074	41	474	36	505

Notes: High income = top quartile; middle income = middle two quartiles; low income = lowest quartile.

Other economic status includes those working part-time, the unemployed and the economically inactive.

Throughout the three nations and in response to all three aspects of welfare provision, women are more supportive of the welfare state than are men. Similarly, support tends to rise as income declines. This is hardly surprising in view of the fact that social provision is generally thought to benefit those on lower incomes more than those on higher incomes and women more than men. So what we seem to be seeing is simply a reflection of self interest at work.

But what of the distinctions we had expected in terms of the theory? We had expected greater divisions between rich and poor over income redistribution in Britain than in either Germany or Sweden. This is borne out. Solidarity between income groups seems strongest in Sweden, in keeping with the tradition of social democracy.

We had also expected gender differences to be particularly large in Germany, but it turns out that, while Germany and Britain are rather similar (in the case of attitudes to redistribution and to benefits for unemployed people), it is Sweden that has the largest gender gap. Could it be that equal opportunities in the formal labour market in Sweden have sharpened the conflicts there, perhaps, because of the difficulties faced by full-time working women in reconciling the demands of their work and domestic responsibilities?

Our third assumption, that the state/private sector division in employment would be reflected most strongly in welfare attitudes in Sweden, is not supported. The division emerges most clearly in Germany.

The fourth suggestion, that full-time employment would relate most clearly to attitudes in corporatist Germany, is confirmed. However, there are also substantial divisions in Britain, perhaps reflecting national political debates which imply that the direct taxes paid by those in work finance the benefits for others.

Finally, we had expected differences in attitudes between the various elements of the welfare state - with pensions, for instance, provoking less controversy than unemployment benefits or income redistribution. While it is true that the average level of support for pensions is higher than in other areas there still seems to be considerable disagreement between the social groups. The very low support of higher income people in Britain and Germany for redistribution and for benefits for unemployed people is striking.

This general picture is confirmed by multivariate analysis which takes all these factors into account simultaneously (see appendix for more details of the models). This brings out the greater divisions between social groups in relation to the strongest interventions in the capitalist market system (income redistribution and support for unemployed people), the significance of unemployment and, most strongly, of income divisions and the greater social solidarity in Sweden.

The most striking point about this analysis in relation to the predictions of 'regime theory', however, is the similarity it displays in the patterns of public attitudes within the different sorts of welfare regimes - in particular the lack of distinction between Germany, Europe's leading corporatist power, and

Britain, its leading liberal-leaning nation. Social democratic Sweden differs from the other two in the small income divisions and in the similarity of views between middle and low income groups. In general, however, British attitudes to welfare cannot be described as being out of step with those in the rest of the EU.

Modernising welfare

A growing political consensus has emerged that welfare states need to reform themselves not only in response to new developments in work and family structure, but also as a means of keeping rising state expenditure (and therefore taxes) under better control. Linked to concerns about unemployment and benefit dependency, debates about modernising welfare also increasingly emphasise employment rather than benefits as the appropriate way to combat low incomes among those of working age. Derived largely from the USA, this approach has been prominent in the proposed reforms of the new Labour government in Britain under the slogan 'Welfare to Work'. Is there any sign that public attitudes, particularly among the unemployed themselves, match this new philosophy of welfare, embodying as it does a move away from maintenance and towards opportunity for those not currently in the labour market?

In the next table we contrast answers to the questions we used earlier about the responsibility of government to provide a job for everyone who wants one and to provide a decent standard of living for the unemployed, and look separately at the answers of those with and without jobs. By this means we can see how far those in receipt of welfare services tend to endorse policies for more active measures (job creation) as against more passive ones (increased benefits).

Jobs *versus* benefits for the unemployed

	Germany		Sweden		Britain	
	Unem-ployed	Em-ployed	Unem-ployed	Em-ployed	Unem-ployed	Em-ployed
% saying government should definitely be responsible for						
Jobs for everyone who wants them	65	34	50	29	40	23
A decent standard of living for the unemployed	47	19	65	32	48	23
Base	*225*	*1804*	*84*	*759*	*40*	*511*

Not surprisingly, perhaps, unemployed people in all three nations prove to be much keener than are those in work to attribute responsibility to governments to provide for both jobs *and* adequate benefits. Both unemployed and employed people are relatively keener on benefits as a solution in Sweden and on jobs in Germany with weaker attitudinal differences in Britain. There thus appears to be no consensus endorsing interventionist measures across the different European welfare regimes.

Conclusion

We have found some differences in the patterns of support for welfare policies between the major European states and in most policy areas a weakening of support over the years. Since that decline is happening in parallel in different countries, there is no evidence of convergence between public attitudes in different countries.

Such differences as we *do* find, do not comply with the assumptions of the dominant strands in welfare state theory. In particular, contrary to the implications of the model, British opinion does not appear to be strikingly less supportive of welfare in general than that in corporatist countries, and is in fact noticeably more supportive of some of the more integrative aspects of provision. The recent trend in welfare policies towards an emphasis on jobs rather than benefits finds sympathy in German popular attitudes, while benefits are favoured in Sweden.

These findings lead to three main conclusions. First, current theoretical frameworks for the analysis of European welfare states are hardly satisfactory in providing a foundation for understanding divisions at the level of public attitudes. Public attitudes, though in some respects still distinctively 'national', seem obstinately to resist conforming to the dominant policy themes of the welfare systems they inhabit.

Secondly, there is no evidence of convergence in public opinion in relation to welfare in different European states. There is evidence of a slight but consistent cross-national shift away from support for government action on welfare but not of a differential impact on countries with different welfare regimes.

Thirdly, as far as public attitudes are concerned, Britain certainly does not emerge as a liberal-leaning welfare regime. It is much closer in its overall attitudes to welfare to countries such as Sweden and Italy than it is to Germany, although the pattern of divisions in attitudes between social groups does not reflect the solidarity found in the more social democratic countries.

Overall, there is no obvious European convergence from which Britain is excluded, nor any sign that Britain's current emphasis on jobs not welfare will lead the way in European welfare reform.

Notes

1. The questions about job provision and the reduction of income differences were also included in 1987 and 1992 surveys, but with rather different wording. Since preliminary analysis suggested that the two wordings are not directly comparable, the 1987 and 1992 data are not covered in this chapter.
2. One problem in the analysis is disentangling people's ideas about issues of principle - what the role of the government in welfare should be - from issues of practice - what their government should be doing for them in the current context, where their views may be influenced by considerations of need, advantage or the incidence of taxation. Some common survey questions tend to conflate these two different elements. Questions about the level of state spending on welfare services may produce answers reflecting concerns about how much the government should spend in a particular area to meet the needs that the respondent perceives, or about the level of engagement that the respondent thinks government should have in meeting a particular need. One answer is to do with the current success of a particular welfare state in providing a service, the other to do with the question of the role of government in welfare provision in general.

   Attitude surveys indicate that respondents are able to discriminate between different questions of this sort and, in particular, between questions of principle and those concerned with current policies. For example, the 1996 ISSP survey included, along with questions about whether the respondent believes it is the responsibility of government to provide various services, some questions about whether government should *spend more* on services in these areas.

	Britain	Western Germany	Sweden
% saying government should spend more or much more on ...			
... unemployment benefits	35	27	43
... health	91	52	77
... old age pensions	78	42	56
% saying government should probably or definitely have responsibility for ...			
... a decent standard of living for the unemployed	78	74	91
... health care for the sick	99	92	96
... a decent standard of living for the old	97	92	98
Base	*993*	*2402*	*1360*

As discussed in the text, there is considerable agreement across countries that have different traditions about the *structure* of welfare provision. But there is considerable variation in support for increased spending, presumably reflecting local factors which will include ideas about the current level of need and how well government is meeting it, the respondent's own conception of personal advantage and interest and views on whether the responsibility lies with government in the first place.

The fact that answers to the two sets of questions vary so substantially (and in the expected direction) suggests that respondents *do* differentiate between current government policies and the principles of state welfare. We can thus feel confident about using the questions in the way that we do in this chapter.

3. The tables show the proportion who say that these services are *definitely* the responsibility of government. When adding those who say that it is *probably* the responsibility of government, the proportion giving this answer rises to over 90 per cent in all five countries.

4. The only sign of real convergence we found seemed to be a result of German reunification, where east Germans seem to be shifting their attitudes towards those of west Germans.

References

Castles, F. and Mitchell, D. (1990), *Three Worlds of Welfare Capitalism or Four?*, Public Policy Programme Discussion Paper no 21, Australian National University, Canberra.

Commission of the European Community (1995), *Social Protection in Europe*, Luxembourg.

Daly, M. (1997) 'Welfare States under Pressure: Cash Benefits in European Welfare States over the Last Ten Years', *Journal of European Social Policy*, **7/2**: 129-46.

Department of Social Security (1998), *A New Contract for Welfare*, cm 3805, London: HMSO.

Esping-Andersen, G. (1990), *Three Worlds of Welfare Capitalism*, Cambridge: Polity Press.

Esping-Andersen, G. (1996), *Welfare States in Transition*, Newbury Park: Sage.

Ferrera, M. (1993), *Modelli di solidarietà*, Bologna: Il Mulino.

Glennerster, H. (1993) 'Paying for Welfare: Issues for the Nineties', in Deakin, N. and Page, R. (eds.) *The Costs of Welfare*, Aldershot: Avebury.

Leibfried, S. (1990), 'The Classification of Welfare State Regimes in Europe', Social Policy Association Annual Conference, University of Bath, July.

Lewis, J. (1992), 'Gender and the development of welfare state regimes', *Journal of European Social Policy*, **2/2**: 159-730.

Myles, J. and Quadagno, J. (1996), 'Recent trends in public pension reform: a comparative view' presented at the Conference on the Reform of the Retirement Income System, Queen's University, Ontario, February 1-2.

OECD (1994), *Revenue Statistics of Member Countries*, Paris: OECD.

OECD (1995), *The Jobs Report*, Paris: OECD.

Oxley, H. and Martin, J. (1991), 'Controlling government spending and deficits: trends in the 1980s and Prospects for the 1990s', *OECD Economic Studies*, **17**, Autumn.

Shola Orloff, A. (1993), 'Gender and the Social Rights of Citizenship: the comparative analysis of gender relations and welfare states', *American Sociological Review*, **58**: 303-28.

Appendix

Logistic regressions of determinants of attitudes to state responsibility

Dependent Variables

v39	Government should definitely be responsible for provision of benefits to the elderly code 1 All other values: code 2
v41	Government should definitely be responsible for provision of benefits to the unemployed: code 1 All other values: code 2
v42	Government should definitely be responsible for redistributing income from better off to worse off: code 1 All other values: code 2

Independent Variables

Low income	Income in bottom quartile: code 1 All other values: code 2
High income	Income in top quartile: code 1 All other values: code 2
Sex	Man: code 1 Woman: code 2
State sector	Employed in state sector or in a nationalised industry: code 1 All other values: code 2
F/T employed	In full-time employment: code 1 All other values: code 2

The following tables show the logistic regression coefficients for the characteristics specified on the left side of the table for each of the three countries.

Each coefficient shows whether that particular characteristic differs significantly from its 'comparison group' (code 2 in the above list of independent variables) in its association with the dependent variable. A positive coefficient indicates that those with the characteristic are more likely than the comparison group to agree that the government has responsibility for provision of benefits for the elderly or for the unemployed, or for redistribution of income.

Two asterisks indicate that the coefficient is statistically significant at a 99% level, and one asterisk that it is significant at a 95% level. Statistical significance and logistic regression techniques are explained in more detail in Appendix I to this Report.

Pensions for the elderly: regression coefficients

	Germany		Sweden		Britain	
Low income	.18		.23	**	.85	**
High income	-.53	**	-.27	*	-.28	
Men	-.25	**	-.11		-.13	
State sector	-.21	*	.19		.13	
F/T employed	-.02		-.41	**	-.20	
Constant	1.37	**	-.15		-2.01	**
% Correct Predictions	55		66		70	
Base	*3518*		*1238*		*989*	

Benefits for unemployed people: regression coefficients

	Germany		Sweden		Britain	
Low income	.59	**	.05		.52	**
High income	-.69	**	-.56	**	-.36	
Men	-.10		-.40	**	-.21	
State sector	-.21	*	.19		.13	
F/T employed	-.28	**	-.62	**	-.41	*
Constant	1.91	**	2.82	**	.91	
% Correct Predictions	78		64		74	
Base	*3518*		*1238*		*989*	

Redistribution from high income to low income: regression coefficients

	Germany		Sweden		Britain	
Low income	.48	**	.23		.65	**
High income	-.93	**	-.99	**	-1.13	**
Men	-.12		-.23		-.02	
State sector	.16		.34	**	-.10	
F/T employed	-.23	**	-.35	**	-.27	
Constant	1.52	**	2.15	**	1.77	**
% Correct Predictions	70		63		69	
Base	*3518*		*1238*		*989*	

5 The rewards of work

Helen Russell [*]

Introduction

In recent years there has been increasing interest in people's attitudes towards paid work - their 'work orientation'. This interest has centred around two issues. The first concerns *commitment* to work, and how this may have been affected by changes in the labour market - rising unemployment, for instance, or job insecurity - as well as by developments in the welfare state. The second concerns the *values* that people attach to work, and whether increasing affluence means that workers now look for more than just a pay-packet when it comes to their jobs.

During the 1980s and 1990s many countries within the EU, including Britain, began to experience levels of unemployment unseen since the Great Depression. This rise in unemployment aroused fears that, with so many of the population idle, an erosion would occur in the social obligation to work (Gallie *et al.*, 1998). Concern was also expressed that the unemployed may become discouraged and lose the will to work. However, others suggested that the experience of unemployment might have the opposite effect. Perhaps the experience of being unemployed might serve to highlight the importance of employment, hence leading to increased work commitment (Jahoda, 1982).

Of course, high unemployment levels do not simply affect the unemployed. They may also lead to those who are in work feeling increasingly insecure about their jobs. Such employee insecurity may also have been affected by the increased use of temporary contracts. However, the relationship between job insecurity and work orientation is by no means clear-cut. On the one

---

[*] Helen Russell is a Research Officer at The Economic and Social Research Institute, Ireland.

hand, it may be that job insecurity reduces workers' commitment to their employers. Employees will not, in other words, feel very loyal towards an employer who does not offer them security of tenure (Lincoln and Kalleberg, 1990). However, on the other hand, it could be argued that the fear of losing their jobs may actually lead to workers working harder, and being more likely to behave as though they were committed to their work (Rose, 1985).

Others suggest that the key factor underlying falling levels of work commitment is not unemployment *per se*, but the way in which government has provided financial help to the unemployed. Some theories about 'the underclass' argue that over-generous welfare provision and inadequate socialisation have created a 'dependency culture' and undermined commitment to employment (Murray, 1990).

Speculation about the values that people attach to different aspects of work has arisen as part of a broader debate about changing values within society in general. Inglehart (1990; 1997) argues that rich industrialised societies are moving from being characterised by materialist values, which emphasise economic and physical security, towards 'post-materialist' values which focus on self-expression and quality of life. Consequently, while in poorer societies individuals will be willing to accept uninteresting, meaningless work for financial gain, in wealthier ones we should expect a 'gradual shift in what motivates people to work: emphasis shifts from maximising one's income and job security toward a growing insistence on interesting and meaningful work' (Inglehart, 1997: 44). The move towards post-material values is also believed to involve a greater focus on non-work activities such as family life and leisure. Such proposed changes in values have been popularised through concepts such as 'downshifting', which has been used to describe people who give up high-powered and well-paid jobs for a simpler, and more fulfilling, way of life.

Within individual societies, the move towards post-materialist values will occur first among the wealthy and more educated (Inglehart, 1997). It is also likely that these values will apply particularly to younger generations, because their early socialisation occurred during periods of greater economic and physical security.

In this chapter we use data from two surveys focusing on attitudes towards work, fielded in 1989 and 1997 as part of the *International Social Survey Programme* (ISSP).[*] The data are used to answer two main questions. First, are unemployment, job insecurity and welfare state provision in the EU linked to a decline in work and organisational commitment? Second, is there any evidence that 'post-materialism' is bringing about a change in what EU citizens want from the work that they do?

To address these questions it is necessary to look both at the characteristics of individuals (their age, for instance, or educational experience) *and* those of the societies within which they live. For instance, societal levels of

---

[*] See the Introduction and Appendices to this Report for further details about ISSP.

unemployment and job insecurity may influence an individual's commitment to their job. Similarly, levels of national wealth may influence the attitudes of citizens towards their work. Further, we might expect that those living in societies with well-developed welfare states will, because of the economic security that this provides, focus less upon the material rewards of work (Inglehart, 1997).

The chapter examines these issues in four EU countries: Britain, Italy, Germany and Sweden (data for Germany will be presented separately for eastern and western Germany, as these two areas vary considerably in many respects that are relevant here)[*]. These four countries were chosen to provide a wide spread in terms of unemployment rates, labour market regulation (which is related to job security) and welfare state regimes. In addition, information is available over time for three of these countries (Britain, Italy and western Germany), allowing the examination of claims about trends in attitudes towards work. Since the debates being examined are essentially concerned with attitudes towards *paid work*, the chapter focuses on those who are currently in paid work or are unemployed.

The chapter is divided into three sections. The first addresses the issue of defining and measuring work orientation. The second examines the proposed link between work and organisational commitment, on the one hand, and unemployment, job insecurity, and welfare state provision on the other. The final section examines the extent to which greater affluence, security and education have resulted in people expecting more from their work than 'material' reward alone.

Definitions and measurement

The chapter examines three different aspects of 'work orientation' - work commitment, organisational commitment, and the value that a person attaches to different work characteristics.

The first of these aspects concerns a person's commitment to work in general, a common definition being the extent to which work is a central life interest. This definition often involves establishing the importance of employment, *relative* to other aspects of life, such as family and leisure (Loscocco and Kalleberg, 1988). Of course, one limitation of this definition is the assumption that a trade-off exists between commitment to employment and family life, despite some evidence that those who are committed to one life role will carry over a similar level of enthusiasm to other roles (Ganon and Hendrickson, 1973; Bielby and Bielby, 1989). The question used here does not impose a direct choice between different spheres of life, but this

---

[*] By western Germany we mean the geographical area known until unification as the Federal Republic of Germany. By eastern Germany we mean the area formerly known as the German Democratic Republic.

trade-off may be implicit. To assess 'work centrality', respondents were asked whether they agreed or disagreed with the statement:

Work is a person's most important activity[1]

Responses to this statement should allow us to examine the extent to which there has been a shift in emphasis towards non-work activities.

Knowing whether work is central to a person's life tells us nothing about *why* it is important. It may be, for instance, that its centrality simply reflects the fact that it provides an income. So another means of measuring general work commitment is to examine whether employment is valued in itself, rather than simply as a source of income (Warr, 1982). This will incorporate both those for whom employment is some form of social or moral 'duty'[2] as well as those who look to employment as a source of self-actualisation. Such a definition by no means implies that those who attach importance to pay are uncommitted to their work - only those with a purely instrumental approach to employment are defined here as uncommitted. To measure non-financial employment commitment respondents were asked to agree or disagree with two statements:

A job is just a way of earning money - no more

I would enjoy having a paid job even if I did not need the money

Not surprisingly, people's answers to these questions are highly correlated, so they are combined here to form a scale. The higher the score on this 'non-financial work commitment' scale, the greater the respondent's commitment.[3] Using such a composite measure increases reliability and minimises any subtle linguistic differences in the individual statements which may remain despite careful translation procedures.

Commitment to work in general can be distinguished from the second aspect of work orientation examined here - organisational commitment. This involves a person's loyalty to a particular organisation and the extent to which he or she shares its goals and values (Lincoln and Kalleberg, 1990). By definition, this type of commitment is only relevant to those with jobs. To assess organisational commitment respondents were asked to agree or disagree with three statements:

I am willing to work harder than I have to in order to help the firm or organisation that I work for to succeed

I am proud to be working for my firm or organisation

I would turn down a job that offered quite a bit more pay in order to stay with this organisation

In addition, they were also asked how likely it was they would try to find a job with another firm or organisation over the next year. Responses to this question, and the three statements, were combined to form an 'organisational commitment' scale[4] on which higher scores indicate greater organisational commitment.

The third aspect of work orientation considered here concerns the *values* people attach to different work rewards or characteristics (what we can call 'work values'). To measure this, respondents were questioned on the importance they attach to a variety of job characteristics. We focus here on two clear categories. The first, relating to what can be called 'extrinsic' rewards, includes job characteristics relating to income, job security and promotion opportunities. The second relates to 'intrinsic' rewards and includes the characteristics of interesting work, independence and discretion in deciding work hours, all of which can be seen as enhancing workers' experience of the tasks they do. The responses to these two categories were used to create 'extrinsic value' and 'intrinsic value' scores, with higher scores indicating higher adherence to the particular values being considered.[5]

Employment commitment and organisational commitment

How do personal attributes and societal level characteristics relate to work and organisational commitment? We begin by assessing the impact of personal experience of unemployment and job insecurity using pooled data from all four countries. We then compare work commitment across the countries to see what national differences exist, and whether these relate to national differences in welfare provision, unemployment rates and levels of job insecurity. Using regression models we can test whether these country differences persist once we control for national differences in individual level characteristics. Finally, we examine trends in work commitment between 1989 and 1997.

Work commitment and employment status

There are two opposing views about the impact of unemployment on a person's work commitment. While some argue that unemployment can lead to a detachment from work and an erosion in work commitment, others suggest it may increase commitment by demonstrating how important work really is. To assess this, we examine the responses of the employed and the unemployed to the 'work centrality' statement and 'non-financial work commitment' scales outlined earlier.

Commitment to work

	Non-financial commitment score	Work most important activity (% agree)	Base
Employed	7.0	39	2856
Unemployed	6.7	51	342
All	6.9	41	3198

This gives mixed support to the competing theories. Certainly, a much higher proportion of the unemployed (51 per cent) than the employed (39 per cent) agree that work is a person's most important activity. On the other hand, the non-financial commitment scores suggest a different story, with the mean score for the unemployed (6.7) being lower than that of the employed (7.0). However, this partly reflects the fact that the unemployed come disproportionately from the unqualified and the working classes, groups who are traditionally less committed than average to employment (Warr, 1982, Gallie et al., 1998). In fact, the commitment score of the unemployed (6.7) is greater than that of semi-skilled and unskilled workers (6.3) and is very similar to the score of those with secondary or lower levels of education (6.7).[6] Therefore, there is little support for the view that unemployment is linked to lower than average levels of work commitment.

Work commitment, organisational commitment and personal job security

Although the use of temporary contracts is increasingly advocated as a means of allowing employers to deal with fluctuations in demand (see, for instance, Atkinson, 1984), we know little about the effects that these types of contracts have upon employees' attitudes towards work. Two contrasting possibilities have been identified. Job insecurity may reduce organisational and employment commitment, with workers feeling that such commitment offers insufficient returns. Alternatively, insecurity may induce higher commitment among workers who are anxious to avoid the prospect of unemployment.

Of the countries considered here, non-permanent contracts are most common in Britain, where only two thirds of workers have open-ended contracts. As the next table shows, this is largely due to the high proportion of workers who have no written contracts (20 per cent). Very short-term contracts are most frequent in Sweden, where five per cent of workers are on contracts of less than one year. Strict labour market regulation means that fixed term contracts are relatively uncommon in Italy, but the thriving informal sector means that three in every twenty Italian workers have no written contract at all.

Types of work contract

	Britain	Western Germany	Eastern Germany	Italy	Sweden
	%	%	%	%	%
No written contract	20	11	7	15	15
Fixed term of less than a year	3	2	2	3	5
Fixed term of a year or more	11	7	9	7	4
No time limit	66	80	82	76	76
Base (all employed)	*527*	*681*	*256*	*461*	*760*

There is a strong relationship between contract status and commitment, both to work in general, and the employing organisation. Those who are on very short-term contracts have lower non-financial work commitment (scoring 6.7, compared to 7.0 among those on permanent contracts) and are less likely to see work as being a person's most important activity (only 28 per cent doing so, compared to 39 per cent of those on permanent contracts). This group also records a lower level of commitment to their organisation than do workers with other types of contracts. Even when we exclude from our organisational commitment scale the item that relates to the likelihood of a person leaving their current employer, those on contracts of less than a year's duration still have significantly lower scores than other workers.

Levels of commitment by type of contract

	Non-financial commitment score	Work most important activity (% agree)	Organisational commitment score	*Base*
No written contract	6.4	40	12.3	*226*
Fixed term (less than year)	6.7	28	10.5	*81*
Fixed term (year plus)	7.1	35	12.1	*163*
No time limit	7.0	39	12.7	*1811*
Self-employed	7.1	48	14.4	*404*
All	7.0	39	12.8	*2685*

Somewhat surprisingly, those on fixed term contracts of over one year do not differ substantially from those on permanent contracts. One explanation for this lies in the fact that almost a third of this group are in the professional or managerial class (this probably reflects the use of short term training contracts for those entering the professions, see Dale and Bamford, 1988). Once occupation is taken into account, having a fixed-term contract of one year or more's duration is linked to lower than average levels of organisational commitment. It is not, however, linked to lower than average commitment on each of our two levels of work commitment (as shown in the appendix to this chapter). Finally, if we take occupational differences into account, those without written contracts have lower non-financial work commitment and lower organisational commitment than those with permanent contracts.

The self-employed display exceptionally high levels of work commitment and organisational commitment. It seems likely that this is due to self-selection: those who start their own businesses are likely to be highly motivated and have a strong work ethic. Furthermore, organisational commitment is likely to mean something quite different to the self-employed than to employees.

These findings support the view that job insecurity is linked to *lower* levels of work and organisational commitment rather than higher commitment. As the organisational commitment measure we use here includes a measure relating to willingness to engage in hard work, the results suggest that employers may gain flexibility at the expense of productivity. However, we cannot rule out the possibility the relationship between job insecurity and commitment may operate the other way round - that those on temporary contracts are there *because* they are less committed to work. It might also be argued that job security is not synonymous with contract length. Even the jobs of workers with permanent contracts may be insecure if, say, they are located in declining industries. And some of those on fixed-term contracts may be assured of long-term employment but not necessarily in the same location.

To take this complexity into account, we examine two additional questions that relate to *perceived* job security. The first requires respondents to agree or disagree with the statement 'my job is secure'. The second asks them how much they worry about losing their job - 'a great deal', 'to some extent', 'a little' or 'not at all'. Not surprisingly, there was a strong correlation between responses to these two questions so these two variables[7] are combined here to form a single index of job insecurity. Using this, we again find a significant correlation between perceived insecurity and both non-financial commitment and organisational commitment.[8] This lends weight to the earlier finding that commitment decreases as insecurity increases.

National differences in work and organisational commitment

We have seen that unemployment and insecurity at an individual level can affect work orientation. However, societal levels of unemployment and insecurity might also have a more general effect on work orientation within society at large. High levels of unemployment and job insecurity might lead to a breakdown in the work ethic, or may actually induce commitment among those competing for increasingly scarce jobs. As discussed earlier, differences in welfare provision have also been cited as sources of national variation in work commitment.

The next table compares the countries considered here in terms of their unemployment rates, job security and levels of state provision for the unemployed. The first column shows that the highest rates of unemployment are in eastern Germany and Italy. So, if unemployment levels within society as a whole lead to lower work commitment it should be evident in these two countries. The second column shows the percentage of employees who are in temporary contracts, with the highest proportions being found in Sweden and Germany. However, as previously noted, job insecurity is not solely determined by the nature of the employment contract. Labour market regulation also matters, particularly the extent to which an open-ended contract guarantees job security. This is indicated in the third column, which shows that in Britain the legal obstacles to an employer terminating a contract via dismissal or redundancy are insignificant. By contrast, in Germany and Italy employment regulation is much stronger and thus workers are more reassured of their security (Emerson, 1988; Grubb and Wells, 1993). Sweden lies between these two extremes. According to this classification we might expect job insecurity to have the biggest influence in Britain. Finally, the table also ranks countries on the basis of their provision for the unemployed. This shows that provision for the unemployed is greatest in Sweden and Germany and is considerably lower in Britain and Italy.

Characteristics of national labour markets and benefit systems

	Unemp-loyment[i]	% employees in temporary jobs[ii]	Obstacles to ending employment[iii]	Unemployment benefit ranking[iv]
Sweden	10.2	12.4	Serious	1
Germany	11.1	10.9	Fundamental	2
- Western	9.1	n.a.	n.a.	-
- Eastern	18.4	n.a.	n.a.	-
UK	7.1	6.8	Insignificant	3
Italy	12.0	7.2	Fundamental	4

[i]   ILO unemployment in 1997, OECD 1998a.
[ii] Data for 1995, European Labour Force Survey 1995.
[iii] Emerson 1988, p791.
[iv] This ranking, where 1 indicates the highest provision, is based on two dimensions - coverage (measured by the proportion of the unemployed who receive benefits) and replacement rate (the extent to which benefits replace previous earnings).[9]

n.a. = not available

When we examine the mean national levels of our measures of work and organisational commitment we find a number of patterns, as shown in the next table. First, work commitment. The non-financial work commitment score is highest in western Germany (7.9). However, the percentage of respondents who agree that work is a person's most important activity is actually highest in eastern Germany, where three out of every five respondents (62 per cent) agree with the statement. Of note is the fact that Britain records the lowest level of commitment on both measures.

National differences in non-financial work commitment do not appear to be related to national unemployment rates or levels of job insecurity . However, responses to the work centrality question do vary according to unemployment levels. Thus, the proportion of respondents who believe work is the most important activity is highest in eastern Germany (where unemployment is highest), and is lowest in Britain (which has the lowest unemployment rate). This supports the hypothesis that mass unemployment highlights the centrality of work for the population as a whole. The fact that a relationship does not emerge using the non-financial commitment measure suggests that mass unemployment forces a recognition of the financial consequences of joblessness. These societal-level findings correspond to the relationships found between unemployment and commitment at the individual level. Then unemployment, though linked to responses to the work centrality question, was not linked to variations in responses to questions tapping non-financial work commitment.

Commitment levels by country

	a. Non-financial commitment score	b. % agree work most important activity	Base for a. and b.	c. Organisational commitment score	Base for c.
Sweden	7.4	42	982	12.7	657
Germany	7.0	46	1106	13.0	772
- Western	7.9	39	766	13.1	565
- Eastern	6.8	62	340	12.9	207
Britain	6.5	25	1635	12.9	472
Italy	6.7	46	535	12.5	443

National patterns of work commitment do not support the argument that high levels of compensation for unemployment will lead to a deterioration in commitment to work. Sweden and Germany provide the most state support to the unemployed, yet the non-financial commitment scores for both countries is high (7.4 and 7.0 respectively). Furthermore, although eastern and western Germany have the same benefit system, there is a wide difference in the responses to the work centrality in each country. Only 39 per cent of those in western Germany believe work is a person's most important activity, compared to 62 per cent of those in eastern Germany.

The findings also fail to support the argument that employment *security* will lead to greater organisational commitment. If this were true we would expect Italian workers to be the most committed to their firms, because in Italy temporary contracts are rare and labour protection is strong. But this is not the case. In fact, organisational commitment is highest in Germany (particularly western Germany) and lowest in Italy. It may be possible, however, that if high levels of state regulation force all employers to offer stable employment, as is the case in Italy, they may be less likely to inspire organisational commitment.

Of course, there remains the possibility that these national differences in work commitment reflect other differences in the characteristics of each nation's population. For instance, the higher than average proportion of unemployed workers in countries with high unemployment levels means that it can be hard to establish whether the key factor linked to work commitment is *individual* unemployment, as opposed to a high level of unemployment within the country *as a whole*. In order to take these sorts of influences into account, we must 'control for' national differences in certain individual characteristics thought to influence work orientations. However, regression models that take into account these characteristics before calculating the work commitment scores for each country, do not dramatically alter the ranking of countries in terms of their scores on our work commitment measures (details of these models can be found in the appendix to this chapter). Within society as a whole, high levels of unemployment do indeed appear to be linked to a high level of importance being attached to work.

Taking into account national differences in individual characteristics does alter the relative position of countries when it comes to levels of organisational commitment. Those in western Germany are no longer the most committed to their employing organisations, now falling below both those in eastern Germany and Britain. However, the differences between countries are small and, even when individual level factors are taken into account, Italians remain as having the lowest levels of organisational commitment - despite enjoying greater security than workers in other countries. Explanations for this distinctiveness could lie in cultural differences or variation in organisational structure and management practices. The large number of small firms in Italy may provide a partial explanation. Previous studies have found that organisational commitment decreases with company size (Lincoln and Kalleberg, 1990), with small firms being unable to offer the wages, benefits, services and opportunities for advancement provided by larger firms.

Changes in work commitment between 1989 and 1997

Work commitment appears to be affected by both the labour market experiences of individuals and societies a whole. But has this commitment changed over time? Much of the debate about work commitment has been prompted by concern about an alleged decline in the work ethic.[10] So we now turn to examine support for the view that work commitment is declining, focusing upon Britain, western Germany and Italy.

Changes in work commitment

	1989	Base	1997	Base	Change
Non-financial work commitment					
A job is 'just a way of earning money' (% disagree)					
Britain	57	*734*	50	*595*	-7
Western Germany	50	*690*	62	*692*	+12
Italy	63	*600*	57	*530*	-6
Would enjoy paid job 'even if I did not need the money' (% agree)					
Britain	65	*734*	58	*595*	-7
Western Germany	62	*690*	73	*692*	+11
Italy	53	*600*	55	*530*	+2
Non-financial commitment score					
Britain	6.8	*734*	6.5	*595*	-.3
Western Germany	6.6	*690*	7.0	*692*	+.4
Italy	6.7	*600*	6.7	*530*	0
All	6.7	*2024*	6.8	*1817*	+.1
Work centrality					
Work 'is a person's most important activity' (% agree)					
Britain	33	*757*	25	*607*	-8
Western Germany	35	*701*	39	*720*	+4
Italy	49	*612*	46	*535*	-3
All	38	*2070*	36	*1862*	-2

Taking the three countries together, there has been very little change in either non-financial commitment to work or our measure of the centrality of work. Certainly the overall data support neither the prediction of declining work commitment nor that of increasing commitment in the light of more difficult labour market conditions. However, there are substantial differences between countries. Over the period of the two surveys, work commitment (both non-financial commitment and work centrality) has increased in western Germany, decreased in Britain and remained fairly stable in Italy.

Previous British studies (Hedges, 1994; Gallie *et al.,* 1998) have found that women's work commitment has increased in recent years while men's has remained static. However, our figures here show a decline in commitment among British men and women on both measures (although the drop has been bigger for men than for women).[11] In Italy and western Germany however, women show a bigger increase in work commitment over time than do men.

As our results refer to only two points in time we need to be wary about drawing strong conclusions about trends. However, taken together with analyses by Bryson & McKay (1997), the evidence suggests that in the second half of the 1990s, work commitment in Britain began to decline. This decline certainly cannot be attributed to an increase in unemployment levels as these were almost identical in 1989 and 1997.[12] Nor does it appear to be due to inadequate socialisation into the work ethic by the young, as commitment increased among those under 24. The decline in work commitment in Britain between 1989 and 1997 does, however, coincide with a big increase in job insecurity (see endnote 12). As insecurity has been found to affect an individual's work commitment, this may partly account for the trend.

The increase in work commitment in western Germany coincides with a significant increase in unemployment in that country, this providing more evidence of the impact of labour market conditions on work commitment. However, a sharp rise in perceived job insecurity in western Germany has not cancelled out this increase in work commitment. In Italy stable employment commitment over time mirrors the stable unemployment and job security conditions during this period (see endnote 12).

Shifting work values?

We have focused so far on people's commitment to work and to the particular organisations for whom they work. However, we are also interested in what people want from work in general - what we have termed 'work values'. Some argue that growing affluence, security and education have resulted in a shift towards what can be called 'post-materialist values', which means, among other things, that people are becoming more concerned with the intrinsic rewards of work and less concerned with more material extrinsic rewards (such as pay and job security). Such changes in values will, it has been argued, be most noticeable among young people, the highly educated and in richer societies, and those with greater welfare state provision (Inglehart, 1997).

Work values and age

We find little evidence that the young are more likely than average to hold 'post-materialist' values when it comes to work. Across the four EU countries we examine here, there are almost no age differences in measures relating to the importance of intrinsic rewards of work (interesting work, independence and autonomy). In fact, those aged under 25 are found to place a slightly greater emphasis than average on *extrinsic* rewards (income, promotion and security). Their mean score on our extrinsic values scale is 3.2 (compared with 3.0 for those aged over 25). The need by younger workers to establish themselves in a career with good long term prospects seems to supersede any 'post-materialist' shift among the young towards more intrinsic benefits such as interesting work or job autonomy.

Extrinsic and instrinsic work values by age

	Extrinsic values score	Intrinsic values score	Base
18-24 years	3.2	3.0	277
25-34 years	3.1	3.1	792
35-44 years	3.0	3.1	869
45-54 years	3.0	3.0	771
Over 54 years	3.0	3.0	489

Work values and education

By contrast, comparing the values attached to work by those with different educational backgrounds does provide some support for the notion that the more highly educated will tend to value intrinsic rewards more than those who are less highly educated. Within the four EU countries considered here, those with university level education place greater importance on intrinsic rewards than do the less highly educated. This remains true even when other differences between these groups are taken into account (for instance, contract length, working hours and occupational position). However, education is not linked to any significant differences in the importance attached to extrinsic work values. The more highly educated value issues such as pay, job security and so on just as much as everyone else - but are more likely to demand interesting work. If these demands are not met it is likely to lead to greater frustration and dissatisfaction among this group.

Extrinsic and instrinsic work values by education level

	Extrinsic values score	Intrinsic values score	Base
Education level reached			
Primary education or below	3.0	3.0	519
Lower or higher secondary	3.1	3.0	1710
University	3.0	3.2	500

National differences in intrinsic and extrinsic work values

Are wealthier countries, or those with more developed welfare states, more likely than average to emphasise the intrinsic characteristics of work, such as fulfilment and interest? Both these national factors are thought to provide a secure background for their citizens, allowing them to turn away from purely material concerns. To examine this we use *per capita* GDP as a summary measure of national wealth, and measure (albeit imperfectly) welfare state development by the proportion of GDP spent on social expenditure.[13] These measures are shown in the following table.

Levels of affluence and welfare by country

	GDP per capita [i] 1997	Social expenditure [ii] (% GDP)
Italy	$20,093	18.2
UK	$20,144	23.4
Sweden	$20,344	38.3
Germany	$22,462	28.7

[i] US Dollars, using current prices and purchasing power parities (source: OECD 1998b).
[ii] Source: OECD 1997, Table 1.4 and Table 2.2.

Differences in the *per capita* GDP between the four countries are small, with the highest rate occuring in Germany and the lowest in Italy. Although we do not have here information on *per capita* GDP in the areas that make up eastern and western Germany, it seems very likely that it is higher in western Germany. Social expenditure is by far the highest in Sweden and is lowest in Italy.

Based on these statistics we would expect an emphasis on intrinsic work values to be most evident in Sweden and western Germany, and to be less common in Britain and Italy. The opposite should be the case with regard to extrinsic work values. There is some support for this notion. The emphasis on extrinsic rewards is lowest in Sweden and highest in Italy. In fact, Sweden is the only country in which extrinsic values receive a *lower* average rating than intrinsic characteristics. This remains true even when other national differences are taken into account, as shown in the appendix to this chapter. The welfare regime in Sweden means that well-being and security is less dependent on the labour market (Esping-Anderson, 1990). This may allow its citizens to focus on other aspects of employment than pay and security alone. National differences in scores on our *intrinsic* work value scale are, however, less consistent with our expectations. Although the Swedes and (western) Germans show a greater preference for intrinsically rewarding work as expected, the values of the Italians follow the same pattern.

Extrinsic and instrinsic work values by country

	Extrinsic values score	Intrinsic values score	Base
Sweden	2.9	3.1	883
Germany	3.1	3.0	1039
- Western	3.1	3.1	722
- Eastern	3.1	2.9	317
Britain	3.1	2.9	604
Italy	3.2	3.1	530

When national differences in the composition of the labour market, education levels and so on, are taken into account, Britain emerges as the country where the proposed shift from extrinsic to intrinsic work values is the *least* advanced (as shown in model C in the appendix to this chapter). Why might this be so? One reason might stem from the fact that Britain has a relatively low per capita GDP. It also has a more unequal distribution of income than the other countries examined here (Atkinson *et al.*, 1995), meaning that national wealth is more unevenly spread. Conversely, demands for material rewards are lowest in Sweden, and demands for intrinsically rewarding work highest in western Germany and Sweden. Both these countries have high standards of living and well developed welfare states which protect their citizens from poverty. These findings do, therefore, lend support to the notion that those living in better-off countries are more likely to emphasise intrinsic work values than those living in less well-off nations.

Changes in extrinsic and intrinsic work values over time

The notion of post-materialism has a very strong temporal dimension, with changes in values being partly linked to the gradual replacement of older cohorts of people by younger cohorts with different values and demands (Inglehart, 1990: 66). But this does not appear to have occurred in the context of attitudes to work. True, if we take data from Britain, Italy and western Germany together, the mean extrinsic value score has decreased very slightly (from 3.2 to 3.1), this being consistent with the post-materialist predictions. However, no increase has taken place in the emphasis being put on intrinsic values (with the average score remaining at 3.3).

Examining the individual questions that make up each scale provides a further insight into changes over time. The next table shows the proportion of people in each country in 1997 thinking that specific extrinsic and intrinsic work values are 'very important'. The figure in brackets is the percentage point change since 1989.

Changes in work values over time
(1997, with change since 1989 shown in brackets)

	Britain		Western Germany		Italy	
Extrinsic values						
% 'very important'						
High income	17	(-1)	14	(-13)	30	(+2)
Job security	64	(+7)	66	(+5)	66	(-1)
Opportunity for advancement	23	(-3)	14	(-15)	25	(-6)
Overall extrinsic value score	**3.1**	**(-.1)**	**3.1**	**(-.1)**	**3.2**	**(0)**
1997 Base (1989 in brackets)	*604*	*(750)*	*722*	*(703)*	*530*	*(611)*
Intrinsic values [1]						
% 'very important'						
Interesting job	49	(+1)	53	(-3)	54	(+2)
Independence	20	(-1)	44	(-4)	34	(-4)
Overall intrinsic value score	**3.2**	**(-.1)**	**3.4**	**(0)**	**3.2**	**(-.1)**
1997 Base (1989 in brackets)	*604*	*(750)*	*722*	*(703)*	*530*	*(511)*

[1] The wording of the question on working hours differs between the two surveys and is thus excluded from the scale presented here.

In both Britain and Germany there has been a significant increase in the proportion of the workforce who take the view that 'job security' is very important. This change coincides with a substantial growth in perceived insecurity in both countries. Conversely, the emphasis on job security remains unchanged in Italy where job incumbents are most sheltered from unemployment.[14] In the main, the importance attached to the other two extrinsic job characteristics (high income and promotion opportunities) has declined between 1989 and 1997. This suggests that the overall trend in extrinsic work values is broadly in line with what we would expect from the notion of post-materialism. However, the trend has been limited by short-term economic changes which have, among other things, increased respondents' desire for job security. When it comes to changes over time in the importance attached to various intrinsic job characteristics, only Britain and Italy show an increase. However, the importance attached to these job characteristics was already high in western Germany.

Conclusion

Fears that mass unemployment has led to a widespread decline in the work ethic appear unfounded. Thus, in western Germany, which has witnessed large increases in unemployment, work commitment has actually risen over time. In fact, our data suggest that high levels of unemployment in society are linked to a *stronger* belief in the importance of work. It would seem that job scarcity apparently highlights the importance of having a job to the workforce in general. A similar process is also evident among individual workers. Those who are currently unemployed place a higher value on work compared to other areas of life than do those who are in paid work. Perhaps the unemployed are in the best position to judge the relative merits of life with, and without, paid work - and their experience leads them to come out in favour of employment.

One trend that appears to have a more *negative* impact on attitudes to work is the recent growth in job insecurity and increased reliance on non-permanent contracts. Fixed-term contracts are found to reduce work commitment and have an extremely damaging effect on organisational commitment. Employers, it seems, are sacrificing productivity and loyalty for short-term flexibility gains. Furthermore, since a growing proportion of the workforce (even amongst the young) judge job security to be a highly desirable job characteristic, employers who use non-permanent contracts may have difficulty in attracting good candidates. Further, as previous studies have linked worries about job security to increased levels of psychological distress (Burchell, 1994), the growth in perceived insecurity could also have consequences for workers' health and absenteeism.

A highly developed welfare state providing generous levels of compensation to the unemployed does *not* seem to be linked to depressed levels of commitment to work. Rather, in Sweden, which has the most extensive welfare regime of the countries studied, non-financial commitment to employment is highest. In fact, it seems that access to an adequate means of support outside employment, rather than leading to disinterest in employment *per se*, serves to decrease the importance attached to extrinsic rewards within work. This result supports one aspect of Inglehart's post-materialist thesis. In addition, individual variations in attitudes to work also provide some support for this thesis. Thus, those with higher qualifications place a higher premium than average on the intrinsic rewards of work. Although changes in work values at the societal level are likely to take some time to become apparent, our research suggests that the importance attached to the extrinsic characteristics of work (apart from job security) is waning, while the emphasis placed on intrinsic rewards remains stable and high. We can only wait to see whether these trends persist in the long term.

Only in Britain has there been a substantial decline in work commitment over time. This decline has occurred alongside an increase in perceived job insecurity and in the use of non-permanent contracts. Increased job insecurity in the guise of 'labour market flexibility' has been pursued at the policy level in Britain and a comparison of labour market regulation in the four countries studied here showed that British workers are by far the worst protected. The refusal of the Conservative government to sign the Social Charter, and the contracting-out of public sector services, are further examples of this policy. The endorsement of the Social Charter by the Labour Party may lead to some improvements in the working conditions of workers on fixed-term contracts and in temporary jobs, as this is an explicit aim of the charter. However, it is less likely to improve the situation for that significant minority of workers who have no written contracts, many of whom will fall outside legal regulation. Furthermore, EU policy-makers have been increasingly recommending greater flexibility in working hours and contracts as a means of reducing unemployment across the EU (European Commission, 1997; OECD, 1994b). If these recommendations are followed through, it is likely that EU work practices will converge towards those operating in Britain, perhaps causing a more widespread downturn in work commitment throughout the EU.

Notes

1. It should be noted that the statement refers to work rather than employment. Consequently, it may be seen to encompass unpaid work in the home as well as paid work.
2. The moral worth of 'hard work' is central to the idea of a Protestant work ethic.
3. This 'non-financial' work commitment scale has a minimum score of 2 and a maximum score of 10.
4. The four item scale has an Alpha of 0.65.
5. Respondents were asked 'how important do *you personally* think the following items are in a job?' The items listed were as follows: job security; high income; good opportunities for advancement; an interesting job; a job that allows someone to work independently; a

job that allows someone to decide their times or days of work. For each of these respondents were asked whether they thought it 'very important', 'important', 'neither important nor unimportant', 'not important' or 'not important at all'. Since very few respondents chose the 'not important at all' category, the final two response categories were combined. An extrinsic value score was calculated by averaging respondents' scores for the first three characteristics and a similar score was calculated for intrinsic values using responses to the last three characteristics (the existence of two groups of work values was first confirmed by factor analysis). The two scales range from zero to four.

6. This is confirmed in the regression model examining non-financial work commitment (see the appendix to this chapter) which finds unemployment to be insignificant in its effect.

7. The correlation coefficient between the two variables, r, is 1.51.

8. The correlation between insecurity and non-financial commitment is -0.09 and with organisational commitment is -0.25. Both are significant at the .001 level.

9. Initial replacement rates for those with full eligibility is 90 per cent of wages in Sweden, 58 per cent in Germany, 16 to 26 per cent in the UK and 15 per cent in Italy (OECD 1991). The 'average' replacement rate in the four countries has been calculated as 29 per cent in Sweden, 28 per cent in Germany, 18 per cent in the UK and 3 per cent in Italy. Details of how this 'average' is calculated can be found in OECD 1994a. The replacement ratios in Italy may be underestimated because they are unlikely to include a number of special compensation schemes such as the *Cassa Integrazione* (see Dell'Argina and Lodovici, 1997 for details). The proportion of unemployed receiving these benefits follows a similar national pattern: coverage stands at 70 per cent in Sweden, 71 per cent in Germany, 59 per cent in the UK and 7 per cent in Italy (European Labour Force Survey 1995, UK Employment Gazette Dec. 1995).

10. Little discussion of changes in organisational commitment over time have taken place, so this issue will not be discussed here.

11. The change in non-financial commitment was −0.36 for men and −.031 for women. The change in work centrality was -8.1 per cent and -5.9 per cent for men and women respectively.

12. Changes in economic structure between 1989 and 1997 surveys were as follows -

	Difference in unemployment rate 1989 and 1997[i]	Difference in % of temporary employees 1989 and 1995[ii]	Difference in % of workers saying job insecure 1989 and 1997[iii]
UK	+0.3	+1.5	+8.7
Western Germany	+3.4	+0.6	+10.0
Italy	+0.9	+0.9	+.0

[i] Source: OECD 1998a and German Labour Force Survey 1996. German and Italian figures refer to 1996.
[ii] European LFS 1989 and 1995. German figure for 1995 includes eastern Germany.
[iii] ISSP 1989 & 1997. % who disagree that 'my job is secure'.

13. This measure of welfare state development is a much broader measure of state support than the figures on benefits for the unemployed reported earlier in the chapter, since it includes spending on pensions, health care, social services and so forth.

14. Unemployment in Italy is mainly concentrated amongst first time job seekers and returners. Only 35 per cent of unemployed men and 22 per cent of unemployed women are job losers (1995 Labour Force Survey).

References

Atkinson, A.B., Rainwater, L. and Smeeding, T. (1995), 'Income Distribution in OECD countries', *OECD Social Policy Studies,* 18.

Atkinson, J. (1984), 'Manpower strategies for flexible organisations', *Personal Management,* August.

Bielby, W.T., and Bielby, D.D. (1989), 'Balancing Commitments to Work and Family in Dual Earner Households', *American Sociological Review,* **54**, 776-789.

Bryson, A. and McKay, S. (1997), 'What about the Workers?' in Jowell, R., Curtice, J., Park, A., Brook, L., Thomson, K. and Bryson, C. (eds.), *British Social Attitudes: the 14th Report,* Aldershot: Ashgate.

Burchell, B. (1994), 'The Effects of Labour Market Position, Job Insecurity and Unemployment on Psychological Health' in Gallie, D., Marsh, C. and Vogler, C. (eds.), *Social Change and the Experience of Unemployment,* Oxford: Oxford University Press.

Dale, A. and Bamford, C. (1988), 'Temporary workers: cause for concern or complacency?', *Work, Employment and Society,* **2/2**.

Dell'Argina, C. and Lodovici, M.S. (1997), 'Policies for the Unemployed and Social Shock Absorbers: The Italian Experience', in Rhodes, M. (ed.), *Southern European Welfare States: Between Crisis and Reform,* London: Frank Cass.

Emerson, M. (1988), 'Regulation or Deregulation of the Labour Market: Policy Regimes for the Recruitment and Dismissal of Employees in the Industrialised Countries', *European Economic Review,* **32**, 775-817.

Esping-Anderson, G. (1990), *The Three Worlds of Welfare Capitalism,* Cambridge: Polity Press.

European Commission (1997), *Employment in Europe 1997,* Luxembourg.

Gallie, D., White, M., Cheng, Y. and Tomlinson, M. (1998), *Restructuring the Employment Relationship,* Oxford: Clarendon Press.

Gannon, L. and Hendrickson, A. (1973), 'Career Orientation and Job Satisfaction among Working Wives', *Journal of Applied Psychology,* **57**, 339-340.

Grubb, D. and Wells, W. (1993), 'Employment Regulation and Patterns of Work in EC Countries', *OECD Economic Studies* No. 21.

Hedges, B. (1994), 'Work in a Changing Climate' in Jowell, R., Curtice, J., Brook, L. and Ahrendt, D. (eds.), *British Social Attitudes: the 11th Report,* Aldershot: Dartmouth Publishing Company.

Inglehart, R. (1990), *Culture Shift in Advanced Industrial Society,* Princeton, New Jersey: Princeton University Press.

Inglehart, R. (1997), *Modernization and Postmodernization: Cultural, Economic, and Political Change in 43 Societies,* Princeton, New Jersey: Princeton University Press.

Jahoda, M. (1982), *Employment and Unemployment: A Social Psychological Analysis,* Cambridge: Cambridge University Press.

Lincoln, J. R. and Kalleberg, A. L. (1990), *Culture, Control and Commitment: A Study of Work Organisation and Work Attitudes in the United States and Japan,* Cambridge: Cambridge University Press.

Loscocco, K. A. and Kalleberg, A. L. (1988), 'Age and the Meaning of Work in the United States and Japan', *Social Forces,* **67**, No. 2, 337-356.

Marsh, C. and Alvaro, J. L. (1990), 'A Cross-Cultural Perspective on the Social and Psychological Distress Caused by Unemployment: A Comparison of Spain and the United Kingdom' *European Sociological Review,* **6**, No. 3.

Murray, C. A. (1990), *The Emerging British Underclass,* London: Institute of Economic Affairs, Health and Welfare Unit.

OECD (1991), *Employment Outlook 1991*, Paris: OECD.

OECD (1994a), *The OECD Jobs Study: Evidence and Explanations. Part II*, Paris: OECD.

OECD (1994b), *The OECD Jobs Study: Facts, Analysis, Strategies,* Paris: OECD.

OECD (1997), *Family, Market and Community: Equity and Efficiency in Social Policy*, Social Policy Studies Number 21.

OECD (1998a), *Quarterly Labour Force Statistics,* Number 1, Paris: OECD Statistics Directorate.

OECD (1998b), *Main Economic Indicators: June 1998*, Paris: Statistics Directorate.

Rose, M. (1985), *Re-working the Work Ethic: Economic Values and Socio-Cultural Politics*, London: Batsford.

Warr, P. (1982), 'A National Study of Non-financial Employment Commitment', *Journal of Occupational Psychology*, **55**, 297-312.

Appendix: Regression model results

The five models presented in the chapter follow. Two multivariate techniques were used: multiple regression and logistic regression. These are explained in more detail in Appendix II to this report.

The models report the *coefficients* for each of the characteristics specified on the left side of the table. Each coefficient shows whether that particular characteristic differs significantly from its 'comparison group' in its association with the 'dependent variable', the variable we are investigating (for example, non-financial work commitment). Details of the comparison group are supplied in brackets. For example, Sweden has been used as the base category for comparisons by country because it represented an extreme case for a number of the explanatory variables that we are interested in. Sweden has the highest proportion of temporary workers, offers the most generous support to the unemployed and has the highest level of welfare spending (this latter feature is considered in relation to extrinsic/intrinsic work values). This choice means that the coefficients reported in the first section of each table tell us whether or not the average scores in Italy, western Germany, eastern Germany and Britain differ significantly from those found in Sweden.

A positive coefficient indicates that those with the characteristic are more committed to work than the comparison group; a negative coefficient that they are less committed. Two asterisks indicate the coefficient is statistically significant at a 99 per cent level, and one asterisk that it is significant at a 95 per cent level.

Model A: Work orientations - all measures

	Non-financial commitment score	Agreement that work is most important activity[1]	Organisation commitment score	Extrinsic values score	Intrinsic values score
Characteristic (comparison group in brackets)					
Constant	6.63	-.18	12.50	2.90	2.97
Country (Sweden)					
Western Germany	-.27**	-.17	.10	.20**	-.01
Eastern Germany	-.50**	.79**	.26	.24**	-.17**
Britain	-.92**	-.69**	.20	.28**	-.23**
Italy	-.62**	.18	-.54**	.35**	-.05
Contract type (permanent job)					
No contract	-.42**	.09	-.45*	-.01	-.08*
Temp. < 1 yr	-.57**	-.31	-2.25**	-.09	.12
Temp. 1 yr +	.07	-.06	-.49*	-.10*	-.00
Self-emp.	.30**	.40**	1.77**	-.15**	.23**
Part-time(full-time)	-.11	-.28	-.12	-.11**	-.02
Socio-economic group(working class[2])					
Prof/Manager	.82**	-.09	1.03**	.02	.12**
Tech + Ass. prof	.44**	-.17	.71**	-.00	.11**
Clerical	.36**	.01	.20	-.00	.08*
Sales/Service	.22	-.09	.17	.01	.07
Unemployed (employed)	.07	.32*	n.a.	-.01	.03
Women (men)	.43**	-.17	-.10	.00	-.00
Age (35-54 yrs)[3]					
18-25 years	.41**	.14	-.80**	.16**	-.03
25-34 years	.12	-.40**	-.21	.06*	.04
Over 54 yrs	-.12	.79**	.55**	.00	-.03
Education level completed (Lwr 2nd or less)[4]					
High Secondary	.24*	-.28*	-.33	-.04	.11**
Third Level	.42**	-.26	-.04	-.02	.17**
University	.53**	-.38**	-.54**	-.06	.16**
Adj. R Square	.12	[5]	.130	.072	.079
Base N	(2742)	(2755)	(2169)	(2821)	(2809)

* significantly different from comparison group (* p <.05 ** p<.005).

1 As the work centrality measure is categorical, we have used logistic regression techniques to model the probability of a person agreeing that work 'is a person's most important activity'. The unexponentiated coefficients are reported, each representing the effect the variable has on the log-odds of agreeing with this statement.

2 Occupational categories are based on the main ISCO88 groupings. Working class-skilled manual were semi/unskilled categories merged together after initial analyses showed no significant differences between the two groups.

3 This base category was chosen in order to provide a big enough reference group so that the constant plus the main country effects could be used to make sensible predictions.

4 There are no respondents in the British survey who have only primary education, therefore the lower secondary and primary categories were combined for the models.

5 Model Chi-square=273 (P< .005).

Model B: Predicted national work commitment and organisational commitment after controlling for individual level characteristics[1]

	Non-financial commitment score	Probability agree work most important activity	Organization commitment score
Sweden	6.6	.46	12.5
Western Germany	6.4 *	.41	12.6
Eastern Germany	6.1 **	.65 **	12.8
Britain	5.7 **	.30 **	12.7
Italy	6.0 **	.50	12.0 **

* significantly different from reference country: Sweden (* p <.05 ** p<.005).

[1] The figures reported apply to men, aged 35-54, employed in a full-time, permanent job in a skilled manual or semi/unskilled occupation, with low levels of education (incomplete secondary school or lower).

Model C: Predicted Scores after controlling for individual level characteristics[1]

	Extrinsic values score	Intrinsic values score
Sweden	2.9	3.0
Western Germany	3.1 **	3.0
Eastern Germany	3.1 **	2.8 **
Britain	3.2 **	2.7 **
Italy	3.3 **	2.9

* significantly different from reference country: Sweden (* p <.05 ** p<.005).

[1] The figures reported apply to men, aged 35-54, employed in a full-time, permanent job in a skilled manual or semi/unskilled occupation, with incomplete secondary or lower education.

6 The greening of Europe

Russell Dalton and Robert Rohrschneider [*]

The decade of the 1990s has in many ways been the one in which environmental issues have finally become a permanent feature of the politics of advanced industrial democracies. Between the 1980s and 1990s in most European states an emerging environmental movement increased its membership, and more importantly became a significant factor in the making of public policy. Green parties often made dramatic, albeit sometimes fleeting, gains in parliamentary elections and such parties now hold seats in several national parliaments in Western Europe. There was a growth in the number of environmental regulations and in the amount of environmental legislation introduced by European national governments (e.g., Klingemann, 1985; Bomberg, 1998). By the beginning of the 1990s, all the larger European states had a ministry devoted to environmental matters, and environmental issues had become an integral part of the policy making process.

Moreover, over the past ten years the environment has become a European-wide - and even global - issue. Increasingly European publics and elites have come to realise that environmental issues transcend national borders. The acid rain in the German Black Forest or the Swedish Kölen Mountains originates with upwind factories in France or England, while German industries, in turn, pollute Eastern Europe; the Swiss chemical spill into the Rhine in 1986 graphically illustrated how the level of pollution of major rivers depended on what occurred upstream. The Chernobyl accident later in

[*] Russell Dalton is a Professor at the University of California, Irvine, and Robert Rohrschneider an Associate Professor at Indiana University.

the same year showed that affluence or distance could not protect one from environmental risk. Thereafter, growing awareness of greenhouse warming and the ozone hole further underscored the global dimension of environmental protection. In response to this, European wide environmental policy making has expanded rapidly (Vogel 1993; Sbragia 1996). For example, both the Single European Act and the Maastricht treaty widened the authority of the EU on environmental matters.

Most scholars and political analysts agree that environmental concerns have increased across Europe during the 1980s and the 1990s (Dalton 1994, ch. 3).[1] As Sharon Witherspoon and Jean Martin noted in the *9th Report*, "not only do surveys attest to it, but increasing numbers of books, consumer guides, newspapers, television programmes, and so forth sell on the basis of their coverage of the environment". Moreover, "[consumer goods] are marketed as being 'environmentally-safe' or 'environmentally-friendly', testifying that manufacturers see a market opportunity in the public's new environmentalism. Politicians from all parties claim that environmental protection is central to their policies". (Witherspoon and Martin, 1992.) The 'greening' of Britain and Europe has been a real change of the past generation.

But what is less clear is the pace and extent of these changes across Europe, and the factors that explain the public's concern for environmental protection. For example, while some reports trumpet the greenness of the British public, other reports point to Britain as the 'dirty man of Europe'. Both views might be correct, but only cross-national analyses can assess Britain's position relative to its neighbours. Furthermore, studies of environmental policy and environmental opinions have hitherto focused on the nations of northern, industrial Europe and not on the wider range of European experiences.

This chapter uses the International Social Survey Programmes' 1993 module to map public opinion on environmental issues across six European Union countries. First of all, we describe the level of public concern in Europe about the environment and examine the environmental values of Europeans. This is followed by an examination of the relationship between levels of concern and environmental values. Then we explore cross-national patterns of personal and political behaviour on environmental matters. To what extent does a green consciousness translate into green action? Are those who are most likely to become active on behalf of the environment also those with the highest levels of concern and the greenest environmental values? The results should help us understand the breadth and depth of environmental sentiments in Europe in the middle of the 1990s, and the prospects for the future of environmentalism in Europe.

The roots of environmental concerns

In broad terms, previous research has presented two contrasting views of the contemporary environmental movement. From one perspective, the rise of environmentalism results from a deterioration in living conditions in advanced industrial democracies, and in the world in general. Increasing population densities, mass consumption, and pollution-generating production methods and technologies create environmental problems that are beyond the ability of the natural environment to absorb. Britain, Germany, and other northern European nations are sometimes cited as illustrations of these developments.

From another perspective, environmentalism has resulted from the very socio-economic progress of advanced industrial democracies (Inglehart 1990, 1997; Dalton 1994). Growing affluence and the development of the modern welfare state mean that the basic needs of western publics for physical and economic security are now satisfied. As a result, younger generations are shifting their priorities towards 'higher-order', non-materialist and libertarian goals, such as self-expression, freedom to choose one's life style, and social equality. From this perspective, the rise of environmentalism primarily reflects a change in the political orientations of the public, rather than changes in the environment.

These contrasting views not only have different explanations for the spread of environmental concerns, they also hold different implications for how societies and governments should respond to increasing demands for action about the environment. If such demands are simply a reflection of concerns that the environment has deteriorated, then progress in improving the quality of the environment should ameliorate the public's worries and reduce the level of political support for the environmental movement. But if those demands reflect changes in the social and political priorities of Western publics, then simply reducing pollution levels may not be a sufficient policy response. Thus, we begin our analyses by examining the two rival explanations of the roots of environmentalism (see also chapter 7 by Bryson and Curtice in this volume).

Perceptions of environmental problems

There are many aspects of the environmental issue that might potentially concern Europeans, ranging from global issues to problems of much more immediate impact. The 1993 ISSP[*] module referred to six potential environmental problems, and asked people to judge each in terms of the threat it posed, first, to the environment in general and, then, to themselves and their families.[2] The responses to the first of these questions are shown in the following table.

---

[*] See the Introduction and Appendices to this Report for further details about ISSP.

Perceived threats to the environment in general

% 'extremely'/ 'very' dangerous:	Car pollution	Nuclear power	Industry pollution	Pesti- cides	Water pollution	Global warming	Base (smallest)
Britain	49	46	56	39	62	55	1157
Ireland	45	84	65	56	72	58	878
Italy	59	69	72	67	76	71	945
Netherlands	25	47	65	41	46	40	1695
Spain	57	75	73	60	75	68	1098
Western Germany*	64	67	81	67	78	80	975

Many Europeans see each of the six problems as posing dangerous risks to the environment. For instance, roughly half or more of the public in each nation see nuclear power stations as a very great risk to the environment - even in a nation such as the Netherlands which does not possess its own nuclear power facilities. There is also considerable apprehension about the dangers of air pollution, water pollution and global warming. (The survey was conducted a few months after the global environmental summit at Rio, where issues of global warming were discussed.) Despite the progress that has been made in each of these areas during the decade preceding this survey, public concerns have not ended.

Levels of concern about the direct impact of environmental problems on the individual and his/her family are however somewhat lower, as the next table shows. For example, 64 per cent of Germans believed that pollution from cars posed an 'extremely dangerous' or 'very dangerous threat to the environment', but only 46 per cent saw an equal threat to their family. In other words, environmental protection is more often seen as a collective need, rather than an immediate personal danger.

---

* By western Germany we mean the geographical area known until unification as the Federal Republic of Germany. By eastern Germany we mean the area formerly known as the German Democratic Republic.

Perceived threats to individual and family

% 'extremely'/ 'very' dangerous:	Car pollution	Nuclear power	Industry pollution	Pesti-cides	Water pollution	Global warming	Base (smallest)
Britain	41	40	46	34	48	48	1153
Ireland	39	76	55	53	62	54	876
Italy	52	63	65	65	68	63	942
Netherlands	11	31	35	23	20	25	1690
Spain	53	69	68	57	71	65	1092
Western Germany	46	58	64	57	58	68	973

Despite the evidence of growing environmental consciousness among the British public (e.g., Witherspoon and Martin,1992; Norris 1997), in general the British public expressed relatively lower levels of environmental concern in comparison to other EU countries. For instance, the British were less concerned with air pollution or water pollution than most other European publics - despite persisting debates about these unresolved environmental problems in Britain. This may partially reflect an idyllic image that Britons hold toward the countryside and nature. In addition, British political elites - from the Thatcher to the Blair administration - have often questioned the claims of environmentalists, arguing, for example, that water quality in Britain is high, when EU statistics presented a contrasting picture. On the other hand, worries about environmental problems tend to be more common among the German, Italian and Spanish publics.

Values and the environment

The claim that increased concern about the environment reflects a change in values rather than the objective state of the environment has been argued most influentially by Ronald Inglehart (1990; 1997). In his theory of postmaterial value Inglehart maintains that younger Europeans have been raised in an environment of relative economic prosperity and security, and thus the values of the younger generation are shifting toward new *postmaterial values*. Postmaterial values emphasise social equality, life style choices, greater participation, and a concern for non-economic issues such as environmental quality. Indeed, in his various writings Inglehart has marshalled an impressive array of data showing that postmaterial values are linked to support for environmental action and support for the environmental movement (also see Rohrschneider, 1991; Dalton, 1994, ch. 3)

Other scholars, however, have argued that the new values which are responsible for growing concern about the environment reflect the development of a broader new environmental consciousness - known as a *New Environmental Paradigm* (NEP) - among the citizenry of advanced industrial societies (Dunlap and van Liere, 1978; Catton and Dunlap, 1980; Milbrath, 1984; Cotgrove, 1982; Dobson, 1995; Eckersly, 1992).   This paradigm supposedly interconnects several specific beliefs. A core element involves beliefs about the relationship between humans and nature, in particular that human needs and values should no longer be supreme. Instead other species are considered to have rights too.   (Dobson, 1995: 49-50; Kempton *et al.*, 1995: ch. 5). In addition, nature should be valued for its own sake, with less emphasis on economic growth. Similarly, supporters of the paradigm are supposedly sceptical of technology, believing that it simply postpones the consequences of past environmental mistakes and can even worsen the damage humankind inflicts on the environment. In addition, there are limits to nature's bounty and human expectations need to be adjusted to reflect those limits. In short, the new environmental paradigm thesis claims that the values of Western publics are changing in fundamental ways which restructure our relationship to the environment, and that these changes stimulate new concerns about environmental issues and behaviour to express these concerns.

 We have examined both approaches to the study of values, starting with Inglehart's theory of postmaterial value. Inglehart's research has indicated that postmaterial value orientations are less developed in Britain, in part because Britain's socio-economic development has lagged behind the rest of Europe since the end of World War II and in part because fewer political groups in Britain are open advocates of these values (Inglehart, 1990; 1997). The 1993 ISSP module contained the four-item index that Inglehart himself and other researchers have used to ascertain the distribution of postmaterialist values (Inglehart, 1990). Respondents were asked the following question:-

> *Looking at the list below, please tick a box next to the **one** thing you think should be [country's] **highest priority**, the **most** important thing it should do.*

> *And which **one** do you think should be [country's] **next highest priority**, the **second** most important thing it should do?*

> *Maintain order in the nation*
> *Give people more say in government decisions*
> *Fight rising prices*
> *Protect freedom of speech*

Those who chose the second and fourth items as their top two priorities are regarded as postmaterialists while those who chose the first and third items are labelled materialists. Those choosing any other combination are regarded as mixed'.   The following table shows the balance of materialists and postmaterialists in each of our six EU countries.

Balance of postmaterialists and materialists

	Postmaterialist	Materialist	**Difference**	base
	%	%	%	
Western Germany	23	24	-1	989
Netherlands	16	23	-7	1653
Italy	13	25	-12	980
Ireland	13	26	-13	941
Britain	12	26	-14	1172
Spain	12	31	-19	1159

We find that materialists outnumber postmaterialists in Britain by 14 points, making Britain more materialist than every other country except Spain. Postmaterialism is most common among the German and Dutch publics.

Assessing public orientations toward the values embedded in the New Environmental Paradigm proved to be more difficult. Although the 1993 ISSP module contained a battery of fourteen relevant items, a variety of methodological tests led us to choose eight which appeared to have the greatest empirical and theoretical reliability.[3] This is the best measure of public support for values which are argued to be part of a New Environmental Paradigm, even though the underlying empirical validity of these measures is still uncertain.

Almost two-thirds of the British, and an even greater proportion in most of the other European nations, express the view that humans should respect nature, and that nature would be at peace without humans (see the appendix to this chapter for details of the wording of this question). But only between a third and a half anywhere endorse the view that animals have the same rights as humans. European publics also display a robust scepticism of science, with as many as one in three in some countries contending that science does more harm than good. While only a quarter of the British public sees economic growth as a threat to the environment, greater numbers in most other nations see a tension between them. Indeed when we look at the answers to all the component items of our scale together, only in the Netherlands is support for the new environmental paradigm lower than it is in Britain.

Mean score on new environmental paradigm index

		base
Italy	4.71	970
Germany	4.23	943
Ireland	4.21	920
Spain	3.66	1092
Britain	3.34	1138
Netherlands	2.96	1716

Note: The index score is simply the number of component propositions with which the respondent agreed. A higher score indicates greater adherence to the values of the paradigm. For details of the component items see the appendix.

The New Environmental Paradigm thus receives only moderate support among Europeans, as one would expect with a challenging political ideology. Moreover, as with postmaterial values, support for this environmental orientation is generally even lower in Britain than elsewhere in Europe.[4] There are certainly environmental concerns and environmental actions in Britain, but in cross-national terms they appear to lack the ideological grounding in values that is among other European publics. As one activist described Britain in an earlier survey of the environmental movement (Dalton, 1994), Britain has environmentalists without environmentalism.

Linking values and environmental perceptions

What is the link between levels of concern about the environment and environmental values? As we argued earlier, some researchers have claimed that levels of concern are primarily influenced by values rather than by the 'objective' state of the environment. Those who value the environment may be more aware of its problems. If so, concern may rise at a time when environmental conditions are actually improving. However, it is less plausible to argue that environmental values are determined by environmental concerns as previous research suggests that such values develop before citizens form opinions about present-day pollution problems (Rohrschneider, 1988: 1990).

We therefore need to assess the impact of environmental values on levels of concern about the environment (Rohrschneider, 1988). If we were to find no relationship between the two, this would suggest that, contrary to the claims of Inglehart and others, environmental concern does simply reflect the objective state of the environment. If, in contrast, we were to find a relationship, this would suggest that environmental concern exists to some degree independently of the actual state of the environment. In order to ensure that our estimates of the impact of values are as accurate as possible, we also enter into our analysis indicators of the social location of our respondents such as income and education, in order to tap respondents' degree of exposure to environmental hazards (as those with less income and less education are more likely to be exposed to such risks). We also take into account the possibility that levels of environmental concern may be a reflection of more traditional left/right values by including an indicator of respondents' attitudes towards income inequality.

Predictors of environmental concern in general

	Britain	Western Germany	Italy	Ireland	Netherlands	Spain
Values						
Postmaterialism	+	+	n.s.	-	+	n.s.
New environmental paradigm	+	+	+	+	+	+
Left/right	+	n.s.	+	+	+	n.s.
Social location						
Higher income	n.s.	+	-	n.s.	n.s.	n.s.
Higher education	n.s.	n.s.	n.s.	+	+	n.s.
Larger town or city	n.a.	n.s.	n.s.	+	+	+
Controls						
Age	-	n.s.	-	-	-	n.s.
Sex (female)	n.s.	n.s.	n.s.	n.s.	+	n.s.

Note: n.s. = not significant at 95% level; n.a. = not available.

The previous table summarises the results when we included all these factors in a regression analysis in which the dependent variable was the total number of times that the respondent stated that an environmental hazard was 'extremely' or 'very' dangerous to the environment as a whole. (Full details of the regression results can be found in the Appendix to this chapter, and a description of regression analysis in the Appendix at the end of the book.) The results strongly suggest that levels of environmental concern are strongly influenced by one's prior values. Adherence to the values embodied in the New Environmental Paradigm is consistently one of the strongest predictors of environmental concern. Even a broader left/right ideological measure - support for reducing income inequalities - is significantly related to perceptions of environmental problems in most nations. Postmaterial values also tend to result in a higher level of environmental concern.[5] Moreover, values appear to exert a particularly strong influence in Britain, suggesting that the limited adherence to postmaterialism and the new environmental paradigm we have noted in Britain is at least a partial explanation for why environmental concerns are also generally lower among the British public.

   In contrast, we find that a person's social location has a limited impact on their levels of concern. Neither income nor education is strongly or consistently related to environmental worries. Urban residents are more likely than those living in more rural environments to perceive environmental problems as dangerous to their families, but even this difference is fairly moderate in comparison to the differences we find amongst those with different values.

How citizens advance the environmental cause

People have multiple opportunities to translate their environmental concerns into actual behaviour. They may join an environmental organisation, be willing to pay more taxes to finance environmental legislation, participate in protests promoting the environmental cause, or become green consumers. Some of these activities require few resources (signing a petition, for instance) while others require a substantial investment, such as organising a demonstration. Some of these activities have direct political relevance, others have less direct effects. We address two questions in this section. First, what actions do Europeans take as a result of their environmental concerns? Second, how active is the British public relative to other Europeans?

We distinguish between three basic types of activities. A first group includes political activities targeted at policy makers, such as organising demonstrations, signing petitions, or joining environmental groups. These activities seek to exert political pressure on policy makers and to motivate them to pass environmentally-friendly policies. Second, we examine personal support for strong environmental policies, even if these come at an economic cost for the individual. This provides a measure of the depth of environmental sentiments. A third set consists of individual actions which might not attract the attention of the mass media or the policy makers, but which directly address environmental problems, that is, changes in personal consumption patterns, such as recycling or driving a car less frequently. Such examples of green consumerism do not attract the media or result in policy changes, but they are equally important in reducing the amount of pollution because waste produced by individual households constitutes a major source of ecological problems.

Political action targeting policy makers

Great Britain does in fact have a long tradition of advancing the environmental cause, reaching as far back as the end of the 19th century (Lowe and Goyder, 1983; Sheail, 1976), especially in its support for nature conservation groups and amenity societies. For instance, the National Trust, founded in 1895, now boasts a membership of over 1 million. The goal of such groups is to achieve environmental protection within the framework of industrial societies, the principles of market economies, and the existing policy process. In recent years, new ecology groups have emerged which reflect alternative values like those of postmaterialism and the New Environmental Paradigm (Dalton, 1994). For instance, Greenpeace and

Friends of the Earth have garnered a large membership in Britain as they have in many other European nations.

Given this long-standing tradition, we expected the British public to endorse and participate in environmental groups. The 1993 ISSP asked: 'Are you a member of a group whose main aim is to preserve or protect the environment?' A substantial proportion of British respondents - five per cent - said they were members of an environmental organisation. This is a significant number, exceeding as it does the combined individual membership of the major political parties (which was found to be just three per cent in the 1994 *British Social Attitudes Survey*). Moreover, the figure is also relatively high when compared with other countries. Among the six countries in the following table, the British public occupies third place, after the Dutch (17 per cent) and the Germans (six per cent).

Environmental political action

	Britain	Germany	Italy	Ireland	Nether-lands	Spain
% member of environmental group	5	6	5	4	17	2
Base	*1247*	*994*	*999*	*956*	*1833*	*1196*
% who in last five years:						
Gave money to environmental group	30	19	14	23	44	10
Signed petition	37	31	24	21	23	15
Demonstration	3	8	7	4	5	6
Base (smallest)	*1116*	*994*	*957*	*950*	*1824*	*1195*

These results are not an artefact of a particular time point - the same pattern emerged in 1989 when the European Community commissioned a survey in all member-states of the EU. When asked whether they had joined a nature conservation or anti-nuclear energy group, the British again turned out to be among the leaders. Five per cent of the British public claimed they belonged to a nature conservation group, second only to the Dutch (20 per cent). Meanwhile, two per cent said they belonged to an anti-nuclear energy group, the highest within the EU. Overall, then the British are among the leaders in Western Europe in terms of membership of both traditional nature conservation groups and the newer more assertive anti-nuclear power groups.

Impressive membership figures convey a strong signal to policy makers, as those groups lobby for specific policies. At the same time, however, once citizens have signed a membership form they may theoretically remain passive - indeed only a small fraction of group members actually becomes intensely involved in the work of an organisation (Dalton, 1994; Norris, 1997). To be effective, the leaders of environmental groups have to translate their membership rosters into political pressure, such as by organising events, and establishing contacts with the mass media to advance their organisations' cause. Large membership figures are insufficient evidence of a viable grass-roots environmental movement - citizens also need to engage in activities which generate pressure on policy makers.

And indeed, the evidence suggests that the British do not just join a group but are also ready to lobby in a traditional way on behalf of the environment. Indeed, the British public leads those of other countries in having given money to environmental groups (30 per cent) and having signed a petition (37 per cent). Such figures are a clear sign of a public which not only joins environmental organisations, but is also ready to support environmental groups in other ways.

But there is one intriguing and we believe telling exception to this general pattern. By comparative standards, the British public is the least willing to join in demonstrations on environmental matters. Only three per cent of Britons said they had participated in an environmental demonstration. Both in absolute and in comparative terms British citizens are evidently substantially more willing to engage in traditional lobbying activities than in direct action tactics. This pattern is not however confined to environmental behaviour. Previous studies of political participation have found that British citizens are generally among the least likely to use unconventional forms of behaviour (Barnes and Kaase, 1979; Topf, 1995). The British appear content to elect representatives or to join organisations, but less inclined than other countries to challenge their representatives directly. Naturally, these activities do sometimes happen, but they occur less frequently in Britain than in other advanced democracies. To a British public accustomed to representative democracy, political behaviours bypassing elected officials apparently do not come easily.

Paying for environmental protection

A second form of green action is expressing support for government action to protect the environment. Contemporary public opinion nearly unanimously endorses stronger measures to protect the environment. For example, in a survey conducted by Gallup before the 1992 environmental summit at Rio, more than 90 per cent of the public in most European nations favoured stronger environmental protection laws for business and industry (Dunlap et al., 1993). An almost equally high proportion favoured laws requiring that all citizens conserve resources and reduce pollution (also see Dalton, 1994, ch. 3; Rüdig, 1993).

Many political analysts discount these apparently high levels of support for environmental action because people do not have to consider the cost of the policies they are backing when they answer such questions. So, the ISSP tried to test the depth of support for environmental action by seeing if people would endorse government actions to protect the environment even when they were reminded of the likely financial burden that would result Three questions were asked:

*How willing would you be to pay **much higher prices** in order to protect the environment?*

*And how willing would you be to pay **much higher taxes** in order to protect the environment?*

*And how willing would you be to **accept cuts in your standard of living** in order to protect the environment?*

As is clear from the next table, British support for the environment diminishes when there are costs attached. The British are the least ready to pay higher prices, the second least willing to accept lower living standards, and the third least prepared when it comes to paying more taxes for the sake of the environment. In none of these instances does a majority of the British public support the pro-environment option. The overall impression is that there is a limited reservoir of support for policies which impose greater financial burdens.

Willingness to accept the costs of higher environmental quality

	Britain	Germany	Italy	Ireland	Nether lands	Spain
% 'very' or 'fairly' willing to:						
Pay higher prices	48	50	68	50	70	52
Pay higher taxes	39	34	38	24	49	44
Accept lower living standards	31	55	52	29	48	45
Base (smallest)	*1207*	*974*	*964*	*944*	*1801*	*1166*

One might argue that Britons are simply more forthright than continental Europeans in answering survey questions or, at a minimum, that they are more realistic when pitting such 'lofty' goals as environmental protection against their short-term economic interests. It is as difficult to rule this possibility out as it is problematic to provide evidence for it. On the other hand we can assess the depth of the reluctance of people in Britain to take steps personally to protect the environment by examining their consumption patterns.

The personal dimension of environmental behaviour

Despite the considerable amount of pollution generated by households, political scientists have paid relatively little attention to green consumer behaviour (McCormick, 1991; Dalton, 1994). One reason for this neglect is undoubtedly that political activities and public opinion are more likely to catch the attention of the mass media and policy makers, and thus attract the attention of political scientists. Personal behaviours, however, are less visible and seemingly lack an overt political component.

However, as we have noted, the sheer volume of pollution generated by households means it is essential to examine what citizens actually do (or are willing to do) in order to help clean up the environment. If we know under what conditions people are willing to adjust their individual behaviour, policy makers may be in a better position to establish incentives to accomplish such changes. In addition, one of the few studies which actually analysed citizens' personal activities suggests that what individuals do in their households is related to their general attitudes about environmental groups (Rohrschneider, 1993). Thus, the seemingly apolitical domain of citizens' behaviour in their individual household is connected at least indirectly to politics.

Not only do personal actions affect a nation's environment, but they may also make it more likely that people will be prepared to take political action in the future. By engaging regularly in activities like recycling or buying organic fruit and vegetables, individuals' respect for the environment is likely to be reinforced on an almost daily basis. While a petition may be signed today and forgotten tomorrow, engaging regularly in a household activity, may well not only reinforce an individual's pre-existing support for ecological protection but also help foster broader sympathies for the environmental cause. Thus, for example, citizens who start to recycle may come to support the introduction of recycling laws which at one time they did not support, and so come to endorse environmental groups and other environmental action.

The 1993 ISSP module contains several questions that examine the personal activities that people undertake to help the environment. The results show the British public displays only a modest level of green consumer. Less than half of Britons reported that they recycled glass, less than a quarter bought organic fruit and vegetables , and less than one in eight tried to cut down on use of their car for the sake of the environment. In contrast, almost 90 per cent of Germans and of the Dutch said they recycled glass. Even if they have made progress over the past decade, the British still lag behind their Northern European neighbours in their green consumer behaviour.

The personal dimension of environmental behaviour

	Britain	Western Germany	Italy	Ireland	Nether-lands	Spain
% who 'always' or 'often':						
Recycle glass	46	87	50	39	85	40
Buy organic fruit & veg	22	53	20	25	18	15
Avoid using car	12	29	17	4	24	6
Base (smallest)	*872*	*757*	*788*	*633*	*1390*	*734*
% who 'always' or 'often' **pay attention to packaging** **before purchasing product**	29	49	37	32	26	-
Base:	*1249*	*1010*	*1000*	*957*	*1803*	
% where environment 'most' or **'very' important consideration** **when last buying vehicle**	19	54	26	16	27	-
Base (all who have chosen/helped to *choose motor vehicle in last 5 years)*	*672*	*525*	*508*	*449*	*1086*	

Of course some of the differences between the countries could be the result of differences in the requirements and opportunities to engage in environmentally friendly behaviour rather than differences in the willingness of citizens to undertake such activities. However, the results in the above table are noteworthy because we have excluded from the figures those who said they did not have the opportunity to undertake the activity in question.[6] It appears that what the British lack is not the opportunity to engage in environmentally friendly behaviour, but the motivation.

Indeed, as our next table shows, the British seem to recognise this picture of themselves. Like the Irish and the Spanish they believe it difficult for someone like themselves to do much about the environment. They are also the least likely of all to claim that they actually do what is right for the environment. These perceptions of themselves suggest the British are at least realistic about what they can and want to do on behalf of nature.

	Britain	Western Germany	Italy	Ireland	Nether-lands	Spain
% disagree:						
It is just too difficult for someone like me to do much about the environment	48	56	67	47	62	46
% agree:						
I do what is right for the environment, even when it costs more or takes more time	46	61	60	61	55	47
Base (smallest)	*1141*	*983*	*983*	*944*	*1806*	*1171*

Overall, we find a unique constellation of behavioural patterns. On the one hand, the British public is more willing than that of other West European countries to belong to environmental groups and to engage in traditional lobbying techniques on behalf of the environment. On the other hand, the British are among the least willing to pay for the costs of environmental protection or to engage in green consumerism. This combination suggests that the environmental movement in Britain may be less able than it is in other countries to challenge established policy makers. Elsewhere, and especially in Germany and the Netherlands, citizens are not only willing to engage in conventional political activities but also to go on demonstrations and to engage in environmentally friendly personal behaviour. But in Great Britain, activism focuses disproportionately on traditional lobbying techniques to the detriment of anything more intense.

Linking values, problem perceptions, and activism

We have already seen that values influence levels of environmental concern, and not just the objective state of the environment. But do values influence willingness to engage in certain sorts of green behaviour? To address this question, we have undertaken regression analysis once more, examining in turn each of our three forms of environmental activism, that is participation in political activities, willingness to incur greater costs to protect the environment, and green consumer behaviour. In each case we have constructed a simple additive index based on the measures of each that we have already presented. We used the same predictors as in our earlier analyses except that we have added our measures of levels of concern about the environment, and excluded income and urban residence. The analyses were conducted separately for all the countries included in the earlier tables but to simplify matters we simply show here the results we obtained when we analysed all our five continental countries together plus those we acquired for Great Britain alone.

Predictors of environmental behaviours in Britain and other EU Countries

	Political Behaviour		Policy Support		Personal Behaviour	
	GB	EU	GB	EU	GB	EU
Perceived Pollution Threat						
To family	n.s.	+	n.s.	-	n.s.	-
To environment as a whole	+	+	+	+	+	+
Values						
Postmaterialism	+	+	+	+	+	+
New Environmental Paradigm	-	+	+	+	+	+
Left/Right	n.s.	n.s.	n.s.	-	n.s.	n.s.
Controls						
Higher Education	+	+	+	+	+	+
Age	-	n.s.	n.s.	n.s.	-	-
Gender (female)	n.s.	n.s.	-	n.s.	+	+

Note: n.s. = not significant at 95% level; n.a. = not available. For full details of the regression results see the Appendix.

All else being equal, we would expect citizens who perceive greater pollution problems to be more active on behalf of the environment. And indeed, among both the British public and that of the other EU nations perceptions of the danger posed by pollution problems to the environment as a whole do exert a strong influence on all three types of behaviours. Citizens with a high level of such concern are substantially more likely to engage in environmental political action, more willing to bear a greater financial burden, and more likely to adopt green consumer actions. Indeed, perceptions of environmental dangers in general emerge as one of the strongest predictors in almost all countries. This finding confirms the results of previous studies of the evolution of support for the environmental movement in Western Europe (Rohrschneider, 1990; Dalton, 1994). Equally our finding that perceptions of the threat posed by pollution to respondents and their families is also in line with the findings of previous research (Rohrschneider, 1988).

Values also shape the propensity to act, but in a more varied way. Those adhering to postmaterial values are more likely to engage in all three types of behaviour. And we should also bear in mind that as those with postmaterial values are also more likely to have a high level of environmental concern, these values also influence behaviour indirectly via their impact on environmental concern. Thus, the overall impact of postmaterialism is consistent with Inglehart's earlier findings (Inglehart, 1990). Conformity with the New Environmental Paradigm also increases the propensity of British citizens to favour strong environmental policies and to adopt green consumer behaviour. Surprisingly, however, these values apparently reduce the British public's propensity to become politically active to protect the environment. One possible explanation may be that the fairly conventional activities commonly organised by British environmental groups are of little appeal to those with such views. In other EU nations, in contrast, where environmental groups are more radical than in Britain, upholding the values of the new environmental paradigm does increase the propensity to support group activities.[7]

Education is also a consistently strong predictor of citizen action. In line with the literature on political participation, better educated individuals are more willing to become politically active, incur greater costs on behalf of nature, and engage in environmentally friendly personal behaviour. Younger people also appear more likely to act, especially when it comes to the personal dimension. But the most important finding of our analysis is that values not only appear to influence people's perceptions of the quality of the environment, but also their propensity to act on those perceptions.

Conclusion

Throughout the 1990s, environmentalism became an increasingly transnational issue, through the activities of the United Nations' Environmental Program and the European Union's expanding authority on environmental matters. Britain has often been labelled a laggard in this process largely as a result of the reluctance of the Conservative administrations of Thatcher and Major. In many ways, British public policy on the environment was out of line with that of the rest of Europe (Bomberg, 1998; Cichowski, 1999).

The goal of this chapter was to determine whether the environmental attitudes of people in Britain are in fact similar to those of other Europeans, despite their governments having somewhat different policies and priorities. We addressed this question in three ways. First, we asked whether the British were as concerned as their counterparts elsewhere in Europe about the threat to their environment, and whether they brought similar values to their consideration of the issue. Second, we asked whether the British were as willing as people elsewhere in Europe to take action to help the environment. And third, we asked whether the links between levels of concern, values and willingness to take action were the same in Britain as elsewhere in Europe.

On the first point, our analyses suggest that while the British public is quite concerned about the potential dangers presented by environmental pollution, they are less so than most other EU countries. Moreover, Britons score relatively low on both postmaterialism and their conformity with the New Environmental Paradigm. Second, as for political action, environmentally-concerned people in Britain are ready to endorse the activities of environmental groups, a pattern which in no small part results from the strong tradition of nature conservation groups in the country. Indeed, British environmental groups receive comparatively strong support even though the British are not as concerned as are other Europeans about the scale of pollution and are less likely to support the alternative values underlying modern environmental movements.

Third, despite this particular British finding, environmental perceptions and values do generally have a strong impact on environmental behaviour. Even in the British case the public's relatively low level of environmental concern and its limited adoption of postmaterial values results in limited enthusiasm for strong environmental policies and green consumer behaviour. As a result British environmental groups are less likely than their German or Dutch counterparts to secure strong public support for assertive environmental action.

Overall, our analyses modify a picture presented in some recent reports in the *British Social Attitudes* series. While the British undoubtedly do more than they have in the past, a majority does not possess those characteristics which in other nations lead to assertive movements challenging established policy-makers. In sum, while the British environmental movement will doubtless continue to be visible and a pressure for political change in Britain, it is likely to continue to be more moderate politically and a more heavily elite-driven phenomenon than in many of its European neighbours.

Notes

1. There are, however, some dissenting voices. See, for example Bramwell (1994).
2. A typical question read: 'In general, do you think that air pollution caused by cars is extremely dangerous for the environment, very dangerous, somewhat dangerous, not very dangerous, or not dangerous at all for the environment? And do you think that air pollution cased by cars is extremely dangerous for you and your family...' The other questions asked about: 1) nuclear power stations, 2) air pollution caused by industry, 3) pesticides and chemicals used in farming, 4) pollution of [the nations'] rivers, lakes, and streams, and 5) a rise in the world's temperature caused by the 'greenhouse effect'.
3. Factor analyses of the full battery of questions (the wording of which is shown in the appendix to this chapter) found that several items phrased in negative terms did not consistently have negative loadings in each country. In addition, the scalability of two items was limited. Because the NEP has not been systematically tested with representative cross-national samples, it is difficult to know whether these results reflect flaws in the measurement or in the underlying theoretical concept. The patterns of correlation for the NEP and postmaterialism reported below also raise questions about what are the core elements of value change and what is their relationship to environmentalism. In the end, we chose to use the eight items that were all worded in a pro-NEP direction, and which together loaded on a first unrotated factor in most nations. Even so, we advise caution in judging the reliability and validity of the resulting NEP scale.
4. It is surprising the Dutch public scores so low on the NEP values. This is not consistent with other measures of environmentalism that we will present for the Dutch public, and is not consistent with Dutch scores on postmaterial values (see above).
5. We expected a strong positive relationship between the NEP and postmaterialism, but these two indices were essentially unrelated in most nations. Other research on environmental values has found a strong relationship between these two measures (e.g., Dalton *et al.* 1999, chapter 7). This may be another indicator of the uncertain validity of the NEP index as discussed in note 3 above. Alternatively, it may be a consequence of

using only the four-item measure of postmaterialism that focuses on only the participatory aspect of postmaterialism.

6. This means in the case of recycling we have excluded from the denominator upon which the figures in the table are based those who said they did not have the facilities locally to recycle glass, in the case of buying organic fruit and vegetables, those who said they did not have access to such products, and in the case of using a car those who said they did not drive.

7. We should however bear in mind our earlier reservation about the validity of our measure of NEP values. The finding that NEP values are negatively associated with political activity in Britain may thus be a methodological artefact. However given that the variable behaves as we would expect in all other respects, our finding may well be an accurate reflection of reality.

References

Barnes, S., Kaase, M. *et al.* (1979), *Political Action,* Beverly Hills: Sage.

Bomberg, E. (1998), *Green Parties and Politics in the European Union,* London: Routledge.

Bramwell, A. (1994), *The Withering of the Greens,* New Haven: Yale University Press.

Catton, W.R. and Dunlap, R. (1980), 'A New Ecological Paradigm for Post-exuberant Sociology', *American Behavioural Scientist,* **24**: 15-47.

Cichowski, R. (1998, forthcoming), 'European Environmental Policy and the European Court of Justice', *Journal of European Public Policy.*

Cotgrove, S. (1982), *Catastrophe or Cornucopia: The Environment, Politics and the Future,* New York: Wiley and Sons.

Dalton, R. (1994), *The Green Rainbow: Environmental Interest Groups in Western Europe,* New Haven: Yale University Press.

Dalton, R. (1999, forthcoming), *Critical Masses: Public Response to the Environmental Consequences of Nuclear Weapons Production in the United States and Russia,* Cambridge: MIT Press.

Dobson, A. (1995), *Green Political Thought,* 2nd Edition, London: Harper/Collins.

Dunlap, R. and Van Liere, K. (1978), 'The New Environmental Paradigm', *The Journal of Environmental Education,* **9**: 10-19.

Dunlap, R., Gallup, G.H. Jr. and Gallup, A.M. (1993), *Health of the Planet Survey,* Princeton, New Jersey: Gallup International Institute.

Eckersley, R. (1992), *Environmentalism and Political Theory: Toward an Ecocentric Approach,* Albany: State University of New York Press.

Kempton, W., Boster, J. and Hartley, J. (1995), *Environmental Values in American Culture,* Cambridge, Mass: MIT Press.

Inglehart, R. (1990), *Culture Shift in Advanced Industrial Society,* Princeton: Princeton University Press.

Inglehart, R. (1997), *Modernization and Postmodernization,* Princeton: Princeton University Press.

Klingemann, H-D. (1985), 'Umweltproblematik in den Wahlprogrammen der etablierten politischen Parteien in der Bundesrepublik Deutschland' in Wildenmann, R. (ed.), *Umwelt, Wirtschaft, Gessellschaft,* Stuttgart: Staatsministeriums Baden-Wuertemmberg.

Lowe, P. and Goyder, J. (1983), *Environmental Groups in Politics,* New York: Allen and Unwin.

McCormick, M. (1991), *British Politics and the Environment,* London: Earthscan.

Milbrath, L. (1984), *Environmentalists: Vanguard for a New Society,* Albany: SUNY Press.

Norris, P. (1997), 'Are we all Greens now? Public Opinion on Environmentalism in Great Britain', *Government and Opposition,* **32**: 320-39.

Rohrschneider, R. (1988), 'Citizen attitudes toward environmental issues: Selfish or selfless?', *Comparative Political Studies,* **21**:347-67.

Rohrschneider, R. (1990), 'Public Opinion Toward New Social Movements: An Empirical Test of Competing Explanations', *American Journal of Political Science*, **34**: 1-30.

Rohrschneider, R. (1991), 'Public opinion toward environmental groups in Western Europe', *Social Science Quarterly*, **72**: 251-66.

Rohrschneider, R. (1993), 'Environmental Belief Systems in Western Europe: A Hierarchical Model of Constraint', *Comparative Political Studies*, **26**: 3-29.

Rüdig, W. (1993), 'Dimensions of Public Concern over Global Warming', paper presented at the 4th Global Warming International Conference, Chicago.

Sbragia, A. (1996), 'Environmental Policy' in Wallace H. and Wallace, W. (eds.), *Policy-making in the European Union*, Oxford: Oxford University Press.

Sheail, J. (1976), *Nature in Trust: The History of Nature Conservation in Britain*, London: Blackie.

Topf, R. (1995), 'Beyond Electoral Participation' in Klingemann, H-D. and Fuchs D. (eds.), *Citizens and the State*, Oxford: Oxford University Press.

Vogel, D. (1993), 'The European Union and the Environment' in Kamienecki, S. (ed.), *Environmental Politics in the International Arena: Movements, Parties, Organizations and Policy*, Albany: State University of New York Press.

Witherspoon, S. and Martin, J. (1992), 'What do we mean by green?' in Jowell, R., Brook, L., Prior, G. and Taylor, B. (eds.), *British Social Attitudes - the 9th Report*, Aldershot: Dartmouth.

Appendix

New Environmental Paradigm

The following table gives full details of the wording and the response distributions for the questions that form part of our New Environmental Paradigm scale.

Distribution of environmental values

	Britain	Germany	Nether-lands	Ireland	Italy	Spain
% say agree or strongly agree						
Biocentric values						
Humans should respect nature because it was created by God	62	74	43	90	84	71
Nature would be at peace and in harmony if only human beings would leave it alone	61	77	32	69	80	64
Animals should have the same moral rights that human beings do	46	50	31	44	50	38
Scepticism of science						
We believe too often in science, and not enough in feelings and faith	50	51	49	66	63	66
Overall, modern science does more harm than good	26	27	14	38	32	30
Economic growth						
Economic growth always harms the environment	26	51	30	32	56	42
Social change						
Any change humans cause in nature - no matter how scientific - will make things worse	37	54	34	43	52	55
Almost everything we do in modern life harms the environment	49	60	31	49	62	65
Base (smallest)	*1138*	*943*	*1716*	*920*	*970*	*1092*

Regression models

The following linear regression models are summarised in the chapter. The tables below show the standardised regression coefficients; coefficients marked with an asterisk are significant at the .05 level.

Model a: predictors of perceived environmental problems

The dependent variable is a count of the number of environmental problems that are perceived to pose an extremely dangerous or very dangerous risk to the environment as a whole.

	Britain	Germany	Italy	Ireland	Nether-lands	Spain
Values						
Postmaterialism	.08*	.10*	.01	-.09*	.13*	.05
New Environmental Paradigm	.31*	.31*	.17*	.14*	.28*	.22*
Left-right	.12*	.04	.08*	.08*	.13*	.00
Social location						
Higher income	.01	.09*	-.11*	.05	-.06	-.05
Higher education	.04	.12	.07	.12*	.10*	-.02
Larger town or city	-	.01	.05	.19*	.07*	.15*
Controls						
Age	-.14*	-.01	-.09*	-.08*	-.13*	-.01
Gender (female)	.00	.05	.08*	.02	.09*	-.01
R Square	.37	.37	.27	.31	.37	.26

Model b: predictors of environmental behaviours in Britain and other EU countries

The dependent variable is the total number of behaviours engaged in by the respondent. See main text for full details of the component indicators.

	Political Behaviour		Policy Support		Personal Behaviour	
	GB	EU	GB	EU	GB	EU
Perceived Pollution Threat						
Pollution threat to family	-.12	.07*	-.11	-.09*	-.04	-.14*
Pollution threat to nation	.37*	.26*	.36*	.26*	.34*	.33*
Values						
Postmaterialism	.12*	.04*	.07*	.13*	.08*	.07*
New Environmental Paradigm	-.10*	.14*	.09*	.05*	.10*	.11*
Left/Right	.04	-.02	-.02	-.04*	.01	.03
Controls						
Higher Education	.16*	.25*	.25*	.18*	.18*	.11*
Age	-.13*	.01	-.04	.01	-.27*	-.16*
Gender (female)	-.02	.01	-.08*	.01	-.07*	.08*
R Square	.18	.12	.15	.10	.20	.10

7 The end of materialism?

Caroline Bryson and John Curtice [*]

Other chapters in this book tend to focus on particular topics addressed by the *International Social Survey Programme* (ISSP). [**] In this chapter we look instead at *all* the areas covered between 1992 and 1996 to identify patterns across a range of different subjects. In particular, we try to assess how far these ISSP data support claims that a global shift in values has been taking place over a number of decades - a shift which rejects the materialism of the past and embraces a new mood of what has been called 'postmaterialism' and, subsequently, 'postmodernisation'.

This thesis has been developed by, and is still most closely associated with, the work of Ronald Inglehart (Inglehart, 1977; Inglehart 1990; Abramson and Inglehart, 1995; Inglehart 1997). It holds that the rise of postwar affluence in regions such as Western Europe, accompanied by the relative absence of war in those areas, has had a profound effect on public attitudes towards a wide range of subjects - with important consequences for the present and future social, economic and political fabric of those societies. To the extent that the thesis holds true, it would suggest that while key British social values may not be similar now to those in the rest of the EU, they are destined to follow the same trajectory.

---

[*] Caroline Bryson is a Research Director at SCPR, and Co-director of the *British Social Attitudes* survey series. John Curtice is Deputy Director of the ESRC Centre for Research into Elections and Social Trends (CREST), and Professor of Politics and Director of the Social Statistics Laboratory at Strathclyde University.
[**] See the Introduction and Appendices to this Report for further details about ISSP.

'Postmaterialism' and 'postmodernisation'

According to Inglehart's original postmaterialist thesis, the attitudes and values of people who were born in the developed world after the Second World War have been shaped by the experience of relative affluence and relative peace during their formative years. Unlike their predecessor generations, they could take relative economic well-being and physical security for granted and, as a result, their ambitions and priorities for themselves and their societies were bound to be rather different. Thus, postwar generations were more concerned with the opportunity to express themselves, to develop their talents and to enhance their quality of life, than with the sheer struggle for survival and security. They were thus less likely than preceding generations had been to regard the advancement of their own and their nation's material welfare as their top priority.

These new values, so the argument goes, expressed themselves above all in the student 'revolutions' of the late 1960s and in the environmental movements of the 1970s and 1980s - both of which were characterised not only by the fact that they were non-materialist in emphasis, but also that they were unconventional in their methods of expression.

More recently, Inglehart (1997) has broadened his theory to encompass the concept of 'postmodernisation' (see Gibbins and Reimer, 1995). He has identified two important stages in the cultural development of modern societies. The first is 'modernisation' during which societies undergo the rapid changes associated with the development of an industrial economy, such as the decline of agriculture, the development of cities and rapid economic growth. Alongside these economic changes, Inglehart argues, important cultural changes also occur, such as the decline of religion, or at any rate, a shift in those religions which emphasise individual experience and away from those which prioritise traditional authority. In this period, societies become more concerned with securing their own material advancement and less constrained by the demands of, say, the extended family. Meanwhile, the vacuum created by the decline in the authority of religious leaders is filled by an expansion of the role of the state.

The next stage of development in advanced societies, according to Inglehart, is 'postmodernisation'. As these developed societies experience relative physical and economic security, the law of diminishing returns comes into play and the marginal utility of further economic growth declines. The result is a further cultural shift. People then place greater emphasis on the need to promote subjective individual well-being and less on objective economic growth, with major consequences for social and moral values. This shift is particularly evident in younger generations who have experienced 'formative affluence'. Accompanying this process is a loss in confidence in the authority of government, in just the same way as a loss of religious authority characterised the period of modernisation. Indeed, according to the theory, postmodern societies are increasingly unwilling to invoke any kind of authority as the basis on which to make moral judgements about individual behaviour.

Not surprisingly, the alleged consequences of this second cultural shift are wide ranging. They include not only greater concern for the environment and a willingness to challenge state authority, but also the development of increasingly liberal views on social and moral issues such as homosexuality or the role of women, a greater emphasis on the intrinsic as opposed to the extrinsic rewards of work, a suspicion of science, an antipathy towards too large a role for the state in the economy, and a decline in at least the more xenophobic forms of nationalism. Inevitably, therefore, these postmodern societies - with their absence of moral consensus and their greater propensity to challenge the authority and legitimacy of government - are relatively difficult to govern. However, for Inglehart this is a price worth paying. He suggests that postmodern man and woman have freed themselves from the yoke of external authority and become model independent-minded and critical citizens that help ensure a healthy democratic society. Little echo here of the concerns expressed by others about the consequences for democracy of a decline in people's trust in government (Lipset and Schneider, 1983).

The ISSP modules provide us with an excellent opportunity to examine the validity of the postmodernisation thesis. Recent modules have covered not just postmaterialism and attitudes towards the environment, but also attitudes towards sex, the role of women, national identity, work, and the role of government, all of which are supposedly affected by the postmodern shift. Meanwhile, the modules enable us to examine not only the kinds of people who support particular values *within* each country, but *across* countries too. The countries we have chosen provide different settings to test the thesis, embracing different levels of economic development and, in particular, different levels of religious affiliation.

We focus here on two questions that we consider to be central to the validity and utility of Inglehart's postmodernisation thesis. First, can we clearly distinguish a transition from modernisation to postmodernisation in terms of people's attitudes and values? And second, are the implications and consequences of postmodernisation and postmaterialism as wide ranging as Inglehart argues?

Why might it be difficult to distinguish between modernisation and postmodernisation? A key reason is that, as Inglehart himself acknowledges, societies share certain characteristics during their modernist and postmodernist phases, most notably a decline in the importance of religion. So, if we are to demonstrate that postmodernisation is occurring, we shall need to show that attitudes to, say, moral issues are not just associated with someone's religious disposition but also with their experience or otherwise of 'formative affluence'. Unless we can demonstrate this there is no necessary reason to believe that any cultural changes that societies may be experiencing are the result of a new phenomenon of postmodernisation rather than just a long-standing process of secularisation and modernisation. Curiously, this vital distinction is not clearly pursued in Inglehart's own work, even though in one of his key analyses he shows there is a clear and consistent difference between Catholic and Protestant countries in the degree of postmodernism they exhibit, as well as in their degree of modernism (Inglehart, 1997: 98). One of our aims here is to fill that gap.

As for our second question, if the concept of postmodernisation exists, we should be able to find broadly the same sorts of people in each of the same countries adopting the same sorts of viewpoints towards each of the subjects we examine. If, on the other hand, we discover - as van Deth and Scarborough (1995a) did in their review of value orientations in Europe - that 'value change does not follow a single developmental path; rather the picture is of divergence, fragmentation, and diversity', we will have to reject the postmodernisation thesis (see Flanagan, 1982, 1987).

Data and method

As noted then, postmodernisation is a theory both about individuals and about countries. It posits that postmodern values will be most prevalent amongst those individuals who have enjoyed the most affluence, especially in their early lives, and that they will also be most prevalent in those countries with the highest sustained levels of material affluence. So, in order to examine the theory we have to examine individual differences within countries, as well as national differences between countries.

For each subject we cover, our primary analytical task is to see whether the differences we find between countries fit the expectations of the thesis. After all, the importance of the postmodernisation thesis lies in the claims it makes about its consequences for whole societies rather than for individuals. Indeed, this is also the form that most of Inglehart's own analysis takes. Once we have done that, we shall go on to relate our analyses of country differences to an analysis of individual or group differences within countries.

We cover five member nations of the EU: Britain, western Germany[*], Sweden, Italy and Spain (though we do not always have complete coverage of all subjects in all countries).[1] Between them the countries vary in terms of their national wealth (a crucial indicator of economic security) and in the character and importance of their religious adherence. As the next table shows, Britain is one of the less affluent countries in the EU. Its GDP per head is well below that of Sweden and Germany, on a par with Italy's and above Spain's. And, as noted in Peter Taylor-Gooby's chapter in this volume, Britain's proportion of welfare spending is lower than in Germany and, especially, Sweden. So, if Inglehart's thesis is broadly correct, we should expect to find that attitudes indicative of postmodernism will be less common in Britain than they are in either Germany or Sweden.

---

[*] By western Germany we mean the geographical area known until unification as the Federal Republic of Germany.

Characteristics of countries

	GDP per head 1994 (1,000 ECU)	Social Protection Benefits as % of GDP 1993	% with degree	% attend church 1+ week	% Catholic	% women aged 15+ economically active 1994
Germany	21.2	29.7	9	13	43	48
Sweden	18.9	39.7	17	4	1	57
Italy	14.8	24.7	5	34	95	34
Britain	14.7	26.7	11	12	10	53
Spain	10.4	23.2	9	22	92	35

Sources: Eurostat, 1996; ISSP, 1995
Note that the data quoted for Britain are for the United Kingdom. Data quoted for Germany are for the whole of that country, not just western Germany.

While Britain's economic characteristics resemble Italy's or Spain's more than Germany's or Sweden's, it has more in common with Germany and (especially) Sweden when it comes to religion. Italy and Spain are overwhelmingly Catholic and still have much higher levels of regular church attendance than any of the other three countries. Moreover, Protestants significantly outnumber Catholics in both Britain and Sweden, while the two groups are found in roughly equal numbers in Germany. So, if religion rather than economic security is what primarily influences the values we are examining, then we would expect Britain to be more like Sweden (especially) and Germany rather than like Spain or Italy.

Like Inglehart, our interest here is in people's underlying values, not merely in a collection of disparate attitudes. These consist of people's overall principles or conceptions about matters of right and wrong, for instance, or their dispositions towards issues of freedom or equality or fairness - a knowledge of which would predict their individual attitudes towards more concrete issues such as the right to abortion, or trial by jury, or their leanings towards, say, redistribution of income (Rokeach, 1973; van Deth and Scarbrough, 1995b). Attitudes towards a single concrete issue may, of course, be influenced by several competing values, as well as being subject to measurement error. So, in order to obtain reliable indicators of adherence or otherwise to particular underlying values, we have constructed scales which summarise respondents' answers to a number of questions on each subject we cover. In other words, if someone has a low score on our environmental concern scale, that person's answers to the series of individual questions which make up the scale suggest a low degree of concern about the environment. (This approach contrasts with that of Inglehart, much of whose evidence rests on the analysis of single items.) In all but one of our scales, the scores range from 1 to 5, with a high score indicating a position consistent with a postmodern view (see the appendix to this chapter for more details).

In developing our scales we have applied stringent tests to ensure that they are indeed reliable measures of a single underlying value. Their construction was informed by an extensive factor analysis of a large number of questions in the relevant ISSP module with a view to identifying groups of theoretically relevant questions, the answers to which clustered together. The scales themselves were formed by adding up the respondent's 'score' across the component items and then dividing by the total number of items. The reliability of the resulting scales was checked using a statistical measure known as Cronbach's alpha (see the appendix to this chapter for further details).[2]

The incidence of postmaterialism

We begin our analysis by looking at the incidence of support for Inglehart's original key value, postmaterialism. This has come to be commonly measured by asking respondents to say which of four objectives they consider to be most important and second most important for their country. This well-established - if shorthand - measure was included in the 1993 ISSP module (which was not administered in Sweden):

> Looking at the list below, please tick a box next to the **one** thing you think should be [country's] **highest priority**, the **most** important thing it should do.

> And which **one** do you think should be [country's] **next highest priority**, the **second** most important thing it should do?

> Maintain order in the nation
> Give people more say in government decisions
> Fight rising prices
> Protect freedom of speech
> (Can't choose)

According to Inglehart's thesis, those who choose the second and fourth items (that focus on the non-material goal of self-expression) are postmaterialists, while those who choose the first and third items (that focus on the material goals of physical and economic security) are materialists. Those who opt for one of each type fall into a 'mixed' group.

The incidence of postmaterialism

	Germany	Britain	Italy	Spain
% classified as:				
Postmaterialist	23	11	12	12
Mixed	56	63	62	57
Materialist	21	26	25	31
Base	*1014*	*1261*	*1000*	*1208*

The distribution of answers in the four of our five countries for which we have data does appear to match the expectations we would derive from Inglehart's work. The incidence of postmaterialism is highest in Germany, the richest of the four, while the incidence of materialism is highest in Spain, the poorest. We should also note, however, that only a minority of respondents fall into one or other group. Most people in all four countries do not apparently see the materialist or postmaterialist options as such stark alternatives as the theory implies they should be. Moreover, while the incidence of postmaterialism may well have increased in Europe in recent years, it is still evidently only a minority orientation (Scarbrough, 1995). Whatever the strength of post-war EU economies may have been, most people have not abandoned their concerns about economic or physical security.

Nonetheless, there do appear to be the national differences on this measure which Inglehart's theory would have predicted. So we now have to establish whether these differences can justifiably be attributed to postmaterialism or to other factors.

Here we introduce a standard statistical model which we will employ throughout this chapter. It contains measures of the characteristics both of respondents and of the countries in which they live to investigate the influence of both factors on values. At both levels - individual and nation - it incorporates measures of income, education and religious attendance so that we can test the relative strength of the impact of 'formative affluence' and religiosity on each of the values we consider.

'Formative affluence' is, however, a difficult concept to operationalise. It should refer to the material well-being of individuals as they were growing up - for instance, family income or occupational level of one or both parents. But such indicators are rarely available in social surveys and, even if they were, would be of doubtful validity either because respondents never knew or could not remember such details. They are certainly not available in any useful form within ISSP data. We are thus required to use as our principal indicator of the affluence of individuals their *current* family income, but - given the difficulties of comparing income levels across countries - we have for this purpose classified individuals merely according to the income quartile in which they fall within their own country. In effect, then, our measure is of relative affluence within each country. In view of the limited amount of social mobility within developed societies, this measure is at least a workable proxy for the relative affluence of individuals when they were young.

To bolster this measure we have, as noted, included in the model a second measure, whether or not the individual has a degree, which, according to Inglehart himself (1997), is another indicator of formative affluence. Individuals who enjoy tertiary education, it is argued, are more likely to have experienced a relatively secure childhood. We should be aware, however, that others have argued that higher education has an *independent* influence on people's values and attitudes for reasons that have nothing to do with 'formative affluence' (Duch and Taylor, 1993; Davis, 1996; Heath *et al.*,

1985). So we will have to treat this variable with some caution. If it turns out to be associated with a postmodern view, while our indicator of income does not, then we should be wary of attributing that association to the impact of formative affluence. On the other hand if both university education *and* income are associated with postmodern values, then such a result would be consistent with Inglehart's expectations.

Finally, we have an indicator of religiosity. We distinguish between respondents according to how frequently they report attending a religious ceremony. Preliminary analysis suggested that for the most part this was a more important distinction than their religious identity *per se* (see also Heath *et al.*, 1993; Jagodzinski and Dobbelaere, 1995). In any event these two measures are correlated as those with a Catholic religious identity are more likely to attend church than are those with a Protestant identity. If our respondents' value scale scores turn out to be strongly associated with religion, and not with income, then again we shall have reason to doubt that those values can be attributed to postmodernisation.

Our measures of the national context simply parallel these individual level indicators. Thus for each respondent we have a measure of the GDP in their country, the proportion with a degree and the proportion who attend church once a week. Inglehart's thesis suggests that formative affluence and a sense of security flow not simply from the circumstances of the individual but also from the wider national context in which they live. Although this implies that it is not just current GDP that matters, but also the record of economic growth over a considerable period, current differences in the level of GDP also largely reflect our selected countries' economic performance throughout much of the post-war period. So, again, if Inglehart's thesis holds, then those living in a country with a high GDP will be more likely to exhibit postmodern attitudes than those living in a country with a lower level of GDP, *independently* of their personal circumstances. Of course, with just five countries, the results of our models will inevitably be more tentative in respect of the role of national context than they are of individual characteristics, but given the variety of contexts they exhibit in terms of wealth and religiosity they will give us a useful indication of the role of national origin as against family background in understanding the formation of values.

Partly because we have limited our statistical model to variables that we can measure at both an individual and national level (income, education level and religiosity), the model does not directly test one of Inglehart's other claims - that younger people, born at a time of greater affluence and security, are more likely to adopt a postmaterialist or postmodernist orientation than are older people. We could have added age consistently to our model, but insofar as it already captures the process of formative affluence, there is no reason to expect that age would be independently associated with a postmodern outlook anyway. Moreover, if we had found such an association, it would not have confirmed or negated Inglehart's postmodernisation thesis. On the other hand, we can include age where appropriate and if - improbably - we were to find that older people were more, not less, likely to express 'postmaterialist' values, then we we would certainly have grounds for doubting that these values formed part of any postmodernisation process.

Applying this model to our measure of postmaterialism does initially provide support for Inglehart's claims. (For full details of the results see model a in the appendix to this chapter.)[3] For instance, those in the highest income quartile in their country are more likely to be postmaterialist in their values, as are those with a degree. On the other hand, the links are limited. So, people in the second and third income quartiles turn out to be no different from people in the fourth quartile. Moreover, religious attendance is at least as strongly associated with the likelihood of holding postmaterialist views as are either individual income or education. Thus, after allowing for the other influences in the model, those who attend church regularly are significantly *less* likely to be postmaterialist than those who almost never attend religious services. It appears then that a rise in postmaterialism is, in part at least, a product of the decline of religion *per se* rather than of a wider and distinctive process of postmodernisation.

But the most substantial departure from the expectations of Inglehart's theory comes from the patterns of association with the character of our different countries. Not unexpectedly, we find that people living in a country with a high level of religious attendance are less likely to be postmaterialist. But, having taken this association into account, it turns out that those living in a country with a high GDP are also slightly *less* likely to be postmaterialist. True, as we noted above, if we look simply at the association between postmaterialism and the richness of a country, postmaterialists are most common in the richest country, Germany. However, our more complex modelling indicates that this pattern can be accounted for more successfully by looking at differences of levels of religiosity and education between the countries.[4] The more religious the country and the *higher* the proportion of its graduates, so the less likely it is to have a postmaterialist orientation.

Adding age to this model does confirm Inglehart's claim that postmaterialist values are more common among younger people. But overall, our results suggest that, even when its comes to the central plank of Inglehart's theory of postmodernisation - postmaterialist values - we find it difficult to conclude that financial security has more impact than secularism.

The environment

No topic has featured more prominently in discussions of the impact of postmaterialism than has the environment. As people become more concerned about the quality of life and less concerned about advancing their material welfare, so - it is argued - they become more concerned about the impact of industrialisation. This growing focus on the environment reveals itself in diverse ways, such as greater support for recycling and greater opposition to nuclear power stations.

Our analysis of the results of the 1993 ISSP module on the environment suggests, however, that 'green' concerns split into two distinct value dimensions, enabling us to construct two separate scales. The first scale is based on items indicating the degree to which people are prepared to take action or suffer financially for the sake of the environment. This measure of 'environmental concern' is in a sense a classic *postmaterialist* scale in that it measures the priority that people give to quality of life rather than material gain. The second scale refers to a quite different dimension of attitudes, all of which suggest, in effect, that nature is best left alone since it is inevitably damaged by human intervention. It encompasses a distrust of science and scientific progress which is supposedly one of the hallmarks of *postmodernisation*. As Dalton and Rohrschneider (in another chapter in this volume) note, these items touch on a group of radical environmental ideas known as the New Environmental Paradigm (Dobson, 1990).

National differences in environmental values

	Mean Scale Score			
	Germany	Britain	Italy	Spain
Environmental concern	3.3	3.1	3.3	3.2
Pro-nature	3.5	3.1	3.6	3.4
Base (smallest)	*1001*	*1179*	*994*	*1207*

The table above shows the average scale score in four of our five countries. The higher the score on the environmental concern scale in the first row, the greater is the willingness of respondents in each country to incur personal disadvantage for the sake of the environment. And the higher the score on the pro-nature scale in the second row, the greater is the belief in each country that scientific progress harms and disrupts nature.

Some important points emerge from these figures. First, since we have already discovered that most people in each country are neither outright materialists nor postmaterialists, it is not surprising, perhaps, that the average respondent is fairly close to the mid-point of 3 on each scale. But, with the sole exception of Britain, the average score on the pro-nature scale is higher than it is on the environmental concern scale. Respondents seemed to find it easier to support rather abstract propositions about the environment, however radical, than to show willingness to incur a personal penalty for the sake of the environment.

Second, there is much less difference between the countries on the environmental concern scale than on the pro-nature scale. Britain has the lowest average score on both scales - not what we might have anticipated given its level of national wealth. Indeed, pro-nature (or anti-science) views are strongest in Italy, the country with the highest level of religious attendance, rather than in Germany, the wealthiest of the four countries.

So the pattern of national similarities and differences does not fit comfortably with the postmaterialist thesis. Moreover, when we model individual differences (see model b in the appendix to this chapter), we discover that the pattern of pro-nature or anti-science views is not, after all, consistent with the expectations of postmodernisation at all. On the contrary, high income and high education are both negatively associated with a pro-nature viewpoint, the opposite of what the postmodernisation thesis would predict. Moreover, when we introduce age into the equation, it emerges that it is older rather than younger people who are likely to be pro-nature. In short, scepticism about the value of scientific progress and beliefs about its negative impact on the environment appear to have little to do with postmodernisation at all. Rather, it appears to be characteristic of the less well-educated, the more religious and and the less well-off. This is the first serious indication that the wide-ranging claims for postmodernisation do not appear to be borne out by the data.

On the other hand, the sorts of people who express environmental *concern* are indeed those whom Inglehart anticipates would do so. Thus we find that the higher a person's income and the better educated they are, the more likely it is that they would in principle be prepared to incur a personal penalty for the sake of the environment. Individual religiosity is not associated with this scale at all.

At a national level we found little difference between our countries in their average scores on this scale: Germany, despite being significantly richer than the other three countries, did not exhibit a higher level of environmental concern. The model finds that it is the religiosity of a country rather than its wealth that is associated with a higher level of environmental concern. In other words, even when we find that the pattern of *individuals* who adopt a postmodern viewpoint is consistent with the thesis, the implications for overall national levels of environmental concern may not be as significant as is claimed.

Moral issues

We have found that attitudes towards the environment, the topic most commonly associated in the literature with a postmaterialist or postmodern viewpoint, do not conform well to the claims of the theory. We now turn to other issues that are supposed to be associated with postmodernism. In particular we look at two moral issues covered in the 1994 ISSP module - the role of women and attitudes towards sex. These sorts of issues should provide a particularly important test of how far the postmodernisation thesis can be taken, since it is well-known that attitudes towards such subjects are closely associated with religion (Heath *et al.*, 1993). If they are the product of postmodernisation, however, they should be associated with financial security and formative affluence too.

National differences in moral values

Mean Scale Score

	Germany	Sweden	Britain	Italy	Spain
Role of women	3.0	3.4	3.3	3.0	3.0
Sexual liberalism	2.5	2.4	2.1	2.0	2.2
Base (smallest)	*1323*	*869*	*729*	*869*	*1837*

Note: exceptionally, the range of scores on this sexual liberalism scale is from 1 to 4 rather than 1 to 5.

Our attitude scale on the role of women is based on several questions tapping people's views on whether women should be expected to fulfil the traditional roles of primary homemaker and mother, or to have a free choice, as men traditionally do, to work outside the home as well as having a family. A postmodern outlook would place less emphasis on the traditional role of women and the family, and more on their freedom to go out to work if they want to. Meanwhile, our attitude scale on sexual liberalism relates to the acceptability or otherwise of various forms of sexual activity ranging from extra-marital sex to homosexuality. Again, we would expect those of a postmodern disposition to regard the freedom of the individual as more important than the moral standards of society and thus to be more liberal or permissive on this scale.

What do we find? On the one hand, the difference between countries on the sexual liberalism scale conforms admirably to postmodernisation thesis. The two most affluent countries, Germany and Sweden, have the highest scores, while Britain is closer in its scores to Italy and Spain, *despite* having neither a high level of Catholicism nor widespread religious adherence. On the other hand, as far as the role of women is concerned, Britain is clearly more liberal in its attitudes than Italy or Spain and closest to Sweden, the country which it most resembles in terms of religiosity (or the lack of it). Instead, it is the Germans - with their high GDP - who prove to be closest to the Italians and Spanish in their attitudes towards the role of women. Indeed, the pattern of national attitudes towards women and work largely reflects the pattern of actual labour market participation by women in those countries - which is highest in Sweden and Britain and lowest in Italy and Spain (see earlier table, 'Characteristics of countries').

This rather mixed support for the postmodernisation thesis is confirmed by our more elaborate modelling of attitudes within each country (see model c in the appendix to this chapter). On both scales there is limited support for the thesis in that those with higher incomes and those with a degree adopt a more liberal position on both scales.[5] Younger people also have more liberal attitudes on both scales. However, our statistical modelling confirms the fact that, as far as attitudes to the role of women are concerned, any association with a country's GDP disappears once we take into account the proportion of women who go out to work in each country - thereby explaining the differences in attitudes between Britain and Sweden on the one hand and Germany on the other.

Moreover, we find that an individual's religiosity or otherwise is much more strongly associated with their propensity towards sexual liberalism than is either their income or their education. For instance, after taking into account all other variables in the model, those who attend a place of worship at least once a week are significantly less liberal or permissive on that scale than those who do not attend at all. But at the same time, our model also shows that sexual liberalism is higher in the more wealthy countries while having a low level of religious attendance, as in Britain, does not necessarily promote sexual liberalism.[6] Once again it is clear that national differences do not simply flow from differences in the social composition of countries.

But perhaps the most important of all about these two scales is that the kinds of people and countries who comprise the more liberal differ so much. This is underlined by the further finding that men are more liberal than women on the sexual liberalism scale, and *vice versa* on the role of women scale. If post-modernisation were truly the overarching and wide-ranging explanation of the development of modern values it is claimed to be, we should surely anticipate a much more consistent pattern of associations than we have found. As we discovered earlier with our environmental scales, we find here again that there are distinctly different patterns of association when the theory suggests they should be uniform or consistent.

The 1994 ISSP module on the family contains one further question that is central to the postmodernisation thesis. Respondents were asked:

> *Which of these would you say is more important in preparing children for life..*
>
> *...to be obedient*
> *or, to think for themselves?*
> *(Can't choose)*

Although only a single dichotomous item, it comes closer than any other question asked in recent modules to capturing the distinction between the traditional view of the importance of external authority as opposed to the postmodern view of self determination. We include it here also because its results conform more closely to Inglehart's theory than any other results we have found. Support for the idea that children should think for themselves is highest in our two richest countries, Sweden (92 per cent) and Germany (88 per cent), compared with only 63 per cent in Spain and 52 per cent in Italy, while Britain comes in between (72 per cent). Meanwhile, when we apply our standard model, we also find that those with a higher income and those with a degree are more likely to take that view, as are those living in a richer and more educated society. And while those who attend a religious ceremony are less likely to think a child should be taught to think for themselves, the religious character of the country in which the respondent lives on this occasion does not make any difference. Of course, the level of support for the idea that children should be taught to think for themselves is well above what we would expect from the incidence of postmaterialism alone, but it is nonetheless an idea which seems to have been fostered by the forces that Inglehart has identified as postmodernisation.

National pride

Inglehart suggests that those of a postmaterialist persuasion are less likely to be nationalistic, patriotic or chauvinistic. They would tend not only to be suspicious of forms of authority such as the state, but their higher degree of security would leave them less inclined to be xenophobic or inward looking (Inglehart 1997: 303-5). On the other hand, since Inglehart's own results suggest that national pride is linked to religiosity, it is of course possible that any decline in patriotism may simply be part of the process of modernisation rather than postmodernisation (Inglehart, 1997: 84-6).

We have developed a scale of national pride from the 1995 ISSP module on national identity.

Differences in national pride

	Germany	Sweden	Britain	Italy	Spain
Mean scale score	2.1	1.7	1.6	1.8	1.6
Base	1240	1268	1025	1087	1221

Note: because postmodernists are expected to have a low level of national pride, a high score on the scale means a *low* level of national pride; the closer to 1, or the furthest from 5, the *greater* is the level of patriotism - or in some cases a sense of national superiority - in that country.

There are, for the most part, few differences between our five countries in their expressed level of national pride (see also the chapter by McCrone and Surridge in this volume). Most people in all the countries express a high level of pride (fairly close to 1 in their scores). The only country which deviates somewhat from the uniform pattern is Germany, whose citizens are significantly less proud than those in the other four nations. This singular difference suggests that the reason has more to do with Germany's particular historical legacy than with postmodernisation, especially given the high levels of national pride in Sweden and Britain. Meanwhile, Britain and Spain - which both contain territories seeking a high degree of autonomy if not independence - lead the others in national pride.

Again our more elaborate modelling finds a certain amount of support for the postmodernisation thesis (see model d in the appendix to this chapter). The relatively well-off and the university-educated are less likely to express pride in their nation, as indeed are the young, though religion also plays a role too. And, solely thanks to the significantly lower level of national pride in Germany, we also find that living in a richer country turns out to be associated with a lower level of national pride. On the other hand, given the absence of any significant differences in the level of national pride in the other four countries, it would clearly be wrong to conclude that as countries become more postmodern in their social character, so their levels of national pride will fall.

Government

Our final exploration of the evidence for a process of postmodernisation is in attitudes towards government. Two separate ISSP modules enable us to look at different and important aspects. The 1992 module on social inequality contains a battery of items that combine to form a scale of attitudes towards inequality and, in particular, the role that government should or should not play in reducing it. (This module was not administered in Spain.) The 1996 module on the role of government contains items on personal 'efficacy', which tap the extent to which citizens feel they can influence government. (Data for this module were not available for Italy.) Limitations of the data available for both of these modules mean that we cannot, however, use our standard regression model to examine the patterns of association for these scales. Instead, we have to rely on more mundane methods.

What might we expect to find if a process of postmodernisation was at work? Inglehart (1997) suggests that one of the consequences of postmodernisation is that people become more convinced of the need to limit the role of the state in the economy. This may partly be accounted for by the fact that the state in many developed societies already consumes a relatively large proportion of GDP and citizens may well see limits to, and diminishing returns from, an expansion of its role. But it is also likely to reflect the fact that material security is already ensured by a large welfare state. Above all, perhaps, it may be part of the wider process of growing distrust of the authority of the state. As a result, although postmaterialists generally have views which lean towards the centre-left of the political spectrum, they tend to adopt pro-market positions on economic matters, traditionally associated with the right.

An element of postmodernism then is scepticism about the role of the state combined with a growing self-confidence on the part of the citizenry to challenge its authority when they think their government is doing something wrong.[7] So, if postmodernisation has taken root, we should anticipate that people living in more affluent and secure countries will have less trust in government and the democratic process than those living in less affluent and secure ones, as well as more belief in their personal political efficacy. This would, of course, be irrespective of the nature of their governments. Rather, it would be a result of the impact that social and economic change has had in raising citizens' expectations of their governments and of democracy itself.

National differences in attitudes towards government

Mean Scale Score

	Germany	Sweden	Britain	Italy	Spain
Tolerance of inequality	1.3	1.5	1.3	0.9	n.a.
Base	*2270*	*730*	*1038*	*995*	
Political efficacy	2.8	2.7	2.8	n.a.	2.7
Base	*2333*	*1206*	*952*		*2473*

n.a. = not available

Note: high scores indicate a high degree of reluctance for the state to intervene in reducing inequality *and* a high degree of political efficacy.

The table shows substantial national differences in public attitudes towards inequality. Thus we find it is those who enjoy the most extensive welfare state provision, that is the Swedes, who are most reluctant to see further action to reduce inequality. And it is the country with the least extensive welfare provision, Italy, which is the least reluctant to see the state intervene more. These results may therefore simply be closely related to the *status quo* in each country, not directly to different attitudes towards inequality. So the Swedes, for instance, may simply be saying that an appropriately large amount is already being devoted to the purpose of reducing inequalities in their society.[8] In any event, here again there is at face value a fairly straightforward confirmation of Inglehart's expectations.

There are, however, reasons for some doubt. Although we are unable to apply our standard model to the inequality scale, we have examined other data to enable us to explore attitudes towards the subject more fully. The ISSP 1993 module on attitudes to the environment not only asked Inglehart's standard four-item indicator of postmaterialism, to which we have already referred, but also asked people whether they agreed or disagreed (using a five-point scale) with two statements about the role of the government in the economy, as follows:

> *Private enterprise is the best way to solve Britain's economic problems*

> *It is the responsibility of government to reduce the differences in income between people with high incomes and those with low incomes*

By summarising the answers (after reversing the scores on the second question) we have derived a short scale indicating whether the respondent is inclined to favour government intervention (low score) or the free market (high score).

If we link our individual respondents' scores on this scale to their scores on the postmaterialist scale, we can test if postmaterialists are actually more inclined to favour the market rather than government intervention in the economy, as the theory suggests they should. In fact we find the opposite. Being postmaterialist is associated with a sympathy for government action rather than market forces.[9] From this evidence it thus appears that the concept of postmaterialism does not, after all, cut across traditional conceptions of what it means to be on the 'left' on politics.[10] Postmaterialists on Inglehart's own postmaterialist scale turn out to be fairly consistently left of centre, even on economic matters. So, when we find the public in an advanced industrial society such as Sweden, with its large welfare state, not wishing to see an expansion of the role of the state, it may well simply reflect satisfaction with the current arrangements rather than any new postmodernist views about the limitations of the state.

Moreover, our political efficacy scale proves to be remarkable for the uniformity of its scores across the countries. Germans and Swedes are no more or less likely than the British or Spanish to believe they can participate effectively in, or influence, the political process. Indeed, other questions in the same module confirm the fact that Germans and Swedes are hardly notable for their propensity to take part in political action. It is the Spaniards who, despite professing much less interest in politics, were nonetheless most likely to report having been on a protest march or demonstration in the last five years (nearly a quarter had done so, compared with fewer than one in five Germans and Swedes, and around one in sixteen in Britain).

In short, neither the incidence of postmaterialist attitudes nor the pattern of economic development in a country produces the pattern of national differences in political efficacy or attitudes to government that the theory predicts they should.

Conclusion

We set ourselves two tasks in this chapter. The first was to test whether we could clearly distinguish postmodernisation from modernisation, that is whether *advanced* industrial societies were experiencing a cultural change different in character from that experienced by societies that had industrialised more recently? In order to pass the test, we needed to establish that the values supposedly influenced by postmodernism are indeed related to indicators of formative affluence and security, *independently* of their association with religiosity.

The postmodernisation thesis did not pass this acid test. True, there are a number of key indicators that are more common among those with high incomes or among younger people. These include Inglehart's own measure of postmaterialism, as well as more liberal attitudes towards the role of women, less national pride, and more environmental concern. But with the sole exception of environmental concern, these values are also less common among those who are more religious. So we can by no means discount the possibility that differences in national wealth are in fact less influential than are differences in national levels of religiosity in explaining variations in these attitudes. We are even unable to rule out the possibility from the evidence available that it is the experience of education itself rather than the formative affluence of which education might be one indicator which is responsible for a supposedly postmodern outlook. In other words, the difference between the impact and process of 'modernisation' as opposed to 'postmodernisation' is not clearly discernible.

Our second task was to examine whether the consequences and implications of postmodernisation were as wide-ranging as has been claimed. Here we have encountered evidence of two kinds that casts doubt upon the thesis. First, we find that several values which are supposedly related to postmodernisation are not. For instance, a belief in the virtues of nature over science is more common among the less well-educated, the less well-off and older people, rather than in each case the reverse, and is also unrelated to the measure of postmaterialism. Moreover, postmaterialism does not appear to be associated with any decline in support for government activity to reduce inequalities. Meanwhile, one's sexual mores appear to be influenced much more by one's religiosity, or lack of it, than by one's own or one's country's affluence. So, if postmodernisation is taking place at all along the lines posited, it is doing so much more selectively than it is supposed to.

Moreover, and perhaps most importantly, we can by no means be clear, even in societies where values might be being influenced by a process of postmodernisation, that the impact on the cultural character of those societies is at all marked. Even on Inglehart's own measure of postmaterialism, most people were neither 'materialist' nor 'postmaterialist'. Moreover, we discovered on many other measures close similarities between our five countries on matters such as political efficacy, national pride (excepting Germany), and, most surprisingly, environmental concern, when - according to the theory - there should have been noticeable differences. Cultural values within the EU seem to vary too little for postmodernisation to be the powerful a force it is claimed to be.

Where does this leave Britain? In the first place, it certainly does not appear to be a distinctively postmodern country. Postmaterialists are relatively scarce, environmental concern is low, national pride is relatively high, and its sexual mores tend towards the illiberal. As it is one of the less affluent members of the EU one should perhaps not be surprised at these results. Yet it turns out in many respects to be even less postmodern in character than both Italy, no richer than Britain, and Spain, which is even less affluent. Britain it seems is thus a little different from the rest of Europe in ways that postmodernisation theory cannot explain. And there is little reason to believe that the difference will disappear.

Notes

1. The post-war economic and political experience of eastern Germany (the area formerly known as the German Democratic Republic) has of course been very different from that of western Germany and is inadequately captured by current measures of national wealth. Meanwhile, exploratory analysis showed that attitudes in eastern Germany differed dramatically from those in western Germany, and from those in the other EU countries chosen. We thus decided to exclude eastern Germany from our analysis. Attitudes there are discussed by Renwick and Tóká in their chapter on differences between Eastern and Western Europe in this volume.

2. Note that where we were unable to form a scale with an alpha close to at least 0.7 (De Vellis, 1991), we excluded that topic from our analysis even though it might be relevant to a discussion of postmodernisation. In particular, we were unable to construct a satisfactory scale which identified those who were particularly concerned about securing intrinsic rewards from work.

3. In the model postmaterialists were given a score of 2, those with a 'mixed' orientation a score of 1, and 'materialists' a score of 0. The resulting variable was treated as an interval level variable. However, we also ran logistic models in which the dependent variable was postmaterialist *versus* not postmaterialist and obtained the same substantive findings.

4. If we exclude the level of religious attendance from our model, % GDP has a weak positive association with the incidence of postmaterialism.

5. Further modelling reveals that the association between attitudes towards the role of women and having a high income is not simply the product of living in a dual earner family where the woman goes out to work.

6. This interpretation of the positive association between a high level of religious attendance in a country and sexual liberalism is confirmed by the fact that if we enter into our model a variable which simply identifies those living in Britain, this variable proves to be significantly negatively associated with sexual liberalism while the term for the level of religious attendance becomes insignificant.

7. It might thus be anticipated that postmodernism should be associated with a high level of personal efficacy and a low level of system efficacy. However, we were unable to construct a satisfactory scale that operationalised the distinction between these two forms of efficacy.

8. Note also that when asked about how much conflict there is in their society between different social groups, Swedes were least likely to say that there was conflict. Thus, as the table shows, less than one in three Swedes think there is a strong conflict between rich and poor in their society compared with around three in five Italians or Britons. And less than one in ten Swedes think there is a strong conflict between the working and the middle class compared with nearly a half of Italians.

	Italy	Britain	Germany	Sweden
Mean score on inequality scale	*4.1*	*3.7*	*3.7*	*3.5*
% thinking strong conflict between ...				
rich and poor	58	61	39	31
working and middle class	45	26	12	8
unemployed and workers	56	46	41	16
Base (smallest)	*971*	*1008*	*2052*	*671*

9. The scale has a beta value of -.07 and is significant at the 1% level when added to our standard model together with age. High scores on the scale indicate a pro-market position, so those favouring such a position are less likely to be postmaterialists.
10. This is despite the fact that, as we would anticipate, those with higher incomes and with a degree are in general more likely to have a relatively right-wing score on our scale. Given their social background, postmaterialists are particularly notable for their left-wing views on economic matters.

References

Abramson, P. and Inglehart, R. (1995), *Value Change in Global Perspective*, Ann Arbor: University of Michigan Press.

Davis, J. (1996), Review of P. Abramson and R. Inglehart, *Value Change in Global Perspective*, *Public Opinion Quarterly*, **60**, 322-31.

De Vellis, R. (1991), *Scale Development: Theory and Applications*, Newbury Park, Ca.: Sage Applied Social Research Methods Series no. 26.

Dobson, A. (1990), *Green Political Thought*, London: Harper/Collins.

Duch, R. and Taylor, M. (1993), 'Postmaterialism and the Economic Condition', *American Journal of Political Science*, **37**, 747-89.

Eurostat (1996), *Facts through Figures: A statistical picture of the European Union*, Luxembourg: Office for Official Publications of the European Union.

Flanagan, S. (1982), 'Changing Values in Advanced Industrial Societies: Inglehart's Silent Revolution from the Perspective of Japanese Findings', *Comparative Political Studies*, **14**, 403-44.

Flanagan, S. (1987), 'Changing Values in Industrial Society Revisited: Towards a Resolution of the Values Debate', *American Political Science Review*, **81**, 1303-19.

Gibbins, J. and Reimer, B. (1995), 'Postmodernism', in van Deth, J. and Scarbrough, E., *The Impact of Values*, Oxford: Oxford University Press.

Heath, A., Jowell, R. and Curtice, J. (1985), *How Britain Votes*, Oxford: Pergamon.

Heath, A., Taylor, B. and Toka, G. (1993), 'Religion, Morality and Politics', in Jowell, R., Brook, L. and Dowds, L. (eds.), *International Social Attitudes: the 10th BSA report*, Aldershot: Dartmouth.

Inglehart, R. (1977), *The Silent Revolution: Changing Values and Political Styles*, Princeton, NJ: Princeton University Press.

Inglehart, R. (1990), *Culture Shift in Advanced Industrial Society*, Princeton, NJ: Princeton University Press.

Inglehart, R. (1997), *Modernization and Postmodernization: Cultural, Economic and Political Change in 43 Societies*, Princeton: Princeton University Press.

Jagodzinski, W. and Dobbelaere, K. (1995), 'Secularisation and Church Religiosity', in van Deth, J. and Scarbrough, E., *Beliefs in Government Volume Four: The Impact of Values*, Oxford: Oxford University Press.

Lipset, S. and Schneider, W. (1983), *The Confidence Gap: Business, Labor and Government in the Public Mind*, New York: Free Press.

Rokeach, M. (1973), *The Nature of Human Values*, New York: Free Press.

Scarbrough, E. (1995), 'Materialist-Postmaterialist Value Orientations', in van Deth, J. and Scarbrough, E. (eds.), *Beliefs in Government Volume Four: The Impact of Values*, Oxford: Oxford University Press.

van Deth, J. and Scarbrough, E. (1995a), 'Perspectives on Value Change', in van Deth, J. and Scarbrough, E. (eds.), *Beliefs in Government Volume Four: The Impact of Values*, Oxford: Oxford University Press.

van Deth, J. and Scarbrough, E. (1995b), 'The Concept of Values', in van Deth, J. and Scarbrough, E. (eds.), *Beliefs in Government Volume Four: The Impact of Values*, Oxford: Oxford University Press.

Appendix

Derivation of the scales

Each scale is based on responses to five or six statements. With the sole exception of the 'sexual liberalism' scale where a four point scale was used, answers to the component statements were recorded on a five point scale as specified. The scale score was calculated by averaging the scores for each respondent on each of the items, giving a maximum value of five and a minimum value of one. Responses to the statements were recoded where necessary so that five equals the postmodern view and one equals the least for all items. Answers of 'can't choose' were recoded as 'Neither agree nor disagree'.

Environmental concern scale
Based on items from the 1993 module on the environment.
Using data from Great Britain, western Germany, Italy and Spain.
Cronbach's alpha of 0.72.
The first three questions asked respondents to respond using a five point scale (Very willing; Fairly willing; Neither willing nor unwilling; Fairly unwilling; Very unwilling; Can't choose).
*How willing would **you** be to pay **much higher <u>prices</u>** in order to protect the environment?*
*And how willing would **you** be to pay **much higher <u>taxes</u>** in order to protect the environment?*
*And how willing would **you** be to **accept cuts in your standard of living** in order to protect the environment?*
The last two questions consisted of statements to which respondents should respond using a five point scale (Strongly agree; Agree; Neither agree nor disagree; Disagree; Strongly disagree; Can't choose).
It is just too difficult for someone like me to do much about the environment
I do what is right for the environment, even when it costs more money or takes more time

Anti-progress scale
Also based on items from the 1993 module on the environment.
Using data from Great Britain, western Germany, Italy and Spain.
Cronbach's alpha of 0.67.
Each question consisted of a statement to which respondents should respond using a five point scale (Strongly agree; Agree; Neither agree nor disagree; Disagree; Strongly disagree; Can't choose).
Any change humans cause in nature - no matter how scientific - is likely to make things worse
Almost everything we do in modern life harms the environment
Nature would be at peace and in harmony if only human beings would leave it alone
Economic growth always harms the environment

Role of women scale
Based on items from the 1994 module on women and the family.
Data from Great Britain, western Germany, Sweden, Italy and Spain.
Cronbach's alpha of 0.76.
Each question consisted of a statement to which respondents should respond using a five point scale (Strongly agree; Agree; Neither agree nor disagree; Disagree; Strongly disagree; Can't choose).
A working mother can establish just as warm a relationship with her children as a mother who does not work
A preschool child is likely to suffer if his or her mother works
All in all, family life suffers when the woman has a full-time job
A job is all right, but what most women really want is a home and children
Being a housewife is just as fulfilling as working for pay
A man's job is to earn money; a woman's job is to look after the home and family

Sexual liberalism scale
Based on items from the 1994 module on women and the family.
Using data from Great Britain, western Germany, Sweden, Italy and Spain.
Cronbach's alpha of 0.69.
Respondent's were asked how right or wrong each of the following were using a four point scale (Always wrong; Almost always wrong; Wrong only sometimes; Not wrong at all)
A man and a woman have sexual relations before marriage
They are in their early teens, say under 16 years old?
A married person having sexual relations with someone other than his or her husband or wife
Sexual relations between two adults of the same sex

National pride scale
Based on items from the 1995 module on national identity.
Using data from Great Britain, western Germany, Sweden, Italy and Spain.
Cronbach's alpha of 0.73.
Each question consisted of a statement to which respondents should respond using a five point scale (Strongly agree; Agree; Neither agree nor disagree; Disagree; Strongly disagree; Can't choose).
I would rather be a citizen of [country] than of any other country in the world
The world would be a better place if people from other countries were more like the [people from country]
Generally speaking [country] is a better place than most other countries
People should support their country even if the country is in the wrong
When my country does well in international sports, it makes me proud to be [from country]

Political efficacy scale
Based on items from the 1996 module on the role of government.
Using data from Great Britain, western Germany, Sweden and Spain.
Cronbach's alpha of 0.62.
Each question consisted of a statement to which respondents should respond using a five point scale (Strongly agree; Agree; Neither agree nor disagree; Disagree; Strongly disagree; Can't choose).
People like me don't have any say about what the government does
The average citizen has considerable influence on politics
Elections are a good way of making governments pay attention to what people think
People we elect as MPs try to keep the promises they have made during the election
Most civil servants can be trusted to do what is best for the country

Inequality scale
Based on items from the 1992 module on social inequality.
Data from Great Britain, western Germany, Sweden and Italy.
Cronbach's alpha of 0.77.
Each question consisted of a statement to which respondents should respond using a five point scale (Strongly agree; Agree; Neither agree nor disagree; Disagree; Strongly disagree; Can't choose).
Inequality continues because it benefits the rich and powerful
Differences in income in [country] are too large
It is the responsibility of the government to reduce the differences in income between people with high incomes and those with low incomes
The government should provide a job for everyone who wants one
The government should provide everyone with a guaranteed basic income

Regression models

Figures quoted are standardised beta coefficients.
** Statistically significant at the 1% level.
* Statistically significant at the 5% level.

Model a: the correlates of postmaterialism

Individual Characteristics
(comparison group in brackets)

Income (lowest quartile)
Highest quartile	.07**
Second highest quartile	.00
Second lowest quartile	-.01

Education (no degree)
Has degree	.06**

Religious attendance (never attends services)
Once a week	-.08**
Once a month	-.07**
Once a year	-.05**

National Context
GDP	-.14*
% with degree	-.64**
% attend church 1+ a week	-.65**

Model b: the correlates of environmentalism

	Environmental Concern	Anti-Progress
Individual Characteristics (comparison group in brackets)		
Income (lowest quartile)		
Highest quartile	.18**	-.14**
Second highest quartile	.10**	-.06**
Second lowest quartile	.06**	-.00
Education (no degree)		
Has degree	.07**	-.07**
Religious attendance (never attends services)		
Once a week	.01	-.01
Once a month	.01	.03
Once a year	-.01	.01
National Context		
GDP	-.25**	-.18**
% with degree	-.80**	-.85**
% attend church 1+ a week	-.79**	-.67**

Model c: the correlates of moral values

	Role of Women	Sexual Liberalism
Individual Characteristics (comparison group in brackets)		
Income (lowest quartile)		
Highest quartile	.16**	.14**
Second highest quartile	.09**	.08**
Second lowest quartile	-.02*	-.03*
Education (no degree)		
Has degree	.11**	.09**
Religious attendance (never attends services)		
Once a week	-.13**	-.35**
Once a month	-.04**	-.18**
Once a year	-.06**	-.15**
National Context		
GDP	.11**	.35**
% with degree	.32**	.06
% attend church 1+ a week	.24**	.13**

Model d: correlates of low national pride

Individual Characteristics	
Income (lowest quartile)	
Highest quartile	.11**
Second highest quartile	.07**
Second lowest quartile	.03*
Education (no degree)	
Has degree	.15**
Religious attendance (never attends services)	
Once a week	-.10**
Once a month	-.08**
Once a year	-.08**
National Context	
GDP	.20**
% with degree	-.24**
% attend church 1+ a week	-.07

8 East meets West

Alan Renwick and Gábor Tóka [*]

The European Union upon which this Report focuses is by no means fixed. Negotiations have already begun that may see the EU's enlargement to include five post-communist countries in Central Europe by the early years of the 21st century, and it is possible that further expansion into Eastern Europe will occur after that. It is often assumed that such a 'widening' of EU membership will prevent any 'deepening' of the role of the Union within the member states. It is argued that an expanded membership will seriously limit the policy options available to the EU, since members will have increasingly disparate characteristics, giving only the most shallow opportunities for integration.

There are indeed many differences between the prospective and the current member states - but how different are the attitudes and values of their inhabitants?   Will enlargement result in increasing diversity of opinion throughout the EU? Or are the views of prospective members not really very different from those expressed within existing EU countries?

Our aims in this chapter are two-fold. First, we shall identify differences in social attitudes between existing EU members and post-communist applicants.   Secondly, we shall attempt to explain those differences, assessing, in particular, whether they reflect primarily the legacy of communist rule or stem from other features that differentiate the two areas. We shall also consider whether attitudes within the EU and the applicant countries are likely to converge or not in the future.

The data come from the *International Social Survey Programme* (ISSP)

[*] Alan Renwick is a PhD student and Gábor Tóka is Assistant Professor at the Department of Political Science, Central European University, Budapest.

surveys conducted in 1991, 1992, 1993 and 1994.[*] We use data from eight
EU countries (Austria, Britain, Ireland, Italy, the Netherlands, Spain, Sweden
and western Germany[**]), which we take to be representative of all of the EU's
member states, although data for all eight are not available for each year. To
represent post-communist applicant countries, we use data from five
countries, including four that are likely to be in the first round of EU
expansion (the Czech Republic, Hungary, Poland and Slovenia), plus one that
may join at a later date (Bulgaria). In addition, data for eastern Germany are
included, in order to assess the effect of communism upon the values and
attitudes of its citizens.

Our focus will be upon three broad themes - religious values, moral values,
and economic values. Under 'moral values' we consider attitudes towards
marriage, women and work, sexual permissiveness, and the punitiveness of
the legal system. Under 'economic values' we consider attitudes towards
left-wing economic policies, income distribution, and concern for the
environment.

All our analyses are based upon data relating to several ISSP questions.
This is essential as translation difficulties make excessive reliance upon any
single question dangerous. The use of several questions also allows us to
construct an index for each dimension, which is not only a useful way of
summarising respondents' attitudes, but is also likely to prove a more reliable
indicator of underlying values than are answers to individual questions.

Why might attitudes differ?

Any differences we find between social attitudes in current EU member
states and in post-communist states could fall into one of two categories -
those that reflect long-term differences pre-dating the communist era, and
those that stem directly from the impact of communist rule itself. This
distinction is important since the latter might be expected to disappear quite
fast (and, indeed, may already have done so), whereas the former can be
expected to be more persistent - perhaps lasting until such time as the level of
economic development in the post-communist countries catches up with that
found in the EU.

There are two relevant long-term differences that pre-date communism.
First, *the level of socio-economic development* in post-communist countries
was always (and remains) lower than that in most existing EU states.
Secondly, the *religious composition* of their populations is quite distinct.
Whereas many of the EU states (particularly the more northerly ones) have

---

[*] See the Introduction and Appendices to this Report for further details about ISSP.
[**] By western Germany we mean the geographical area known until unification as the Federal
Republic of Germany. By eastern Germany we mean the area formerly known as the German
Democratic Republic.

substantial Protestant populations, the five post-communist countries in our sample are overwhelmingly Catholic or Orthodox.

Both these differences are associated with particular patterns in social attitudes. For instance, lower socio-economic development and a religious balance skewed towards Catholicism and Orthodoxy rather than Protestantism are likely to be associated with more traditional attitudes when it comes to the role of marriage, law and order, the place of women and sexual morals.

As regards the legacy of communist rule, we can identify four mechanisms through which it may have had an impact upon current attitudes: those of indoctrination, repression, change in social structure and the post-communist backlash.

Indoctrination was widespread in the communist countries, particularly in the fields of economic policy, egalitarianism and the role of women, leading us to expect more left-wing economic policy attitudes, more favourable attitudes to egalitarianism, and more acceptance of the role of women in the workplace than might otherwise have been the case. It would also be expected to lead to weaker religious beliefs and, because of the emphasis placed on industrial progress, to less concern for the environment.

Repression took place on several fronts. Public debate on many social issues was often suppressed, and the activities of the churches were severely curtailed. The lack of public debate could be expected to lead to slower attitude change over time, to a fossilisation of those traditional values not affected by indoctrination, and thus to a tendency towards conservatism. This needs, however, to be set against the effect of suppressing the churches, which might be expected to weaken the role of traditional moral teachings over such matters as sexual norms and the place of women.

Radical *social change* was deliberately promoted in numerous spheres. For example, the employment of women was both boosted and celebrated, and education levels greatly increased in many communist countries. The greater employment of women could be expected to lead to increased acceptance of a role for women in the workplace, and raised education levels might be expected to have a broad range of liberalising effects.

Finally, it is important to remember that there has also been a substantial *backlash* against communist rule in all of the post-communist countries considered here. The backlash has tended to be strongest in those areas where the message or impact of communism was clearest - so we might expect it to promote inegalitarian views and right-wing attitudes towards economic policy. It may also lead to increasingly anti-authoritarian views on other issues.

Of course, the effects of these different mechanisms upon social attitudes may at times be contradictory. For example, when it comes to religious values, the effect of repressing religious teachings under communism must be weighed against the likely consequences of a backlash against such repression. And while a growth in religiosity after the collapse of communism might promote conservative attitudes towards marriage, these sit uneasily alongside some of the likely effects of social change and an anti-authoritarian backlash.

Examining differences between East and West

Because our aim is to examine differences in values and attitudes between EU and post-communist countries we use some key data at a *national* (rather than individual) level. We do not want to assess, for example, whether a Protestant person has different attitudes from a Catholic person - but whether attitudes in broadly Protestant countries are different from attitudes in generally Catholic countries. So it is the *context* of a Protestant or Catholic (or Orthodox) tradition that is important here, not individuals' religious allegiance.

We have already seen that there are two broad reasons as to why the attitudes of those living in EU and post-communist countries might vary - namely, trends that pre-date communism and the impact of communism itself. To disentangle these explanations our analyses take into account, or 'control for', indicators of two of the key differences that pre-date communism, such that any subsequent differences that we find are more likely to reflect the legacy of communism. To achieve this, we use data relating to two national dimensions, economic development and religion. For each dimension, we have two alternative measures. In the case of economic development, we use either GDP per capita or the average level of education. In the case of religion, we either use a measure relating to the proportion of Protestants within the country or one that reflects the level of church attendance. Any single analysis will include only one of the two measures for each dimension (as the two are so closely related to one another), with our choice in each case being determined by which measure is most closely related to the attitudes under consideration. This is explained in more detail in the appendix to this chapter.

This approach cannot, of course, differentiate perfectly between the effects of communism and any longer-term legacies. Our explanatory measures relating to the latter are clearly not independent of whether the countries have experienced communism. Nevertheless, the procedure does help to differentiate between the various mechanisms through which communist experience may have influenced attitudes.

The results of this approach are presented in tables throughout the chapter. However, in order to account for all the factors at the same time, and to comment adequately on the results, a multivariate (regression) analysis was also conducted, the details of which are described in the appendix to this chapter. The tables also show 'scores' for all the EU members together and for all the post-communist countries together, to show how similar or different the two regions are, as well as a combined score for all the countries considered in the chapter.[1]

Traditional religious beliefs

Our index measuring traditional religious beliefs is drawn from five questions dealing with belief in life after death, the devil, heaven, hell and religious miracles asked in the 1991 ISSP survey on religion (the exact question wordings are given in Appendix III). The next table shows the average index scores of each country, organised by GDP and national levels of church attendance. In order to make the tables easier to read, the post-communist applicant countries and eastern Germany are shown in italics, while the current EU member states (except eastern Germany) are shown in Roman type.

Traditional religious beliefs

Average country index scores by church attendance and GDP[2]
(higher score = more religious; lower score = less religious)

1992 GDP per capita ($)	High/moderate church attendance		Low church attendance	
20,000	W Germany	-1.6		
18,000	Austria	-1.2		
17,500	Italy	0.3		
17,200			Netherlands	-2.5
15,900			Britain	-1.3
12,000	Ireland	2.0		
10,700	*Slovenia*	-2.8		
6,500			*E Germany*	-5.2
5,380			*Hungary*	-4.0
4,400	*Poland*	1.0		

Mean index scores:

Current EU members (excluding E Germany)	- 0.9
Former communist countries (including E Germany)	- 1.6
Combined	- 1.0

Note: means are weighted by population size

The table clearly shows that, with the exception of Poland, traditional religious beliefs are rather weak in the post-communist countries. Indeed, eastern Germany and Hungary have the lowest scores of any of the countries considered. Secondly, and unsurprisingly, strength of religious beliefs is associated with average frequency of church attendance, as shown by the fact that those countries in the left hand column tend to have higher scores than those in the right hand column. What is more intriguing is a third finding, that countries with higher GDP tend to have stronger religious beliefs than countries with lower GDP (shown by the fact that countries towards the top of the table have higher scores than countries towards the bottom), contradicting much existing research on the subject (Jagodzinski and Dobbelaere, 1995). This apparent paradox is, however, resolved when the effect of communism is taken into account in the multivariate modelling. The explanation hinges on the fact that there is an association between low levels of GDP and past experience of communism. It is the *latter* that is linked to the relatively low levels of religiosity, which, in turn, is negatively related to GDP among both post-communist countries and EU member states, when they are considered separately. So the experience of communism appears to have been to reduce traditional religious values, presumably through indoctrination (the ideology of atheism), the repression of the churches, and social change. The backlash against the communist period does not appear to have led to a revival in religious beliefs large enough to reverse this effect of communism.

Overall then, an EU expanded to include post-communist countries would actually cover a population with *weaker* religious beliefs than is now the case. Nevertheless, as is shown by the mean index scores in the table, the effect of this change would be very small once the relative sizes of post-communist countries are taken into account. Most of the post-communist countries, with the exception of Poland, are comparatively small - and it is Poland which stands out as having the strongest religious beliefs of any of the post-communist countries considered.

Moral values

Support for the institution of marriage

The index of support for the institution of marriage is drawn from six questions asked in the 1994 ISSP survey on family and gender roles (the exact question wordings are given in Appendix III). The next table shows the average index scores of each country, again arranged by GDP and national levels of church attendance.

Support for marriage

Average country index scores by church attendance and GDP
(higher score = more supportive; lower score = less supportive)

1994 GDP per capital ($)	High/moderate church attendance		Low church attendance	
19,660	W Germany	-3.1		
18,580			Sweden	-4.9
17,980			Britain	-2.5
17,940			Netherlands	-4.8
17,500	Austria	-3.6		
17,180	Italy	-2.3		
14,060	Ireland	-1.2		
13,120	Spain	-2.6		
8,110	*Slovenia*	-2.8		
7,350			*Czech Republic*	-2.1
5,950			*E Germany*	-3.6
5,700			*Hungary*	-1.9
4,920	*Poland*	0.0		
3,830			*Bulgaria*	0.6

Mean index scores:

Current EU members (excluding E Germany)	-2.9
Former communist countries (including E Germany)	-1.3
Combined	-2.5

Note: means are weighted by population size

The table shows that support for marriage tends to be greater in the post-communist applicant countries than it is in the existing EU member states, suggesting that the incorporation of these countries into the EU would lead to a strengthening of traditional values in this respect. But it should be said that support is no more than lukewarm in any of the countries we examined (bearing in mind that a score of zero represents a neutral attitude). As we would expect, higher church attendance is associated with more traditional attitudes on marriage, while higher levels of GDP are associated with less traditional attitudes. However, even once these two characteristics are taken into account, the legacy of communism is still found to have a significant (though slight) association with greater traditionalism in attitudes towards marriage. Two plausible explanations for this exist. The first is that a backlash against communism's suppression of church teachings has revived traditional values. However, this is inconsistent with our finding that any such backlash has not been strong enough to reverse the tendency of communism to reduce traditional religious values. More likely is that the repression of social debate during communism has slowed down value change and fossilised those value systems that existed prior to communism.

Women and work

The index for attitudes towards women and work is drawn from six questions asked in the 1994 ISSP survey on family and gender roles (the exact question wordings are given in Appendix III). As with the previous tables, we organise our findings by GDP - but this time we refer to the religious composition of the country instead of levels of church attendance (as this proved to have a stronger relationship with attitudes towards women and work).

Attitudes to women and work

Average country index scores by religious composition and GDP
(higher score = more in favour of working women;
lower score = more against working women)

1994 GDP per capita ($)	High % Protestants		Low % Protestants	
19,660	W Germany	0.8		
18,580	Sweden	1.9		
17,980	Britain	1.8		
17,940	Netherlands	1.2		
17,500			Austria	0.9
17,180			Italy	-0.5
14,060			Ireland	1.0
13,120			Spain	0.4
8,110			Slovenia	-0.5
7,350			Czech Republic	-0.9
5,950	E Germany	3.3		
5,700			Hungary	-1.8
4,920			Poland	-0.2
3,830			Bulgaria	-1.0

Mean index scores

Current EU members (excluding E Germany)	0.8
Former communist countries (including E Germany)	-0.1
Combined	0.6

Note: means are weighted by population size

Once more the post-communist countries (with the notable exception of eastern Germany) are the most conservative in their attitudes, suggesting that enlarging the EU would cause attitudes in the EU as a whole to become more conservative. As one might expect, countries where Protestantism is the dominant religion tend to be more liberal in their attitudes towards the role of women, while predominantly Catholic or Orthodox countries are more traditionalist. Similarly, higher GDP levels are also related to a more liberal view. However, as was the case with attitudes towards marriage, the multivariate analysis shows that differences between current EU members and post-communist countries cannot be explained solely by reference to these factors. The experience of communism also appears to be associated with more traditionalist views, one possibility being that it has tended to impede value change. This effect has overshadowed any effects of social change and of the declining role of the church.

Sexual permissiveness

To examine attitudes towards sexual permissiveness we consider four questions dealing with the acceptability of various sexual relations asked on the 1994 ISSP survey about family and gender roles (the exact question wordings are given in Appendix III). The table shows the average index scores of each country, organised by GDP and levels of church attendance.

Sexual permissiveness

Average country index scores by church attendance and GDP
(higher score = more permissive; lower score = less permissive)

1994 GDP per capita ($)	High/moderate church attendance		Low church attendance	
19,660	W Germany	0.0		
18,580			Sweden	-0.4
17,980			Britain	-2.0
17,940			Netherlands	0.5
17,500	Austria	-1.6		
17,180	Italy	-2.5		
14,060	Ireland	-4.5		
13,120	Spain	-1.6		
8,110	*Slovenia*	-1.6		
7,350			*Czech Republic*	-0.2
5,950			*E Germany*	0.2
5,700			*Hungary*	-2.0
4,920	*Poland*	-3.4		
3,830			*Bulgaria*	-3.1

Mean index scores:

Current EU members (excluding E Germany)	-1.5
Former communist countries (including E Germany)	-2.2
Combined	-1.7

Note: means are weighted by population size

The table again shows that the post-communist countries are more conservative when it comes to sexual attitudes than are the existing members of the EU. So the inclusion of these countries in the EU would lead to its covering a slightly more conservative population than is currently the case. Not surprisingly, higher church attendance is associated with more conservatism when it comes to sexual issues, while higher GDP is associated with greater permissiveness.

However, multivariate modelling shows that once church attendance and GDP are taken into account, communism actually has a small *liberalising* effect upon attitudes towards sexuality. In other words, once their levels of church attendance and GDP are taken into account, the communist countries are slightly *more* liberal when it comes to attitudes towards sex than we would predict. One possible explanation for this could be the weakening of church teachings and the promotion of social change that took place under the previous communist regime (particularly the promotion of education, which tends to be associated with more liberal attitudes in this sphere). An alternative possibility is that such attitudes towards sexuality reflect a backlash against communist authoritarianism, and an embracing of liberal values and behaviour. But neither of these interpretations is easily reconciled with the finding that the experience of communism is linked to traditional attitudes towards marriage and the role of women - it would be arbitrary to give such explanations here where they were rejected in each of the previous cases. Our findings on sexual attitudes can therefore be described only as a paradox that must await further investigation.

Punitiveness of the legal system

For a direct measure of such anti-authoritarianism, we turn to our index of attitudes towards the punitiveness of the legal system. This is derived from two questions about stiffer sentences and the death penalty asked in the 1991 ISSP survey (the exact question wordings are given in Appendix III). As was the case when examining attitudes towards women and work, we organise our findings by GDP and the religious composition of the country.

Attitudes on the punitiveness of the legal system

Average country index scores by religious composition and GDP
(higher score = more punitive; lower score = less punitive)

1992 GDP per capita ($)	High % Protestants		Low % Protestants	
20,000	W Germany	0.4		
18,000			Austria	0.8
17,500			Italy	1.4
17,200	Netherlands	1.1		
15,900	Britain	1.4		
12,000			Ireland	1.0
10,700			Slovenia	1.3
6,500	E Germany	1.3		
5,380			Hungary	2.7
4,400			Poland	2.1

Mean index score

Current EU members (excluding E Germany)	1.1
Former communist countries (including E Germany)	2.0
Combined	1.3

Note: means are weighted by population size

Once again, the post-communist countries tend to be more conservative than the existing members of the EU, with populations in the post-communist countries being significantly more likely to favour stiffer sentencing and the use of the death penalty than are those in existing EU member states. This is partly explained by the religious composition of the post-communist countries and by their lower GDP levels - the Catholic and Orthodox churches have more punitive attitudes than do the Protestant churches, and lower GDP levels are also associated with stronger punitivism. In fact, multivariate analysis shows that once GDP and religion are taken into account, the effect of communism is actually a *liberalising* one - as was the case with attitudes towards sexuality. Unlike in the case of sexuality, however, an explanation for the present findings does present itself - namely, that a backlash against communism - specifically, against communist authoritarianism - affects attitudes towards punitivism while having no direct effect upon attitudes to marriage, the role of women or sexuality. Of particular relevance here is the fact that opposition to the excessively heavy hand of the law was an important element of the opposition to communist rule during the 1980s. The data we use were collected in 1991, at a time when the liberal backlash against communist authoritarianism was particularly strong. Circumstantial evidence suggests that subsequent experience of rising crime has led to the development of more punitive attitudes.

Moral values - East and West

We have considered four attitude dimensions that relate to moral values - attitudes towards marriage, women and work, sexuality and the punitiveness of the legal system. In all four cases we find that post-communist countries are more conservative than the existing EU member states. Consequently, the enlargement of the EU would tend to cause attitudes in the EU as a whole to become more conservative, although this effect would be muted by the relatively small populations in the countries we are considering here.

In all cases, a substantial amount of the variation we found is due to socio-economic and religious differences between post-communist and EU countries. It is true that these characteristics do, to a certain degree, reflect the policies of the communist era. But they are also the product of trends that substantially pre-date that period. Their importance suggests that differences between East and West in Europe are deep-rooted, and that they are certainly not merely short-term reflections of a communist past. In fact, when it comes to attitudes towards sexuality and the punitiveness of the legal system, communism appears to have produced a degree of convergence between EU countries and post-communist countries.

When we look in detail at the effect of communism on attitudes and values, once levels of economic development and religious difference are taken into account, the picture is rather contradictory. In two respects (attitudes towards the role of marriage and towards women and work) communism appears to have reinforced conservative attitudes. But in the other two respects (attitudes towards sexuality and towards the punitiveness of the legal system) communism seems to have promoted liberalism. It is not difficult to provide plausible explanations for each of these findings - the various mechanisms through which communism might be expected to influence attitudes often work in opposite directions, making it easy to explain almost any result that is reached. The difficulty is, of course, that it is unsatisfactorily *ad hoc* to suggest that one mechanism may have been more influential with respect to one attitudinal dimension, and another mechanism of greater significance to another, unless we are able to provide a theoretical justification for these differences.

One such theoretically grounded explanation for the liberalising effect of communism on attitudes to punishment is that this reflects a backlash against communist authoritarianism and the heavy hand of the law. It is more paradoxical, however, why communism should apparently have had a permissive effect upon sexual attitudes while seemingly promoting conservatism in respect of both marriage and the role of women. We might in particular expect that attitudes relating to marriage and sexual behaviour would follow similar patterns. Why attitudes on sexual issues fail to follow what is apparently the general trend is a paradox that cannot be satisfactorily explained without further research.

Economic values

Support for left-wing economic policies

Our index on support for left-wing economic policies is drawn from two questions about whether private enterprise is the best way to solve a country's economic problems and about the responsibility of government to reduce income differences, both of which were included in the 1993 ISSP survey (the exact question wordings are given in Appendix III). Preliminary analysis suggested that the best two explanatory factors were GDP and church attendance.

Support for left-wing economic policies

Average country index scores by church attendance and GDP
(higher score = more left-wing; lower score = more right-wing)

1993 GDP per capita ($)	High/moderate church attendance		Low church attendance	
19,400	W Germany	-0.3		
17,200			Netherlands	0.0
17,000			Britain	0.4
16,700	Italy	0.1		
13,100	Ireland	0.5		
12,700	Spain	0.3		
7,600	*Slovenia*	0.5		
7,200			*Czech Republic*	-0.2
6,300			*E Germany*	0.5
5,500			*Hungary*	0.8
4,680	*Poland*	0.8		
3,800			*Bulgaria*	1.2

Mean index scores:

EU members (excluding E Germany)	0.1
Former communist countries (including E Germany)	0.6
Combined	0.2

Note: means are weighted by population size

As the table shows, support for left-wing economic policies is significantly stronger in the post-communist countries than it is in the existing EU member states. Consequently, an EU *including* the five applicant countries considered here would, in economic terms, be more left-wing than that of today.

As with other studies (for example, Haller, Höllinger and Raubal, 1990; Knutsen, 1995; Roller, 1995), we find that higher GDP is associated with greater support for right-wing economic policies. Higher church attendance, meanwhile, is associated with greater support for left-wing policies, though this effect is not statistically significant. Once differences in GDP and church attendance are taken into account, however, the effect of communism is to promote *right-wing* attitudes on economic policy. Although it would seem at first glance that communist policies succeeded in producing populations that are unusually left-wing in their economic attitudes, this is not, in fact, the case. Rather, the left-wing orientation of these countries is better explained by other factors (particularly their lower GDP). While we might expect communist rule and the social changes it fostered to have promoted attitudes favouring more left-wing economic policies, what we find here is clear evidence of a backlash against communist rule, a popular rejection of communist policies and the espousal of more market-oriented economic strategies.

It might be pointed out that the data used for this index were collected in 1993 - during the early years of post-communism, when right-wing parties were elected to governmental office in almost all of the countries under consideration.   Attitudes on economic policy have been highly volatile in these countries during the 1990s, with early enthusiasm for the market later being followed, at least on the mass level, by a shift to more statist views on matters of economic policy (Markowski and Tóka, 1995; Mateju and Vlachova, 1997).   Nevertheless, most of this leftward shift seems to have occurred before rather than after the 1993 ISSP surveys were conducted.   As a result, it is likely that our findings do indeed have lasting significance.

Income redistribution

The index on income redistribution or economic egalitarianism is developed from four questions asked in the 1992 ISSP survey (the exact question wordings are given in Appendix III).   Rather than GDP (used in the previous tables), educational attainment emerged as the best measure relating to socio-economic development, and so the table is organised by this as well as by levels of church attendance.

Support for income redistribution

Average country index scores by church attendance and educational level
(higher score = more in favour of income redistribution;
lower scores = more against income redistribution)

Educational attainment*	High/moderate church attendance		Low church attendance	
66			Czechoslovakia	1.6
65			Britain	2.2
65	Slovenia	2.0		
64			Sweden	0.7
60	Poland	1.5		
59			Bulgaria	3.1
57			E Germany	3.8
56	Austria	2.3		
56	W Germany	2.1		
55			Hungary	2.5
53	Italy	2.2		

Mean index scores

EU members (excluding E Germany)	2.1
Former communist countries (including E Germany)	2.2
Combined	2.2

Note: means are weighted by population size

* Educational attainment is measured for each individual and then a country 'mean' score calculated. The higher the score, the higher the level of educational attainment reached. For further details see the appendix to this chapter.

The post-communist countries show very slightly higher levels of egalitarianism than the existing members of the EU.   This effect is strengthened when levels of church attendance and educational attainment are taken into account (as high levels in both are associated with lower levels of support for egalitarianism). Here, in contrast with support for left-wing economic policies, the evidence is that communist ideology and indoctrination have indeed had a lasting impact on attitudes in the countries concerned, making them more egalitarian than one would otherwise expect. This apparent conflict in findings is not as implausible as it might seem at first. While our index of support for left-wing economic policies is geared towards the specificities of the economic order, our measure of support for income redistribution is concerned more with the broad principles by which the economy operates. And it was the *governments* of the communist countries and their *specific policies* that were considered to have failed in the last years of communist rule, not the general goal of a more egalitarian world. Indeed, many of the anti-Communist reformers in the region during the 1980s advocated a 'third way' in economic policy that was built upon strongly egalitarian principles.

Concern for the environment

The index on concern for the environment is drawn from four questions asked in the 1993 ISSP survey (the exact question wordings are given in Appendix III). Preliminary analysis suggested that the best two explanatory factors were GDP and religious composition.

Environmental concerns

Average country index scores by religious composition and GDP
(higher score = more environmentalist; lower score = less environmentalist)

1993 GDP per capita ($)	High % of Protestants		Low % of Protestants	
19400	W Germany	0.8		
17200	Netherlands	1.3		
17000	Britain	0.1		
16700			Italy	0.3
13100			Ireland	-1.8
12700			Spain	0.6
7600			*Slovenia*	-0.1
7200			*Czech Republic*	-1.4
6300	*E Germany*	-0.8		
5500			*Hungary*	-2.2
4680			*Poland*	-0.5
3800			*Bulgaria*	-0.1

Mean index score

EU members (excluding E Germany)	0.5
Former communist countries (including E Germany)	-0.9
Combined	0.2

Note: means are weighted by population size

As the table shows, the populations of the post-communist countries are considerably less concerned about the environment than those in the EU. As would be predicted, high levels of GDP are strongly related to environmental concern. Rather more curiously, we find that largely Protestant countries exhibit lower levels of environmental concern than do predominantly Catholic or Orthodox countries.

The multivariate analysis shows that the low levels of environmental concern in the post-communist countries can be explained in part by the lower levels of material well-being seen in those countries, but that this is not sufficient to explain all of the difference between the regions. Two possible explanations present themselves. One is that current attitudes reflect communist indoctrination, and that the view that it is acceptable to pursue industrial progress at the cost of environmental damage is one that has taken hold among the populations of these countries. However, the importance of environmental issues within the anti-Communist movements of the 1980s suggests that this explanation may not be entirely plausible. An alternative explanation is that the low level of environmental concern in these countries is a short-term product of the severe economic recessions that they have undergone during the 1990s. It is highly plausible that environmental concern will fluctuate strongly with the economic cycle, as perceptions of personal material well-being change (Taylor, 1997). Given the severity of the downturn that has been experienced in the post-communist region during the early 1990s, it is hardly surprising that the levels of environmental concern found should be lower than would be predicted simply on the basis of levels of GDP.

Economic values - East and West

Our findings suggest that, while the economic policies of communism have been rejected, its ultimate goal of egalitarianism continues to be strongly held. Many of the post-communist applicant countries are more egalitarian in this respect than existing members of the EU, and they appear to be economically more left-wing only before their low income levels are taken into account. They also display less concern for the environment than do the current EU member states, reflecting their lower levels of material well-being and the severe recessions that they have recently undergone.

Conclusions

What do these findings tell us about the likely impact of the EU's eastward expansion on social attitudes within the EU as a whole? Although various differences in attitudes between the existing member states and the post-communist applicants have been identified, there are many reasons for thinking that we should not exaggerate the impact of enlargement on mass opinion within the EU.

First, most attitude differences occur within, not between, the borders of individual countries.   In trying to account for the difference between two people's attitudes, the country they are from matters far less than other characteristics (such as age or educational attainment).   Only in the case of traditional religious beliefs does country make a substantial difference.

Furthermore, in most cases only a small fraction of the difference between countries reflects the communist legacy.   In most respects the post-communist countries differ just as much among themselves as do current EU member states.   Only when it comes to environmental concern, attitudes towards punishment, and support for left wing economics does having a communist past appear to account for a substantial percentage of the difference in attitudes between countries (accounting for a third or more of this variation, which, it is worth stressing once more, is dwarfed by the magnitude of within-country variation).   This suggests that the impact of communism on public attitudes was limited, and that no single generic type of communism ever really existed.

It is likely that the already small gap between attitudes in the post-communist countries and the existing EU member states will decrease further as a consequence both of EU enlargement and the currently high rates of economic growth in Eastern Europe.   An additional reason for attitude change in the post-communist countries may be the fact that attitudes are less 'crystallised' in these countries - where there has been little free public debate - and may thus be more likely to change once such debate occurs.   This can be tested by examining the extent to which responses to different questions about a similar subject are coherent (or correlate) with one another.   If attitudes are clearly crystallised we would expect to find high levels of correlation.   And average correlations are indeed lower in post-communist countries than in the EU countries for all but two of the eight sets of attitude questions we examine.   The exceptions to this concern attitudes to do with traditional religious beliefs (on which there has been as little public debate in the post-war West as in the East) and support for left-wing economic policies (which have been the subject of very intense public contestation in nearly all East European countries since the late eighties).

Finally, when it comes to attitudes towards economic policy issues, generational replacement may also serve to reduce any discrepancy between East and West.   In our EU member states we found no relationship between age and attitudes towards economic policy (with the exception of the Netherlands, where the young are more left-wing).   In contrast, in our post-communist countries, the young are significantly more right-wing than average in their attitudes towards economic policy issues.   This is hardly surprising - those less exposed to communist ideology and more affected by any post-communist backlash might be expected to be more right-wing than those in older cohorts.   Consequently, as these generations gradually replace older ones, the gap between EU and post-communist states might be expected to diminish still further.   This is not the case for any of the other attitudes and values explored in this chapter (where the differences between EU and non-EU nations in the relationship of attitudes to age is minimal).

Social attitudes in post-communist countries do indeed differ from those held by current EU members. Post-communist states are morally more conservative and economically more left-wing and egalitarian than the current EU member states, and they are characterised by less concern for the environment. To a large degree, this simply reflects differences between the two areas in their levels of socio-economic development and in the nature of religiosity. However, it also reflects the direct legacy of the communist experience, with the repression of social debate under communism leading to the fossilisation of existing, traditional moral values. Only when other, stronger, forces are at work does it seem that the overall impact of communist experience and the subsequent post-communist backlash has been to promote liberalism. And, while communist ideology appears to have had a lasting effect through its promotion of egalitarian values, it has also led to a considerable backlash against left-wing economic policies.

Although clear differences exist between the attitudes of East and West, these must not be exaggerated. Indeed, there is reason to believe that these differences are already in decline, reflecting generational attitude change, economic progress and the rejuvenation of social debate in the post-communist world.

Notes

1. When calculating the overall mean index scores we weighted each country by its population size in order to allow the assessment of the potential effects of enlargement to be understood. Given that most of the applicant countries have small populations, the impact of their admittance on EU-wide attitudes would clearly be over-estimated were this weighting not carried out.
2. All GDP figures are for purchasing power parity.

References

Haller, M., Höllinger, F. and Raubal, O. (1990), 'Leviathan or welfare state? The role of government in six advanced Western nations' in Alwin, D., Becker, J., Davis, J., Haller, M., Höllinger, F., Jowell, R., Küchler, M., Morrow, B., Raubal, O. and Smith, T. *Attitudes to Inequality and the Role of Government,* Rijswijk: Sociaal en Cultureel Planbureau.

Jagodzinski, W. and Dobbelaere, K. (1995), 'Secularization and church religiosity' in Deth, J. and Scarbrough, E. (eds.), *Beliefs in Government Volume Four: The Impact of Values,* Oxford: Oxford University Press.

Knutsen, O. (1995), 'Left-right materialist value orientation' in Deth, J. and Scarbrough, E. (eds.), *Beliefs in Government Volume Four: The Impact of Values,* Oxford: Oxford University Press.

Markowski, R. and Tóka, G. (1995), 'Left turn in Hungary and Poland five years after the collapse of communism' *Sisyphus: Social Studies* 1 **(IX 1993),** 75-100.

Mateju, P. and Vlachova, K. (1997), 'The crystallisation of political attitudes and political spectrum in the Czech Republic' *Working Papers of the Research Project 'Social Trends'* 9/1997, Prague: Institute of Sociology.

Roller, E. (1995), 'Socioeconomic equality - one goal of the welfare state' in Borre, O. and Scarbrough, E. (eds.), *Beliefs in Government Volume Three: The Scope of Government,*

Oxford: Oxford University Press.

Taylor, B. (1997), 'Green in word ...', in Jowell, R., Curtice, J., Park, A., Brook, L., Thomson, K. and Bryson, C. (eds), *British Social Attitudes: the 14th Report*, Aldershot: Ashgate.

Appendix

The regression analyses referred to in the text were run using pooled cross-national data sets. In addition to using standard country-specific weights where necessary, data for each country were weighted to correspond to that country's total population in the period around 1993. Respondents with missing values (i.e. no, or 'can't say' responses) on any of the variables used to construct the attitude index in question were left out of the respective analysis.

Independent variables

The impact of communism was assessed by regressing the attitude indices on a dummy variable called Communism, which distinguished between former communist and other countries (coded as 1 and 0, respectively) and the predicted country means of the attitude indices (called Predicted) derived from a previous regression of the given attitude index on two independent variables. These two independent variables were:

- *either* GDP per capita
  or the mean level of education in the population aged 25 years or older, and
- *either* average frequency of church attendance in the adult population
  or the percentage of Protestants among adults belonging to a Christian church.

In the case of the religious composition, we make the choice on the basis of the measure that has the highest correlation with that attitude scale. The choice between GDP and education is slightly more complicated: GDP is strongly (negatively) correlated with whether a country has experienced communism, so any correlation between GDP and the attitude scale scores may in fact be spurious, being caused by the correlations of communism itself with both GDP and attitudes. GDP is therefore preferred to education only if it shows a higher correlation with the attitude scale than education *and* the sign of this correlation is the same in both the post-communist and the current-EU parts of the sample.

These variables were obtained as follows:

GDP per capita: purchasing power parity figures as reported in the annual editions of the CIA World Fact Book. This source is the only one available to us that gives comparable figures for Eastern and Western Europe. Since GDP estimates based on purchasing power parity are not available for 1991, 1992 GDP figures are used in the analysis of the 1991 ISSP data.
Average education levels are taken from the last pre-1995 ISSP data set available for each country. Level of education was recoded as 0=none, 25=incomplete primary, 50=at least primary completed, 75=at least secondary completed, 100=university degree.
Church attendance is taken from the last pre-1995 ISSP data set available for each country. Frequency of church attendance was recoded as 100=at least once a week, 67=1-3 times a month, 33=less frequently, 0=never.
Proportion of Protestants (among adults belonging to a Christian church) is taken from the last pre-1995 ISSP data set available for each country.

The country means of these variables were then used as independent variables in our regression analyses.

Dependent variables

The attitude indices are based on the summation of the responses to several different questions and were all scaled so that an index value of 0 expresses a neutral attitude - for instance that the respondent answered all questions with the 'neither agree nor disagree' response option, or that on the various questions he or she signalled exactly as many times a positive as a negative attitude towards the given attitude object. The higher the value a respondent has on an index, the more positive attitudes he or she has towards the issue in question.

The **traditional religious beliefs** index was constructed as 12.5 - V34 - V35 - V36 - V37 - V38, where the variables come from the 1991 data set and record responses to the following questions using a four-point scale (1=definitely yes; 2=probably yes; 3=probably not; 4=definitely not):

> *Do you believe in ...*
> *[V34] ... life after death?*
> *[V35] ... the Devil?*
> *[V36] ... Heaven?*
> *[V37] ... Hell?*
> *[V38] ... religious miracles?*

The index thus runs from +7.5 (most religious) to -7.5 (least religious).

The **marriage** index was constructed as V25 + V26 + V27 - V19 - V22 - V23, where the variables come from the 1994 data set and record responses to the following questions using the same five-point agree-disagree scale (1=agree strongly; 2=agree; 3=neither agree nor disagree; 4=disagree; 5= disagree strongly):

> *Do you agree or disagree that ...*
> *[V19] ... married people are generally happier than unmarried people?*
> *[V22] ... it is better to have a bad marriage than no marriage at all?*
> *[V23] ... people who want children ought to get married?*
> *[V25] ... it is all right for a couple to live together without intending to get married?*
> *[V26] ... it is a good idea for a couple who intend to get married to live together first?*
> *[V27] ... divorce is usually the best solution when a couple can't seem to work out their marriage problems?*

The index thus runs from +12 (most pro-marriage) to -12 (least pro-marriage).

The **women and work** index was constructed as V5 + V6 + V7 + V8 - V4 - V9 - 6, where V5 to V9 are variables in the 1994 data set and record responses to the following questions on a five-point agree-disagree scale (1=strongly agree; 2=agree; 3=neither agree nor disagree; 4=disagree; 5=strongly disagree):

> *Do you agree or disagree that ...*
> *[V4] ... a working mother can establish just as warm and secure a relationship with her children as a mother who does not work?*
> *[V5] ... that a pre-school child is likely to suffer if his or her mother works?*
> *[V6] ... that all in all, family life suffers when the woman has a full-time job?*
> *[V7] ... that a job is all right, but what most women really want is a home and children?*
> *[V8] ... that being a housewife is just as fulfilling as working for pay?*
> *[V9] ... that having a job is the best way for a woman to be an independent person?*

The index thus runs from +12 (most in favour of working women) to -12 (most against working women).

The **sexual permissiveness** index was constructed as V45 + V46 + V47 + V48 - 12, where the variables come from the 1994 data set and record responses to the following questions using a five-point scale (1=always wrong; 2=almost always wrong; 3=it depends - this response option was only offered in Spain; 4= wrong only sometimes; 5=not wrong at all):

*[V45] Do you think it is wrong or not wrong if a man and a woman have
sexual relations before marriage?*
*[V46] What if they are in their early teens, say under 16 years old, in that
case is it ...*
*[V47] What about a married person having sexual relations with someone
other than his or her husband or wife, is it ...*
*[V48] And what about sexual relations between two adults of the same sex,
is it ...*

The index thus runs from +8 (most permissive) to -8 (least permissive).

The **punitiveness** index was constructed as 6 - V7 - V8, where the variables come from the
1991 data set and record responses to the following questions on a five-point agree-disagree
scale (1=strongly agree; 2=agree; 3=neither agree nor disagree; 4=disagree; 5=strongly
disagree):

*Here are some measures to deal with crime. Some people are in favour of
them while others are against them. Do you agree or disagree that ...*
[V7] ...criminals should be given stiffer sentences?
*[V8] ... people convicted of murder should be subject to the death
penalty?*

The index thus runs from +4 (most punitive) to -4 (least punitive).

The **support for left-wing economic policies** index was constructed as V5 - V6, where the
variables come from the 1993 data set and record responses to the following questions using
a five-point agree-disagree scale (1=strongly agree; 2=agree; 3=neither agree nor disagree;
4=disagree; 5=strongly disagree):

How much do you agree or disagree with each of these statements?
*[V5] Private enterprise is the best way to solve <the respondent's
country's> economic problems.*
*[V6] It is the responsibility of the government to reduce the differences in
income between people with high incomes and those with low incomes.*

The index thus runs from +4 (left-wing) to -4 (right-wing).

The **income redistribution** index was constructed as V23 + V24 - V56 - V57, where the
variables come from the 1992 data set and record responses to the following questions using
a five-point agree-disagree scale (1=strongly agree; 2=agree; 3=neither agree nor disagree;
4=disagree; 5=strongly disagree):

Please show how much you agree or disagree with each statement ...
*[V23] ... Large differences in income are necessary for <the respondent's
country's> prosperity.*
*[V24] ... Allowing business to make good profits is the best way to
improve everyone's standard of living.*
*[V56] ... Differences in income in <the respondent's country> are too
large.*
*[V57] ... It is the responsibility of the government to reduce the
differences in income between people with high incomes and those with
low incomes.*

The index thus runs from +8 (most pro income redistribution) to -8 (most anti income
redistribution).

The **concern for the environment** index was constructed as 6 + V13 - V24 - V25 - V26,
where the variables come from the 1993 data set and record responses to the following
questions using the same five-point agree-disagree scale for V13 and a different scale for
variables V24 to V26 (where 1=very willing; 2=fairly willing; 3=neither willing nor
unwilling; 4=fairly unwilling; 5=very unwilling):

*Please tick one box [respond using the card] for each of these statements
to show how much you agree or disagree with it.*

[V13] We worry too much about the future of the environment and not enough about prices and jobs today.
How willing would you be ...
[V24] ... to pay much higher prices in order to protect the environment?
[V25] ... to pay much higher taxes in order to protect the environment?
[V26] ... to accept cuts in your standard of living in order to protect the environment?

The index thus runs from +8 (most environmentalist) to -8 (least environmentalist).

Regression analyses of the contextual determinants of social attitudes

The table entries below are metric regression coefficients. Each dependent variable was regressed first on two independent variables (either GDP per capita or average educational level and either the proportion of Protestants or mean church attendance rate in the respective countries). The predicted value of the dependent variable derived from this equation became, alongside a dummy variable distinguishing between former communist and other countries, one of the independent variables in the second regression. The two initial independent variables and the Communism dummy entered the third equation simultaneously.

	Independent variables:							
Dependent variable:	GDP per capita	Educ level	Protes-tants	Church attend	Predicted value	Commu-nism	Adj R^2	N (un-weighted)
RelBeli	.086**	-	-	.085**	-	-	.091	*9785*
RelBeli	-	-	-	-	.987**	-.393**	.092	*9785*
RelBeli	-.237**	-	-	.081**	-	-4.36**	.104	*9785*
Marriage	-.118**	-	-	.032**	-	-	.044	*15606*
Marriage	-	-	-	-	.958**	.128	.045	*15606*
Marriage	-.072**	-	-	.033**	-	.611**	.045	*15606*
PermSex	.054**	-	-	-.045**	-	-	.045	*13957*
PermSex	-	-	-	-	1.04**	.188*	.045	*13957*
PermSex	.153**	-	-	-.042**	-	1.29**	.047	*13957*
WomWork	.030**	-	.026**	-	-	-	.048	*16231*
WomWork	-	-	-	-	.965**	-.272**	.049	*16231*
WomWork	-.178**	-	.031**	-	-	-2.64**	.054	*16231*
Punish	-.088**	-	-.003**	-	-	-	.061	*11308*
Punish	-	-	-	-	2.09**	-1.39**	.070	*11308*
Punish	-.213**	-	-.003**	-	-	-1.72**	.072	*11308*
LeftEcon	-.055**	-	-	.001	-	-	.031	*12405*
LeftEcon	-	-	-	-	1.85**	-.634**	.035	*12405*
LeftEcon	-.113**	-	-	-.001	-	-.749**	.035	*12405*
Egalitar	-	-.078**	-	-.024**	-	-	.020	*10952*
Egalitar	-	-	-	-	1.12**	.371**	.023	*10952*
Egalitar	-	-.089**	-	-.027**	-	.373**	.023	*10952*
Environ	.117**	-	-.004**	-	-	-	.027	*12671*
Environ	-	-	-	-	.542**	-.666**	.028	*12671*
Environ	.062**	-	-.003**	-	-	-.691**	.028	*12671*

* = significant at 5% level
** = significant at 1% level

9 How Britain views the EU

Geoffrey Evans [*]

Other chapters in this book compare British attitudes with those in the rest of the EU to discover how far they coincide or differ. This chapter, in contrast, is not concerned with similarities and differences. It asks instead whether or not the British public *wants* Britain to be part of an integrated Europe in the first place.

The importance of this question is incontestable. Whether expressed via headlines in The Sun or through episodic rows in parliament, disputes about Britain's part in the integration of Europe continue, evincing charged feelings on either side about national loyalties and economic security. Now, with the prospect of a referendum on European Monetary Union (EMU) shortly after the next general election, these disputes are sure to become still more heated.

The issue of Britain's role in the EU has already had a profound effect on British politics. In recent years, for instance, it was the key axis of division in the Conservative Party's leadership elections of 1990, 1995 and 1997, and it spawned a new - if short-lived - political party, the Referendum Party, which fought many seats in the 1997 election.

Our interest here is in what the British *public* thinks about the EU and in whether it is exercised about the issue in much the same way as politicians and journalists clearly are. Although the creation, expansion and consolidation of the EU is, of course, primarily due to the efforts of politicians over the years, it has been aided by a 'permissive consensus' of the citizenry within many member countries (Lindberg and Scheingold, 1970). The intriguing question now is whether the issue of monetary union will stir up more public disquiet than have other moves towards integration (see, for

---

[*] Geoffrey Evans is Faculty Fellow at Nuffield College, Oxford.

example, Franklin *et al.*, 1994). In Britain at any rate, it is likely to need more than mere public acquiescence to carry the day in a referendum following a sustained anti-campaign, which is bound to centre not only on the well-worn issues of national identity and sovereignty, but also on the new issue of a potentially confusing transition to an unfamiliar new currency.

This chapter assesses British public opinion towards the EU, using both the most recent module of questions in the 1997 *British Social Attitudes* survey, and an analysis of trends derived from questions about the EU that the series has asked regularly since its inception in 1983. We also draw on data from the *British General Election Studies*. We first examine trends in public support for and attitudes towards the general issue of European integration and its consequences, taking in the particular issue of monetary union *en route*, and then move on to examine the range of factors underpinning these attitudes.

Changing attitudes

The issue of European integration has never been a stable political issue. Its nature and significance have changed markedly over the years and we would expect such changes to be reflected in public attitudes. The 1990s has witnessed particularly rapid shifts and may well have had the biggest domestic political impact, but it is important to examine these developments in the broader perspective of longer term trends.

In the next table, we see the responses to a question on attitudes towards membership of the EU which was asked in each *British Social Attitudes* survey from the start of the series in 1983 until 1991, and then again in 1997. It was also asked in the 1992 *British General Election Study*.

Do you think Britain should continue to be a member of the European Union or should it withdraw?[1]

	1983	1984	1985	1986	1987	1988	1990	1991	1992	1997
	%	%	%	%	%	%	%	%	%	%
Continue	53	48	56	61	63	68	76	77	72	55
Withdraw	42	45	38	33	31	26	19	16	22	28
Don't know	5	6	6	6	6	6	5	6	6	17
Base	*1719*	*1645*	*1769*	*3066*	*2766*	*2930*	*2698*	*1422*	*2834*	*1355*

Note: All data are from the *British Social Attitudes* series, except for 1992 which are from the *British General Election Study*.

There were steady increases in British public acceptance of EU membership from the early 1980s until 1991, starting off the period in 1983 with less than 50 per cent support and rising to over 75 per cent support by 1991. The impression up to that time was of a population slowly becoming accustomed to, and even perhaps comfortable with, being part of the European community. But in 1992 there was a small but significant fall in acceptance and by 1997 the former secular upward trend had dramatically reversed itself.

What then has happened since 1991 to precipitate such a reversal? A clue can be found in the answers to another question that has been asked since 1992, which gives people a fuller and rather more realistic set of options than the stark choice in the first question between Britain's either staying in the EU or leaving it. It more closely reflects the changing terms of the debate about *degrees* of integration and the strength of the links rather than about the pros and cons of departure from the EU.

Do you think Britain's long-term policy should be to ...

	1992	1993	1994	1995	1996	1997
	%	%	%	%	%	%
... leave the EU	10	11	11	14	19	17
... stay in the EU and try to reduce the EU's powers	30	25	25	23	39	29
... leave things as they are	16	23	21	20	19	18
... stay in the EU and try to increase the EU's powers	28	24	28	28	8	16
... work for the formation of a single European government	10	9	8	8	6	7
Don't know	7	8	7	6	9	13
Base	*2855*	*1461*	*1165*	*1227*	*1196*	*1355*

Note: All data are from *British Social Attitudes* series, except for 1992 which are from the *British General Election Study*.

The answers to this question confirm the recent downward trend in attitudes towards integration: the proportion favouring closer links with the EU fell from 38 per cent in 1992 to a low point of 14 per cent in 1996, and then recovered somewhat to 23 per cent a year later. Indeed, 1996 seems to have been a particularly bad year for public support for the EU, possibly as a result of the BSE crisis which broke in the spring of that year (Curtice and Jowell, 1998). The most recent survey shows a rise in the proportion of 'don't know' responses thus indicating increased uncertainty. Looked at over the full period covered, we can say that the proportion of respondents actually seeking to leave the EU has grown considerably (from 10 per cent in 1992 to 17 per cent in 1997), but it is still quite small. The proportion of respondents who seek to weaken the EU's influence even though remaining part of the union has remained fairly constant, while the proportion seeking closer links has clearly fallen.

Combining the evidence from these two tables, we can conclude that the start of the decade may well have been the high watermark of British support for European integration. What we are seeing now may be the start of a longer term decline or simply a temporary reaction to some of the events that have dominated news coverage of the EU in the period - among which are the Exchange Rate Mechanism (ERM) fiasco of 1992, serious Conservative Party splits on the issue throughout the period, the rise and fall of the Referendum Party, the long-running BSE crisis and an increasing focus on monetary union as *the* European issue and, as we shall see, the ambivalent (bordering on downright hostile) British response to it.

Support for particular aspects of integration

There will, of course, be many debates in coming years about the exact nature of further moves towards European integration and how far each development impinges on member states' internal policies and practices. In that context, *general* support for, or opposition towards, the abstract concept of European integration (of the sort we have been examining so far here) is not necessarily the best indicator of where people are likely to stand on specific aspects of integration. We need to discover in more concrete terms which aspects of integration people support or oppose,[2] not least because that is the way in which integration actually proceeds.

In the present political climate, British participation (or not) in a single European currency is comfortably the most dominant item on the immediate agenda. We asked:

Which come closest to your view?

	1992	1993	1994	1995	1996	1997
Should Britain...	%	%	%	%	%	%
...replace the pound by a single currency	21	15	17	18	13	17
...use both the pound and a new European currency in Britain	21	16	18	18	16	17
...keep the pound as the only currency for Britain	54	66	62	62	68	61
Don't know	4	3	4	4	3	6
Base	*2855*	*1461*	*1165*	*1227*	*1196*	*1355*

Note: All data are from the *British Social Attitudes* series, except for 1992 which are from the *British General Election Study*.

As we can see, only a small minority (17 per cent) of the public are at present content to lose the pound as their currency, and a further 17 per cent would be prepared to see a new European currency phased in alongside the pound. Indeed, the proportion wishing to keep the pound as the only currency for Britain has never dipped below half. It now stands at 61 per cent, having been as high as 66 per cent in 1993 in the wake of Britain's unseemly withdrawal from the ERM, and 68 per cent during the early stages of the BSE crisis in 1996. Even with the presumed weight of government support behind the proposition, a referendum victory on Britain's adoption of the Euro will be hard to achieve. As noted, it will involve overcoming not only the usual inertia about giving up things British for things European, but also in this case the fear of abandoning the familiar metric by which people are used to judging the value of their goods and services.

But monetary union is only one of a number of steps towards integration. Other policy areas - including aspects of taxation, defence, immigration, pollution control, employment policy, science policy and law enforcement - are all candidates for harmonisation at some point or other. Would people be more or less prepared to contemplate ceding national control over these sorts of policies? We included a series of questions in the 1997 survey (most of which were also in the 1994 survey) asking respondents to choose between national, EU or joint control over various aspects of governance.

The EU and decision making in specific areas

Decisions about...		Who should mostly make decisions?		
		EU	Individual governments	Both equally
... taxes	%	2	76	11
... how much farmers should produce	%	13	51	25
... immigration	%	14	57	19
... defence	%	14	51	25
... the rights of people at work	%	16	50	24
... funding scientific research	%	19	33	34
... stop drug trafficking	%	28	17	46
... controlling pollution	%	30	29	32

Base: 1080

Not surprisingly, perhaps, public opinion is in general very reluctant to hand over singular British control to the EU in most of the policy areas we asked about. Indeed, even those respondents who approve in principle of giving more influence to the EU then seem to balk at most of the possible concrete manifestations of integration. On the other hand, there is more acceptance of EU involvement in some aspects of governance than in others. So, while three-quarters of respondents oppose EU control over taxation, over half opposed it over agricultural quotas, immigration policy, defence and working practices. In response to a further question about rights at work, only 38 per cent of people subscribed to the proposition (to which we invited their agreement or disagreement) that "the British government should sign up to the Social Chapter so that British workers have the same rights at work as everyone else in Europe".

But opposition falls to around one-third when it comes to more global issues such as scientific research and pollution, and to one sixth when it comes to the fight against drug trafficking. In fact, in each of these last three, there is majority support for some EU involvement, and quite a bit of support for the EU to be the main decision-maker.

Notably, these attitudes have hardly changed since our last reading in 1994 (see Evans, 1995: 114 for an equivalent table for 1994). So, despite the increase since then in Euroscepticism more generally, it has not spread to attitudes towards these *specific* aspects of policy.

Public ambivalence about the EU

Coherence of attitudes

Analysis of the 1994 *British Social Attitudes* survey showed that even pro-EU respondents resisted the notion of European parliamentary control over British policy decisions (Evans, 1995). As with many other difficult political choices, principle and practice often diverge. Indeed, studies of political attitudes over the years in diverse political systems have uncovered marked differences between attitudes towards abstract principles on the one hand and their translation into concrete policies on the other (Converse, 1964; Sniderman *et al.,* 1991). What we may have seen over time in relation to the EU, however, with the microscope so sharply focused on it in recent years, is a growing *convergence* between the abstract and the concrete. Thus, people's formerly more positive attitudes to integration *in principle* may have moved closer to their more negative attitudes towards integration *in practice*.

To investigate this further, we must look at how people's views cohere and whether this has changed over time as the EU has become a more salient public issue. In the next table, we take two related issues - support for Britain's continued membership of the EU, and support for a single European currency - and investigate the extent to which those who hold a pro-European view on the first issue also hold a pro-integration view on the second issue. More importantly, we look at how the coincidence between these two viewpoints has changed over time. At the bottom of the table we give a summary measure of the link between the two positions by means of an 'odds ratio'. The higher the odds ratio, the more consistent are the viewpoints.

Relationship between attitudes to
British membership of the EU and EMU

	1993	1994	1995	1996	1997
% who want to leave EU					
- Among those who want to keep the pound	15	17	18	26	25
- Among those who want to replace the pound	3	3	3	5	3
The gap between the two groups	+12	+14	+15	+21	+22
Odds-ratios for pro *versus* anti closer integration by keep *versus* replace the pound	6.4	5.7	5.4	8.7	10.4
Base	*1461*	*1165*	*1227*	*1196*	*1355*

The strength of the link between public support for British membership of the EU and British adoption of a single European currency has increased over the years. Put another way, respondents who do not want to lose the pound have over the years become increasingly likely to oppose British membership of the EU altogether. It may well be merely that the politicisation of EU issues in the 1990s has had most impact on those who were already Eurosceptic on specific issues. But it has probably also enabled people to appreciate more clearly than before the implications of integration and thus to revise their attitudes accordingly.

This same process can be observed below in the odds ratios for support/opposition to integration and support for decision-making powers at EU *versus* national level on various issues.

Relationship between attitudes to British membership of the EU and appropriate level of policy-making in various areas

Odds ratios
(The higher the odds ratio, the more consistent the attitudes)

	1994	1997
Taxes	3.5	8.8
Immigration	6.8	8.7
Defence	4.9	4.2
The rights of people at work	4.8	8.0
Controlling pollution	3.8	4.6
Base	*975*	*1080*

Over the three years from 1994 to 1997 there were big increases in the relationship between attitudes towards integration and views on control over taxation and workers' rights and more modest increases in their association with views on control over immigration.

Knowledge about the EU

In as little as four years, then, the links between support for EU membership and attitudes towards monetary union have strengthened markedly. That is true too of the links between support for EU membership and other policies - in particular those to do with economic regulation. It seems that, as the EU has become more and more salient politically, so people have become more internally consistent in their attitudes towards the EU. Put another way, the drop in support for British participation in the EU may reflect a greater awareness than before of the direction of EU policy towards closer integration and a reluctance to go in that direction. On the other hand, the greater public antipathy than before towards the EU might reflect a continued ignorance of the facts and a corresponding susceptibility to the more hostile of the anti-European campaigning that have emerged in recent years. In the former case, a growth in knowledge about the EU might undermine support for it - something of an irony given that the Brussels bureaucracy has been active in trying to increase knowledge about what the EU does and means. In the latter case, an informed public might become less susceptible than now to scare stories about the excesses of 'Brussels bureaucrats'.

One bit of evidence to determine which is the more likely explanation arises from a 'Deliberative Poll' on the EU carried out by SCPR in 1995, in which a national sample of adults (whose prior views on the EU had been elicited) took part in a weekend of discussion, debate and information, at the end of which they were asked for their views again.[3] In this experiment, there was a marked *increase* in public support for the EU with greater knowledge (Curtice and Gray, 1995), suggesting that more information about the EU might provide a basis for greater popular endorsement. Moreover, as much psychological research has shown, the more knowledge-based are one's attitudes, the more likely they are to be robust. In other words, informed citizens tend to be surer of their opinions than are uninformed citizens and are less easily won over by counter campaigns (Ajzen and Fishbein, 1980). So it is a matter of some importance as to how much support for, or opposition to, the aims of the EU is to be found among the well-informed and how much among the ill-informed.

The problem is that knowledge about such a complex topic as the EU is not easy to assess in the context of a survey such as the *British Social Attitudes* without special questions designed to measure it. So, in 1997, we developed six statements specifically designed to tap respondents' knowledge of the EU.[4] Respondents were asked to say which were true (three, as indicated) and which false. In the next table we show the proportions who identified the true and false statements correctly.

Knowledge about the EU

		Correct	Incorrect	Don't know
Britain's income tax rules are decided in Brussels (false)	%	74	9	17
Britain doesn't have any European Commissioners at the moment (false)	%	60	14	26
Elections to the European Parliament are held every five years (true)	%	59	11	30
The EU has fifteen members (true)	%	48	15	36
Norway is a member of the EU (false)	%	40	28	31
Hungary has applied to join the EU (true)	%	38	16	45

Base: 1355

Whether one should regard these responses as showing public knowledge or ignorance is a matter of opinion. In any event, the average respondent got 3.2 right answers (out of six), but the numbers of 'don't know' responses (average 32 per cent) were very high, and - of the remainder - we would expect 50 per cent to get it right by chance alone. Yet, on all the statements, the proportion who gave correct answers outnumbered those who gave incorrect ones, mostly by a very large margin.

The levels of knowledge of each issue seem to reflect the immediate relevance of that issue to Britain. Thus, people are more secure in the knowledge that British taxes are not set in Brussels, that Britain does indeed have European Commissioners and that elections to the European Parliament take place every five years, than they are about, say, the relationship of Norway or Hungary to the EU.

In addition, given the fact that newspapers, especially some of the tabloid ones, tend rarely to provide such facts and figures, it is probably fair to describe the level of public knowledge about the EU as rather impressive. As many as 63 per cent of tabloid readers, compared to 18 per cent of readers of broadsheet newspapers, said that they got to know very little or nothing at all from their newspaper about Britain's relationship with the EU. This may in part reflect a Eurosceptic bias of many of the tabloids, at least according to their readers. Over half (56 per cent) of tabloid readers thought that, if "there is an argument between Britain and the EU", their paper would usually side with Britain, while much the same proportion of broadsheet readers thought that their paper would usually give "equal weight to both sides". In response, however, the newspapers would doubtless argue that they tend to give their readers what they want.

Two types of Euroscepticism?

So, is support for, or opposition to, the EU fuelled by knowledge or does it thrive on relative ignorance? Certainly, the heartland of support for European integration is to be found among the generally more informed 'chattering classes' (Evans, 1995; Evans, 1999). But this does not necessarily mean that opposition to the EU is mainly confined to the ill-informed. According to our quiz scores, it is the case that people who want Britain to leave the EU are less informed than those who do not. But it would be misleading to take this single figure as an indication that Euroscepticism is in general grounded in ignorance. In the next table we look at answers which show a rather more complicated picture.

Knowledge about EU by attitudes to the EU

	Mean quiz score
Do you think Britain's long-term policy should be to ...	
Leave the EU	3.10
Stay in the EU and try to reduce the EU's powers	3.76
Leave things as they are	3.01
Stay in the EU and try to increase the EU's powers	3.57
Work for the formation of a single European government	3.55
Don't know	1.75

Base: 1355

Those who offer no opinion are by far the least knowledgeable. But of those who offer an opinion, we find that those who want Britain to stay in an EU with reduced powers are actually more informed than those who either wish to increase the EU's powers or those who want full integration. These informed Eurosceptics are likely to take some convincing of the merits of further integration.

Further analysis confirms our earlier findings (Evans, 1995) that support for the EU is higher among the young, the highly educated, the middle classes and men, and that there appears to have been little change in the social characteristics of supporters and opponents in the last three years. The levels of 'don't know' responses are also lower among these groups. These informed Eurosceptics are likely to take some convincing of the merits of further integration as their opinions are not without a firm knowledgeable foundation. The outliers in terms of knowledge, education and social class are those who do not know what they think about European integration and, to a lesser degree, those who want to withdraw completely from the EU.

What underlies attitudes towards the EU?

Previous research into attitudes towards European integration has come up with various competing explanations of the factors underlying public support or opposition. Some commentators have emphasised economic motivations for supporting the growth of the EU (Eichenberg and Dalton, 1993; Gabel and Palmer, 1995; Anderson and Reichert, 1996). Some have emphasised growing cosmopolitanism in response to changing values (Inglehart, 1977, Inglehart, Rabier and Reiff 1991). Others have discovered the failure to create a postnational identity as a source of opposition to the EU (Deflem and Pampel, 1996). And still others attribute the causes of support or opposition to the influence of positive or negative cues from parties (Flickinger, 1994; Anderson, 1998). It is clearly beyond the scope of this chapter to analyse these various strands, but we can provide a picture here of where the main pockets of support and opposition lie and, in particular, how the two sorts of Eurosceptic - the well-informed and the ill-informed - differ from one another.

Economic and political self-interest

One obvious source of support for, or opposition towards, integration is people's view of its likely economic and political costs and benefits. We therefore asked respondents whether they thought that closer links with the EU would give Britain more or less influence in the world and whether they thought it would make Britain stronger or weaker economically.

Effect of closer links with the EU

Closer links with the EU would give Britain ...	1993	1994	1995	1997
	%	%	%	%
More influence in the world	30	32	27	30
Less influence in the world	16	17	17	15
Would make no difference	48	46	51	44
Don't know	6	6	5	11
Closer links with the EU would make Britain ...	%	%	%	%
Stronger economically	36	40	32	33
Weaker economically	22	20	20	20
Would make no difference	31	29	39	32
Don't know	12	10	9	15
Base	*1461*	*1165*	*1227*	*1355*

Twice as many people thought that closer links with the EU would give Britain more influence in the world (30 per cent) than those who thought the opposite (15 per cent). Similarly, a third thought that closer links with the EU would make Britain stronger economically, while only fifth thought the opposite.

It is hardly surprising that people's answers to these questions are strongly linked to their attitudes to more or less integration. But it is certainly surprising that we find that public opinion on the economic and political costs and benefits of closer links with the EU have not, in fact, changed in any systematic way since we first included the questions in the *British Social Attitudes* series in 1993. This is despite the drop in general support for integration over the same period. Underlying perceptions of the EU and its role seem to survive independently of people's views of the merits or otherwise of further integration.

Given the importance of monetary union, it is worth examining in detail what people think will happen if Britain enters the EMU. As the next table shows, views are mixed. Only a small proportion believes it will have a beneficial effect on mortgage rates and a majority believe that trade with Europe will be enhanced. On the other hand, a larger minority believes it will increase unemployment in Britain and a majority believes that Britain will lose its ability to set its own tax and spending plans.

If Britain joins the single currency ...

	All respondents	Those who would like to replace £	Those who would like to keep £ only
Percent who agree that...			
... unemployment in Britain will become higher	32	14	42
... mortgage rates will become lower	9	16	7
... Britain will lose its ability to decide its own tax and spending plans	59	36	71
... Britain will trade more successfully in Europe	54	88	42
Base	*1355*	*225*	*839*

As the table shows, people's views about the consequences of Britain's joining EMU are predictably associated with their support or otherwise for joining. So, as many as 42 per cent of those who oppose the Euro in Britain also believe that it would bring about more unemployment, compared with only 14 per cent of those who want Britain to adopt the Euro as a single currency.

Perceived threats to culture and national identity

Another possible explanation of people's support for or opposition to the EU is their attitudes towards the preservation of cultural and national identity.

For instance, concerns about levels of immigration are apparent either explicitly or implicitly in many Western societies. These concerns are always likely to surface in debates about the removal of passport controls within the EU, or about the ceding of national powers of immigration control to the EU. We asked our sample whether "all passport controls between countries in the EU should be removed", and more than twice as many people opposed the idea than supported it (54 per cent, compared with 25 per cent).

There is, of course, the expected relationship between attitudes to passport controls and attitudes to European integration. Thus, while 36 per cent of those who would like to see passport controls removed also support an extension of EU powers, only 19 per cent of those who favour the retention of national passport controls do so.

There is also a link between attitudes to integration and concern over the possible threat that it might pose to cultural traditions. Overall, some 45 per cent of respondents agree with the proposition that "in a united Europe, the various nations will lose their culture and individuality". Of these, 29 per cent came from the small group who want to leave the EU, while only 12 per cent came from the group who want to strengthen the EU's powers.

Interestingly, though, national identity *per se* did not prove a strong source of opposition to European integration. When we tested whether there was any conflict between feelings of, say, 'Britishness' and endorsing European integration, we found too weak a relationship to matter. A similar lack of conflict between feelings of national pride and support for European integration has been observed in other EU member states (Domm, 1998). So, although people's attitudes to European integration are by no means based solely on economic considerations, other factors seem to play a smaller role in explaining variation.

The EU and political partisanship

We turn now to the effects that parties might have on attitudes towards the EU. Parties seek both to form opinion and, if they wish to be electorally successful, to respond to public attitudes and preferences. Most commentary on British public attitudes towards European integration have emphasised the role of party political leadership in influencing public opinion. In recent years, however, the signals sent to the party faithful have been going through a state of flux. The Labour Party, for instance, shifted from advocating withdrawal from the European Economic Community without a referendum in 1983, to strong support by 1989 (George and Rosamund, 1992; Heath and Jowell, 1994), and then to a rather less fixed position just before and since the last election. The Conservatives, in contrast, who were the main pro-European party of the 1970s, have become markedly more Eurosceptical ever since and openly split over the issue - with, perhaps, damaging electoral consequences (Evans, 1998). Not surprisingly, however, such divisions between party supporters are less clear-cut.

Britain's long-term EU policy, by vote in 1992 and 1997

	1992			1997		
	Conser-vative	Labour	Lib Dem	Conser-vative	Labour	Lib Dem
	%	%	%	%	%	%
to leave the EU	20	14	21	17	16	14
to stay in the EU and try to reduce the EU's powers	42	24	28	59	39	41
to leave things as they are	15	21	16	11	16	16
to stay in the EU and try to increase the EU's powers	11	21	19	5	13	15
to work for the formation of a single European govt	5	9	7	4	9	6
Base	*1105*	*829*	*414*	*637*	*1096*	*387*

Note: data from the 1992 and 1997 *British General Election Studies*

Using data from the *British General Election Studies*, we find that voters in all main parties have become more Eurosceptic in the period 1992 to 1997. In 1992, Labour voters were a little less likely than Conservative voters to favour withdrawal, but by 1997 this difference had disappeared. At the same time, there is a noticeable convergence in the attitudes of Labour and Liberal Democrat supporters and hence the increased appearance of isolation of the Conservatives - probably a result of the more hard-core character of the reduced Conservative vote in 1997 than of actual vote switching by people with strong attitudes on Europe. On the other hand, there is also some evidence to support the view that attitudes to Europe did have a smallish effect on the 1997 vote (Evans, 1998; Heath et al., 1998).

In the main, however, it is politicians themselves who are most in dispute over the EU. We know this from the results of the British Candidate Survey, also conducted in 1997.[5] While over eight in ten Conservative MPs wished to reduce EU influence, only one in ten Labour MPs did so. Similar patterns were found in 1992 (Evans, 1995). This is in sharp contrast to public attitudes which are much more ambivalent and less polarised. This is not perhaps surprising, as only 36 per cent of respondents agreed with the statement that "it doesn't really matter which party wins the next general election, Britain's relations with the EU will stay much the same".

Conclusions

Underlying the thrust of this chapter has been a concern to address the issue of whether Britain can be part of Europe without alienating public opinion to a degree that many, including the leaders of the main political parties, would find unacceptable. In recent years we have seen clear evidence of declining support for integration as people have linked their policy preferences on issues such as EMU to their attitude towards integration more generally. It is not simply a case of a need for education about the EU: as we have seen, the most informed are also often those who want European influence to be limited. Indeed, as we have argued above, recent increases in attention to European issues probably underlie the drop in support for integration.

At the same time, the recent small recovery of pro-integration attitudes between 1996 and 1997 suggests that the cause is by no means in inexorable decline. It also remains the case that only a small (though slowly growing) proportion of people favour British withdrawal from the EU. Even most informed Eurosceptics, people who are likely to be influential as 'opinion formers', do not support British withdrawal. That option is favoured most by the less well-informed on Europe and the less highly educated generally.

We should note too that British scepticism about the EMU is not in any way unique. Surveys in Germany, Austria, Denmark, Sweden and Finland all attest to the fact that majorities of those populations are also opposed to monetary union. Indeed, as in Britain, public attitudes in other EU member states witnessed a steady increase in support for the EU until 1991. Only after the Maastricht Treaty in December of that year did levels of public support begin to drop almost everywhere with little subsequent recovery (Royal Institute of International Affairs, 1997). Yet, despite growing public scepticism, countries like Germany nonetheless continue to play a central role in the integrative process. So the British do not seem unusual among member states either in their reduced support for integration in general or in their particular scepticism about monetary union.

How far then does British public support for, and opposition to, different options for Britain's role in the EU actually extend? We tackled that broad question head-on in the 1997 survey by asking plainly whether Britain should use its influence in future to help turn the EU into either a "trading bloc alone" or a "closer political and economic union". This broad dichotomy is, in a sense, the nub of the issue for the future of Britain's role in the EU, at the heart of what the broad direction of Britain's policy ought to be. And, predictably perhaps, the British public turns out to be split perfectly down the middle in their responses, with 44 per cent supporting each option.

Given this divided state of public opinion, how might the issue unfold over the next few years with a referendum on EMU in prospect? A great deal will depend on how the political parties behave. Particularly as far as the Conservatives are concerned, since their policies are still more in flux, they will have to decide whether outright Euroscepticism is likely to be a vote winner or loser, bearing in mind that serious party splits on any issue tend to be vote losers. They will know that attitudes towards the EU have not in the past been *strong* determinants of voting intention, nor linked consistently with any single party. So the Conservative calculus (as if this were really all that mattered in determining party policies) would involve weighing the potential benefit of championing and marshalling a reasonably promising anti-integration campaign, against the potential harm of damaging their party fabric and losing some core and influential support in the process.

The Labour Party in contrast will have its own problems. It has promised a referendum and given its unambiguous support to eventual British membership of the EMU. It has a large and, for the moment anyway, impervious majority in the House of Commons. The idea of a referendum has strong public support. Indeed, only 15 per cent of our 1997 respondents believed that it should be up to MPs to decide "whether or not Britain should replace the pound by a single European currency". Three-quarters (74 per cent) opted instead for a referendum. Labour Party strategists will be aware, however, that the way people are likely to vote in a referendum on joining the EMU will not turn solely on attitudes to Britain's future role in the EU. Even if it did, we have seen that the public's ambivalence about the EU suggests that the result is far from certain. Added to this problem, however, is the near-certainty that for many voters the issue at stake will not be Britain's role in the EU but the much more salient one, perhaps, of a fear of a change in their currency.

The only absolute certainty is that this story will run and run.

Notes

1. The wording of questions about the EU has altered over the years to fit common usage. This question referred to 'the EEC - the Common Market' until 1989; to 'EC - the Common Market' in 1990; to 'the European Community' in 1991 and 1992; and to the 'European Union' in 1997. This chapter refers to 'the EU' throughout.
2. Given the vulnerability of survey responses to the framing and wording of questions it is always wise to look beyond a single indicator of pro- anti-integration sentiment. Thus Evans (1995) finds rather different estimates of trends in support depending on which questions are used to assess it. Using figures obtained from the Eurobarometer series, Janssen (1991) also presents evidence on the difficulties of interpreting trends in attitudes towards integration using just a single item.
3. See Fishkin (1995) and Luskin *et al.* (1998).
4. Such 'knowledge quizzes' have been used effectively to examine knowledge of other areas on which the public might be considered to be hazily informed, such as science and technology (Durant *et al.*, 1989) and the political system (Martin *et al.*, 1993), and to look at the relationship between knowledge and public attitudes (Evans and Durant, 1995; Park, 1995).
5. The 1997 British Representation Study was a national survey of prospective parliamentary candidates and MPs from all major parties standing in the 1997 British general election. The project was directed by Pippa Norris in collaboration with Joni Lovenduski, Anthony Heath, Roger Jowell and John Curtice. The figures presented here are based on samples of 57 Conservative and 161 Labour MPs.

References

Ajzen, I. and Fishbein, M. (1980), *Understanding Attitudes and Predicting Social Behavior*, Englewood Cliffs NJ.: Prentice Hall.

Anderson, C.J. (1998 forthcoming), 'When in doubt use proxies: attitudes towards domestic politics and support for European integration', *Comparative Political Studies*, **31**.

Anderson, C.J. and Reichert, M.S. (1996), 'Economic benefits and support for membership in the EU: a cross-national analysis', *Journal of Public Policy*, **15**: 231-49.

Converse, P. (1964), 'The structure of belief systems in mass publics' in Apter, D. (ed.) *Ideology and Discontent*, New York: Free Press.

Curtice, J. and Gray, R. (1995), 'Deliberative poll shows voters keen on Europe when fully informed', *New Statesman and Society*, 16th June.

Curtice, J. and Jowell, R. (1998), 'Is there really a demand for constitutional change?', *Scottish Affairs*, Special Issue on Understanding Constitutional Change.

Deflem, M. and Pampel, F.C. (1996), 'The myth of postnational identity: popular support for European unification', *Social Forces*, **75**: 119-43.

Domm, R. (1998), *Public Opinion for European Integration: Interpreting the Evidence*. Unpublished M.Phil Thesis, University of Oxford.

Durant, J.R. Evans, G. and Thomas, G.P. (1989), 'The public understanding of science', *Nature*, **340**: 11-14.

Eichenberg, R.C. and Dalton, R.J. (1993), 'Europeans and the European Community: the dynamics of public support for European integration', *International Organization*, **47**: 507-34.

Evans, G. (1995), 'The state of The Union: attitudes towards Europe', in Jowell, R., Curtice, J., Park, A. and Brook, L. (eds.) *British Social Attitudes: the 12th Report*, Aldershot: Dartmouth.

Evans, G. (1998 forthcoming), 'Euroscepticism and Conservative electoral support: how an asset became a liability', *British Journal of Political Science,* **28**.

Evans, G. and Durant, J.R. (1995), 'The relationship between knowledge and attitudes in the public understanding of science in Britain', *Public Understanding of Science*, **4**: 57-74.

Evans, G. (1999 forthcoming), 'Europe: A New Electoral Cleavage?', Evans, G. and Norris, P. (eds.) *A Critical Election? The 1997 British Election in Long-term Perspective,* London: Sage.

Evans, G., Heath, A. and Payne, C. (1999 forthcoming), 'Class: Labour as a Catch-All Party?' Evans, G. and Norris, P. (eds.) *A Critical Election? The 1997 British Election in Long-term Perspective,* London: Sage.

Fishkin, J.S. (1995), *The Voice of the People: public opinion and democracy*, New Haven: Yale University Press.

Flickinger, R.S. (1994), 'British political parties and public attitudes towards the European Community: leading, following or getting out of the way?', Broughton, D.,Farrell, D.M., Denver, D. and Rallings, C. (eds.) *British Elections and Parties Yearbook 1994*, London: Frank Cass.

Franklin, M., Marsh, M. and McLaren, L. (1994), 'Uncorking the bottle: popular opposition to European unification in the wake of Maastricht', *Journal of Common Market Studies* **32**: 455-72.

Gabel, M. and Palmer, H.D. (1995), 'Understanding variation in public support for European integration', *European Journal of Political Research*, **27**: 3-19.

George, S. and Rosamund, B. (1992), 'The European Community' in Smith, M.J. and Spear, J. (eds.) *The Changing Labour Party*, London: Routledge.

Heath, A. and Jowell, R. (1994), 'Labour's policy review' in Heath, A., Jowell, R. and Curtice, J. (eds.) *Labour's Last Chance?*, Aldershot: Dartmouth.

Heath, A., Jowell, R., Taylor, B. and Thomson, K. (1998), 'Euroscepticism and the Referendum Party' in Denver, D., Fisher, J., Cowley, P. and Pattie, C. (eds.) *British Elections and Parties Review, Vol 8: The 1997 General Election*, London: Frank Cass.

Inglehart, R. (1977), *The Silent Revolution*, Princeton: Princeton University Press.

Inglehart, R., Rabier, J.-R. and Reiff, K. (1991), 'The evolution of public attitudes towards European integration: 1970-86', in Reiff, K. and Inglehart, R. (eds.), *Eurobarometer: The dynamics of European Public Opinion,* London: Macmillan.

Janssen, J.I.H. (1991), 'Postmaterialism, cognitive mobilization and public support for European integration' *British Journal of Political Science*, **21**: 443-68.

Lindberg L.N. and Scheingold S.A. (1970), *Europe's Would-be Polity,* Englewood Cliffs NJ: Prentice-Hall.

Luskin, R.C., Fishkin, J.S., Jowell, R. and Park, A. (1998) 'Learning and Voting in Britain: Insights from the Deliberative Poll' presented at the annual meeting of the International Society of Political Psychology, July 12-15, 1998, Montreal, Canada.

Martin, J., Heath, A., Ashworth, K. and Jowell, R. (1993), *Development of a Short Quiz to Measure Political Knowledge*, JUSST Working Paper 21, London: SCPR.

Park, A. 'Teenagers and their politics' in Jowell, R., Curtice, J., Park, A., Brook, L. and Ahrendt, D. (eds) (1995), *British Social Attitudes: the 12th Report*, Aldershot: Dartmouth.

Royal Institute of International Affairs (1997), *An Equal Partner: Britain's role in a changing Europe*, London: Royal Institute of International Affairs.

Sniderman, P.M., Tetlock, P.E. and Brody, R.A. (1991), *Reasoning and Choice: Explorations in Political Psychology,* Cambridge: Cambridge University Press.

Acknowledgement

SCPR is grateful to the Gatsby Charitable Foundation for their financial support for the 1997 *British Social Attitudes* survey, which enabled us to ask the questions reported in this chapter, and to the Royal Institute of International Affairs for their help in designing the module.

Appendix I
Technical details of the surveys

This appendix describes in brief the various surveys on which the data presented in this report are based.

The data for the chapter by Geoffrey Evans is drawn from a module of questions about Europe asked in the 1997 *British Social Attitudes* survey. The data for all the other chapters stem from annual national surveys conducted by countries participating in the *International Social Survey Programme* (ISSP). Since 1985, the members of the ISSP[1] have each undertaken to run a short survey on an agreed topic, usually as a bolt-on to large national surveys. Further information about the annual national surveys conducted by the countries participating in the ISSP between 1985 and 1997 may be obtained from the respective organisations that conduct them, or from the German *Zentralarchiv* (ZA) at the University of Cologne. The details provided in this Appendix are derived from the ISSP Codebooks published by the *Zentralarchiv*[2] (ZA, 1993; 1995a; 1995b; 1996; 1998) and from its web site: http://www.issp.org/homepage.htm.

This Report largely focuses on data from the modules fielded between 1991 and 1997. The 1985 to 1990 surveys are introduced only where they provide a time series for the 1991 to 1997 modules. Technical information in this appendix also concentrates on the 1991 to 1997 surveys. Details are given for all ISSP member countries from the EU and Eastern Europe included within the Report.

EU countries included in this Report

Austria

The Institut für Soziologie (IS) at the University of Graz is responsible for the Austrian part of the ISSP. The IS conducts the Austrian social survey - *Sozialer Survey Österreich (SSÖ)* to which the ISSP is often a self-completion supplement. In years when the SSÖ is not being fielded ISSP modules are administered alongside other surveys carried out by the IS.

The samples used by SSÖ and other surveys containing ISSP modules are designed to be representative of adults in the republic of Austria and use a three-stage sampling method:

- *sampling points* are selected within each Bundesland (region) according to the population size of each point;

- *households* within each sampling point are selected using addresses drawn randomly from the electoral register;

- *individuals* are randomly selected for interview in each household, using a fixed random number.

The 1991 and 1992 modules were fielded together in 1993. The 1993 and 1994 modules were also combined and were fielded in 1995/6. The fieldwork was carried out as follows:

1992	*Social Inequality II,* **and** *1991 module* Religion	:	Feb - March 1993 (SSÖ)
1994	*Family and Changing Gender Roles II,* **and** *1993 module Environment I*	:	Dec 1995 - Jan 1996
1995	*National Identity*	:	June - July 1995
1996	*Role of Government III*	:	Information not available
1997	*Work Orientations II*	:	Information not available

Response rates are as follows:

	1992[1]		1994		1995	
	No	%	No	%	No	%
Issued			1472		1548	
Adjusted sample (eligible)			1387	100	1466	100
Completed ISSP q'aires	1027		977	70	1007	69

[1] The ZA codebook does not contain full details for 1992

The datasets are weighted using data from the most recent Austrian Mizrocensus. In 1995 the weighting criteria were:

> Bundesland
> Size of community
> Sex
> Age
> Employment status / Professional status

Further information may be obtained from:

> Professor Dr. Max Haller
> Institute of Sociology
> University of Graz
> Universitatsstrase 15/G4
> 8010 Graz
> AUSTRIA
> MAX.HALLER@KFUNIGRAZ.AC.AT
> http://www.kfunigraz.ac.at/sozwww/

Britain

In Britain, the ISSP questions are fielded in the *British Social Attitudes* (BSA) surveys - an annual survey series that has been running since 1983. It is designed and carried out by SCPR, core-funded by the Gatsby Charitable Foundation, one of the Sainsbury Family Charitable Trusts, and financially supported by additional contributions from government departments, other research bodies and foundations, quasi-government organisations and industry. Data are collected by computer-assisted personal interview and on a follow-up self-completion questionnaire (on which the ISSP questions are asked).

Each survey is designed to yield a representative sample of adults aged 18 and over, living in private households. Since 1993, the sampling frame for the survey has been the Postcode Address File (PAF), a list of addresses (or postal delivery points) compiled by the Post Office. Between 1983 and 1990, the Electoral Register (ER) was used as the sampling frame. In 1991 a 'split-run' experiment was carried out using ER and PAF sampling. This confirmed that a change from ER to PAF would have a minimal impact, if any, on response rates or sample composition. The PAF sampling method involves a multi-stage design, with three separate stages of selection. In a typical year:

- *postcode sectors* are selected systematically from a list of all postal sectors in Great Britain, with probability proportional to the number of addresses in each sector. Before selection, postal sectors are stratified on the basis of Registrar General's Standard Region, population density and percentage of owner occupation;

- *addresses* are selected in each of the 200 sectors, by starting from a random point on the list and choosing each address at a fixed interval, giving a sample of 6,000 addresses;

- one *individual* at each address is chosen by a random procedure selecting from all those in the household eligible for inclusion in the sample (adults aged over 18).

Fieldwork is carried out during the spring of each year, the bulk of interviewing generally taking place in April and May. In 1992 and 1997 the procedures differed because in those years SCPR carried out post-election studies. In 1992 there was no BSA and the ISSP module was implemented as a postal self-completion questionnaire and sent to respondents of the 1991 survey who had said they were willing to help again, had returned a self-completion questionnaire in 1991 and had *not* been selected to take part in the ISSP environment module pilot in April 1992. In 1997, a smaller version of the BSA was run in addition to the post-election study. It was fielded earlier in the year with the bulk of fieldwork taking place in February to April. The response rates for the six surveys are as follows:

	1991		1992		1993		1994	
	No	%	No	%	No	%	No	%
Issued	4752		2067		4928		6000	
In scope (eligible)	4378	100	1920	100	4309	100	5320	100
Interview achieved	2918	67	n.a.		2945	68	3469	65
Self completion q'aire returned								
(i) Both versions	2481	57	n.a.		2567	60	2929	55
(ii) ISSP version	1257	57	1053	55	1261	59	993	56
Proportion of respondents to the main q'aire who returned the ISSP q'aire		85		n.a.		87		84

	1995		1996		1997	
	No	%	No	%	No	%
Issued	6000		6000		2490	
In scope (eligible)	5251	100	5374	100	2136	100
Interview achieved	3633	69	3662	68	1355	63
Self completion q'aire returned						
(i) Both versions	3135	60	3119	58	n.a.	
(ii) ISSP version	1058	61	1002	57	1080	51
Proportion of respondents to the main q'aire who returned the ISSP q'aire		86		85		80

Note: in 1991 and 1993 two (randomly allocated) versions of the questionnaire were fielded with the ISSP question on one version (half the sample); from 1994 to 1996 the number of versions increased to three each year with the ISSP question on one version (a third of the sample). In 1997 only one version of the questionnaire was fielded.

A more detailed statement of response, by questionnaire version and by Standard Region, is included in Appendix B of the annual Technical Reports of the *British Social Attitudes* survey.

Where necessary, two postal reminders are sent to respondents in an effort to obtain the self-completion supplement. Since the overall proportion returning the supplement each year is high, no weighting is applied to correct for differential non-response.

Each year the data are weighted. Firstly, the PAF does not contain any information about how many 'dwelling units' there are at each address; so in cases where we find that there are several dwelling units at the same postal address corrective weights need to be applied. The data are also weighted to take account of the fact that individuals in large households have a lower chance than individuals in small households of being included in the sample. Users of the *Zentralarchiv* Codebooks should note that the tabulated data presented there are unweighted; for most purposes, analysts should use weighted data.

Full technical details of the six surveys can be found in Brook *et al.* (1992), Brook *et al.* (1993), Ahrendt and Brook (1995), Brook *et al.* (1996), Lilley *et al.* (1997), Lilley *et al.* (1998), Bryson *et al.* (1999 forthcoming). Further information may be obtained from:

> Alison Park
> SCPR
> Northampton Square
> London EC1V 0AX
> BRITAIN
> A.Park@scpr.ac.uk

Germany

ALLBUS (*Allgemeine Bevölkerungsumfrage der Sozialwissenschaftern*), conducted biennially since 1980, is the German general social survey and, like BSA, is a replicating time-series. The research and development side of ALLBUS is carried out at the *Zentrum für Umfragen, Methoden und Analysen* (ZUMA) in Mannheim. The *Zentralarchiv für Empirische Sozialforschung* (ZA) in Cologne archives and distributes the data and provides ALLBUS codebooks. ALLBUS was extended to cover eastern Germany[*] in 1990. In even years between 1986 and 1996 the German ISSP was fielded as part of the ALLBUS, in 1991 it was fielded as part of a special

---

[*] By western Germany we mean the geographical area known until unification as the Federal Republic of Germany. By eastern Germany we mean the area formerly known as the German Democratic Republic.

post-reunification ALLBUS, in 1993 and 1998 it was fielded as part of the *Sozialwissenschaften-Bus* (an omnibus survey organised for social science researchers), and in 1995 and 1997 it was conducted as a stand alone mail survey.

Each survey is designed to be a representative sample of adults (aged 18 and over) living in private households in Germany, including German speaking foreigners. A three-stage stratified design is used: selection of sampling points; selection of households within those points by a random route method; and at each household selection of an eligible German national or German speaking foreigner. The fieldwork is contracted out. The ISSP data are collected on a self-completion questionnaire. When fielded with the ALLBUS it is filled in following the main ALLBUS interview. Fieldwork was carried out as follows:

1991	*Religion I*	:	May - July 1991 (ALLBUS Baseline)
1992	*Social Inequality II*	:	May - June 1992 (ALLBUS)
1993	*Environment I*	:	May - July 1993 (SOWI-BUS)
1994	*Family and Changing Gender Roles II*	:	Feb - April 1994 (East) May 1994 (West) (ALLBUS)
1995	*National Identity*	:	March - May 1995 (mail survey using panel of 1994 respondents)
1996	*Role of Government III*	:	February - June 1996 (ALLBUS)
1997	*Work Orientations II*	:	February - May 1997 (mail survey using panel of 1996 respondents)

The table below shows the response rates in each year:

| | 1991 | | | | 1992 | | | |
| | Western Germany | | Eastern Germany | | Western Germany | | Eastern Germany | |
	No	%	No	%	No	%	No	%
Issued	2900		2720		4650		2100	100
Adjusted sample (eligible)	2875	100	2712	100	4625	100	2100	55
Achieved interviews	1517	53	1544	57	2400	52	1148	52
Completed ISSP q'aires	1346	50	1486	55	2297	50	1094	
% of respondents who returned the ISSP q'aire		89		96		96		95

| | 1993 | | | | 1994 | | | |
| | Western Germany | | Eastern Germany | | Western Germany | | Eastern Germany | |
	No	%	No	%	No	%	No	%
Issued	1680		1680		4847		2174	
Adjusted sample (eligible)	1440	100	1498	100	4402	100	2007	100
Achieved interviews	n.a.		n.a.		2342	53	1108	55
Completed ISSP q'aires	1014	70	1092	73	2324	53	1097	55
% of respondents who returned the ISSP q'aire		n.a.		n.a.		99		99

| | 1995 | | | | 1996 | | | |
| | Western Germany | | Eastern Germany | | Western Germany | | Eastern Germany | |
	No	%	No	%	No	%	No	%
Issued	2342		1108		4939		2246	
Adjusted sample (eligible)	2259	100	1092	100	4430	100	2058	100
Achieved interviews	n.a.		n.a.		2402	54	1116	54
Completed ISSP q'aires	1282	57	612	56	2361	53	1109	54
% of respondents who returned the ISSP q'aire		n.a.		n.a.		98		99

| | 1997 | | | |
| | Western Germany | | Eastern Germany | |
	No	%	No	%
Issued	2519		1192	
Adjusted sample (eligible)	2398	100	1124	100
Achieved interviews	n.a.		n.a.	
Completed ISSP q'aires	1192	50	513	47
% of respondents who returned the ISSP q'aire		n.a.		n.a.

The datasets are not weighted. Further details are given in Bandilla *et al.* (1992) and Braun *et al.* (1993), Wasmer *et al.* (1996), Harkness, J. (1996a), Harkness, J. (1996b), Harkness, J. (1998). Further information may be obtained from:

> Dr. Janet A. Harkness
> ZUMA
> B2,1 PO BOX 12 21 55
> 68072 Mannheim
> GERMANY
> harkness@zuma-mannheim.de
> http://www.issp.org

Italy

The *Indagine Sociale Italiana* (ISI) is an annual series of surveys carried out by the *Ricerca Sociale e di Marketing Institute* (EURISKO) in Milan. Since 1985, the surveys have included the ISSP questionnaire modules, administered either as a self-completion supplement to the main ISI questionnaire or as an interviewer-assisted supplement. EURISKO also co-operates with POLEIS, a research centre at Bocconi University, on the ISSP survey.

The sample for each ISI survey is designed to be representative of the population of Italy aged between 18 and 74. A national two stage probability sample is used selecting:

- *small geographical areas or administrative units* are selected to yield a probability sample of primary sampling units (PSUs); areas and units had been pre-stratified according to sex, age and population density;

- a pre-specified number of *households* (or dwelling units) within each PSU;

- one *individual* (aged 18 to 74) is selected within each household by quota methods.

Comparable response rates cannot be calculated owing to the use of quota sampling methods.

				Achieved interviews
1991	*Religion I*	:	April 1990	983
1992	*Social Inequality II*	:	Information not available	996
1993	*Environment I*	:	May 1993	1000
1994	*Family and Changing Gender Roles II*	:	June - July 1994	1021
1995	*National Identity*	:	November 1995	1094
1996	*Role of Government III*	:	Information not available	-
1997	*Work Orientations II*	:	Information not available	-

Corrective weights have been applied to the data for all six surveys to adjust for population size, sex, age and occupation (based on 1991 Census estimates).

Further information may be obtained from:

Giovanna Guidorossi
EURISKO
Via Monte Rosa 15
20149 Milano
ITALY
WALDEN@IDEA.IT

The Netherlands

The ISSP in the Netherlands is the responsibility of the *Sociaal en Cultureel Planbureau* (SCP) in the Hague. SCP is a government agency which conducts surveys on social and cultural welfare issues in the Netherlands, as mandated by its terms of reference (see SCP, 1986). It conducts an annual face-to-face survey *Cultural Change in The Netherlands* and normally fields the ISSP module with this as a self-completion questionnaire for respondents to fill out after the main interview. In 1996 it was not possible to include the ISSP module because another government survey took precedence. SCP produces a biennial publication *The Social and Cultural Report* which covers matters such as health care, employment, social security, the media and issues relating to political participation and the government. An English version is available.

Samples are drawn from a list of addresses as used by the postal service. All towns with 15,000 addresses or more are selected, with a sample of smaller towns chosen at random (their chance of selection being proportional to their size).

At each sampling point, interviewers are provided with a 'starting address', from which they proceed to other addresses according to strict 'random route' guidelines. At each household, the interviewer attempts to interview the 'head of household'; where there are more than one (for example husband and wife) one is selected for interview according to predetermined rules. If they fail to achieve an interview at any address (after at least three calls) they are given a new 'starting address' and seek and interview in the same way. Comparable response rates cannot be calculated owing to the use of replacement starting addresses.

				Achieved interviews
1991	*Religion I*	:	Throughout the year	1638
1992	*Social Inequality II*	:	Not fielded	-
1993	*Environment I*	:	October 1993 - January 1994	1852
1994	*Family and Changing Gender Roles II*	:	October 1994 - January 1995	1968
1995	*National Identity*	:	September '95 - January 1996	2031
1996	*Role of Government III*	:	Not fielded	-
1997	*Work Orientations II*	:	October 1997 - January 1998	2032

No weights are applied to the data. For more information contact:

Jos Becker
Ministry of VWS/SCP
Parnassusplein 5
2511 VX The Hague
NETHERLANDS
J.BECKER@SCP.NL

Republic of Ireland

In common with some other ISSP member countries, the Republic of Ireland has no suitable regular national survey on which to field the annual ISSP module. Since 1988, ISSP modules have been fielded as part of nation-wide special purpose surveys.

For each survey, two stage probability samples are drawn, the first stage being District Electoral Divisions and the second, electors aged 18 and over. The fieldwork timetable and the response rates are set out below:

1991	*Religion I*	:	September - November 1991
1992	*Social Inequality II*	:	Not fielded
1993	*Environment I*	:	September - October 1993
1994	*Family and Changing Gender Roles II*	:	March 1994
1996	*Role of Government III,* **and** *1995 module National Identity*	:	May - June 1996
1997	*Work Orientations II*	:	Not fielded

	1991		1993		1994[1]		1996	
	No	%	No	%	No	%	No	%
Issued	1575		1500		-		1869	
Adjusted sample (eligible)	1374	100	1243	100	-	-	1700	100
Completed ISSP q'aires	1005	73	957	77	938		998	59

[1]Full details are not available for 1994

Weighting has been used since 1996 using Labour Force Survey statistics for controls on the basis of gender, age cohort and marital status. Further information can be obtained from:

> Conor Ward
> SSRC
> (Social Science Research Centre)
> University College Dublin
> Dublin 4
> REPUBLIC OF IRELAND
> ACOOGAN@ACADAMH.UCD.IE

Spain

The responsibility for fielding ISSP modules is divided between two organisations in Spain, the *Centro de Investigaciones Sociologicas* (CIS), a public non-profit survey research institute, and *Analisis Sociologicos Economicos y Politicos* (ASEP), a private consultancy firm whose main purpose is social, economic and political research. The two bodies carry out the work in alternate years.

The sample is designed to be representative of adults aged 18 and over living in private households in Spain, including the Canary and Balearic Islands, but not Ceuta or Melilla.

Stratified random samples are drawn using the 1991 Census as the source. The municipalities of each of the 17 Autonomous Communities are divided into categories depending on the size of their population. Municipalities are then randomly selected within each category, and within these, electoral sections are also randomly selected. Then random routes are used to select households, and respondents are selected using Kish grids.

The ZA Codebooks do not give information about response rates.

				Achieved interviews
1992	*Social Inequality II*	:	Not fielded	-
1993	*Environment I*	:	July 1994 (ASEP)	1208
1994	*Family and Changing Gender Roles II*	:	September 1994 (CIS)	2494
1995	*National Identity*	:	June 1995 (ASEP)	1230
1996	*Role of Government III*	:	January 1996 (CIS)	-[1]
1997	*Work Orientations II*	:	April 1997 (ASEP)	1211

[1] No information is available for 1996 response

In the years when ASEP fielded the modules (1993, 1995, 1997) optional weights can be applied according to gender and age groups. CIS does not use weighting.

Further information can be obtained from:

> Pilar del Castillo
> CIS
> (Centro de Investigaciones Sociòlógicas)
> Montalbán 8
> 28014 Madrid
> SPAIN
> P.CASTILLO@SOCIOL.ES
>
> Juan Diez-Nicolás
> ASEP
> (Anàlisis Sociòlógicos Económicos y Politicos)
> Pº de la Castellana 173, 5º Izquierda
> 28046 Madrid
> SPAIN
> 100613.2721@COMPUSERVE.COM

Sweden

The ISSP is the responsibility of the Department of Sociology, University of Umeå. Sweden joined the ISSP programme in 1992 having conducted a one-off survey in 1991 which replicated the 1987 ISSP Social Inequality I module. The first full survey Sweden conducted was the 1994 Family and Changing Gender Roles II module. The fieldwork is carried out by public and private opinion polling organisations.

In 1992 and 1994 the sample was designed to be representative of the Swedish population aged between 18 and 74 years; from 1995 it included those aged 18 to 76. It is a one-stage full probability sample of individuals drawn from the Register of the Total Population. The fieldwork, using separate postal surveys, was carried out as follows:

1992	*Social Inequality*	:	February - April 1991 (a Swedish survey on attitudes to inequality using the 1987 ISSP module)
1993	*Environment I*	:	Not fielded
1994	*Family and Changing Gender Roles II*	:	February - May 1994
1995	*National Identity*	:	February - May 1995
1996	*Role of Government III*	:	February - May 1996
1997	*Work Orientations II*	:	February - May 1997

The unweighted response rates are shown below:

	1992		**1994**		**1995**	
	No	%	No	%	No	%
Issued	1498		2000		2000	
Adjusted sample (eligible)	1453	100	1988	100	1988	100
Completed ISSP q'aires	808	56	1272	64	1296	65

	1996		**1997**	
	No	%	No	%
Issued	2000		1999	
Adjusted sample (eligible)	1992	100	1982	100
Completed ISSP q'aires	1238	62	1276	64

Each year a subsample is drawn among those who have still not responded after two subsequent reminders. 50% of them are then selected for telephone interviewing (in 1997 the figure was 70%). Respondents from this subsample are weighted and any calculations should be made using the weight.

Further information can be obtained from:

Stefan Svallfors
Dept. of Sociology
University of Umeå
901 87 UMEÅ
SWEDEN
STEFAN.SVALLFORS@SOC.UMU.SE
http://www.umu.se/soc/

Eastern European countries included in this Report

Bulgaria

The ISSP in Bulgaria was conducted by the Institute for Trade Union and Social Research in Sofia until 1994. Since then the Agency for Social Analyses (ASA), an independent public research organisation has taken over responsibility for the survey. ASA began conducting annual national general social surveys in late 1994. There was no fieldwork in 1996, so the 1996 module was fielded in 1997. The sampling method is a two stage cluster sample, designed to be representative of the Bulgarian population of adults aged 18 or over. At the first stage clusters are randomly selected using the smallest units available in the 1992 population census. At the second stage territorial units within each cluster are selected and at each address one respondent was selected using a Kish grid.

1992	*Social Inequality II*	:	March 1993
1993	*Environment I*	:	March 1994
1994	*Family and Changing Gender Roles II*	:	March 1995
1995	*National Identity*	:	November - December 1995
1997	*Work Orientations II and 1996 module Role of Government III*	:	February - May 1997

	1992		1993		1994	
	No	%	No	%	No	%
Issued	1575		1370		1327	
Adjusted sample (eligible)	1494	100	1260	100	1145	100
Completed ISSP q'aires	1198	80	1183	94	1126	98

	1995		1997	
	No	%	No	%
Issued	1200		1100	
Adjusted sample (eligible)	1159	100	1062	100
Completed ISSP q'aires	1004	87	1012	95

In 1993 and 1994 weighting was calculated using data from the 1992 census. In 1995 the weighting variable was based on education, and in 1997 it was based on education, age and gender. Further information can be obtained from:

Lilia Dimova
Agency for Social Analyses
1 Macedonia Square
1040 Sofia
BULGARIA
ASA@MBOX.CIT.BG

Czech Republic / Czechoslovakia

The Institute of Sociology in the Academy of Sciences of the Czech Republic, Prague, was established in 1990 and is principally focused on the study of Czech society and social issues. The ISSP is fielded as a stand alone survey rather than being attached to a major national survey. The 1992 survey was the last to be conducted across Czechoslovakia as the formation of the separate Czech and Slovakian Republics has meant that the series is now conducted by the respective countries individually. The sample is drawn by multi-stage random selection. In 1992 it involved two stages, first localities were selected and then individuals within these strata were randomly selected using information from the Czechoslovakian Central Register of Population. In 1993 three stages were used to select localities, electoral sectors (voting lists used in the 1992 elections with a population aged 20+), and then respondents. Exclusive quotas were used to bring in 18 and 19 year olds. Access to the Central Register of Population has not been allowed since 1993, so alternative sampling frames have had to be found in subsequent years. In 1994 and 1995, three stages were used again but the sampling frame consisted of households rather than individuals. Quotas were not needed for 18 and 19 year olds as individuals aged 16 to 75 were selected from households. In 1996 and 1997, the sampling used a three stage design from a database of all households paying for electricity, gas, or TV and radio licences in the Czech Republic. The use of quota sampling and substitution means that comparable response rates cannot be calculated.

				Achieved interviews
1992	*Social Inequality II*	:	October - November 1992	1101
1993	*Environment I*	:	November 1993	961
1994	*Family and Changing Gender Roles II*	:	September 1994	1024
1995	*National Identity*	:	October - November 1995	1111
1996	*Role of Government III*	:	October - December 1996	1100
1997	*Work Orientations II*	:	September - December 1997	1080

Weighting can and should be applied to the 1995 dataset as low educated respondents are underrepresented. Weighting has not been applied to any other year.

The Institute publishes two journals which draw on data from the surveys, the Czech Sociological Review (in English) and *Sociologický Casopis* (in Czech), as well as the bulletin *Data a Fakta* (Data and Facts).

Further information can be obtained from:

> Klara Plecita
> Institute of Sociology
> Academy of Sciences of the Czech Republic
> Jilska 1
> 110 00 Praha 1
> CZECH REPUBLIC
> VLACHOVA@SOC.CAS.CZ

Hungary

Each year *Tärsadalomkutátsi Informatikai Egyesulés* (TÁRKI) carries out a national survey representative of the population of Hungary aged 18 and over (TÁRKI-OMNIBUSZ) and the ISSP is usually fielded with this. Apart from 1994 and 1995 (see below) samples are selected in two stages, the first consisting of a cluster of 'settlements' and the second of individuals. Random selection of individuals is based on files at the Population Register Bureau which provide names, home addresses and year of birth. Thus the representativeness of the issued sample is controlled in respect of region, age and gender. Each year respondents are drawn either from a 'fresh' sample or from a 'follow-up' sample of people interviewed earlier. For fresh samples, the Population Register Bureau usually provide 50 to 100 per cent substitute addresses in addition to those issued for the main sample. Thus for a survey of 3,000 cases interviewers would be given 3,000 main cases and 1,500 to 3,000 substitute addresses. When an interview is not achieved, a substitute sample member is randomly selected. This sampling technique was different in 1994 and 1995 because the files at the Population Register Bureau were not available as a consequence of new legislation about personal rights. Sample drawing was still random and was expected to be representative of the Hungarian adult population with regard to sex, age and regional distribution. The procedure used in 1994 and 1995 was based on three stages:

- *Settlements* were selected, weighted by population size taking four types of residential area into consideration (Budapest, county seat town and village);

- *Households* were selected randomly using the 1990 registration data from the Central Statistical Office;

- *Individuals* were then selected randomly from the household members by interviewers using a Kish grid. Only persons over 18 were selected.

In 1991 weighting was applied to the data to correct for over-representation of people with secondary and tertiary education, but researchers are advised to use the weight only to check the results obtained with unweighted data. Since 1992 all the data have been weighted as necessary using the 1990 and 1995 censuses to make the samples representative of the population in terms of region, age group, gender and education. The following table details when the fieldwork was carried out and the number of questionnaires received each year. For the 1991 survey, a random sub-sample of 1,000 adults and 500 substitute addresses was drawn from the 3,000 nation-wide random sample of 1989 TÁRKI survey respondents. The 1992 and 1993 surveys used sub-samples drawn from 3,000 persons interviewed for TÁRKI questionnaires in 1992. The 1994 survey, fielded as part of the post-election study, used a 'fresh' sample. In 1995, 1996 and 1997 'fresh' samples were used and the questionnaires were fielded as part of large TÁRKI surveys. Comparable response rates cannot be calculated owing to the use of substituted addresses.

				Achieved interviews
1991	*Religion I*	:	April - May 1991	1000
1992	*Social Inequality II*	:	October 1992	1250
1993	*Environment I*	:	November - December 1993	1167
1994	*Family and Changing Gender Roles II*:		May - June 1994	1500
1995	*National Identity*	:	October - November 1995	1000
1996	*Role of Government III*	:	October 1996	1500
1997	*Work Orientations II*	:	January 1997	1500

Further information can be obtained from:

> Dr. Peter Robert
> TÁRKI
> (Social Research Informatics Centre)
> Victor Hugo u. 18-22
> 1132 Budapest
> HUNGARY
> ROBERT@TARKI.HU

Poland

The Institute for Social Studies (ISS) at the University of Warsaw, founded in 1991, conducts the *Polish General Social Survey* (PGSS) with which the ISSP is usually fielded; in 1991, however, the ISSP was linked with a national study of work values conducted in co-operation with Cornell University. The ISS is affiliated with the Institute for Social Research,

University of Michigan, and is a member of the Inter-University Consortium for Political and Social Research (ICPSR).

The surveys use a random sample of private households drawn in four stages:

- *primary sampling units* (strata) were selected consisting of:
  - all cities having more than 100,000 inhabitants (in the case of five cities having larger number of inhabitants city districts were established as separate strata);
  - all cities with fewer than 100,000 inhabitants, grouped into four categories according to the number of inhabitants (fewer than 10,000, 10-19 thousand, 20-49 thousand, and 50-100 thousand);
  - rural areas, divided into eight regions;

- *single cities or communities* were then selected separately from each primary unit consisting of cities under 100,000 inhabitants or rural areas. The number of secondary sampling units was proportional to the size of the primary sampling unit they were selected from. All cities having more than 100,000 inhabitants (or their district) automatically became secondary sampling units. Finally, 223 secondary sampling units were selected;

- *households* from each secondary sampling unit were selected. In case of units representing cities having more than 100,000 inhabitants, the number of households drawn was proportional to the size of the unit. Through this procedure 2000 addresses of households were selected;

- *individuals* were selected by interviewers who collected information about the month and year of birth for each person in the household and then selected a respondent from all persons 18 years old or more, using a special selection table (unique for every household).

The fieldwork was carried out as follows:

1991	*Religion I*	:	November - December 1991
1992	*Social Inequality II*	:	No information available (PGSS)
1993	*Environment I*	:	May - June 1993 (PGSS)
1994	*Family and Changing Gender Roles II*	:	May - June 1994 (PGSS)
1995	*National Identity*	:	May - June 1995 (PGSS)
1996	*Role of Government III*	:	No information available
1997	*Work Orientations II*	:	No information available

The response rates are detailed below:

| | **1991** | | **1992** | | **1993** | | **1994** | |
	No	%	No	%	No	%	No	%
Issued	1450		2000		2000		2000	
Adjusted sample (eligible)	1291	100	1947	100	1947	100	1946	100
Completed ISSP q'aires	1063	82	1647	85	1641	84	1597	82

| | **1995** | |
	No	%
Issued	2000	
Adjusted sample (eligible)	1967	100
Completed ISSP q'aires	1598	81

The data were weighted in 1992, 1993 and 1994 on the basis of age, gender and type of residence.

Further information can be obtained from:

> Bogdan Cichomski
> ISS
> (Institute for Social Studies)
> University of Warsaw
> Stawki 5/7
> 00-183 Warsaw
> POLAND
> CICHOM@SAMBA.ISS.UW.EDU.PL
> http://andante.iss.uw.edu.pl/iss/pgss/pgsshome.html

Slovenia

The Public Opinion and Mass Communication Research Centre in the Faculty of Social Sciences, University of Ljubljana has been conducting the Slovene Public Opinion Survey (SJM) since 1968. Additional details can be found in Blejec (1970).

The ISSP modules are fielded with the SJM with half the sample selected to answer the ISSP questions. The survey is a representative probability survey of the residential population which uses systematic multi-stage sampling, drawing data from the Central Register of Population. The use of a replacement procedure for non-response means that comparable response rates cannot be calculated.

				Achieved interviews
1991	*Religion I*	:	November - December 1991	2080
1992	*Social Inequality II*	:	February 1992	1049
1993	*Environment I, and 1994 module Family and Changing Gender Roles II*	:	October - November 1993	1032
1995	*National Identity*	:	November 1994	1036
1996	*Role of Government III*	:	November - December 1996	1004
1997	*Work Orientations II*	:	November 1997	1005

Further information can be obtained from:

> Niko Toš
> Public Opinion and Mass Communications Research Centre
> Faculty for Social Sciences
> University of Ljubljana
> Kardeljeva ploscad 5
> 1000 Ljubljana
> SLOVENIA
> CJMMKSJM@UNI-LJ.SI

Other ISSP member countries

The principal contact names are underlined.

Australia:

> Jonathan Kelley
> Mariah Evans
> International Survey Centre, RSSS
> The Australian National University
> Canberra ACT 0200
> AUSTRALIA
> JONATHAN.KELLEY@ANU.EDU.AU
> http://www.international-survey.org

Bangladesh:

> Q. K. Ahmad
> Chairman of Bangladesh Unnyan Parishad
> 33, Road 4
> Dahanmondi R.A.
> P.O. Box 5007 (New Market)
> Dhaka-1205
> BANGLADESH
> QKA.BUP@DRIK.BGD.TOOLNET.ORG

Canada:

> Alan Frizzell
> Heather Pyman
> School of Journalism and Mass Communications
> Survey Center
> Carleton University
> 346 St. Patrick's Building
> Ottawa
> CANADA KIS 5B6
> AFRIZZ@CCS.CARLETON.CA

Chile: Carla Lehmann
                          Centro de Estudios Publicos
                          Monsenor Sótero Sanz 175
                          Providencia
                          Santiago
                          CHILE
                          HBEYER@IACTIVA.CL

Cyprus: Bambos Papageorgiou
                          Center of Applied Research
                          Cyprus College
                          6 Diogenes Street
                          Engomi
                          P.O. Box 2006
                          Nicosia
                          CYPRUS
                          PPAPAGEO@STING.CYCOLLEGE.AC.CY
                          http://www.cycollege.ac.cy/research/car/car.htm

Denmark: Jørgen Goul Andersen
                          Department of Economics, Politics and Public
                             Administration
                          Aalorg University
                          Fibigerstraede 1
                          DK-9220 Aalborg
                          DENMARK

France: Yannik Lemel
                          FRANCE-ISSP Association
                          (Centre de Recherche en Economie et
                             Statistique)
                          Laboratoire de Sociologie Quantitative
                          Bâtiment Malakoff 2 - Timbre J350
                          15, Boulevard Gabriel Péri
                          92245 Malakoff Cedex
                          FRANCE
                          VOULAMA@ENSAE.FR

P. Brechon
B. Cautres
CIDSP (Centre d'Information des Données
  Socio-Politique)
Institut d'Etudes Politiques de Grenoble
Domaine Universitaire
BP 45
38402 Saint Martin D'Heres Cedex
FRANCE
BRECHON@CIDSP.UPMF-GRENOBLE.FR
CAUTRES@CIDSP.UPMF-GRENOBLE.FR

L. Chauvel
M. Forse
OFCE (Observatoire Française des
  Conjonctures Economiques)
69, Quai d'Orsay
75340 Paris Cedex 07
FRANCE
CHAUVEL@OFCE.SCIENCES-PO.FR
FORSE@OFCE.SCIENCES-PO.FR

A. Degenne
LASMAS (Laboratoire d'Analyse Secondaire et
  de Méthodes Appliquées en Sociologie)
59-61, rue Pouchet
75849 Paris Cedex 07
FRANCE

Israel: Noah Lewin-Epstein
Eppie Yuchtman-Yaar
Dept. of Sociology and Anthropology
Tel Aviv University
PO BOX 39040, Ramat Aviv
69978 Tel Aviv
ISRAEL
NOAH1@SPIRIT.TAU.AC.IL
EPPIE@SPIRIT.TAU.AC.IL

Japan: Noriko Onodera
                    NHK, Broadcasting Culture Research Institute
                    Public Opinion Research Division
                    2-1-1 Atago
                    Minato-ku
                    Tokyo
                    105 JAPAN
                    ONODERA@CULTURE.NHK.OR.JP

Latvia: Aivars Tabuns
                    Institute of Philosophy and Sociology
                    Akademijas Laukums 1
                    LV-1940
                    Riga
                    LATVIA
                    atabuns@lza.ac.lv

New Zealand: Philip Gendall
                    Department of Marketing
                    Massey University
                    Private Bag 11222
                    Palmerston North
                    NEW ZEALAND
                    P.GENDALL@MASSEY.AC.NZ

Norway: Knut Kalgraff Skjåk
                    Bjørn Henrichsen
                    Knud Knudsen
                    Vigdis Kvalheim
                    NSD (Norwegian Social Science Data Services)
                    Hans Homboesgt 22
                    5007 Bergen
                    NORWAY
                    SKJAK@NSD.UIB.NO
                    http://www.uib.no/nsd/

Philippines: Linda Luz Guerrero,
                                Mahar Mangahas, Mercedes Abad,
                                Felipe Miranda, Steven Rood, Ricardo Abad
                                Social Weather Stations, Inc.
                                PSSC Building
                                Commonwealth Avenue
                                Diliman
                                Quezon City 1101
                                PHILIPPINES
                                GUERRERO@SWS.ORG.PH
                                http://www.sws.org.ph

Portugal: Manuel Villaverde Cabral
                                Jorge Vala
                                Instituto de Ciencias Sociais
                                University of Lisbon
                                Av. Forças Armadas
                                Edif. I.S.C.T.E.D.
                                1600 Lisbon
                                PORTUGAL
                                MVCABRAL@ICS.UL.PT
                                http://www.ics.ul.pt/scilu.htm

Russia: Ludmila Khakhulina
                                Tatjana Zaslavskaya
                                The Center for Public Opinion and Market
                                  Research
                                17, Nikolskaya
                                Moscow 103012
                                RUSSIA, CIS
                                LKHAKHUL@SKULL.CC.FC.UL.PT

Slovak Republic: Magdalena Piscova
                                Institute of Sociology
                                Slovak Academy of Sciences
                                Klemensova 19
                                81364 Bratislava
                                SLOVAK REPUBLIC
                                SUPISCOV@KLEMENS.SAVBA.SK

South Africa: James Servada
                           Central Statistical Service
                           Steyn's Arcade
                           274 Schoeman Street
                           Pretoria 0002
                           South Africa
                           JamesS@css.pwv.gov.za

USA: Tom W. Smith
                           James A. Davis
                           NORC
                           (National Opinion Research Center)
                           1155 East 60th Street
                           Chicago, IL 60637
                           USA
                           SMITHT@NORCMAIL.UCHICAGO.EDU
                           http://www.norc.uchicago.edu/

Notes

1. ISSP membership has risen from its four 'founding fathers' in 1985 to 31 countries in 1998.
2. 1991: Ref. ZA-No. 2150; 1992: Ref. ZA-No. 2240; 1993: Ref. ZA-No. 2450; 1994: Ref. ZA-No. 2620; 1995: Ref. ZA-No. 2880.

References

Ahrendt, D. and Brook, L. (1995), *British Social Attitudes, 1993 Survey: Technical Report*, London: SCPR.

Bandilla, W., Gabler, S. and Wiedenbeck, M. (1992), *Methodenberict zum DFG-Projekt ALLBUS Baseline-Studie 1991*, ZUMA-Arbeitsbericht, No. 92/04, Mannheim: ZUMA.

Blejec, M. (1970), *Nacrti in analiza vzorcev za ankete "Slovensko javno mnenje"*, SLM68, *SLM69 in SLM70*, Ljubljana: VSSPN.

Braun, M., Eilinghoff, C., Gabler, S. and Wiedenbeck, M. (1993), *Methodenbericht zur Allgemeinen Bevolkerungsunfrage der Sozialwissenschaften, ALLBUS 1992*, ZUMA Arbeitsbericht, No. 93/01, Mannheim: ZUMA.

Brook, L., Taylor, B., and Prior, G. (1992), *British Social Attitudes, 1991 Survey: Technical Report*, London: SCPR.

Brook, L., Dowds, L. and Ahrendt, D. (1993), *British Social Attitudes, 1992 Survey: Technical Report*, London: SCPR.

Brook, L., Chaudhary, C., Park, P. and Thomson, K. (1996), *British Social Attitudes, 1994 Survey: Technical Report*, London: SCPR.

Bryson, C., Jarvis, L., Park, A. and Thomson, K. (1999 forthcoming), *British Social Attitudes 1997 survey: Technical Report*, London: SCPR.

Harkness, J. (1996a), *ISSP 1993 Environment, ZUMA report on the German study*, ZUMA Arbeitsbericht No. 96/06, Mannheim: ZUMA.

Harkness, J. (1996b) *ISSP 1995, National Identity, ZUMA report on the German study*, ZUMA Arbeitsbericht No. 96/10, Mannheim: ZUMA.

Harkness, J. (1998), *ISSP 1997, Work Orientations, ZUMA report on the German study*, ZUMA Arbeitsbericht (forthcoming), Mannheim: ZUMA.

Lilley, S-J., Brook, L., Park, A. and Thomson, K. (1997), *British Social Attitudes, 1995 Survey: Technical Report*, London: SCPR.

Lilley, S-J., Brook, L., Bryson, C., Jarvis, L., Park, A. and Thomson, K. (1998), *British Social Attitudes, 1996 Survey: Technical Report*, London: SCPR.

SCP (Social and Cultural Planning Office) (1986), *Social and Cultural Report 1986*, Rijswijk: SCP.

Wasmer, M., Koch, A., Harkness, J. and Gabler, S. (1996), *Methodenbericht zum ALLBUS/ISSP 1996*, ZUMA Arbeitsbericht No. 1996/08, Mannheim: ZUMA.

ZA (Zentralarchiv fur Empirische Sozialforschung) (1993), *International Social Survey Programme: Religion - 1991*, Codebook ZA-No. 2150, Mannheim: ZA.

ZA (Zentralarchiv fur Empirische Sozialforschung) (1995a), *International Social Survey Programme: Social Inequality II - 1992*, Codebook ZA-No. 2310, Mannheim: ZA.

ZA (Zentralarchiv fur Empirische Sozialforschung) (1995b), *International Social Survey Programme: Environment - 1993*, Codebook ZA-No. 2450, Mannheim: ZA.

ZA (Zentralarchiv fur Empirische Sozialforschung) (1996), *International Social Survey Programme: Family and Changing Gender Roles II - 1994*, Codebook ZA-No. 2620, Mannheim: ZA.

ZA (Zentralarchiv fur Empirische Sozialforschung) (1998), *International Social Survey Programme: National Identity - 1995*, Codebook ZA-No. 2880, Mannheim: ZA.

Appendix II
Notes on presentation of the data

Notes on tabulations

1. Unless otherwise stated, figures in the tables are from the *International Social Survey Programme* dataset, except for the chapter by Geoffrey Evans where figures are from the 1997 *British Social Attitudes* survey.
2. Tables are percentaged as indicated.
3. In tables, '*' indicates less than 0.5 per cent but greater than zero, and '-' indicates zero.
4. Percentages equal to or greater than 0.5 have been rounded up (e.g. 0.5 per cent = one per cent; 36.5 per cent = 37 per cent).
5. Where ISSP data are used, respondents answering 'don't know' or not giving an answer are excluded from the base, unless otherwise stated. However, where data from the main *British Social Attitudes* dataset are used, such respondents are included in the base - in line with the convention of earlier *British Social Attitudes* Reports. Such answers are not necessarily shown in the tables and this, together with the effects of rounding and weighting, means that percentages will not always add up to 100 per cent.
6. Where tables show the base (the number of respondents who answered the question), this is printed in small italics. The bases are *un*weighted unless otherwise stated.

Sampling errors

No sample precisely reflects the characteristics of the population it represents because of both sampling and non-sampling errors. If a sample were designed as a random sample (if every adult had an equal and independent chance of inclusion in the sample) then we could calculate the sampling error of any percentage, p, using the formula:

$$s.e.\ (p) = \sqrt{\frac{p(100-p)}{n}}$$

where n is the number of respondents on which the percentage is based. Once the sampling error had been calculated, it would be a straightforward exercise to calculate a confidence interval for the true population percentage. For example, a 95 per cent confidence interval would be given by the formula:

$$p \pm 1.96 \times s.e.(p)$$

Clearly, for a simple random sample (srs), the sampling error depends only on the values of p and n. However, simple random sampling is almost never used in practice because of its inefficiency in terms of time and cost.

 As outlined in Appendix I, most ISSP samples, including that used for the *British Social Attitudes* survey, are clustered samples, using a stratified multi-stage design. With a complex design like this, the sampling error of a percentage giving a particular response is not simply a function of the number of respondents in the sample and the size of the percentage; it also depends on how that percentage response is spread within and between sample points. The complex design may be assessed relative to simple random sampling by calculating a range of design factors (DEFTs) associated with it, where

$$DEFT = \sqrt{\frac{\text{Variance of estimator with complex design, sample size } n}{\text{Variance of estimator with srs design, sample size } n}}$$

and represents the multiplying factor to be applied to the simple random sampling error to produce its complex equivalent. A design factor of one means that the complex sample has achieved the same precision as a simple random sample of the same size. A design factor greater than one means the complex sample is less precise than its simple random sample equivalent. If the DEFT for a particular characteristic is known, a 95 per cent confidence interval for a percentage may be calculated using the formula:

$$p \pm 1.96 \times complex\ sampling\ error\ (p)$$

$$= p \pm 1.96 \times DEFT \times \sqrt{\frac{p(100-p)}{n}}$$

For examples of the calculations of complex sampling errors and design effects on *British Social Attitudes* data, see Appendix I to Jowell *et al.* (1997).

Analysis techniques

Attitude scales

A useful way of summarising the information from a number of questions on one topic is to construct an additive index (DeVellis, 1991; Spector, 1992). This approach, which has been used by a number of authors in this Report, rests on the assumption that there is an underlying - 'latent' - attitudinal dimension which characterises the answers to all the questions within the index. If so, scores on the index as a whole are likely to be a more reliable indication of the underlying attitudinal dimension than the answers to any one question. Details of the construction of the indices used in this Report are given in the appendices to the relevant chapters.

Regression

Regression analysis aims to summarise the relationship between a 'dependent' variable and one or more 'independent' variables. It shows how well we can estimate a respondent's score on the dependent variable from knowledge of their scores on the independent variables. It is often undertaken to support a claim that the phenomena measured by the independent variables cause the phenomenon measured by the dependent variable. However, the causal ordering, if any, between the variables cannot be verified or falsified by the technique. Causality can only be inferred through special experimental designs or through assumptions made by the analyst.

All regression analysis assumes that the relationship between the dependent and each of the independent variables takes a particular form. In *linear regression*, the most common form of regression analysis, it is assumed that the relationship can be adequately summarised by a straight line. This means that a one point increase in the value of an independent variable is assumed to have the same impact on the value of the dependent variable on average irrespective of the previous values of those variables.

Strictly speaking the technique assumes that both the dependent and the independent variables are measured on an interval-level scale, although it may sometimes still be applied even where this is not the case. For example, one can use an ordinal variable (e.g. a Likert scale) as a *dependent* variable if one is willing to assume that there is an underlying interval level scale and the difference between the observed ordinal scale and the underlying interval scale is due to random measurement error. Categorical or nominal data can be used as *independent* variables by converting them into dummy or binary variables; these are variables where the only valid scores are 0 and 1, with 1 signifying membership of a particular category and 0 otherwise.

The assumptions of linear regression can cause particular difficulties where the *dependent* variable is binary. The assumption that the relationship between the dependent and the independent variables is a straight line means that it can produce estimated values for the dependent variable of less than 0 or greater than 1. In this case it may be more appropriate to assume that the relationship between the dependent and the independent variables takes the form of an S-curve, where the impact on the dependent variable of a one-point increase in an independent variable becomes progressively less the closer the value of the dependent variable approaches 0 or 1. *Logistic regression* is an alternative form of regression which fits such an S-curve rather than a straight line. The technique can also be adapted to analyse multinomial non-interval level dependent variables, that is, variables which classify respondents into more than two categories.

The two statistical scores most commonly reported from the results of regression analyses are:

A measure of variance explained: This summarises how well all the independent variables combined can account for the variation in respondent's scores in the dependent variable. The higher the measure, the more accurately we are able in general to estimate the correct value of each respondent's score on the dependent variable from knowledge of their scores on the independent variables.

A parameter estimate: This shows how much the dependent variable will change on average, given a one unit change in the independent variable (while holding all other independent variables in the model constant). The parameter estimate has a positive sign if an increase in the value of the independent variable results in an increase in the value of the dependent variable. It has a negative sign if an increase in the value of the independent variable results in a decrease in the value of the dependent variable. If the parameter estimates are standardised, it is possible to compare the relative impact of different independent variables; those variables with the largest standardised estimates can be said to have the biggest impact on the value of the dependent variable.

Regression also tests for the statistical significance of parameter estimates. A parameter estimate is said to be significant at the five per cent level, if the range of the values encompassed by its 95 per cent confidence interval (see also section on sampling errors) are either all positive or all negative. This means that there is less than a five per cent chance that the association we have found between the dependent variable and the independent variable is simply the result of sampling error and does not reflect a relationship that actually exists in the general population.

Factor analysis

Factor analysis is a statistical technique which aims to identify whether there are one or more apparent sources of commonality to the answers given by respondents to a set of questions. It ascertains the smallest number of *factors* (or dimensions) which can most economically summarise all of the variation found in the set of questions being analysed. Factors are established where respondents who give a particular answer to one question in the set, tend to give the same answer as each other to one or more of the other questions in the set. The technique is most useful when a relatively small number of factors is able to account for a relatively large proportion of the variance in all of the questions in the set.

The technique produces a *factor loading* for each question (or variable) on each factor. Where questions have a high loading on the same factor then it will be the case that respondents who give a particular answer to one of these questions tend to give a similar answer to the other questions. The technique is most commonly used in attitudinal research to try to identify the underlying ideological dimensions which apparently structure attitudes towards the subject in question.

References

DeVellis, R.F. (1991), 'Scale development: theory and applications', *Applied Social Research Methods Series*, **26**, Newbury Park: Sage.

Jowell, R., Curtice, J., Park, A., Brook, L., Thomson, K. and Bryson, C. (1997), *British Social Attitudes: the 14th Report - The end of Conservative values?*, Aldershot: Ashgate.

Spector, P.E. (1992), 'Summated rating scale construction: an introduction', *Quantitative Applications in the Social Sciences*, **82**, Newbury Park: Sage.

Appendix III
The questionnaires

The findings which are reported in Chapters 1-8 are based mainly on the seven *International Social Survey Programme* (ISSP) questionnaire modules run in 1991, 1992, 1993, 1994, 1995, 1996, and 1997, with reference for time-series purposes to the earlier ISSP surveys. The English language versions of the questionnaires are reproduced below. Question numbers of the English language version correspond to the question numbers used in SCPR's *British Social Attitudes* survey.

The following ISSP questionnaires are included:

1985	*Role of Government I*
1986	*Social Networks*
1987	*Inequality I*
1988	*Family and Changing Gender Roles I*
1989	*Work Orientations I*
1990	*Role of Government II*
1991	*Religion*
1992	*Inequality II*
1993	*Environment*
1994	*Family and Changing Gender Roles II*
1995	*National Identity*
1996	*Role of Government III*
1997	*Work Orientations II*

Additional questions on the environment were fielded as a separate REAP (*Research into Environment Attitudes and Perceptions in Five EC Countries*) module in 1993. These are shown at the end of the 1993 ISSP module.

Chapter 9 uses data from the 1997 *British Social Attitude* survey. The relevant sections of this questionnaire are included at the end of the appendix. Some of these questions were asked in the face-to-face part of the *British Social Attitudes* interview. Since the face-to-face interview is conducted using computer-assisted interviewing, the questionnaire listing is derived from the Blaise program in which the questionnaire is written. For ease of reference, each item has been allocated a question number. Gaps in the numbering system indicate items that are essential components of the Blaise program but which are not themselves questions, and so have been omitted. The SPSS variable name is given, in brackets and italics, above each question. Above the variable names are the filter instructions. A filter instruction should be considered as staying in force until the next filter instruction.

INTERNATIONAL SOCIAL SURVEY PROGRAMME

1985 MODULE

ROLE OF GOVERNMENT

(ENGLISH LANGUAGE VERSION)

- 1 -

2.01 Suppose a newspaper got hold of confidential government papers about defence plans and wanted to publish them.

PLEASE TICK ONE BOX

	(✓)
Should the newspaper be allowed to publish the papers?	[1]
OR	
Should the government have the power to prevent publication?	[2]
Can't choose	[8]

b) Now suppose the confidential government papers were about economic plans.

PLEASE TICK ONE BOX

	(✓)
Should the newspaper be allowed to publish the papers?	[1]
OR	
Should the government have the power to prevent publication?	[2]
Can't choose	[8]

2.02 In general, would you say that people should obey the law without exception, or are there exceptional occasions on which people should follow their consciences even if it means breaking the law?

PLEASE TICK ONE BOX

	(✓)
Obey the law without exception	[1]
Follow conscience on occasions	[2]
Can't choose	[8]

- 2 -

2.03 There are many ways people or organisations can protest against a government action they strongly oppose. Please show which you think should be allowed and which should not be allowed by ticking a box on each line.

PLEASE TICK ONE BOX ON EACH LINE

Should it be allowed?

	Defin-itely	Proba-bly	Probably not	Definitely not	Can't choose
A. Organising public meetings to protest against the government					
B. Publishing pamphlets to protest against the government					
C. Organising protest marches and demonstrations					
D. Occupying a government office and stopping work there for several days					
E. Seriously damaging government buildings					
F. Organising a nationwide strike of all workers against the government					

2.04 There are some people whose views are considered extreme by the majority.

a) First, consider people who want to overthrow the government by revolution. Do you think such people should be allowed to ...

PLEASE TICK ONE BOX ON EACH LINE

	Defin-itely	Proba-bly	Probably not	Definitely not	Can't choose
i) ... hold public meetings to express their views?					
ii) ... teach 15 year olds in schools?					
iii) ... publish books expressing their views?					

b) Second, consider people who believe that whites are racially superior to all other races. Do you think such people should be allowed to ...

PLEASE TICK ONE BOX ON EACH LINE

	Defin-itely	Proba-bly	Probably not	Definitely not	Can't choose
i) ... hold public meetings to express their views?					
ii) ... teach 15 year olds in schools?					
iii) ... publish books expressing their views?					

/continued over ...

- 4 -

2.07 The government has a lot of different pieces of information about people which computers can bring together very quickly. Is this ...

PLEASE TICK ONE BOX

- ... a very serious threat to individual privacy,
- a fairly serious threat,
- not a serious threat,
- or - not a threat at all to individual privacy?
- Can't choose

(Office use only: 20,11)

2.08 Some people think those with high incomes should pay a larger proportion (percentage) of their earnings in taxes than those who earn low incomes. Other people think that those with high incomes and those with low incomes should pay the same proportion (percentage) of their earnings in taxes.

Do you think those with high incomes should ...

PLEASE TICK ONE BOX

- ... pay a much larger proportion,
- pay a larger proportion,
- pay the same proportion as those who earn low incomes,
- pay a smaller proportion,
- or - pay a much smaller proportion?
- Can't choose

(Office use only: 20,12)

2.09 What is your opinion of the following statement: It is the responsibility of the government to reduce the differences in income between people with high incomes and those with low incomes.

PLEASE TICK ONE BOX

- Agree strongly
- Agree
- Neither agree nor disagree
- Disagree
- Disagree strongly

(Office use only: 20,13)

- 3 -

2.05 Suppose the police get an anonymous tip that a man with a long criminal record is planning to break into a warehouse.

Do you think the police should be allowed, without a Court Order....

PLEASE TICK ONE BOX ON EACH LINE

	Defin-itely	Proba-bly	Probably not	Definitely not	Can't choose	
i) ... to keep the man under surveillance?						20,22
ii) ... to tap his telephone?						20,23
iii) ... to open his mail?						20,24
iv) ... to detain the man overnight for questioning?						20,25

b) Now, suppose the tip is about a man without a criminal record.

Do you think the police should be allowed, without a Court Order ...

PLEASE TICK ONE BOX ON EACH LINE

	Defin-itely	Proba-bly	Probably not	Definitely not	Can't choose	
i) ... to keep the man under surveillance?						20,26
ii) ... to tap his telephone?						20,27
iii) ... to open his mail?						20,28
iv) ... to detain the man overnight for questioning?						20,29

2.06 All systems of justice make mistakes, but which do you think is worse:

PLEASE TICK ONE BOX

- to convict an innocent person?
- OR
- to let a guilty person go free?
- Can't choose

(Office use only: 20,30)

- 5 -

2.10 Please show whether you agree or disagree with each of the following statements.

PLEASE TICK ONE BOX ON EACH LINE

	Agree strongly	Agree	Neither agree nor disagree	Disagree	Disagree strongly
A. A person whose parents are rich has a better chance of earning a lot of money than a person whose parents are poor					
B. A person whose father is a professional person has a better chance of earning a lot of money than a person whose parents are poor					
C. In Britain what you achieve in life depends largely on your family background					

2.11 Would you say that opportunities for university education are, in general, better or worse, for women than for men?

PLEASE TICK ONE BOX

- Much better for women
- Better for women
- No difference
- Worse for women
- Much worse for women
- Can't choose

2.12 How about job opportunities for women: do you think they are, in general, better or worse than job opportunities for men with similar education and experience?

PLEASE TICK ONE BOX

- Much better for women
- Better for women
- No difference
- Worse for women
- Much worse for women
- Can't choose

2.13 And how about income and wages: compared with men who have similar education and jobs - are women, in general, paid better or worse than men?

PLEASE TICK ONE BOX

- Women are paid much better
- Women are paid better
- No difference
- Women are paid worse
- Women are paid much worse
- Can't choose

- 6 -

2.14 Here are three things the government might do. Some people are in favour of them while other people are against them. Please tick one box for each statement to show how you feel.

PLEASE TICK ONE BOX ON EACH LINE

	Strongly in favour	In favour	Neither in favour nor against	Against	Strongly against
A. The government should increase opportunities for women in business and industry					
B. The government should increase opportunities for women to go to university					
C. Women should be given preferential treatment when applying for jobs or promotions					

2.15 And now a few questions about education. Here are some things that might be taught in school. How important is it that schools teach each of these to 15 year olds?

PLEASE TICK ONE BOX ON EACH LINE

	Essential, must be taught	Very important	Fairly important	Not very important	Not needed, should not be taught	Can't choose
A. Reading, writing and mathematics						
B. Sex education						
C. Respect for authority						
D. History, literature and the arts						
E. Ability to make one's own judgements						
F. Job training						
G. Science and technology						
H. Concern for minorities and the poor						
J. Discipline and orderliness						

OFFICE USE ONLY

20,32 20,33 20,34 20,37 20,38 20,39 20,40 20,41 20,42 20,43 20,44 20,45 20,46 20,47 20,48 20,49 20,50 20,51

— 7 —

2.16 How do you feel about opportunities for young people to go to university?

PLEASE TICK ONE BOX

		OFFICE USE ONLY
Should opportunities be ...	(✓)	
... increased a lot,	[1]	
increased a little,	[2]	
kept the same as now,	[3]	20,52
reduced a little,	[4]	
or − reduced a lot?	[5]	
Can't choose	[6]	

2.17 Some people think the government should provide financial assistance to university students. Others think the government should not provide such aid. In each of the circumstances listed below should the government provide grants that would not have to be paid back, provide loans which the student would not have to pay back, or should the government not provide any financial assistance?

PLEASE TICK ONE BOX ON EACH LINE

	Government should give grants	Government should make loans	No Government assistance	Can't choose	OFFICE USE ONLY
A. For students whose parents have a low income	[1]	[2]	[3]	[4]	20,53
B. For students who have outstanding exam results in secondary school	[1]	[2]	[3]	[4]	20,54
C. For students who have average exam results and middle income parents	[1]	[2]	[3]	[4]	20,55

— 8 —

2.18 Sometimes public authorities intervene with parents in raising their children. Please show in each of the following cases how far you think public authorities should go in dealing with a 10 year old child and his or her parents:

PLEASE TICK ONE BOX ON EACH LINE

	Public Authorities should				OFFICE USE ONLY
	Take no action	Give warnings or counselling	Take the child from its parents	Can't choose	
A. The child uses drugs and the parents don't do anything about it.	[1]	[2]	[3]	[8]	20,56
B. The child frequently skips school and the parents don't do anything about it	[1]	[2]	[3]	[8]	20,57
C. The parents regularly let the child stay out late at night without knowing where the child is	[1]	[2]	[3]	[8]	20,58
D. The parents fail to provide the child with proper food and clothing	[1]	[2]	[3]	[8]	20,59
E. The parents regularly beat the child	[1]	[2]	[3]	[8]	20,60
F. The parents refuse essential medical treatment for the child because of their religious beliefs	[1]	[2]	[3]	[8]	20,61
G. The parents refuse to send their child to school because they wish to educate the child at home	[1]	[2]	[3]	[8]	20,62
H. The parents allow the child to watch violent or pornographic films	[1]	[2]	[3]	[8]	20,63

2.19 Do you think that ....

PLEASE TICK ONE BOX ON EACH LINE

	Agree strongly	Agree	Neither agree nor disagree	Disagree	Disagree strongly	OFFICE USE ONLY
A. ... the wearing of seat belts in cars should be required by law?	[1]	[2]	[3]	[4]	[5]	20,44
B. ... smoking in public places should be prohibited by law?	[1]	[2]	[3]	[4]	[5]	20,45
C. ... all employees should be required to retire at an age set by law?	[1]	[2]	[3]	[4]	[5]	20,46

- 9 -

2.20 Please show whether you agree or disagree with each of the following statements.

PLEASE TICK ONE BOX ON EACH LINE

	Agree	Disagree	Can't choose
A. The public has little control over what politicians do in office			
B. The average person can get nowhere by talking to public officials			
C. The average citizen has considerable influence on politics			
D. The average person has much to say about running local government			
E. People like me have much to say about government			
F. The average person has a great deal of influence on government decisions			
G. The government is generally responsive to public opinion			
H. I am usually interested in local elections			
J. By taking an active part in political and social affairs the people can control world affairs.			
K. Taking everything into account, the world is getting better			

2.21 Here are some things the government might do for the economy. Please show which actions you are in favour of and which you are against.

PLEASE TICK ONE BOX ON EACH LINE

	Strongly in favour	In favour	Neither in favour nor against	Against	Strongly against
A. Control of wages by legislation					
B. Control of prices by legislation					
C. Cuts in government spending					
D. Government financing of projects to create new jobs					
E. Less government regulation of business					
F. Support for industry to develop new products and technology					
G. Supporting declining industries to protect jobs					
H. Reducing the working week to create more jobs					

- 10 -

2.22 Listed below are various areas of government spending. Please show whether you would like to see more or less government spending in each area.

Remember that if you say "much more", it might require a tax increase to pay for it.

PLEASE TICK ONE BOX ON EACH LINE

	Spend much more	Spend more	Spend the same as now	Spend less	Spend much less	Can't choose
A. The environment						
B. Health						
C. The police and law enforcement						
D. Education						
E. The military and defence						
F. Old age pensions						
G. Unemployment benefits						
H. Culture and the arts						

2.23 Do you consider the amount of income tax that your household has to pay is...

PLEASE TICK ONE BOX

...much too high,

too high,

about right,

too low,

or - much too low?

Can't choose

Does not apply

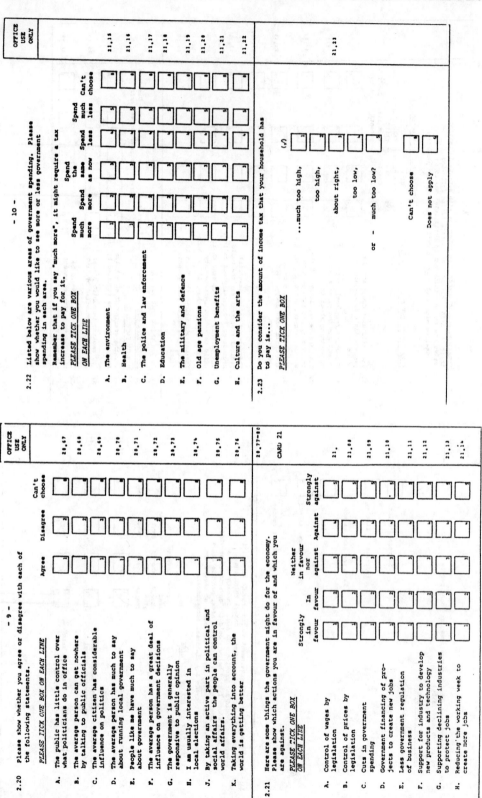

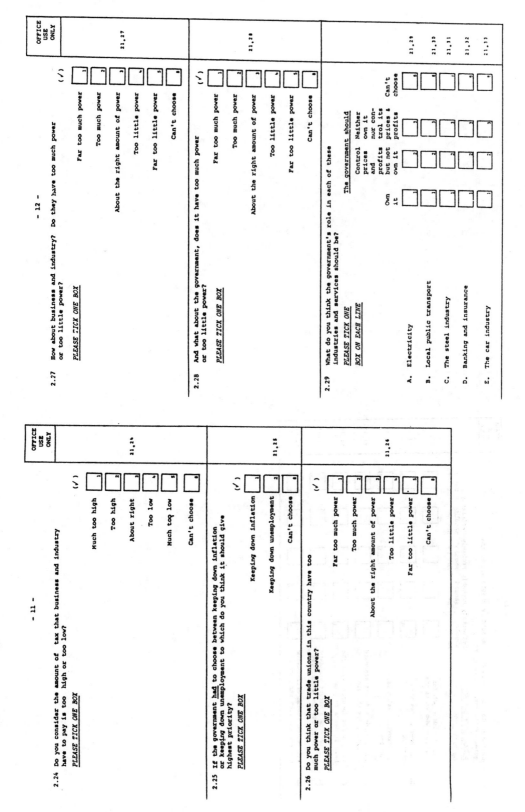

- 11 -

2.24 Do you consider the amount of tax that business and industry
have to pay is too high or too low?

PLEASE TICK ONE BOX

	(✓)
Much too high	1
Too high	2
About right	3
Too low	4
Much too low	5
Can't choose	6

OFFICE USE ONLY: 21.24

2.25 If the government had to choose between keeping down inflation
or keeping down unemployment to which do you think it should give
highest priority?

PLEASE TICK ONE BOX

	(✓)
Keeping down inflation	1
Keeping down unemployment	2
Can't choose	8

OFFICE USE ONLY: 21.25

2.26 Do you think that trade unions in this country have too
much power or too little power?

PLEASE TICK ONE BOX

	(✓)
Far too much power	1
Too much power	2
About the right amount of power	3
Too little power	4
Far too little power	5
Can't choose	8

OFFICE USE ONLY: 21.26

- 12 -

2.27 How about business and industry? Do they have too much power
or too little power?

PLEASE TICK ONE BOX

	(✓)
Far too much power	1
Too much power	2
About the right amount of power	3
Too little power	4
Far too little power	5
Can't choose	8

OFFICE USE ONLY: 21.27

2.28 And what about the government, does it have too much power
or too little power?

PLEASE TICK ONE BOX

	(✓)
Far too much power	1
Too much power	2
About the right amount of power	3
Too little power	4
Far too little power	5
Can't choose	8

OFFICE USE ONLY: 21.28

2.29 What do you think the government's role in each of these
industries and services should be?

*PLEASE TICK ONE
BOX ON EACH LINE*

	Own it	Control prices and profits but not own it	Neither own it nor control its prices & profits	Can't choose	
	The government should				
A. Electricity	1	2	3	9	21.29
B. Local public transport	1	2	3	9	21.30
C. The steel industry	1	2	3	9	21.31
D. Banking and insurance	1	2	3	9	21.32
E. The car industry	1	2	3	9	21.33

- 13 -

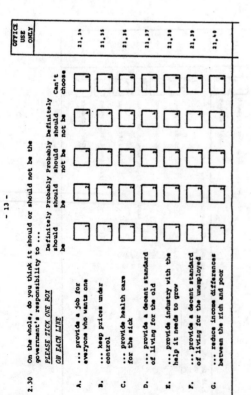

2.30 On the whole, do you think it should or should not be the government's responsibility to ...

PLEASE TICK ONE BOX ON EACH LINE

	Definitely should be	Probably should be	Probably should not be	Definitely should not be	Can't choose	OFFICE USE ONLY
A. ... provide a job for everyone who wants one	☐	☐	☐	☐	☐	21,34
B. ... keep prices under control	☐	☐	☐	☐	☐	21,35
C. ... provide health care for the sick	☐	☐	☐	☐	☐	21,36
D. ... provide a decent standard of living for the old	☐	☐	☐	☐	☐	21,37
E. ... provide industry with the help it needs to grow	☐	☐	☐	☐	☐	21,38
F. ... provide a decent standard of living for the unemployed	☐	☐	☐	☐	☐	21,39
G. ... reduce income differences between the rich and poor	☐	☐	☐	☐	☐	21,40

INTERNATIONAL SOCIAL SURVEY PROGRAMME

1986 MODULE

SOCIAL NETWORKS

(ENGLISH LANGUAGE VERSION)

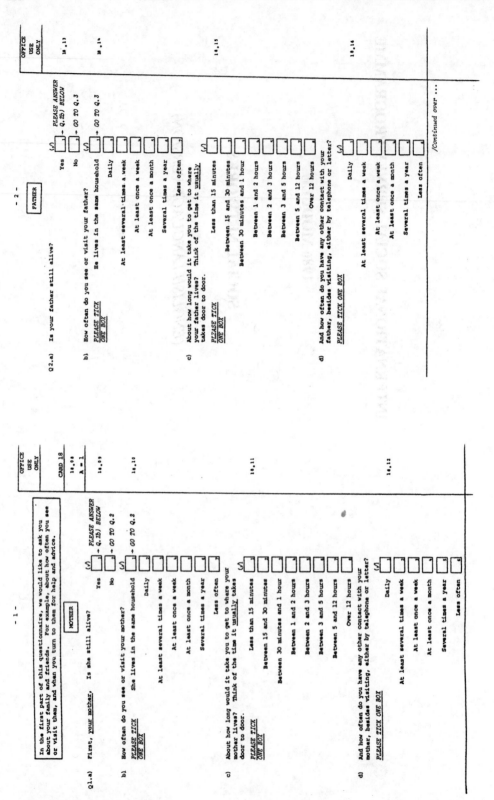

- 1 -

OFFICE USE ONLY

CARD 18
18,08
A = 1

In the first part of this questionnaire, we would like to ask you about your family and friends. For example, about how often you see or visit them, and when you turn to them for help and advice.

[MOTHER]

Q1.a) First, your mother. Is she still alive?

Yes ☐ → PLEASE ANSWER Q.1b) BELOW
No ☐ → GO TO Q.2

18,09

b) How often do you see or visit your mother?

She lives in the same household ☐ → GO TO Q.2
Daily ☐
At least several times a week ☐
At least once a week ☐
At least once a month ☐
Several times a year ☐
Less often ☐

18,10

PLEASE TICK ONE BOX

c) About how long would it take you to get to where your mother lives? Think of the time it usually takes door to door.

Less than 15 minutes ☐
Between 15 and 30 minutes ☐
Between 30 minutes and 1 hour ☐
Between 1 and 2 hours ☐
Between 2 and 3 hours ☐
Between 3 and 5 hours ☐
Between 5 and 12 hours ☐
Over 12 hours ☐

18,11

PLEASE TICK ONE BOX

d) And how often do you have any other contact with your mother, besides visiting, either by telephone or letter?

Daily ☐
At least several times a week ☐
At least once a week ☐
At least once a month ☐
Several times a year ☐
Less often ☐

18,12

PLEASE TICK ONE BOX

- 2 -

OFFICE USE ONLY

[FATHER]

Q2.a) Is your father still alive?

Yes ☐ → PLEASE ANSWER Q.2b) BELOW
No ☐ → GO TO Q.3

18,13

b) How often do you see or visit your father?

He lives in the same household ☐ → GO TO Q.3
Daily ☐
At least several times a week ☐
At least once a week ☐
At least once a month ☐
Several times a year ☐
Less often ☐

18,14

PLEASE TICK ONE BOX

c) About how long would it take you to get to where your father lives? Think of the time it usually takes door to door.

Less than 15 minutes ☐
Between 15 and 30 minutes ☐
Between 30 minutes and 1 hour ☐
Between 1 and 2 hours ☐
Between 2 and 3 hours ☐
Between 3 and 5 hours ☐
Between 5 and 12 hours ☐
Over 12 hours ☐

18,15

PLEASE TICK ONE BOX

d) And how often do you have any other contact with your father, besides visiting, either by telephone or letter?

Daily ☐
At least several times a week ☐
At least once a week ☐
At least once a month ☐
Several times a year ☐
Less often ☐

18,16

PLEASE TICK ONE BOX

/Continued over ...

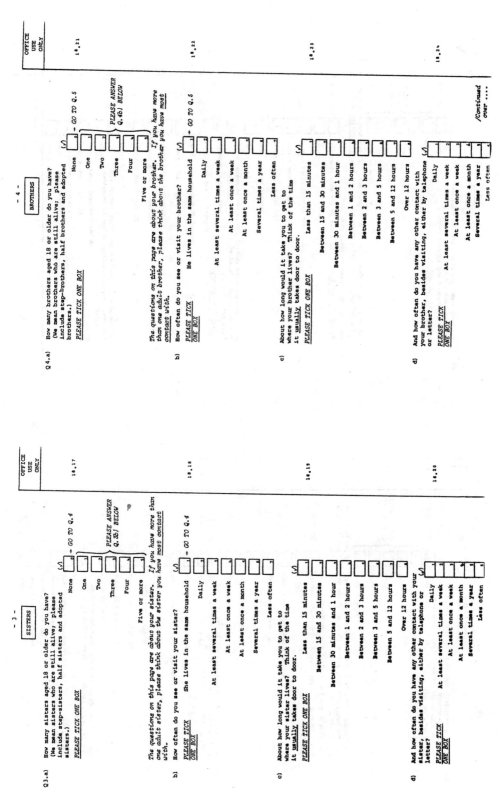

- 3 -

SISTERS

Q3.a) How many sisters aged 18 or older do you have?
(We mean sisters who are still alive; please include step-sisters, half sisters and adopted sisters.)

PLEASE TICK ONE BOX

None → GO TO Q.4
One ⎤
Two ⎥
Three ⎬ PLEASE ANSWER Q.3b) BELOW
Four ⎥
Five or more ⎦

The questions on this page are about your sister. If you have more than one adult sister, please think about the sister you have most contact with.

b) How often do you see or visit your sister?

PLEASE TICK ONE BOX

She lives in the same household → GO TO Q.4
Daily
At least several times a week
At least once a week
At least once a month
Several times a year
Less often

c) About how long would it take you to get to where your sister lives? Think of the time it usually takes door to door.

PLEASE TICK ONE BOX

Less than 15 minutes
Between 15 and 30 minutes
Between 30 minutes and 1 hour
Between 1 and 2 hours
Between 2 and 3 hours
Between 3 and 5 hours
Between 5 and 12 hours
Over 12 hours

d) And how often do you have any other contact with your sister, besides visiting, either by telephone or letter?

PLEASE TICK ONE BOX

Daily
At least several times a week
At least once a week
At least once a month
Several times a year
Less often

OFFICE USE ONLY

18.17

18.18

18.19

18.20

- 4 -

BROTHERS

Q4.a) How many brothers aged 18 or older do you have?
(We mean brothers who are still alive; please include step-brothers, half brothers and adopted brothers.)

PLEASE TICK ONE BOX

None → GO TO Q.5
One ⎤
Two ⎥
Three ⎬ PLEASE ANSWER Q.4b) BELOW
Four ⎥
Five or more ⎦

The questions on this page are about your brother. If you have more than one adult brother, please think about the brother you have most contact with.

b) How often do you see or visit your brother?

PLEASE TICK ONE BOX

He lives in the same household → GO TO Q.5
Daily
At least several times a week
At least once a week
At least once a month
Several times a year
Less often

c) About how long would it take you to get to where your brother lives? Think of the time it usually takes door to door.

PLEASE TICK ONE BOX

Less than 15 minutes
Between 15 and 30 minutes
Between 30 minutes and 1 hour
Between 1 and 2 hours
Between 2 and 3 hours
Between 3 and 5 hours
Between 5 and 12 hours
Over 12 hours

d) And how often do you have any other contact with your brother, besides visiting, either by telephone or letter?

PLEASE TICK ONE BOX

Daily
At least several times a week
At least once a week
At least once a month
Several times a year
Less often

/Continued over ....

OFFICE USE ONLY

18.21

18.22

18.23

18.24

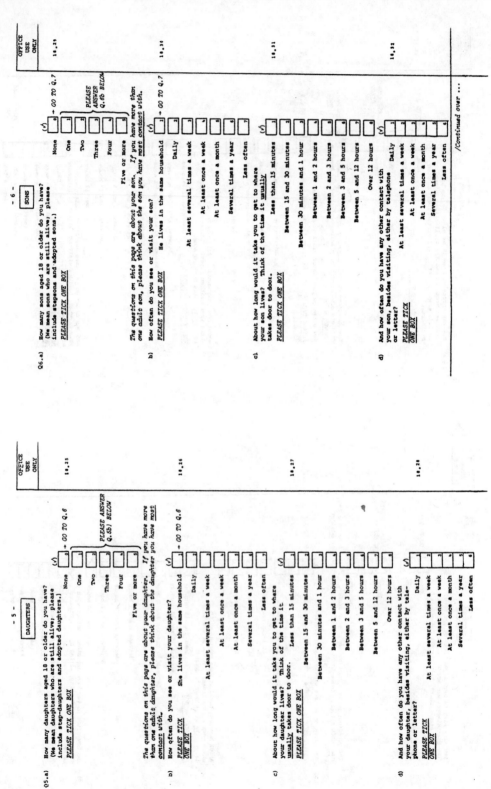

- 5 -

DAUGHTERS

OFFICE USE ONLY

Q5.a) How many daughters aged 18 or older do you have? (We mean daughters who are still alive; please include step-daughters and adopted daughters.)

PLEASE TICK ONE BOX

(✓)
None → GO TO Q.6
One
Two   PLEASE ANSWER Q.5b) BELOW
Three
Four
Five or more

The questions on this page are about your daughter. If you have more than one adult daughter, please think about the daughter you have most contact with.

b) How often do you see or visit your daughter?   She lives in the same household → GO TO Q.6

PLEASE TICK ONE BOX
Daily
At least several times a week
At least once a week
At least once a month
Several times a year
Less often

c) About how long would it take you to get to where your daughter lives? Think of the time it usually takes door to door.

PLEASE TICK ONE BOX
Less than 15 minutes
Between 15 and 30 minutes
Between 30 minutes and 1 hour
Between 1 and 2 hours
Between 2 and 3 hours
Between 3 and 5 hours
Between 5 and 12 hours
Over 12 hours

d) And how often do you have any other contact with your daughter, besides visiting, either by telephone or letter?

PLEASE TICK ONE BOX
Daily
At least several times a week
At least once a week
At least once a month
Several times a year
Less often

- 6 -

SONS

OFFICE USE ONLY

Q6.a) How many sons aged 18 or older do you have? (We mean sons who are still alive; please include stepsons and adopted sons.)

PLEASE TICK ONE BOX

(✓)
None → GO TO Q.7
One
Two   PLEASE ANSWER Q.6b BELOW
Three
Four
Five or more

The questions on this page are about your son. If you have more than one adult son, please think about the son you have most contact with.

b) How often do you see or visit your son?   He lives in the same household → GO TO Q.7

PLEASE TICK ONE BOX
Daily
At least several times a week
At least once a week
At least once a month
Several times a year
Less often

c) About how long would it take you to get to where your son lives? Think of the time it usually takes door to door.

PLEASE TICK ONE BOX
Less than 15 minutes
Between 15 and 30 minutes
Between 30 minutes and 1 hour
Between 1 and 2 hours
Between 2 and 3 hours
Between 3 and 5 hours
Between 5 and 12 hours
Over 12 hours

d) And how often do you have any other contact with your son, besides visiting, either by telephone or letter?

PLEASE TICK ONE BOX
Daily
At least several times a week
At least once a week
At least once a month
Several times a year
Less often

/Continued over ...

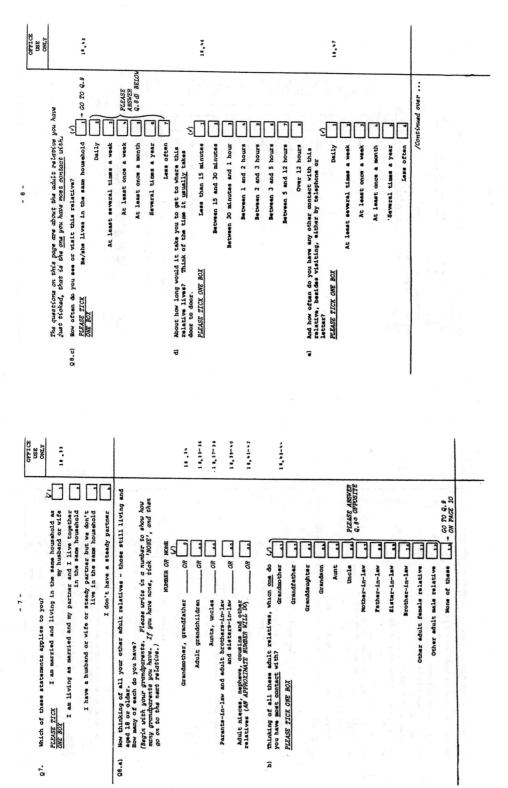

- 7 -

OFFICE USE ONLY

Q7. Which of these statements applies to you?

PLEASE TICK ONE BOX

- I am married and living in the same household as my husband or wife
- I am living as married and my partner and I live together in the same household
- I have a husband or wife or steady partner but we don't live in the same household
- I don't have a steady partner

Q8.a) Now thinking of all your other adult relatives - those still living and aged 18 or older.

How many of each do you have?

(Begin with your grandparents. Please write in a number to show how many grandparents you have. If you have none, tick 'NONE', and then go on to the next relative.)

NUMBER OR NONE

- Grandmother, grandfather _____ OR
- Adult grandchildren _____ OR
- Aunts, uncles _____ OR
- Parents-in-law and adult brothers-in-law and sisters-in-law _____ OR
- Adult nieces, nephews, cousins and other relatives (AN APPROXIMATE NUMBER WILL DO) _____ OR

b) Thinking of all these adult relatives, which one do you have most contact with?

PLEASE TICK ONE BOX

- Grandmother
- Grandfather
- Granddaughter
- Grandson
- Aunt
- Uncle → PLEASE ANSWER Q.8c OPPOSITE
- Mother-in-law
- Father-in-law
- Sister-in-law
- Brother-in-law
- Other adult female relative
- Other adult male relative
- None of these → GO TO Q.9 ON PAGE 10

- 8 -

OFFICE USE ONLY

The questions on this page are about the adult relative you have just ticked, that is the one you have most contact with.

Q8.c) How often do you see or visit this relative?

PLEASE TICK ONE BOX

- He/she lives in the same household → GO TO Q.9
- Daily
- At least several times a week
- At least once a week ⎱ PLEASE ANSWER Q.8d BELOW
- At least once a month
- Several times a year
- Less often

d) About how long would it take you to get to where this relative lives? Think of the time it usually takes door to door.

PLEASE TICK ONE BOX

- Less than 15 minutes
- Between 15 and 30 minutes
- Between 30 minutes and 1 hour
- Between 1 and 2 hours
- Between 2 and 3 hours
- Between 3 and 5 hours
- Between 5 and 12 hours
- Over 12 hours

e) And how often do you have any other contact with this relative, besides visiting, either by telephone or letter?

PLEASE TICK ONE BOX

- Daily
- At least several times a week
- At least once a week
- At least once a month
- Several times a year
- Less often

/Continued over ...

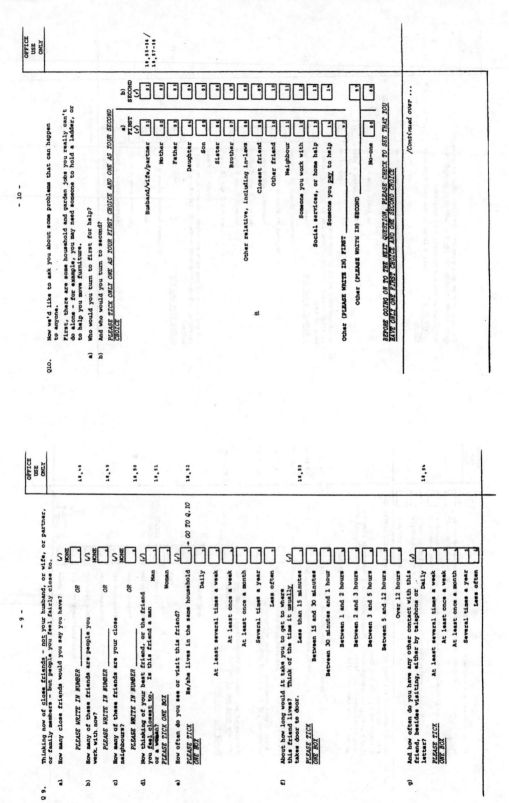

- 9 -

Q 9. Thinking now of close friends - not your husband, or wife, or partner, or family members - but people you feel fairly close to.

a) How many close friends would you say you have?
PLEASE WRITE IN NUMBER ____ OR NONE []

b) How many of these friends are people you work with now?
PLEASE WRITE IN NUMBER ____ OR NONE []

c) How many of these friends are your close neighbours?
PLEASE WRITE IN NUMBER ____ OR NONE []

d) Now thinking of your best friend, or the friend you feel closest to. Is this friend a man or a woman?
PLEASE TICK ONE BOX
Man []
Woman []

e) How often do you see or visit this friend?
PLEASE TICK ONE BOX
He/she lives in the same household → GO TO Q.10 []
Daily []
At least several times a week []
At least once a week []
At least once a month []
Several times a year []
Less often []

f) About how long would it take you to get to where this friend lives? Think of the time it usually takes door to door.
PLEASE TICK ONE BOX
Less than 15 minutes []
Between 15 and 30 minutes []
Between 30 minutes and 1 hour []
Between 1 and 2 hours []
Between 2 and 3 hours []
Between 3 and 5 hours []
Between 5 and 12 hours []
Over 12 hours []

g) And how often do you have any other contact with this friend, besides visiting, either by telephone or letter?
PLEASE TICK ONE BOX
Daily []
At least several times a week []
At least once a week []
At least once a month []
Several times a year []
Less often []

OFFICE USE ONLY: 18,48 ; 18,49 ; 18,50 ; 18,51 ; 18,52 ; 18,53 ; 18,54

- 10 -

Q10. Now we'd like to ask you about some problems that can happen to anyone.

First, there are some household and garden jobs you really can't do alone - for example, you may need someone to hold a ladder, or to help you move furniture.

a) Who would you turn to first for help?

b) And who would you turn to second?

PLEASE TICK ONLY ONE AS YOUR FIRST CHOICE AND ONE AS YOUR SECOND CHOICE

	a) FIRST	b) SECOND
Husband/wife/partner	[]	[]
Mother	[]	[]
Father	[]	[]
Daughter	[]	[]
Son	[]	[]
Sister	[]	[]
Brother	[]	[]
Other relative, including in-laws	[]	[]
Closest friend	[]	[]
Other friend	[]	[]
Neighbour	[]	[]
Someone you work with	[]	[]
Social services, or home help	[]	[]
Someone you pay to help	[]	[]
Other (PLEASE WRITE IN FIRST) ____	[]	
Other (PLEASE WRITE IN) SECOND ____		[]
No-one	[]	[]

BEFORE GOING ON TO THE NEXT QUESTION, PLEASE CHECK TO SEE THAT YOU HAVE ONLY ONE FIRST CHOICE AND ONE SECOND CHOICE

OFFICE USE ONLY: 18,55-56 / 18,57-58

/Continued over ...

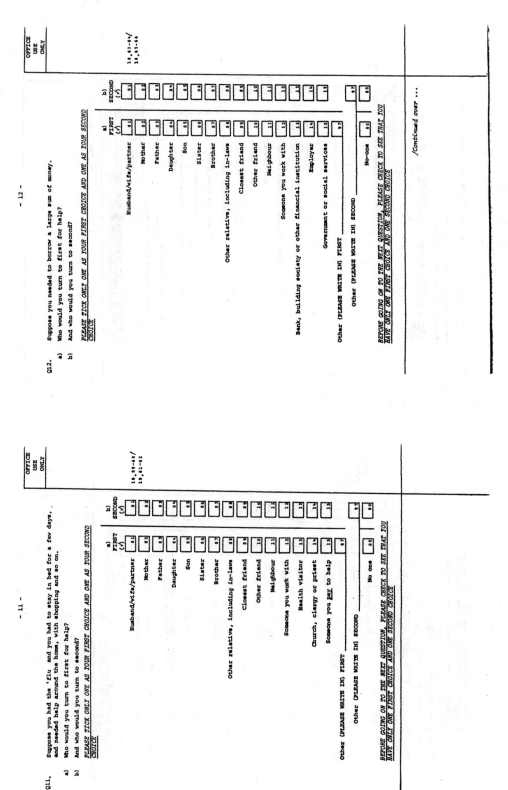

- 11 -

Q11. Suppose you had the 'flu and you had to stay in bed for a few days, and needed help around the home, with shopping and so on.

a) Who would you turn to first for help?

b) And who would you turn to second?

PLEASE TICK ONLY ONE AS YOUR FIRST CHOICE AND ONE AS YOUR SECOND CHOICE

	a) FIRST (✓)	b) SECOND (✓)
Husband/wife/partner	01	01
Mother	02	02
Father	03	03
Daughter	04	04
Son	05	05
Sister	06	06
Brother	07	07
Other relative, including in-laws	08	08
Closest friend	09	09
Other friend	10	10
Neighbour	11	11
Someone you work with	12	12
Health visitor	13	13
Church, clergy or priest	14	14
Someone you pay to help	15	15
Other (PLEASE WRITE IN) FIRST _____	97	
Other (PLEASE WRITE IN) SECOND _____		97
No one	00	00

BEFORE GOING ON TO THE NEXT QUESTION, PLEASE CHECK TO SEE THAT YOU HAVE ONLY ONE FIRST CHOICE AND ONE SECOND CHOICE

OFFICE USE ONLY

18,59-60/
18,61-62

- 12 -

Q12. Suppose you needed to borrow a large sum of money.

a) Who would you turn to first for help?

b) And who would you turn to second?

PLEASE TICK ONLY ONE AS YOUR FIRST CHOICE AND ONE AS YOUR SECOND CHOICE

	a) FIRST (✓)	b) SECOND (✓)
Husband/wife/partner	01	01
Mother	02	02
Father	03	03
Daughter	04	04
Son	05	05
Sister	06	06
Brother	07	07
Other relative, including in-laws	08	08
Closest friend	09	09
Other friend	10	10
Neighbour	11	11
Someone you work with	12	12
Bank, building society or other financial institution	13	13
Employer	14	14
Government or social services	15	15
Other (PLEASE WRITE IN) FIRST _____	97	
Other (PLEASE WRITE IN) SECOND _____		97
No-one	00	00

BEFORE GOING ON TO THE NEXT QUESTION, PLEASE CHECK TO SEE THAT YOU HAVE ONLY ONE FIRST CHOICE AND ONE SECOND CHOICE

OFFICE USE ONLY

18,63-84/
18,65-66

/Continued over ...

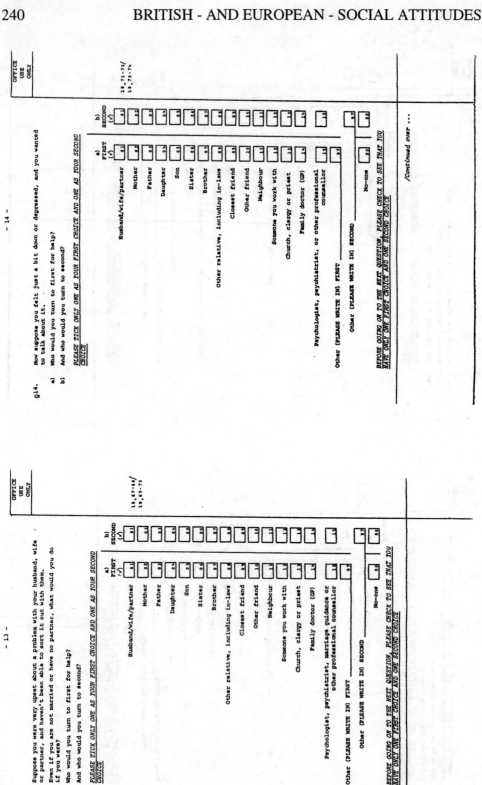

- 13 -

OFFICE USE ONLY

Q13. Suppose you were very upset about a problem with your husband, wife or partner, and haven't been able to sort it out with them.

Even if you are not married or have no partner, what would you do if you were?

a) Who would you turn to first for help?

b) And who would you turn to second?

PLEASE TICK ONLY ONE AS YOUR FIRST CHOICE AND ONE AS YOUR SECOND CHOICE

	a) FIRST (✓)	b) SECOND (✓)
Husband/wife/partner		
Mother		
Father		
Daughter		
Son		
Sister		
Brother		
Other relative, including in-laws		
Closest friend		
Other friend		
Neighbour		
Someone you work with		
Church, clergy or priest		
Family doctor (GP)		
Psychologist, psychiatrist, marriage guidance or other professional counsellor		
Other (PLEASE WRITE IN) FIRST		
Other (PLEASE WRITE IN) SECOND		
No-one		

11,47-68/
11,69-70

BEFORE GOING ON TO THE NEXT QUESTION, PLEASE CHECK TO SEE THAT YOU HAVE ONLY ONE FIRST CHOICE AND ONE SECOND CHOICE

- 14 -

OFFICE USE ONLY

Q14. Now suppose you felt just a bit down or depressed, and you wanted to talk about it.

a) Who would you turn to first for help?

b) And who would you turn to second?

PLEASE TICK ONLY ONE AS YOUR FIRST CHOICE AND ONE AS YOUR SECOND CHOICE

	a) FIRST (✓)	b) SECOND (✓)
Husband/wife/partner		
Mother		
Father		
Daughter		
Son		
Sister		
Brother		
Other relative, including in-laws		
Closest friend		
Other friend		
Neighbour		
Someone you work with		
Church, clergy or priest		
Family doctor (GP)		
Psychologist, psychiatrist, or other professional counsellor		
Other (PLEASE WRITE IN) FIRST		
Other (PLEASE WRITE IN) SECOND		
No-one		

11,71-72/
11,73-74

BEFORE GOING ON TO THE NEXT QUESTION, PLEASE CHECK TO SEE THAT YOU HAVE ONLY ONE FIRST CHOICE AND ONE SECOND CHOICE

/Continued over ...

- 15 -

Q15.   And suppose you needed advice about an important change in your
       life - for example about a job, or moving to another part of the
       country.

a)   Who would you turn to first for help?

b)   And who would you turn to second?

*PLEASE TICK ONE ONLY AS YOUR FIRST CHOICE AND ONE ONLY AS YOUR SECOND
CHOICE*

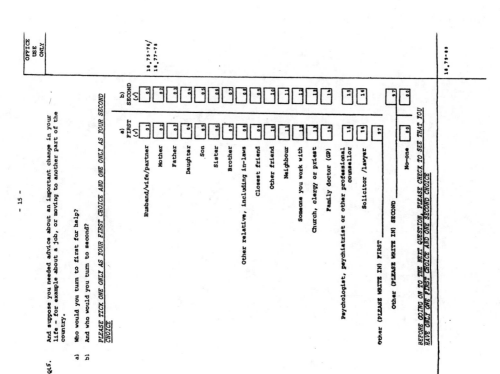

	a) FIRST (✓)	b) SECOND (✓)
Husband/wife/partner	01	01
Mother	02	02
Father	03	03
Daughter	04	04
Son	05	05
Sister	06	06
Brother	07	07
Other relative, including in-laws	08	08
Closest friend	09	09
Other friend	10	10
Neighbour	11	11
Someone you work with	12	12
Church, clergy or priest	13	13
Family doctor (GP)	14	14
Psychologist, psychiatrist or other professional counsellor	15	15
Solicitor /lawyer	16	16
Other (PLEASE WRITE IN) FIRST	97	
Other (PLEASE WRITE IN) SECOND		97
No-one	00	00

*BEFORE GOING ON TO THE NEXT QUESTION, PLEASE CHECK TO SEE THAT YOU
HAVE ONLY ONE FIRST CHOICE AND ONE SECOND CHOICE*

INTERNATIONAL SOCIAL SURVEY PROGRAMME

1987 MODULE

SOCIAL INEQUALITY

(ENGLISH LANGUAGE VERSION)

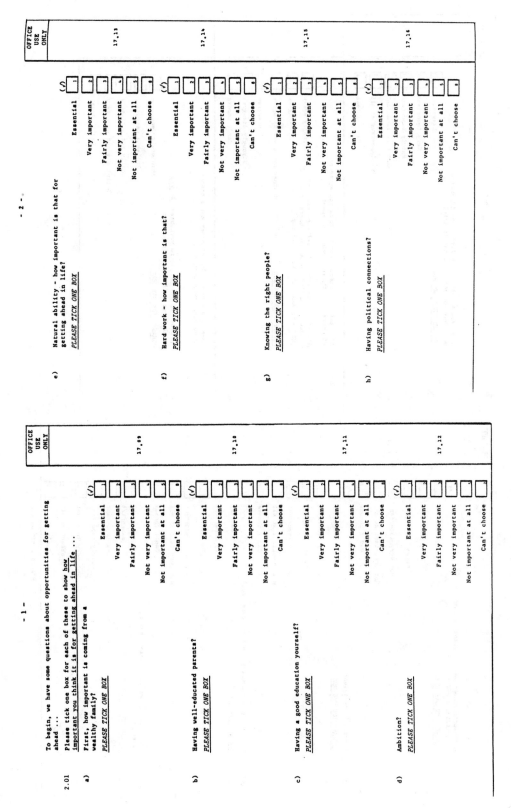

- 1 -

2.01 To begin, we have some questions about opportunities for getting ahead ...

Please tick one box for each of these to show how important you think it is for getting ahead in life ...

a) First, how important is coming from a wealthy family?
PLEASE TICK ONE BOX

Essential
Very important
Fairly important
Not very important
Not important at all
Can't choose

OFFICE USE ONLY 17,09

b) Having well-educated parents?
PLEASE TICK ONE BOX

Essential
Very important
Fairly important
Not very important
Not important at all
Can't choose

17,10

c) Having a good education yourself?
PLEASE TICK ONE BOX

Essential
Very important
Fairly important
Not very important
Not important at all
Can't choose

17,11

d) Ambition?
PLEASE TICK ONE BOX

Essential
Very important
Fairly important
Not very important
Not important at all
Can't choose

17,12

- 2 -

e) Natural ability - how important is that for getting ahead in life?
PLEASE TICK ONE BOX

Essential
Very important
Fairly important
Not very important
Not important at all
Can't choose

OFFICE USE ONLY 17,13

f) Hard work - how important is that?
PLEASE TICK ONE BOX

Essential
Very important
Fairly important
Not very important
Not important at all
Can't choose

17,14

g) Knowing the right people?
PLEASE TICK ONE BOX

Essential
Very important
Fairly important
Not very important
Not important at all
Can't choose

17,15

h) Having political connections?
PLEASE TICK ONE BOX

Essential
Very important
Fairly important
Not very important
Not important at all
Can't choose

17,16

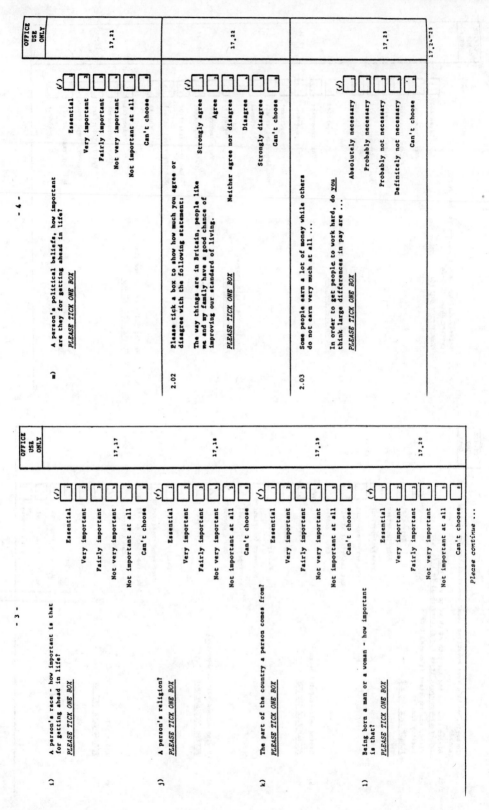

- 3 -

i) A person's race - how important is that for getting ahead in life?
PLEASE TICK ONE BOX

- Essential
- Very important
- Fairly important
- Not very important
- Not important at all
- Can't choose

17,17

j) A person's religion?
PLEASE TICK ONE BOX

- Essential
- Very important
- Fairly important
- Not very important
- Not important at all
- Can't choose

17,18

k) The part of the country a person comes from?
PLEASE TICK ONE BOX

- Essential
- Very important
- Fairly important
- Not very important
- Not important at all
- Can't choose

17,19

l) Being born a man or a woman - how important is that?
PLEASE TICK ONE BOX

- Essential
- Very important
- Fairly important
- Not very important
- Not important at all
- Can't choose

17,20

Please continue ...

- 4 -

m) A person's political beliefs, how important are they for getting ahead in life?
PLEASE TICK ONE BOX

- Essential
- Very important
- Fairly important
- Not very important
- Not important at all
- Can't choose

17,21

2.02 Please tick a box to show how much you agree or disagree with the following statement:

The way things are in Britain, people like me and my family have a good chance of improving our standard of living.
PLEASE TICK ONE BOX

- Strongly agree
- Agree
- Neither agree nor disagree
- Disagree
- Strongly disagree
- Can't choose

17,22

2.03 Some people earn a lot of money while others do not earn very much at all ...

In order to get people to work hard, do you think large differences in pay are ...
PLEASE TICK ONE BOX

- Absolutely necessary
- Probably necessary
- Probably not necessary
- Definitely not necessary
- Can't choose

17,23

17,24-25

OFFICE USE ONLY

- 5 -

2.04 Do you agree or disagree with each of these statements?

PLEASE TICK ONE BOX ON EACH LINE

	Strongly agree	Agree	Neither Agree nor disagree	Disagree	Strongly disagree	Can't choose	OFFICE USE ONLY
a) People would not want to take extra responsibility at work unless they were paid extra for it.	1	2	3	4	5	8	17,26
b) Workers would not bother to get skills and qualifications unless they were paid extra for having them.	1	2	3	4	5	8	17,27
c) Inequality continues because it benefits the rich and powerful.	1	2	3	4	5	8	17,28
d) No-one would study for years to become a lawyer or doctor unless they expected to earn a lot more than ordinary workers.	1	2	3	4	5	8	17,29
e) Large differences in income are necessary for Britain's prosperity.	1	2	3	4	5	8	17,30
f) Allowing business to make good profits is the best way to improve everyone's standard of living.	1	2	3	4	5	8	17,31
g) Inequality continues to exist because ordinary people don't join together to get rid of it.	1	2	3	4	5	8	17,32

Please continue ...

- 6 -

2.05 We would like to know what you think people in these jobs actually earn.

Please write in how much you think they usually earn each year, before taxes.

(Many people are not exactly sure about this, but your best guess will be close enough. This may be difficult; but it is important, so please try.)

Please write in how much they actually earn each year, before tax

		OFFICE USE ONLY
a) First, about how much do you think a bricklayer earns?	£	17,37-38
b) A doctor in general practice?	£	17,39-44
c) A bank clerk?	£	17,45-50
d) The owner of a small shop?	£	17,51-56
e) The chairman of a large national company?	£	17,57-62
f) A skilled worker in a factory?	£	17,64-69
g) A farm worker?	£	17,70-75
h) A secretary?	£	18,09-14
i) A city bus driver?	£	18,15-20
j) An unskilled worker in a factory?	£	18,21-26
k) A cabinet minister in the national government?	£	18,27-33

- 7 -

2.06 Next, what do you think people in these jobs ought to be paid - how much do you think they should earn each year before taxes, regardless of what they actually get?

Please write in how much they should earn each year, before tax

		OFFICE USE ONLY
a)	First, about how much do you think a bricklayer should earn? .... £	18,34-39
b)	A doctor in general practice? .... £	18,40-45
c)	A bank clerk, how much should s/he earn? £	18,46-51
d)	The owner of a small shop? .... £	18,52-57
e)	The chairman of a large national company? .... £	18,58-64
f)	A skilled worker in a factory? ...... £	18,65-70
g)	A farm worker? .... £	18,71-76
h)	A secretary? .... £	19,09-14
i)	A city bus driver? .... £	19,15-20
j)	An unskilled worker in a factory? ... £	19,21-26
k)	A cabinet minister in the national government? .... £	19,27-33

Please continue ...

- 8 -

2.07 Please show how much you agree or disagree with each statement....

PLEASE TICK ONE BOX ON EACH LINE

	Agree strongly	Agree	Neither agree nor disagree	Disagree	Disagree strongly	Can't choose	OFFICE USE ONLY
a) Differences in income in Britain are too large.	□	□	□	□	□	□	19,34
b) It is the responsibility of the government to reduce the differences in income between people with high incomes and those with low incomes.	□	□	□	□	□	□	19,35
c) The government should provide more chances for children from poor families to go to university.	□	□	□	□	□	□	19,36
d) The government should provide a job for everyone who wants one.	□	□	□	□	□	□	19,37
e) The government should spend less on benefits for the poor.	□	□	□	□	□	□	19,38
f) The government should provide a decent standard of living for the unemployed.	□	□	□	□	□	□	19,39
g) The government should provide everyone with a guaranteed basic income.	□	□	□	□	□	□	19,40

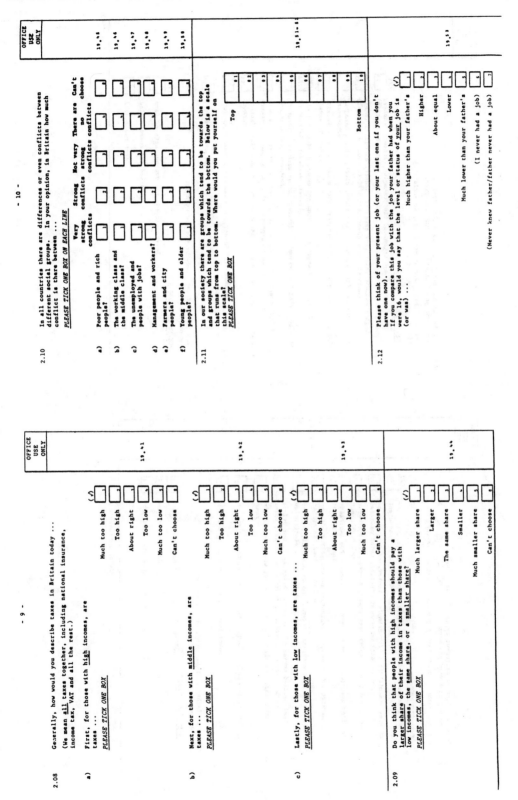

- 10 -

2.10 In all countries there are differences or even conflicts between different social groups. In your opinion, in Britain how much conflict is there between ...

PLEASE TICK ONE BOX ON EACH LINE

	Very strong conflicts	Strong conflicts	Not very strong conflicts	There are no conflicts	Can't choose
a) Poor people and rich people?					
b) The working class and the middle class?					
c) The unemployed and people with jobs?					
d) Management and workers?					
e) Farmers and city people?					
f) Young people and older people?					

2.11 In our society there are groups which tend to be towards the top and groups which tend to be towards the bottom. Below is a scale that runs from top to bottom. Where would you put yourself on this scale?
PLEASE TICK ONE BOX

Top
01
02
03
04
05
06
07
08
09
10
Bottom

2.12 Please think of your present job (or your last one if you don't have one now).
If you compare this job with the job your father had when you were 16, would you say that the level or status of *your* job is (or was) ...

Much higher than your father's
Higher
About equal
Lower
Much lower than your father's
(I never had a job)
(Never knew father/father never had a job)

- 9 -

2.08 Generally, how would you describe taxes in Britain today ...

(We mean *all* taxes together, including national insurance, income tax, VAT and all the rest.)

a) First, for those with *high* incomes, are taxes ...
PLEASE TICK ONE BOX

Much too high
Too high
About right
Too low
Much too low
Can't choose

b) Next, for those with *middle* incomes, are taxes ...
PLEASE TICK ONE BOX

Much too high
Too high
About right
Too low
Much too low
Can't choose

c) Lastly, for those with *low* incomes, are taxes ...
PLEASE TICK ONE BOX

Much too high
Too high
About right
Too low
Much too low
Can't choose

2.09 Do you think that people with high incomes should pay a *larger share* of their income in taxes than those with low incomes, *the same share*, or a *smaller share*?

PLEASE TICK ONE BOX

Much larger share
Larger
The same share
Smaller
Much smaller share
Can't choose

- 11 -

2.13a Here is a list of different types of jobs. Which type did your <u>father</u> have when you were 16?
(If your <u>father</u> did not have a job then, please give the job he used to have.)
PLEASE TICK ONE BOX

	OFFICE USE ONLY
Professional and technical (for example: doctor, teacher, engineer, artist, accountant)	01
Higher administrator (for example: banker, executive in big business, high government official, union official)	02
Clerical (for example: secretary, clerk, office manager, bookkeeper)	03
Sales (for example: sales manager, shop owner, shop assistant, insurance agent)	04
Service (for example: restaurant owner, police officer, waiter, barber, caretaker)	05
Skilled worker (for example: foreman, motor mechanic, printer, tool and die maker, electrician)	06
Semi-skilled worker (for example: bricklayer, bus driver, cannery worker, carpenter, sheet metal worker, baker)	07
Unskilled worker (for example: labourer, porter, unskilled factory worker)	08
Farm (for example: farmer, farm labourer, tractor driver)	09
(Never knew father/father never had job)	10

19.54-55

b) Was your father self-employed, or did he work for someone else?
PLEASE TICK ONE BOX

Self-employed, had own business or farm	1
Worked for someone else	2
(Never knew father/father never had job)	3

19.56

19.57

Please continue ...

- 12 -

2.14a And how about your <u>first</u> job - the first job you had after you finished full-time education?
(Even if that was many years ago, we would still like to know about it.)
PLEASE TICK ONE BOX

	OFFICE USE ONLY
Professional and technical (for example: doctor, teacher, engineer, artist, accountant)	01
Higher administrator (for example: banker, executive in big business, high government official, union official)	02
Clerical (for example: secretary, clerk, office manager, bookkeeper)	03
Sales (for example: sales manager, shop owner, shop assistant, insurance agent)	04
Service (for example: restaurant owner, police officer, barber, waitress, caretaker)	05
Skilled worker (for example: foreman, motor mechanic, printer, seamstress, electrician)	06
Semi-skilled worker (for example: bricklayer, bus driver, cannery worker, carpenter, sheet metal worker, baker)	07
Unskilled worker (for example: labourer, porter, unskilled factory worker)	08
Farm (for example: farmer, farm labourer, tractor driver)	09
(Never had a job)	10

19.58-59

b) Were you self-employed, or did you work for someone else?
PLEASE TICK ONE BOX

Self-employed, had own business or farm	1
Worked for someone else	2
(Never had a job)	3

19.60

19.61-62

- 13 -

2.15a And how about your job now?

(If you are not working now, please tell us about your last job.)

PLEASE TICK ONE BOX

	OFFICE USE ONLY
Professional and technical (for example: doctor, teacher, engineer, artist, accountant)	
Higher administrator (for example: banker, executive in big business, high government official, union official)	
Clerical (for example: secretary, clerk, office manager, bookkeeper)	
Sales (for example: sales manager, shop owner, shop assistant, insurance agent)	
Service (for example: restaurant owner, police officer, waitress, barber, caretaker)	
Skilled worker (for example: foreman, motor mechanic, printer, seamstress, electrician)	
Semi-skilled worker (for example: bricklayer, bus driver, cannery worker, carpenter, sheet metal worker, baker)	
Unskilled workers (for example: labourer, porter, unskilled factory worker)	
Farm (for example: farmer, farm labourer, tractor driver)	
(Never had a job)	19,63-64

b) Are you self-employed, or do you work for someone else?

PLEASE TICK ONE BOX

Self-employed, have own business or farm	
Work for someone else	
(Never had a job)	19,65

INTERNATIONAL SOCIAL SURVEY PROGRAMME

1988 MODULE

WOMEN AND THE FAMILY

(ENGLISH LANGUAGE VERSION)

FIELDED IN BRITAIN IN 1989

- 1 -

2.01 To begin, we have some questions about women.
Do you agree or disagree ...?
PLEASE TICK ONE BOX ON EACH LINE

	Strongly agree	Agree	Neither agree nor disagree	Disagree	Strongly disagree	Can't choose	
a. A working mother can establish just as warm and secure a relationship with her children as a mother who does not work.	☐	☐	☐	☐	☐	☐	1808
b. A pre-school child is likely to suffer if his or her mother works.	☐	☐	☐	☐	☐	☐	1809
c. All in all, family life suffers when the woman has a full-time job.	☐	☐	☐	☐	☐	☐	1810
d. A woman and her family will all be happier if she goes out to work.	☐	☐	☐	☐	☐	☐	1811
e. A job is all right, but what most women really want is a home and children.	☐	☐	☐	☐	☐	☐	1812
f. Being a housewife is just as fulfilling as working for pay.	☐	☐	☐	☐	☐	☐	1813
g. Having a job is the best way for a woman to be an independent person.	☐	☐	☐	☐	☐	☐	1814
h. Both the husband and wife should contribute to the household income.	☐	☐	☐	☐	☐	☐	1815
i. A husband's job is to earn money; a wife's job is to look after the home and family.	☐	☐	☐	☐	☐	☐	1816
j. I would enjoy having a job even if I didn't need the money.	☐	☐	☐	☐	☐	☐	1817

Do you agree or disagree ...

Please continue ...

- 2 -

2.02 Do you think that women should work outside the home full-time, part-time or not at all under these circumstances?
PLEASE TICK ONE BOX ON EACH LINE

	Work full-time	Work part-time	Stay at home	Can't choose	
a. After marrying and before there are children?	☐	☐	☐	☐	1818
b. When there is a child under school age?	☐	☐	☐	☐	1819
c. After the youngest child starts school?	☐	☐	☐	☐	1820
d. After the children leave home?	☐	☐	☐	☐	1821

2.03 Think of a child under 3 years old whose parents both have full-time jobs.
How suitable do you think each of these childcare arrangements would be for the child?

	Very suitable	Somewhat suitable	Not very suitable	Not at all suitable	Can't choose	
a. A state or local authority nursery?	☐	☐	☐	☐	☐	1822
b. A private creche or nursery?	☐	☐	☐	☐	☐	1823
c. A childminder or baby-sitter?	☐	☐	☐	☐	☐	1824
d. A neighbour or friend?	☐	☐	☐	☐	☐	1825
e. A relative?	☐	☐	☐	☐	☐	1826

2.04a If you were advising a young woman, which of the following ways of life would you recommend?
PLEASE TICK ONE BOX ONLY

To live alone, without a steady partner? ☐
To live with a steady partner, without marrying? ☐
To live with a steady partner for a while, and then marry? ☐
To marry without living together first? ☐
Can't choose ☐

1827

Please continue ...

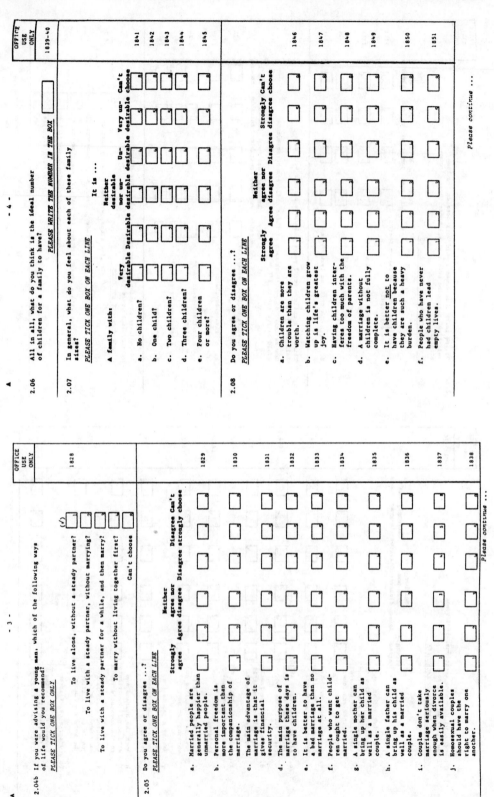

- 3 -

2.04b If you were advising a young man, which of the following ways of life would you recommend?

PLEASE TICK ONE BOX ONLY

To live alone, without a steady partner?

To live with a steady partner, without marrying?

To live with a steady partner for a while, and then marry?

To marry without living together first?

Can't choose

2.05 Do you agree or disagree ...?
PLEASE TICK ONE BOX ON EACH LINE

	Strongly agree	Agree	Neither agree nor disagree	Disagree	Disagree strongly	Can't choose
a. Married people are generally happier than unmarried people.						
b. Personal freedom is more important than the companionship of marriage.						
c. The main advantage of marriage is that it gives financial security.						
d. The main purpose of marriage these days is to have children.						
e. It is better to have a bad marriage than no marriage at all.						
f. People who want children ought to get married.						
g. A single mother can bring up her child as well as a married couple.						
h. A single father can bring up his child as well as a married couple.						
i. Couples don't take marriage seriously enough when divorce is easily available.						
j. Homosexual couples should have the right to marry one another.						

Please continue ...

- 4 -

2.06 All in all, what do you think is the ideal number of children for a family to have?

PLEASE WRITE THE NUMBER IN THE BOX

2.07 In general, what do you feel about each of these family sizes?

PLEASE TICK ONE BOX ON EACH LINE

It is ...

A family with:	Very desirable	Desirable	Neither desirable nor undesirable	Undesirable	Very undesirable	Can't choose
a. No children?						
b. One child?						
c. Two children?						
d. Three children?						
e. Four children or more?						

2.08 Do you agree or disagree ...?
PLEASE TICK ONE BOX ON EACH LINE

	Strongly agree	Agree	Neither agree nor disagree	Disagree	Strongly disagree	Can't choose
a. Children are more trouble than they are worth.						
b. Watching children grow up is life's greatest joy.						
c. Having children interferes too much with the freedom of parents.						
d. A marriage without children is not fully complete.						
e. It is better not to have children because they are such a heavy burden.						
f. People who have never had children lead empty lives.						

Please continue ...

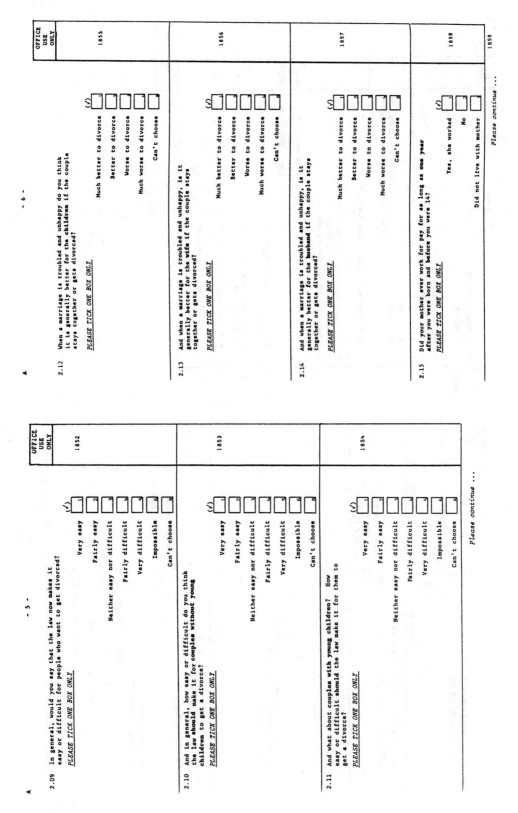

- 6 -

OFFICE USE ONLY

2.12 When a marriage is troubled and unhappy do you think it is generally better for the children if the couple stays together or gets divorced?

PLEASE TICK ONE BOX ONLY

Much better to divorce
Better to divorce
Worse to divorce
Much worse to divorce
Can't choose

1855

2.13 And when a marriage is troubled and unhappy, is it generally better for the wife if the couple stays together or gets divorced?

PLEASE TICK ONE BOX ONLY

Much better to divorce
Better to divorce
Worse to divorce
Much worse to divorce
Can't choose

1856

2.14 And when a marriage is troubled and unhappy, is it generally better for the husband if the couple stays together or gets divorced?

PLEASE TICK ONE BOX ONLY

Much better to divorce
Better to divorce
Worse to divorce
Much worse to divorce
Can't choose

1857

2.15 Did your mother ever work for pay for as long as one year after you were born and before you were 14?

PLEASE TICK ONE BOX ONLY

Yes, she worked
No
Did not live with mother

1858

1859

Please continue ...

- 5 -

OFFICE USE ONLY

2.09 In general, would you say that the law now makes it easy or difficult for people who want to get divorced?

PLEASE TICK ONE BOX ONLY

Very easy
Fairly easy
Neither easy nor difficult
Fairly difficult
Very difficult
Impossible
Can't choose

1852

2.10 And in general, how easy or difficult do you think the law should make it for couples without young children to get a divorce?

PLEASE TICK ONE BOX ONLY

Very easy
Fairly easy
Neither easy nor difficult
Fairly difficult
Very difficult
Impossible
Can't choose

1853

2.11 And what about couples with young children? How easy or difficult should the law make it for them to get a divorce?

PLEASE TICK ONE BOX ONLY

Very easy
Fairly easy
Neither easy nor difficult
Fairly difficult
Very difficult
Impossible
Can't choose

1854

Please continue ...

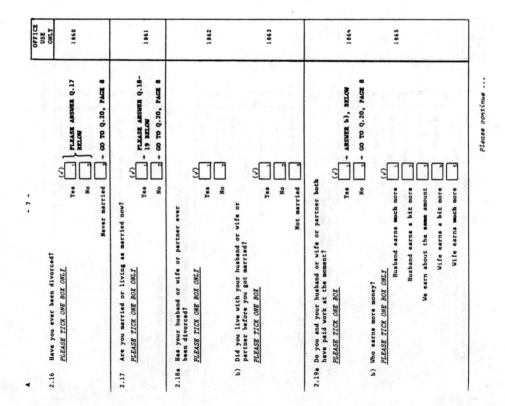

- 41A -

		Col/Code	Skip to
INTERVIEWER TO COMPLETE:		1471	
A903a) RESPONDENT IS:	Man	1 →	Q.904
	Woman	2 →	b)
IF WOMAN:		1472	
b) RESPONDENT IS: (SEE CODE 1, Q.900)	Married	1	c)
	Not married	2	Q.904
IF MARRIED WOMAN:		1473	
c) RESPONDENT: Has children (SEE H/H GRID Q.901) OR Has had children (CODE 1 AT Q.902)		1 →	d)
	Has not	2 →	Q.904

IF MARRIED WOMAN WITH CHILDREN (CODE 1 AT Q.903c)

CARD F7

d) Please use this card to say whether you worked full-time, part-time or not at all ...

READ a)-d) BELOW AND CODE ONE FOR EACH

	Worked full-time	Worked part-time	Stayed at home	Does not apply		
a) ... after marrying and before you had children?	1	2	3	8	1474	
b) ... and what about when a child was under school age?	1	2	3	8	1475	
c) ... after the youngest child started school?	1	2	3	8	1476	
d) ... and how about after the children left home?	1	2	3	8	1477	

1478-80 SPARE
1506-07 CARD 15

- 7 -

	OFFICE USE ONLY

2.16 Have you ever been divorced?
PLEASE TICK ONE BOX ONLY
Yes → PLEASE ANSWER Q.17 BELOW
No → GO TO Q.20, PAGE 8
Never married   1860

2.17 Are you married or living as married now?
PLEASE TICK ONE BOX ONLY
Yes → PLEASE ANSWER Q.18-19 BELOW
No → GO TO Q.20, PAGE 8
Not married   1861

2.18a Has your husband or wife or partner ever been divorced?
PLEASE TICK ONE BOX ONLY
Yes
No   1862

b) Did you live with your husband or wife or partner before you got married?
PLEASE TICK ONE BOX
Yes
No
Not married   1863

2.19a Do you and your husband or wife or partner both have paid work at the moment?
PLEASE TICK ONE BOX
Yes → ANSWER b), BELOW
No → GO TO Q.20, PAGE 8   1864

b) Who earns more money?
PLEASE TICK ONE BOX ONLY
Husband earns much more
Husband earns a bit more
We earn about the same amount
Wife earns a bit more
Wife earns much more   1865

Please continue ...

INTERNATIONAL SOCIAL SURVEY PROGRAMME

1989 MODULE

WORK ORIENTATIONS

(ENGLISH LANGUAGE VERSION)

- 1 -

1. Suppose you could change the way you spend your time, spending more time on some things and less time on others.

Which of the things on the following list would you like to spend more time on, which would you like to spend less time on and which would you like to spend the same amount of time on as now?

PLEASE TICK ONE BOX ON EACH LINE

	Much more time	A bit more time	Same time as now	A bit less time	Much less time	Can't choose/ Doesn't apply	OFFICE USE ONLY
							CARD 19
a. Time in a paid job?	1	2	3	4	5	8	1908
b. Time doing household work?	1	2	3	4	5	8	1909
c. Time with your family?	1	2	3	4	5	8	1910
d. Time with your friends?	1	2	3	4	5	8	1911
e. Time in leisure activities?	1	2	3	4	5	8	1912
f. Time to relax?	1	2	3	4	5	8	1913

2. Please tick one box for each statement below to show how much you agree or disagree with it, thinking of work in general.

PLEASE TICK ONE BOX ON EACH LINE

	Strongly agree	Agree	Neither Agree nor disagree	Disagree	Strongly Disagree	Can't choose	OFFICE USE ONLY
a. A job is just a way of earning money - no more.	1	2	3	4	5	8	1914
b. I would enjoy having a paid job even if I did not need the money.	1	2	3	4	5	8	1915
c. Work is a person's most important activity.	1	2	3	4	5	8	1916

Please continue ...

- 2 -

3. Are you the person responsible for doing the general domestic duties - like cleaning, cooking, washing and so on - in your household?

PLEASE TICK ONE BOX ONLY

	OFFICE USE ONLY
Yes, I am mainly responsible	1
Yes, I am equally responsible with someone else	2
No, someone else is mainly responsible	3

1917

4. Think of two people doing the same kind of work. What do you personally think should be important in deciding how much to pay them?

Looking at the things below, please write '1' in the box next to the thing you think should be most important.

Then write '2' next to the thing you think should be next most important. And '3' next to the thing you think should be third most important. Leave the other boxes blank.

Write 1,2 and 3 in THREE boxes: leave the other boxes blank

		OFFICE USE ONLY
In deciding on pay for two people doing the same kind of work how important should be ...		
... how long the employee has been with the firm?	☐	1918
... how well the employee does the job?	☐	1919
... the experience of the employee in doing the work?	☐	1920
... the standard rate - giving both employees the same pay?	☐	1921
... the age of the employee?	☐	1922
... the sex of the employee?	☐	1923
... the employee's family responsibilities?	☐	1924
... the employee's education and formal qualifications?	☐	1925
OR TICK: Can't choose	8	1926

Please continue ...

- 3 -

5. How much do you agree or disagree with these two statements?

PLEASE TICK ONE BOX ON EACH LINE

	Strongly agree	Agree	Neither agree nor disagree	Disagree	Strongly disagree	Can't choose	OFFICE USE ONLY
a. There will always be conflict between management and workers because they are really on opposite sides.	☐	☐	☐	☐	☐	☐	1927
b. Workers need strong trade unions to protect their interests.	☐	☐	☐	☐	☐	☐	1928

6. From the following list, please tick one box for each item to show how important you personally think it is in a job.

PLEASE TICK ONE BOX ON EACH LINE

How important is ...	Very important	Important	Neither important nor unimportant	Not important	Not important at all	Can't choose	OFFICE USE ONLY
a. ... job security?	☐	☐	☐	☐	☐	☐	1929
b. ... high income?	☐	☐	☐	☐	☐	☐	1930
c. ... good opportunities for advancement?	☐	☐	☐	☐	☐	☐	1931
d. ... a job that leaves a lot of leisure time?	☐	☐	☐	☐	☐	☐	1932
e. ... an interesting job?	☐	☐	☐	☐	☐	☐	1933
f. ... a job that allows someone to work independently?	☐	☐	☐	☐	☐	☐	1934
g. ... a job that allows someone to help other people?	☐	☐	☐	☐	☐	☐	1935
h. ... a job that is useful to society?	☐	☐	☐	☐	☐	☐	1936
i. ... a job with flexible working hours?	☐	☐	☐	☐	☐	☐	1937

Please continue ....

1938-40

- 4 -

7. Suppose you were unemployed and couldn't find a job. Which of the following problems do you think would be the worst?

Please write '1' in the box next to the worst thing. Then write '2' beside the next worst thing. And '3' beside the third worst thing. Leave the other boxes blank.

	Write 1,2 and 3 in THREE boxes: Leave the other boxes blank	OFFICE USE ONLY
Lack of contact with people at work	☐	1941
Not enough money	☐	1942
Loss of self-confidence	☐	1943
Loss of respect from friends and acquaintances	☐	1944
Family tensions	☐	1945
Loss of job experience	☐	1946
Not knowing how to fill one's time	☐	1947
OR TICK: Can't choose	☐	1948

8. Suppose you were working and could choose between different kinds of jobs. Which of the following would you personally choose?

PLEASE TICK ONE BOX ONLY

a. I would choose ...

		OFFICE USE ONLY
... being an employee	☑ ☐ ☐	1949
... being self-employed		
Can't choose		

PLEASE TICK ONE BOX ONLY

b. I would choose ...

		OFFICE USE ONLY
... working in a small firm	☑ ☐ ☐	1950
... working in a large firm		
Can't choose		

Please continue ....

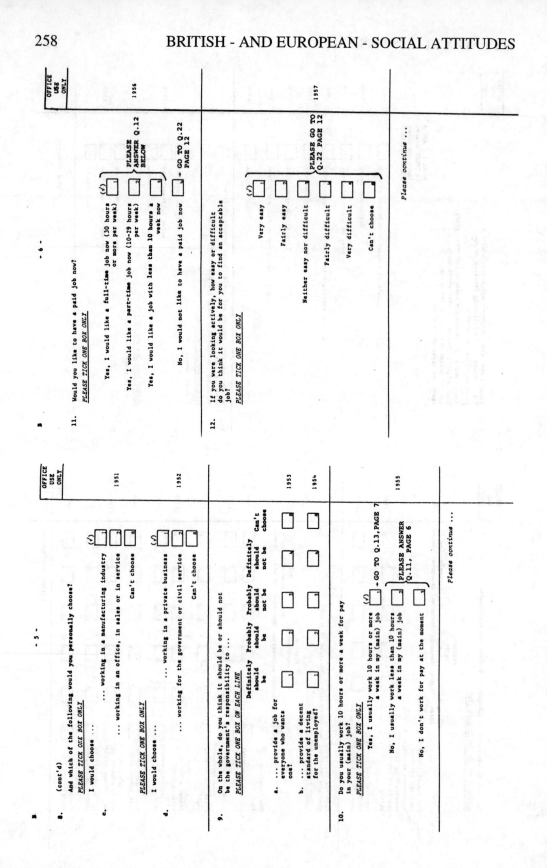

- 5 -

8. (cont'd)

And which of the following would you personally choose?
PLEASE TICK ONE BOX ONLY

I would choose ...

c. ... working in a manufacturing industry [1]
... working in an office, in sales or in service [2]
Can't choose [8]

OFFICE USE ONLY — 1951

PLEASE TICK ONE BOX ONLY

I would choose ...

d. ... working in a private business [1]
... working for the government or civil service [2]
Can't choose [8]

OFFICE USE ONLY — 1952

9. On the whole, do you think it should be or should not be the government's responsibility to ...
PLEASE TICK ONE BOX ON EACH LINE

	Definitely should be	Probably should be	Probably should not be	Definitely should not be	Can't choose	
a. ... provide a job for everyone who wants one?	[1]	[2]	[3]	[4]	[8]	1953
b. ... provide a decent standard of living for the unemployed?	[1]	[2]	[3]	[4]	[8]	1954

10. Do you usually work 10 hours or more a week for pay in your (main) job?
PLEASE TICK ONE BOX ONLY

Yes, I usually work 10 hours or more a week in my (main) job [1] → GO TO Q.13, PAGE 7

No, I usually work less than 10 hours a week in my (main) job [2]

No, I don't work for pay at the moment [3]
} PLEASE ANSWER Q.11, PAGE 6

OFFICE USE ONLY — 1955

Please continue ...

- 6 -

11. Would you like to have a paid job now?
PLEASE TICK ONE BOX ONLY

Yes, I would like a full-time job now (30 hours or more per week) [1]

Yes, I would like a part-time job now (10-29 hours per week) [2]

Yes, I would like a job with less than 10 hours a week now [3]
} PLEASE ANSWER Q.12 BELOW

No, I would not like to have a paid job now [4] → GO TO Q.22 PAGE 12

OFFICE USE ONLY — 1956

12. If you were looking actively, how easy or difficult do you think it would be for you to find an acceptable job?
PLEASE TICK ONE BOX ONLY

Very easy [1]

Fairly easy [2]

Neither easy nor difficult [3]

Fairly difficult [4]

Very difficult [5]

Can't choose [8]

PLEASE GO TO Q.22 PAGE 12

OFFICE USE ONLY — 1957

Please continue ...

- 7 -

PLEASE ANSWER Q.13 - Q.21 ABOUT YOUR MAIN JOB.

13. Which of the following statements best describes your feelings about your job?

PLEASE TICK ONE BOX ONLY

In my job ...

   ... I only work as hard as I have to ☐ 1

   ... I work hard, but not so that it interferes with the rest of my life ☐ 2

   ... I make a point of doing the best work I can, even if it sometimes does interfere with the rest of my life ☐ 3

   Can't choose ☐ 8

OFFICE USE ONLY

1958

14. Think of the number of hours you work, and the money you earn in your main job, including any regular overtime.

If you had only one of these three choices which of the following would you prefer?

PLEASE TICK ONE BOX ONLY

   Work longer hours and earn more money ☐ 1

   Work the same number of hours and earn the same money ☐ 2

   Work fewer hours and earn less money ☐ 3

   Can't choose ☐ 8

1959

Please continue ...

- 8 -

OFFICE USE ONLY

15. Think of two people doing the same kind of work in your place of work. What do you personally think is important in deciding how much to pay them?

Looking at the things below, please write '1' in the box next to the thing you think is most important at your place of work.

Then write '2' next to the thing you think is next most important. And '3' next to the thing you think is third most important. Leave the other boxes blank.

Write 1, 2 and 3 in THREE boxes. Leave the other boxes blank

At your workplace, in deciding on pay for two people doing the same kind of work, how important is ....

   ... how long the employee has been with the firm? ☐ 1960

   ... how well the employee does the job? ☐ 1961

   ... the experience of the employee in doing the work? ☐ 1962

   ... the standard rate - giving both employees the same pay? ☐ 1963

   ... the age of the employee? ☐ 1964

   ... the sex of the employee? ☐ 1965

   ... the employee's family responsibilities? ☐ 1966

   ... the employer's education and formal qualifications? ☐ 1967

OR TICK: Can't choose ☐ 1968

Please continue ...   1969-70

- 9 -

16. For each of these statements about your (main) job, please tick one box to show how much you agree or disagree that it applies to your job.

PLEASE TICK ONE BOX ON EACH LINE

	Strongly agree	Agree	Neither agree nor disagree	Disagree	Strongly disagree	Can't choose	OFFICE USE ONLY
a. My job is secure	☐	☐	☐	☐	☐	☐	197!
b. My income is high	☐	☐	☐	☐	☐	☐	1972
c. My opportunities for advancement are high	☐	☐	☐	☐	☐	☐	1973
d. My job leaves a lot of leisure time	☐	☐	☐	☐	☐	☐	1974
e. My job is interesting	☐	☐	☐	☐	☐	☐	1975
f. I can work independently	☐	☐	☐	☐	☐	☐	1976
g. In my job I can help other people	☐	☐	☐	☐	☐	☐	1977
h. My job is useful to society	☐	☐	☐	☐	☐	☐	1978
i. My job has flexible working hours	☐	☐	☐	☐	☐	☐	1979

Please continue ...

1980

- 10 -

17. Now some more questions about your working conditions. Please tick one box for each item below to show how often it applies to your work.

PLEASE TICK ONE BOX ON EACH LINE

How often ...	Always	Often	Sometimes	Hardly ever	Never	Can't choose	OFFICE USE ONLY
							CARD 20
a. ... do you come home from work exhausted?	☐	☐	☐	☐	☐	☐	2008
b. ... do you have to do hard physical work?	☐	☐	☐	☐	☐	☐	2009
c. ... do you find your work stressful?	☐	☐	☐	☐	☐	☐	2010
d. ... are you bored at work?	☐	☐	☐	☐	☐	☐	2011
e. ... do you work in dangerous conditions?	☐	☐	☐	☐	☐	☐	2012
f. ... do you work in unhealthy conditions?	☐	☐	☐	☐	☐	☐	2013
g. ... do you work in physically unpleasant conditions?	☐	☐	☐	☐	☐	☐	2014

18. And which of the following statements about your work is most true?

PLEASE TICK ONE BOX ONLY

		OFFICE USE ONLY
My job allows me to design or plan most of my daily work	☐	
My job allows me to design or plan parts of my daily work	☐	
My job does not really allow me to design or plan my daily work	☐	2015

Please continue ...

- 11 -

19. If you lost your job for any reason, and were looking actively for another one, how easy or difficult do you think it would be for you to find an acceptable job?

PLEASE TICK ONE BOX ONLY

	(✓)	
Very easy	☐	
Fairly easy	☐	
Neither easy nor difficult	☐	2016
Fairly difficult	☐	
Very difficult	☐	
Can't choose	☐	

20. In general, how would you describe relations at your workplace ...

PLEASE TICK ONE BOX ON EACH LINE

	Very good	Quite good	Neither good nor bad	Quite bad	Very bad	Can't choose	
a. ... between management and employees?	☐	☐	☐	☐	☐	☐	2017
b. ... between workmates/ colleagues?	☐	☐	☐	☐	☐	☐	2018

21. How satisfied are you in your (main) job?

PLEASE TICK ONE BOX ONLY

	(✓)	
Completely satisfied	☐	
Very satisfied	☐	
Fairly satisfied	☐	
Neither satisfied nor dissatisfied	☐	2019
Fairly dissatisfied	☐	
Very dissatisfied	☐	
Completely dissatisfied	☐	
Can't choose	☐	2020

Please continue ...

INTERNATIONAL SOCIAL SURVEY PROGRAMME

1990 MODULE

ROLE OF GOVERNMENT II

(ENGLISH LANGUAGE VERSION)

- 1 -

L.

20.1 In general, would you say that people should obey the law without exception, or are there exceptional occasions on which people should follow their consciences even if it means breaking the law?

PLEASE TICK ONE BOX

		OFFICE USE ONLY
Obey the law without exception	☐	
Follow conscience on occasions	☐	2121
Can't choose	☐	

20.2 There are many ways people or organisations can protest against a government action they strongly oppose.

Please show which you think should be allowed and which should not be allowed by ticking a box on each line.

PLEASE TICK ONE BOX ON EACH LINE

	Should it be allowed?					OFFICE USE ONLY
	Defin-itely	Prob-ably	Probably not	Definitely not	Can't choose	
Organising public meetings to protest against the government	☐	☐	☐	☐	☐	2122
Publishing pamphlets to protest against the government	☐	☐	☐	☐	☐	2123
Organising protest marches and demonstrations	☐	☐	☐	☐	☐	2124
Occupying a government office and stopping work there for several days	☐	☐	☐	☐	☐	2125
Seriously damaging government buildings	☐	☐	☐	☐	☐	2126
Organising a nationwide strike of all workers against the government	☐	☐	☐	☐	☐	2127

Please continue ......

- 2 -

L.

20.3 There are some people whose views are considered extreme by the majority.

First, consider people who want to overthrow the government by revolution. Do you think such people should be allowed to ...

PLEASE TICK ONE BOX ON EACH LINE

	Defin-itely	Prob-ably	Probably not	Definitely not	Can't choose	OFFICE USE ONLY
i) ... hold public meetings to express their views?	☐	☐	☐	☐	☐	2128
ii) ... publish books expressing their views?	☐	☐	☐	☐	☐	2129

20.4 Second, consider people who believe that whites are racially superior to all other races. Do you think such people should be allowed to ...

PLEASE TICK ONE BOX ON EACH LINE

	Defin-itely	Prob-ably	Probably not	Definitely not	Can't choose	
i) ... hold public meetings to express their views?	☐	☐	☐	☐	☐	2130
ii) ... publish books expressing their views?	☐	☐	☐	☐	☐	2131

20.5 Suppose the police get an anonymous tip that a man with a long criminal record is planning to break into a warehouse.

PLEASE TICK ONE BOX ON EACH LINE

Do you think the police should be allowed, without a Court Order ...

	Defin-itely	Prob-ably	Probably not	Definitely not	Can't choose	
i) ... to keep the man under surveillance?	☐	☐	☐	☐	☐	2132
ii) ... to tap his telephone?	☐	☐	☐	☐	☐	2133
iii) ... to open his mail?	☐	☐	☐	☐	☐	2134
iv) ... to detain the man over-night for questioning?	☐	☐	☐	☐	☐	2135

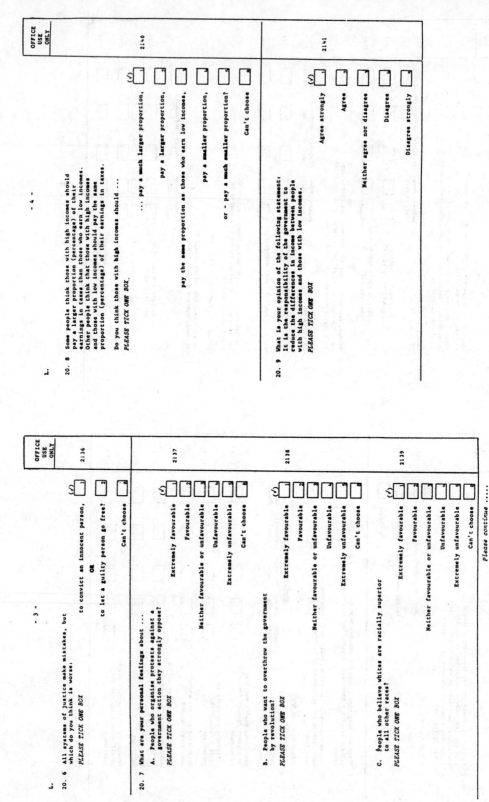

- 4 -

L.

20. 8 Some people think those with high incomes should pay a larger proportion (percentage) of their earnings in taxes than those who earn low incomes. Other people think that those with high incomes and those with low incomes should pay the same proportion (percentage) of their earnings in taxes.

Do you think those with high incomes should ...

PLEASE TICK ONE BOX.

... pay a much larger proportion,

pay a larger proportion,

pay the same proportion as those who earn low incomes,

pay a smaller proportion,

or - pay a much smaller proportion?

Can't choose

OFFICE USE ONLY   2140

20. 9 What is your opinion of the following statement:
It is the responsibility of the government to reduce the differences in income between people with high incomes and those with low incomes.

PLEASE TICK ONE BOX

Agree strongly

Agree

Neither agree nor disagree

Disagree

Disagree strongly

OFFICE USE ONLY   2141

- 3 -

L.

20. 6 All systems of justice make mistakes, but which do you think is worse:

PLEASE TICK ONE BOX

to convict an innocent person,

OR

to let a guilty person go free?

Can't choose

OFFICE USE ONLY   2136

20. 7 What are your personal feelings about ....

A. People who organise protests against a government action they strongly oppose?

PLEASE TICK ONE BOX

Extremely favourable

Favourable

Neither favourable or unfavourable

Unfavourable

Extremely unfavourable

Can't choose

2137

B. People who want to overthrow the government by revolution?

PLEASE TICK ONE BOX

Extremely favourable

Favourable

Neither favourable or unfavourable

Unfavourable

Extremely unfavourable

Can't choose

2138

C. People who believe whites are racially superior to all other races?

PLEASE TICK ONE BOX

Extremely favourable

Favourable

Neither favourable or unfavourable

Unfavourable

Extremely unfavourable

Can't choose

2139

Please continue ......

- 5 -

2.10 Here are some things the government might do for the economy. Please show which actions you are in favour of and which you are against.

PLEASE TICK ONE BOX ON EACH LINE

	Strongly in favour of	In favour of	Neither in favour of nor against	Against	Strongly against	OFFICE USE ONLY
A. Control of wages by law	1	2	3	4	5	2142
B. Control of prices by law	1	2	3	4	5	2143
C. Cuts in government spending	1	2	3	4	5	2144
D. Government financing of projects to create new jobs	1	2	3	4	5	2145
E. Less government regulation of business	1	2	3	4	5	2146
F. Support for industry to develop new products and technology	1	2	3	4	5	2147
G. Support for declining industries to protect jobs	1	2	3	4	5	2148
H. Reducing the working week to create more jobs	1	2	3	4	5	2149

2.11 Listed below are various areas of government spending. Please show whether you would like to see more or less government spending in each area.

Remember that if you say "much more", it might require a tax increase to pay for it.

PLEASE TICK ONE BOX ON EACH LINE

	Spend much more	Spend more	Spend the same as now	Spend less	Spend much less	Can't choose	OFFICE USE ONLY
A. The environment	1	2	3	4	5	8	2150
B. Health	1	2	3	4	5	8	2151
C. The police and law enforcement	1	2	3	4	5	8	2152
D. Education	1	2	3	4	5	8	2153
E. The military and defence	1	2	3	4	5	8	2154
F. Old age pensions	1	2	3	4	5	8	2155
G. Unemployment benefits	1	2	3	4	5	8	2156
H. Culture and the arts	1	2	3	4	5	8	2157

Please continue .....

- 6 -

2.12 If the government had to choose between keeping down inflation or keeping down unemployment, to which do you think it should give highest priority?

PLEASE TICK ONE BOX

- Keeping down inflation 1
- Keeping down unemployment 2
- Can't choose 8

OFFICE USE ONLY: 2158

2.13 Do you think that trade unions in this country have too much power or too little power?

PLEASE TICK ONE BOX

- Far too much power 1
- Too much power 2
- About the right amount of power 3
- Too little power 4
- Far too little power 5
- Can't choose 8

OFFICE USE ONLY: 2159

2.14 How about business and industry? Do they have too much power or too little power?

PLEASE TICK ONE BOX

- Far too much power 1
- Too much power 2
- About the right amount of power 3
- Too little power 4
- Far too little power 5
- Can't choose 8

OFFICE USE ONLY: 2160

- 7 -

2.15 And what about the government, does it have too much power or too little power?

PLEASE TICK ONE BOX

		OFFICE USE ONLY
Far too much power	☐	2161
Too much power	☐	
About the right amount of power	☐	
Too little power	☐	
Far too little power	☐	
Can't choose	☐	

2.16 In general, how good would you say trade unions are for the country as a whole?

PLEASE TICK ONE BOX

		OFFICE USE ONLY
Excellent	☐	2162
Very good	☐	
Fairly good	☐	
Not very good	☐	
Not good at all	☐	
Can't choose	☐	

2.17 What do you think the government's role in each of these industries and services should be?

PLEASE TICK ONE BOX ON EACH LINE

	The government should:				OFFICE USE ONLY
	Own it	Control prices and profits but not own it	Neither own it nor control its prices & profits	Can't choose	
A. Electricity	☐	☐	☐	☐	2163
B. The steel industry	☐	☐	☐	☐	2164
C. Banking and insurance	☐	☐	☐	☐	2165

Please continue .....

- 8 -

2.18 On the whole, do you think it should or should not be the government's responsibility to ....

PLEASE TICK ONE BOX ON EACH LINE

		Definitely should be	Probably should be	Probably should not be	Definitely should not be	Can't choose	OFFICE USE ONLY
A.	... provide a job for everyone who wants one	☐	☐	☐	☐	☐	2166
B.	... keep prices under control	☐	☐	☐	☐	☐	2167
C.	... provide health care for the sick	☐	☐	☐	☐	☐	2168
D.	... provide a decent standard of living for the old	☐	☐	☐	☐	☐	2169
E.	... provide industry with the help it needs to grow	☐	☐	☐	☐	☐	2170
F.	... provide a decent standard of living for the unemployed	☐	☐	☐	☐	☐	2171
G.	... reduce income differences between the rich and poor	☐	☐	☐	☐	☐	2172
H.	... give financial help to university students from low-income families	☐	☐	☐	☐	☐	2173
I.	... provide decent housing for those who can't afford it	☐	☐	☐	☐	☐	2174

2.19 How interested would you say you personally are in politics?

PLEASE TICK ONE BOX

		OFFICE USE ONLY
Very interested	☐	2175
Fairly interested	☐	
Somewhat interested	☐	
Not very interested	☐	
Not at all interested	☐	
Can't choose	☐	

2176-80

INTERNATIONAL SOCIAL SURVEY PROGRAMME

1991 MODULE

RELIGION

(ENGLISH LANGUAGE VERSION)

	OFFICE USE ONLY

1

A 2.01 If you were to consider your life in general these days, how happy or unhappy would you say you are, on the whole?

PLEASE TICK ONE BOX ONLY

CARD 19

                       (✓)

Very happy   □ 1

Fairly happy   □ 2

Not very happy   □ 3

Not at all happy   □ 4

Can't choose   □ 8

1921

A 2.02 On the whole, do you think it should or should not be the government's responsibility to ...

PLEASE TICK ONE BOX ON EACH LINE

	Definitely should be	Probably should be	Probably should not be	Definitely should not be	Can't choose
a. Provide a job for everyone who wants one?	□ 1	□ 2	□ 3	□ 4	□ 8
b. Reduce income differences between the rich and poor?	□ 1	□ 2	□ 3	□ 4	□ 8

1922

1923

A 2.03 Here are some measures to deal with crime. Some people are in favour of them while others are against them. Do you agree or disagree that ...

PLEASE TICK ONE BOX ON EACH LINE

	Strongly agree	Agree	Neither agree nor disagree	Disagree	Strongly disagree	Can't choose
a. People who break the law should be given stiffer sentences?	□ 1	□ 2	□ 3	□ 4	□ 5	□ 8
b. People convicted of murder should be subject to the death penalty?	□ 1	□ 2	□ 3	□ 4	□ 5	□ 8

1924

1925

Please continue ...

2

A 2.04 Do you think it is wrong or not wrong if a man and a woman have sexual relations before marriage?

PLEASE TICK ONE BOX ONLY

          (✓)

Always wrong   □ 1

Almost always wrong   □ 2

Wrong only sometimes   □ 3

Not wrong at all   □ 4

Can't choose   □ 8

1926

A 2.05 What about a married person having sexual relations with someone other than his or her husband or wife, is it ...

PLEASE TICK ONE BOX ONLY

          (✓)

Always wrong   □ 1

Almost always wrong   □ 2

Wrong only sometimes   □ 3

Not wrong at all   □ 4

Can't choose   □ 8

1927

A 2.06 And what about sexual relations between two adults of the same sex, is it ...

PLEASE TICK ONE BOX ONLY

          (✓)

Always wrong   □ 1

Almost always wrong   □ 2

Wrong only sometimes   □ 3

Not wrong at all   □ 4

Can't choose   □ 8

1928

A 2.07 Do you think the law should or should not allow a woman to obtain a legal abortion ...

PLEASE TICK ONE BOX ON EACH LINE

	Definitely should allow it	Probably should allow it	Probably should not allow it	Definitely should not allow it	Can't choose	OFFICE USE ONLY
a. If there is a strong chance of a serious defect in the baby?	1	2	3	4	8	1929
b. If the family has a very low income and cannot afford any more children?	1	2	3	4	8	1930

A 2.08 Do you personally think it is wrong or not wrong for a woman to have an abortion ...

PLEASE TICK ONE BOX ON EACH LINE

	Always wrong	Almost always wrong	Wrong only sometimes	Not wrong at all	Can't choose	OFFICE USE ONLY
a. If there is a strong chance of a serious defect in the baby?	1	2	3	4	8	1931
b. If the family has a very low income and cannot afford any more children?	1	2	3	4	8	1932

A 2.09 How much do you agree or disagree ...

PLEASE TICK ONE BOX ON EACH LINE

	Strongly agree	Agree	Neither agree nor disagree	Disagree	Strongly disagree	Can't choose	OFFICE USE ONLY
a. A husband's job is to earn the money; a wife's job is to look after the home and family	1	2	3	4	5	8	1933
b. All in all, family life suffers when the woman has a full-time job	1	2	3	4	5	8	1934

A 2.10 Consider the situations listed below. Do you feel it is wrong or not wrong if ...

PLEASE TICK ONE BOX ON EACH LINE

	Not wrong	A bit wrong	Wrong	Seriously wrong	Can't choose	OFFICE USE ONLY
a. A taxpayer does not report all of his income in order to pay less income tax?	1	2	3	4	8	1935
b. A person gives the government incorrect information about himself to get government benefits that he is not entitled to?	1	2	3	4	8	1936

A 2.11 How much confidence do you have in ...

PLEASE TICK ONE BOX ON EACH LINE

	Complete confidence	A great deal of confidence	Some confidence	Very little confidence	No confidence at all	Can't choose	OFFICE USE ONLY
a. The British parliament?	1	2	3	4	5	8	1937
b. Business and industry?	1	2	3	4	5	8	1938
c. The Civil Service?	1	2	3	4	5	8	1939
d. Churches and religious organisations?	1	2	3	4	5	8	1940
e. Courts and the legal system?	1	2	3	4	5	8	1941
f. Schools and the educational system?	1	2	3	4	5	8	1942

Please continue ...

3

A 2.12 How much do you agree or disagree with each of the following?

PLEASE TICK ONE BOX ON EACH LINE

	Strongly agree	Agree	Neither agree nor disagree	Disagree	Strongly disagree	Can't choose	OFFICE USE ONLY
a. Politicians who do not believe in God are unfit for public office	1	2	3	4	5	6	1943
b. Religious leaders should not try to influence how people vote in elections	1	2	3	4	5	6	1944
c. It would be better for Britain if more people with strong religious beliefs held public office	1	2	3	4	5	6	1945
d. Religious leaders should not try to influence government decisions	1	2	3	4	5	6	1946

A 2.13 Do you think that churches and religious organisations in this country have too much power or too little power?

PLEASE TICK ONE BOX ONLY

		OFFICE USE ONLY
Far too much power	1	1947
Too much power	2	
About the right amount of power	3	
Too little power	4	
Far too little power	5	
Can't choose	6	

Please continue ...

A 2.14 Please tick one box below to show which statement comes closest to expressing what you believe about God.

PLEASE TICK ONE BOX ONLY

		OFFICE USE ONLY
I don't believe in God	1	1948
I don't know whether there is a God and I don't believe there is any way to find out	2	
I don't believe in a personal God, but I do believe in a Higher Power of some kind	3	
I find myself believing in God some of the time, but not at others	4	
While I have doubts, I feel that I do believe in God	5	
I know God really exists and I have no doubts about it	6	

A 2.15 How close do you feel to God most of the time?

PLEASE TICK ONE BOX ONLY

		OFFICE USE ONLY
Don't believe in God	1	1949
Not close at all	2	
Not very close	3	
Somewhat close	4	
Extremely close	5	
Can't choose	6	

A 2.16 Which best describes your beliefs about God?

PLEASE TICK ONE BOX ONLY

		OFFICE USE ONLY
I don't believe in God now and I never have	1	1950
I don't believe in God now, but I used to	2	
I believe in God now, but I didn't used to	3	
I believe in God now and I always have	4	
Can't choose	8	

8

A 2.19 How much do you agree or disagree with each of the following?
PLEASE TICK ONE BOX ON EACH LINE

	Strongly agree	Agree	Neither agree nor disagree	Disagree	Strongly disagree	Can't choose	OFFICE USE ONLY
a. There is a God who concerns Himself with every human being personally	1	2	3	4	5	8	1957
b. There is little that people can do to change the course of their lives	1	2	3	4	5	8	1958
c. To me, life is meaningful only because God exists	1	2	3	4	5	8	1959
d. In my opinion, life does not serve any purpose	1	2	3	4	5	8	1960
e. The course of our lives is decided by God	1	2	3	4	5	8	1961
f. Life is only meaningful if you provide the meaning yourself	1	2	3	4	5	8	1962
g. We each make our own fate	1	2	3	4	5	8	1963

A 2.20 How often have you felt as though you were ...
PLEASE TICK ONE BOX ON EACH LINE

	Never in my life	Once or twice	Several times	Often	Can't say	OFFICE USE ONLY
a. Really in touch with someone who had died?	1	2	3	3	8	1964
b. Close to a powerful, spiritual force that seemed to lift you out of yourself?	1	2	3	3	8	1965

7

A 2.17 Do you believe in ...
PLEASE TICK ONE BOX ON EACH LINE

	Yes, definitely	Yes, probably	No, probably not	No, definitely not	Can't choose	OFFICE USE ONLY
a. Life after death?	1	2	3	4	8	1951
b. The Devil?	1	2	3	4	8	1952
c. Heaven?	1	2	3	4	8	1953
d. Hell?	1	2	3	4	8	1954
e. Religious miracles?	1	2	3	4	8	1955

A 2.18 Which one of these statements comes closest to describing your feelings about the Bible?
PLEASE TICK ONE BOX ONLY

		OFFICE USE ONLY
The Bible is the actual word of God and it is to be taken literally, word for word	1	1956
The Bible is the inspired word of God but not everything should be taken literally, word for word	2	
The Bible is an ancient book of fables, legends, history and moral teachings recorded by man	3	
This does not apply to me	4	
Can't choose	8	

Please continue ...

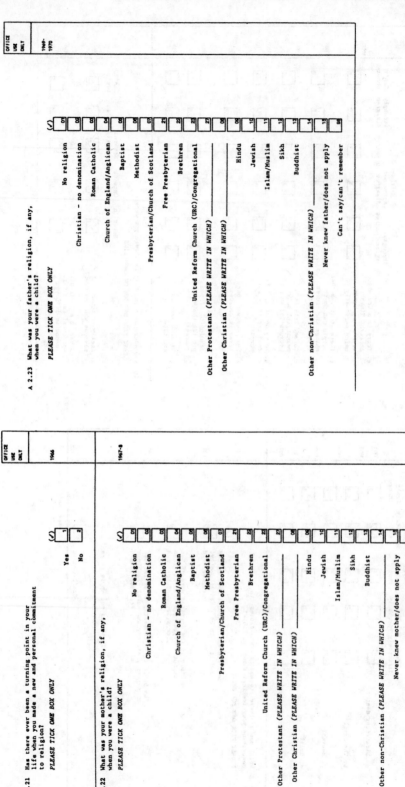

OFFICE USE ONLY

1969-1970

10

A 2.23 What was your father's religion, if any, when you were a child?

PLEASE TICK ONE BOX ONLY

- No religion — 01
- Christian - no denomination — 02
- Roman Catholic — 03
- Church of England/Anglican — 04
- Baptist — 05
- Methodist — 06
- Presbyterian/Church of Scotland — 07
- Free Presbyterian — 21
- Brethren — 22
- United Reform Church (URC)/Congregational — 27
- Other Protestant *(PLEASE WRITE IN WHICH)* — 08
- Other Christian *(PLEASE WRITE IN WHICH)* — 09
- Hindu — 10
- Jewish — 11
- Islam/Muslim — 12
- Sikh — 13
- Buddhist — 14
- Other non-Christian *(PLEASE WRITE IN WHICH)* — 15
- Never knew father/does not apply —
- Can't say/can't remember — 98

OFFICE USE ONLY

1966

1967-8

9

A 2.21 Has there ever been a turning point in your life when you made a new and personal commitment to religion?

PLEASE TICK ONE BOX ONLY

- Yes — 1
- No — 2

A 2.22 What was your mother's religion, if any, when you were a child?

PLEASE TICK ONE BOX ONLY

- No religion — 01
- Christian - no denomination — 02
- Roman Catholic — 03
- Church of England/Anglican — 04
- Baptist — 05
- Methodist — 06
- Presbyterian/Church of Scotland — 07
- Free Presbyterian — 21
- Brethren — 22
- United Reform Church (URC)/Congregational — 27
- Other Protestant *(PLEASE WRITE IN WHICH)* — 08
- Other Christian *(PLEASE WRITE IN WHICH)* — 09
- Hindu — 10
- Jewish — 11
- Islam/Muslim — 12
- Sikh — 13
- Buddhist — 14
- Other non-Christian *(PLEASE WRITE IN WHICH)* — 15
- Never knew mother/does not apply —
- Can't say/can't remember — 98

Please continue ...

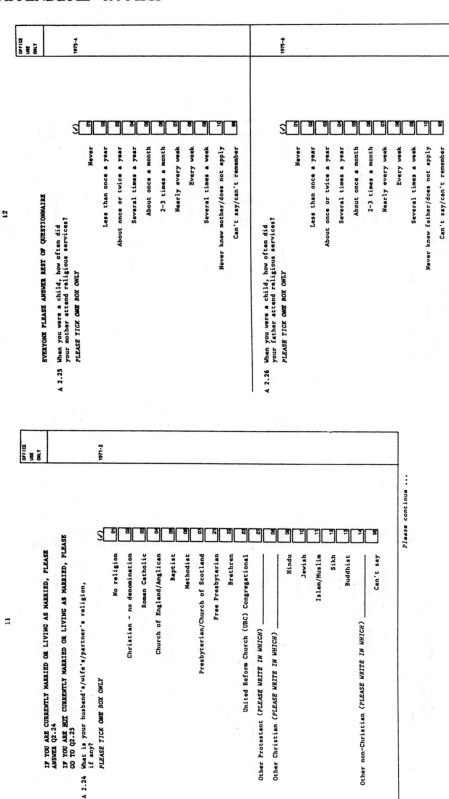

1975-4

12

EVERYONE PLEASE ANSWER REST OF QUESTIONNAIRE

A 2.25 When you were a child, how often did
your mother attend religious services?

PLEASE TICK ONE BOX ONLY

Never

Less than once a year

About once or twice a year

Several times a year

About once a month

2-3 times a month

Nearly every week

Every week

Several times a week

Never knew mother/does not apply

Can't say/can't remember

1975-6

A 2.26 When you were a child, how often did
your father attend religious services?

PLEASE TICK ONE BOX ONLY

Never

Less than once a year

About once or twice a year

Several times a year

About once a month

2-3 times a month

Nearly every week

Every week

Several times a week

Never knew father/does not apply

Can't say/can't remember

1971-2

11

IF YOU ARE CURRENTLY MARRIED OR LIVING AS MARRIED, PLEASE
ANSWER Q2-24

IF YOU ARE NOT CURRENTLY MARRIED OR LIVING AS MARRIED, PLEASE
GO TO Q2.25

A 2.24 What is your husband's/wife's/partner's religion,
if any?

PLEASE TICK ONE BOX ONLY

No religion

Christian - no denomination

Roman Catholic

Church of England/Anglican

Baptist

Methodist

Presbyterian/Church of Scotland

Free Presbyterian

Brethren

United Reform Church (URC) Congregational

Other Protestant *(PLEASE WRITE IN WHICH)*

Other Christian *(PLEASE WRITE IN WHICH)*

Hindu

Jewish

Islam/Muslim

Sikh

Buddhist

Other non-Christian *(PLEASE WRITE IN WHICH)*

Can't say

Please continue ...

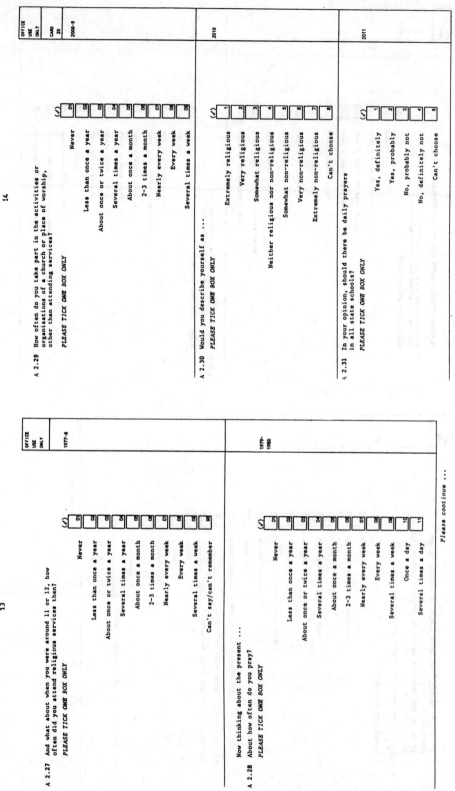

14

A 2.29 How often do you take part in the activities or organisations of a church or place of worship, other than attending services?

PLEASE TICK ONE BOX ONLY

OFFICE USE ONLY — CARD 20 — 2008-9

- Never
- Less than once a year
- About once or twice a year
- Several times a year
- About once a month
- 2-3 times a month
- Nearly every week
- Every week
- Several times a week

A 2.30 Would you describe yourself as ...

PLEASE TICK ONE BOX ONLY

2010

- Extremely religious
- Very religious
- Somewhat religious
- Neither religious nor non-religious
- Somewhat non-religious
- Very non-religious
- Extremely non-religious
- Can't choose

A 2.31 In your opinion, should there be daily prayers in all state schools?

PLEASE TICK ONE BOX ONLY

2011

- Yes, definitely
- Yes, probably
- No, probably not
- No, definitely not
- Can't choose

13

A 2.27 And what about when you were around 11 or 12, how often did you attend religious services then?

PLEASE TICK ONE BOX ONLY

OFFICE USE ONLY — 1977-8

- Never
- Less than once a year
- About once or twice a year
- Several times a year
- About once a month
- 2-3 times a month
- Nearly every week
- Every week
- Several times a week
- Can't say/can't remember

Now thinking about the present ...

A 2.28 About how often do you pray?

PLEASE TICK ONE BOX ONLY

1979-1980

- Never
- Less than once a year
- About once or twice a year
- Several times a year
- About once a month
- 2-3 times a month
- Nearly every week
- Every week
- Several times a week
- Once a day
- Several times a day

Please continue ...

15

2.32 How much do you agree or disagree with each of the following statements?

PLEASE TICK ONE BOX ON EACH LINE

	Strongly agree	Agree	Neither agree nor disagree	Disagree	Strongly disagree	Can't choose	
a. Right and wrong should be based on God's laws	1	2	3	4	5	8	2012
b. Right and wrong should be decided by society	1	2	3	4	5	8	2013
c. Right and wrong should be a matter of personal conscience	1	2	3	4	5	8	2014

2.33 Some books or films offend people who have strong religious beliefs. Should books and films that attack religions be prohibited by law or should they be allowed?

PLEASE TICK ONE BOX ONLY

Definitely should be prohibited	1
Probably should be prohibited	2
Probably should be allowed	3
Definitely should be allowed	4
Can't choose	8

2015

Please continue ...

2016 SPARE

16

A 2.34 Now thinking about the present. How often do you attend religious services?

PLEASE TICK ONE BOX

Never	1
Less than once a year	2
About once or twice a year	3
Several times a year	4
About once a month	5
2-3 times a month	6
Nearly every week	7
Every week	8
Several times a week	9

2017

A 2.35 Now please think about something different. Please tick one box on each line below to show whether you think each statement is true or false.

PLEASE TICK ONE BOX ON EACH LINE

	Definitely true	Probably true	Probably not true	Definitely not true	Can't choose	
a. Good luck charms sometimes do bring good luck	1	2	3	4	8	2018
b. Some fortune tellers really can foresee the future	1	2	3	4	8	2019
c. Some faith healers really do have God-given healing powers	1	2	3	4	8	2020
d. A person's star sign at birth, or horoscope, can affect the course of their future	1	2	3	4	8	2021

2022-2030 SPARE

INTERNATIONAL SOCIAL SURVEY PROGRAMME

1992 MODULE

SOCIAL INEQUALITY II

(ENGLISH LANGUAGE VERSION)

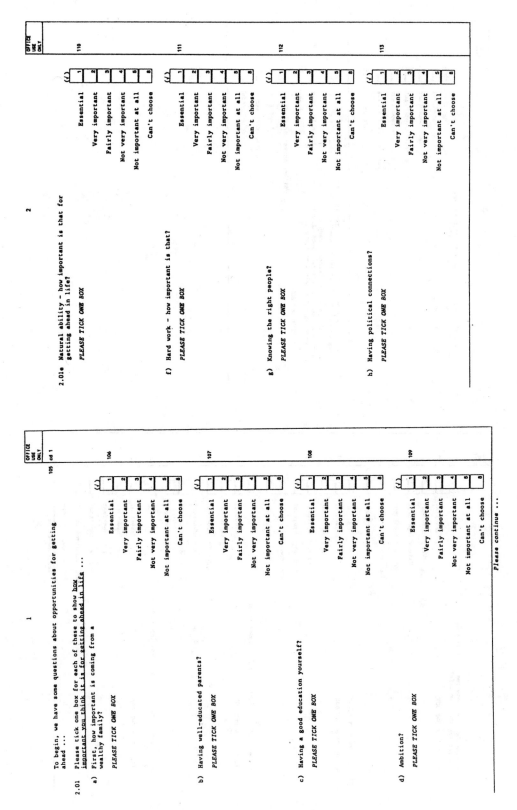

OFFICE USE ONLY 105 cd 1

1

To begin, we have some questions about opportunities for getting ahead ...

2.01 Please tick one box for each of these to show how important you think it is for getting ahead in life ...

a) First, how important is coming from a wealthy family?

PLEASE TICK ONE BOX

Essential — 1
Very important — 2
Fairly important — 3
Not very important — 4
Not important at all — 5
Can't choose — 8

106

b) Having well-educated parents?

PLEASE TICK ONE BOX

Essential — 1
Very important — 2
Fairly important — 3
Not very important — 4
Not important at all — 5
Can't choose — 8

107

c) Having a good education yourself?

PLEASE TICK ONE BOX

Essential — 1
Very important — 2
Fairly important — 3
Not very important — 4
Not important at all — 5
Can't choose — 8

108

d) Ambition?

PLEASE TICK ONE BOX

Essential — 1
Very important — 2
Fairly important — 3
Not very important — 4
Not important at all — 5
Can't choose — 8

109

Please continue ...

OFFICE USE ONLY

2

2.01e Natural ability - how important is that for getting ahead in life?

PLEASE TICK ONE BOX

Essential — 1
Very important — 2
Fairly important — 3
Not very important — 4
Not important at all — 5
Can't choose — 8

110

f) Hard work - how important is that?

PLEASE TICK ONE BOX

Essential — 1
Very important — 2
Fairly important — 3
Not very important — 4
Not important at all — 5
Can't choose — 8

111

g) Knowing the right people?

PLEASE TICK ONE BOX

Essential — 1
Very important — 2
Fairly important — 3
Not very important — 4
Not important at all — 5
Can't choose — 8

112

h) Having political connections?

PLEASE TICK ONE BOX

Essential — 1
Very important — 2
Fairly important — 3
Not very important — 4
Not important at all — 5
Can't choose — 8

113

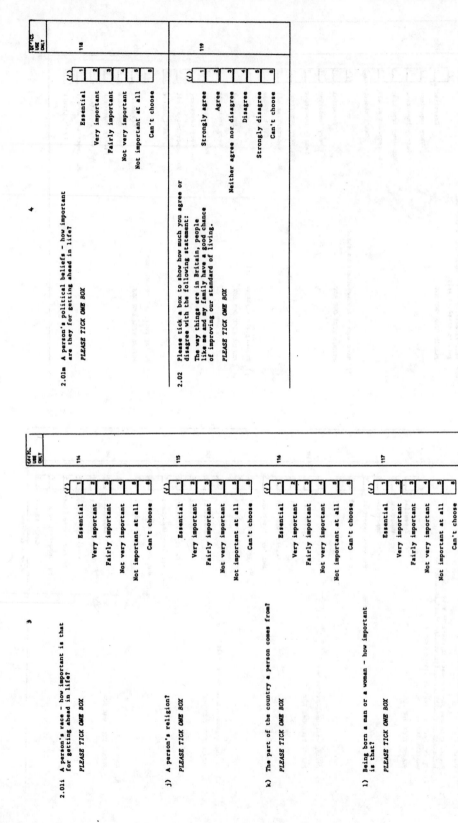

3

2.01i A person's race - how important is that for getting ahead in life?

PLEASE TICK ONE BOX

Essential	1
Very important	2
Fairly important	3
Not very important	4
Not important at all	5
Can't choose	8

114

j) A person's religion?

PLEASE TICK ONE BOX

Essential	1
Very important	2
Fairly important	3
Not very important	4
Not important at all	5
Can't choose	8

115

k) The part of the country a person comes from?

PLEASE TICK ONE BOX

Essential	1
Very important	2
Fairly important	3
Not very important	4
Not important at all	5
Can't choose	8

116

l) Being born a man or a woman - how important is that?

PLEASE TICK ONE BOX

Essential	1
Very important	2
Fairly important	3
Not very important	4
Not important at all	5
Can't choose	8

117

Please continue ...

4

2.01m A person's political beliefs - how important are they for getting ahead in life?

PLEASE TICK ONE BOX

Essential	1
Very important	2
Fairly important	3
Not very important	4
Not important at all	5
Can't choose	8

118

2.02 Please tick a box to show how much you agree or disagree with the following statement:

The way things are in Britain, people like me and my family have a good chance of improving our standard of living.

PLEASE TICK ONE BOX

Strongly agree	1
Agree	2
Neither agree nor disagree	3
Disagree	4
Strongly disagree	5
Can't choose	8

119

OFFICE USE ONLY

2.03 Do you agree or disagree with each of these statements?
PLEASE TICK ONE BOX ON EACH LINE

	Strongly agree	Agree	Neither agree nor disagree	Disagree	Strongly disagree	Can't choose	
a) People would not want to take extra responsibility at work unless they were paid extra for it.	1	2	3	4	5	8	120
b) Workers would not bother to get skills and qualifications unless they were paid extra for having them.	1	2	3	4	5	8	121
c) Inequality continues because it benefits the rich and powerful.	1	2	3	4	5	8	122
d) No-one would study for years to become a lawyer or doctor unless they expected to earn a lot more than ordinary workers.	1	2	3	4	5	8	123
e) Large differences in income are necessary for Britain's prosperity.	1	2	3	4	5	8	124
f) Allowing business to make good profits is the best way to improve everyone's standard of living.	1	2	3	4	5	8	125
g) Inequality continues to exist because ordinary people don't join together to get rid of it.	1	2	3	4	5	8	126

Please continue ...

2.04 We would like to know what you think people in these jobs actually earn.

Please write in how much you think they *usually* earn each year, before taxes.

(Many people are not exactly sure about this, but your best guess will be close enough. This may be difficult, but it is important, so please try.)

Please write in how much they actually earn each year, before tax

		Office use only
a) First, about how much do you think a skilled worker in a factory earns?	£	206-11
b) A doctor in general practice?	£	212-17
c) A shop assistant in a department store?	£	218-23
d) The chairman of a large national company?	£	224-29
e) A solicitor?	£	230-35
f) The owner of a small shop?	£	236-41
g) A farm worker?	£	242-47
h) The owner-manager of a large factory?	£	248-53
i) An Appeal Court judge?	£	254-59
j) An unskilled worker in a factory?	£	260-65
k) A cabinet minister in the national government?	£	266-71

2.05 Next, what do you think people in these jobs *ought* to be paid - how much do you think they should earn each year before taxes, regardless of what they actually get?

Please write in how much they should earn each year, before tax

		Office use only
a) First, about how much do you think a skilled worker in a factory *should* earn?	£	306-11
b) A doctor in general practice?	£	312-17
c) A shop assistant in a department store?	£	318-23
d) The chairman of a large national company?	£	324-29
e) A solicitor?	£	330-35
f) The owner of a small shop?	£	336-41
g) A farm worker?	£	342-47
h) The owner-manager of a large factory?	£	348-53
i) An Appeal Court judge?	£	354-59
j) An unskilled worker in a factory?	£	360-65
k) A cabinet minister in the national government?	£	366-71

2.06 Please show how much you agree or disagree with each statement ...
PLEASE TICK ONE BOX ON EACH LINE

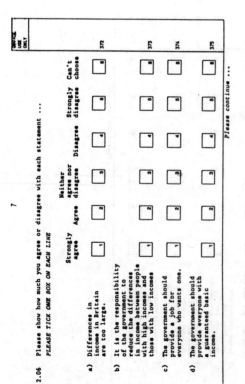

	Strongly agree	Agree	Neither agree nor disagree	Disagree	Strongly disagree	Can't choose	
a) Differences in income in Britain are too large.	1	2	3	4	5	6	372
b) It is the responsibility of the government to reduce the differences in income between people with high incomes and those with low incomes	1	2	3	4	5	6	373
c) The government should provide a job for everyone who wants one.	1	2	3	4	5	6	374
d) The government should provide everyone with a guaranteed basic income.	1	2	3	4	5	6	375

Please continue ...

7

2.07 Generally, how would you describe taxes in Britain today ...
(We mean all taxes together, including national insurance, income tax, VAT and all the rest.)

a) First, for those with high incomes, are taxes ...

PLEASE TICK ONE BOX

- 1 Much too high
- 2 Too high
- 3 About right
- 4 Too low
- 5 Much too low
- 6 Can't choose

376

b) Next, for those with middle incomes, are taxes ...

PLEASE TICK ONE BOX

- 1 Much too high
- 2 Too high
- 3 About right
- 4 Too low
- 5 Much too low
- 6 Can't choose

377

c) Lastly, for those with low incomes, are taxes ...

PLEASE TICK ONE BOX

- 1 Much too high
- 2 Too high
- 3 About right
- 4 Too low
- 5 Much too low
- 6 Can't choose

378

2.08 Do you think that people with high incomes should pay a larger share of their income in taxes than those with low incomes, the same share, or a smaller share?

PLEASE TICK ONE BOX

- 1 Much larger share
- 2 Larger
- 3 The same share
- 4 Smaller
- 5 Much smaller share
- 6 Can't choose

379

8

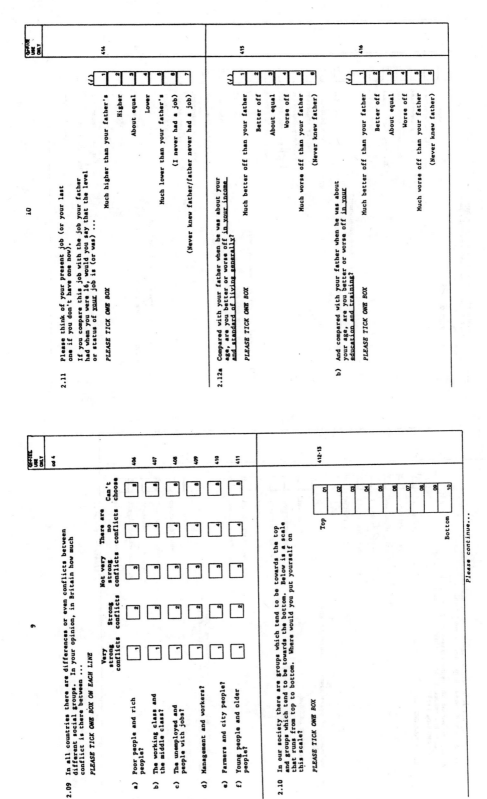

2.09 In all countries there are differences or even conflicts between different social groups. In your opinion, in Britain how much conflict is there between ...

PLEASE TICK ONE BOX ON EACH LINE

	Very strong conflicts	Strong conflicts	Not very strong conflicts	There are no conflicts	Can't choose	
a) Poor people and rich people?	1	2	3	4	8	406
b) The working class and the middle class?	1	2	3	4	8	407
c) The unemployed and people with jobs?	1	2	3	4	8	408
d) Management and workers?	1	2	3	4	8	409
e) Farmers and city people?	1	2	3	4	8	410
f) Young people and older people?	1	2	3	4	8	411

2.10 In our society there are groups which tend to be towards the top and groups which tend to be towards the bottom. Below is a scale that runs from top to bottom. Where would you put yourself on this scale?

PLEASE TICK ONE BOX

412-13

Top 01 / 02 / 03 / 04 / 05 / 06 / 07 / 08 / 09 / 10 Bottom

Please continue...

2.11 Please think of your present job (or your last one if you don't have one now).
If you compare this job with the job your father had when you were 16, would you say that the level or status of your job is (or was) ...

PLEASE TICK ONE BOX

Much higher than your father's	1	414
Higher	2	
About equal	3	
Lower	4	
Much lower than your father's	5	
(I never had a job)	6	
(Never knew father/father never had a job)	7	

2.12a Compared with your father when he was about your age, are you better or worse off in your income and standard of living generally?

PLEASE TICK ONE BOX

Much better off than your father	1	415
Better off	2	
About equal	3	
Worse off	4	
Much worse off than your father	5	
(Never knew father)	6	

b) And compared with your father when he was about your age, are you better or worse off in your education and training?

PLEASE TICK ONE BOX

Much better off than your father	1	416
Better off	2	
About equal	3	
Worse off	4	
Much worse off than your father	5	
(Never knew father)	6	

9

10

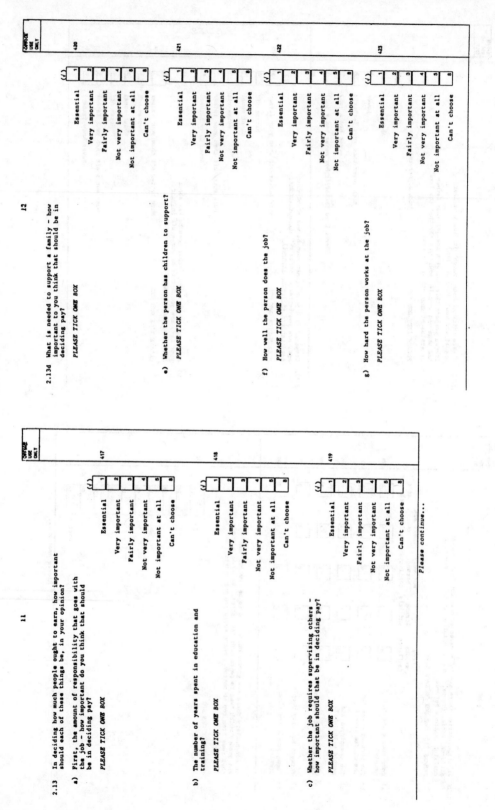

11

2.13 In deciding how much people ought to earn, how important should each of these things be, in your opinion?

a) First, the amount of responsibility that goes with the job - how important do you think that should be in deciding pay?

PLEASE TICK ONE BOX

417

Essential
Very important
Fairly important
Not very important
Not important at all
Can't choose

b) The number of years spent in education and training?

PLEASE TICK ONE BOX

418

Essential
Very important
Fairly important
Not very important
Not important at all
Can't choose

c) Whether the job requires supervising others - how important should that be in deciding pay?

PLEASE TICK ONE BOX

419

Essential
Very important
Fairly important
Not very important
Not important at all
Can't choose

Please continue...

12

2.13d What is needed to support a family - how important to you think that that should be in deciding pay?

PLEASE TICK ONE BOX

420

Essential
Very important
Fairly important
Not very important
Not important at all
Can't choose

e) Whether the person has children to support?

PLEASE TICK ONE BOX

421

Essential
Very important
Fairly important
Not very important
Not important at all
Can't choose

f) How well the person does the job?

PLEASE TICK ONE BOX

422

Essential
Very important
Fairly important
Not very important
Not important at all
Can't choose

g) How hard the person works at the job?

PLEASE TICK ONE BOX

423

Essential
Very important
Fairly important
Not very important
Not important at all
Can't choose

OFFICE USE ONLY

13

2.14a If incomes became more equal in Britain, some people would get higher incomes and some would get lower incomes. Do you think your income ...

PLEASE TICK ONE BOX

	OFFICE USE ONLY
	424

... would definitely go up — 1

would probably go up — 2

would stay the same — 3

would probably go down — 4

would definitely go down — 5

Can't choose — 6

b) And if incomes in Britain became less equal, do you think your income ...

PLEASE TICK ONE BOX

	425

... would definitely go up — 1

would probably go up — 2

would stay the same — 3

would probably go down — 4

would definitely go down — 5

Can't choose — 6

Please continue...

14

Now a few questions about yourself and your background...

2.15a Here is a list of different types of jobs. Which type did your father have when you were 16?

(If your father did not have a job then, please give the job he used to have.)

PLEASE TICK ONE BOX

	OFFICE USE ONLY
	426-27

(✓)

Professional and technical (for example: doctor, teacher, engineer, artist, accountant) — 01

Higher administrator (for example: banker, executive in big business, high government official, union official) — 02

Clerical (for example: secretary, clerk, office manager, bookkeeper) — 03

Sales (for example: sales manager, shop owner, shop assistant, insurance agent) — 04

Service (for example: restaurant owner, police officer, waiter, barber, caretaker) — 05

Skilled worker (for example: foreman, motor mechanic, printer, tool and die maker, electrician) — 06

Semi-Skilled worker (for example: bricklayer, bus driver, cannery worker, carpenter, sheet metal worker, baker) — 07

Unskilled worker (for example: labourer, porter, unskilled factory worker) — 08

Farm (for example: farmer, farm labourer, tractor driver) — 09

(Never knew father/father never had job) — 10

b) Was your father self-employed, or did he work for someone else?

PLEASE TICK ONE BOX

	428

(✓)

Self-employed, had own business or farm — 1

Worked for someone else — 2

(Never knew father/father never had job) — 3

INTERNATIONAL SOCIAL SURVEY PROGRAMME

1993 MODULE

ENVIRONMENT

(ENGLISH LANGUAGE VERSION)

OFFICE USE ONLY

1

2.01 Which of these would you say is more important in preparing children for life ...

PLEASE TICK ONE BOX ONLY

... to be obedient,

OR

... to think for themselves?

Can't choose

2.02 How much do you agree or disagree with each of these statements?

PLEASE TICK ONE BOX ON EACH LINE

	Strongly agree	Agree	Neither agree nor disagree	Disagree	Strongly disagree	Can't choose
a. Private enterprise is the best way to solve Britain's economic problems						
b. It is the responsibility of the government to reduce the differences in income between people with high incomes and those with low incomes						

2.03a Looking at the list below, please tick a box next to the one thing you think should be Britain's highest priority, the most important thing it should do.

PLEASE TICK ONE BOX ONLY

Highest priority

Britain should....

Maintain order in the nation

Give people more say in government decisions

Fight rising prices

Protect freedom of speech

Can't choose

b. And which one do you think should be Britain's next highest priority, the second most important thing it should do?

PLEASE TICK ONE BOX ONLY

Next highest priority

Britain should ...

Maintain order in the nation

Give people more say in government decisions

Fight rising prices

Protect freedom of speech

Can't choose

OFFICE USE ONLY

2

2.04 How much do you agree or disagree with each of these statements?

PLEASE TICK ONE BOX ON EACH LINE

	Strongly agree	Agree	Neither agree nor disagree	Disagree	Strongly disagree	Can't choose
a. We believe too often in science, and not enough in feelings and faith						
b. Overall, modern science does more harm than good						
c. Any change humans cause in nature - no matter how scientific - is likely to make things worse						
d. Modern science will solve our environmental problems with little change to our way of life						

2.05 And please tick one box for each of these statements to show how much you agree or disagree with it.

PLEASE TICK ONE BOX ON EACH LINE

	Strongly agree	Agree	Neither agree nor disagree	Disagree	Strongly disagree	Can't choose
a. We worry too much about the future of the environment and not enough about prices and jobs today						
b. Almost everything we do in modern life harms the environment						
c. Animals should have the same moral rights that human beings do						
d. Human beings should respect nature because it was created by God						

2.06 How much do you agree or disagree with each of the following statements?

PLEASE TICK ONE BOX ONLY

	Strongly agree	Agree	Neither agree nor disagree	Disagree	Strongly disagree	Can't choose
a. People worry too much about human progress harming the environment						
b. Nature would be at peace and in harmony if only human beings would leave it alone						
c. In order to protect the environment Britain needs economic growth						
d. It is right to use animals for medical testing if it might save human lives						
e. Nature is really a fierce struggle for survival of the fittest						
f. Economic growth always harms the environment						

2.07 Please tick one box to show which statement is closest to your views.

PLEASE TICK ONE BOX ONLY

- Nature is sacred because it is created by God
- Nature is spiritual or sacred in itself
- Nature is important, but not spiritual or sacred
- Can't choose

2.08a How willing would you be to pay much higher prices in order to protect the environment?

PLEASE TICK ONE BOX ONLY

- Very willing
- Fairly willing
- Neither willing nor unwilling
- Fairly unwilling
- Very unwilling
- Can't choose

b. And how willing would you be to pay much higher taxes in order to protect the environment?

PLEASE TICK ONE BOX ONLY

- Very willing
- Fairly willing
- Neither willing nor unwilling
- Fairly unwilling
- Very unwilling
- Can't choose

c. And how willing would you be to accept cuts in your standard of living in order to protect the environment?

PLEASE TICK ONE BOX ONLY

- Very willing
- Fairly willing
- Neither willing nor unwilling
- Fairly unwilling
- Very unwilling
- Can't choose

2.09 How much do you agree or disagree with each of these statements?

PLEASE TICK ONE BOX ON EACH LINE

	Strongly agree	Agree	Neither agree nor disagree	Disagree	Strongly disagree	Can't choose
a. It is just too difficult for someone like me to do much about the environment	☐	☐	☐	☐	☐	☐
b. I do what is right for the environment, even when it costs more money or takes more time	☐	☐	☐	☐	☐	☐

2.10 For each statement below, just tick the box that comes closest to your opinion of how true it is.

PLEASE TICK ONE BOX ON EACH LINE

In your opinion, how true is this?	Definitely true	Probably true	Probably not true	Definitely not true	Can't choose
a. 'All radioactivity is made by humans'	☐	☐	☐	☐	☐
b. 'Antibiotics can kill bacteria but not viruses'	☐	☐	☐	☐	☐
In your opinion, how true is this?					
c. 'Astrology - the study of star signs - has some scientific truth'	☐	☐	☐	☐	☐
d. 'Human beings developed from earlier species of animals'	☐	☐	☐	☐	☐
e. 'All man-made chemicals can cause cancer if you eat enough of them'	☐	☐	☐	☐	☐

2.11 And for each of these statements, just tick the box that comes closest to your opinion of how true it is.

PLEASE TICK ONE BOX ON EACH LINE

In your opinion, how true is this?	Definitely true	Probably true	Probably not true	Definitely not true	Can't choose
a. 'If someone is exposed to any amount of radioactivity, they are certain to die as a result'	☐	☐	☐	☐	☐
b. 'Some radioactive waste from nuclear power stations will be dangerous for thousands of years'	☐	☐	☐	☐	☐
c. 'The greenhouse effect is caused by a hole in the earth's atmosphere'	☐	☐	☐	☐	☐
In your opinion, how true is this?					
d. 'Every time we use coal or oil or gas, we contribute to the greenhouse effect'	☐	☐	☐	☐	☐
e. 'All pesticides and chemicals used on food crops cause cancer in humans'	☐	☐	☐	☐	☐
f. 'Human beings are the main cause of plant and animal species dying out'	☐	☐	☐	☐	☐
g. 'Cars are not really an important cause of air pollution in Britain'	☐	☐	☐	☐	☐

OFFICE USE ONLY

5

2.12a In general, do you think that *air* pollution caused by *cars* is ...
PLEASE TICK ONE BOX ONLY

... extremely dangerous for the environment,
very dangerous,
somewhat dangerous,
not very dangerous,
or, not dangerous at all for the environment?
Can't choose

73

b. And do you think that *air* pollution caused by *cars* is ...
PLEASE TICK ONE BOX ONLY

... extremely dangerous for you and your family,
very dangerous,
somewhat dangerous,
not very dangerous,
or, not dangerous at all for you and your family?
Can't choose

74

c. Within the next ten years, how likely do you think it is that there will be a large increase in ill-health in Britain's cities as a result of *air* pollution caused by *cars*?
PLEASE TICK ONE BOX ONLY

Certain to happen
Very likely to happen
Fairly likely to happen
Not very likely to happen
or - Certain **not** to happen
Can't choose

75

OFFICE USE ONLY

6

2.13a In general, do you think that *nuclear* power stations are ...
PLEASE TICK ONE BOX ONLY

... extremely dangerous for the environment,
very dangerous,
somewhat dangerous,
not very dangerous,
or, not dangerous at all for the environment?
Can't choose

76

b. And do you think that *nuclear* power stations are ...
PLEASE TICK ONE BOX ONLY

... extremely dangerous for you and your family,
very dangerous,
somewhat dangerous,
not very dangerous,
or, not dangerous at all for you and your family?
Can't choose

77

2.14a In general, do you think that *air* pollution caused by industry is ...
PLEASE TICK ONE BOX ONLY

... extremely dangerous for the environment,
very dangerous,
somewhat dangerous,
not very dangerous,
or, not dangerous at all for the environment?
Can't choose

78

b. And do you think that *air* pollution caused by industry is ...
PLEASE TICK ONE BOX ONLY

... extremely dangerous for you and your family,
very dangerous,
somewhat dangerous,
not very dangerous,
or, not dangerous at all for you and your family?
Can't choose

79

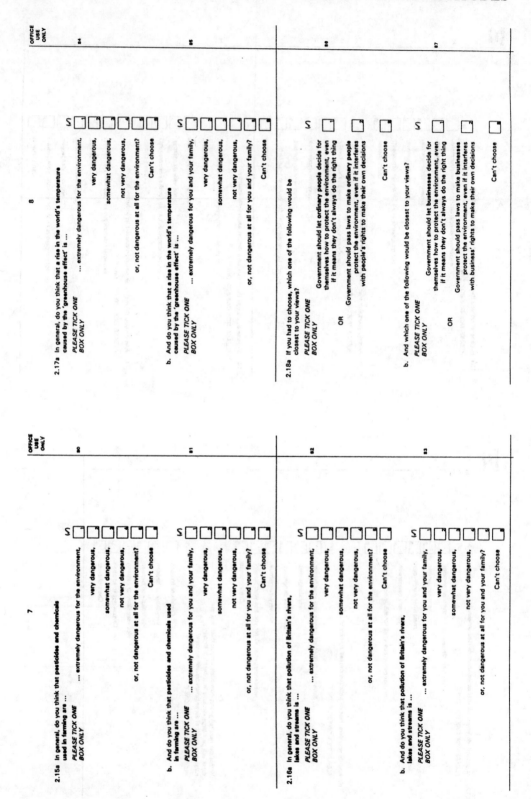

8

2.17a In general, do you think that a rise in the world's temperature caused by the 'greenhouse effect' is ...

PLEASE TICK ONE
BOX ONLY

... extremely dangerous for the environment,

very dangerous,

somewhat dangerous,

not very dangerous,

or, not dangerous at all for the environment?

Can't choose

b. And do you think that a rise in the world's temperature caused by the 'greenhouse effect' is ...

PLEASE TICK ONE
BOX ONLY

... extremely dangerous for you and your family,

very dangerous,

somewhat dangerous,

not very dangerous,

or, not dangerous at all for you and your family?

Can't choose

2.18a If you had to choose, which one of the following would be closest to your views?

PLEASE TICK ONE
BOX ONLY

Government should let ordinary people decide for themselves how to protect the environment, even if it means they don't always do the right thing

OR

Government should pass laws to make ordinary people protect the environment, even if it interferes with people's rights to make their own decisions

Can't choose

b. And which one of the following would be closest to your views?

PLEASE TICK ONE
BOX ONLY

Government should let businesses decide for themselves how to protect the environment, even if it means they don't always do the right thing

OR

Government should pass laws to make businesses protect the environment, even if it interferes with business' rights to make their own decisions

Can't choose

7

2.15a In general, do you think that pesticides and chemicals used in farming are ...

PLEASE TICK ONE
BOX ONLY

... extremely dangerous for the environment,

very dangerous,

somewhat dangerous,

not very dangerous,

or, not dangerous at all for the environment?

Can't choose

b. And do you think that pesticides and chemicals used in farming are ...

PLEASE TICK ONE
BOX ONLY

... extremely dangerous for you and your family,

very dangerous,

somewhat dangerous,

not very dangerous,

or, not dangerous at all for you and your family?

Can't choose

2.16a In general, do you think that pollution of Britain's rivers, lakes and streams is ...

PLEASE TICK ONE
BOX ONLY

... extremely dangerous for the environment,

very dangerous,

somewhat dangerous,

not very dangerous,

or, not dangerous at all for the environment?

Can't choose

b. And do you think that pollution of Britain's rivers, lakes and streams is ...

PLEASE TICK ONE
BOX ONLY

... extremely dangerous for you and your family,

very dangerous,

somewhat dangerous,

not very dangerous,

or, not dangerous at all for you and your family?

Can't choose

9

2.19a How often do you make a special effort to sort glass or tins or plastic or newspapers and so on for recycling?
PLEASE TICK ONE BOX ONLY

Always ☐
Often ☐
Sometimes ☐
Never ☐
(Recycling not available where I live) ☐

b. And how often do you make a special effort to buy fruits and vegetables grown without pesticides or chemicals?
PLEASE TICK ONE BOX ONLY

Always ☐
Often ☐
Sometimes ☐
Never ☐
(Not available where I live) ☐

c. And how often do you **refuse** to eat meat for moral or environmental reasons?
PLEASE TICK ONE BOX ONLY

Always ☐
Often ☐
Sometimes ☐
Never ☐

d. And how often do you **cut back** on driving a car for environmental reasons?
PLEASE TICK ONE BOX ONLY

Always ☐
Often ☐
Sometimes ☐
Never ☐
(I do not have or cannot drive a car) ☐

10

2.20 Are you a member of any group whose main aim is to preserve or protect the environment?
PLEASE TICK ONE BOX ONLY

Yes ☐
No ☐

2.21 In the last five years, have you...
PLEASE TICK ONE BOX ON EACH LINE

Yes, I have / No, I have not

a. ... signed a petition about an environmental issue?
b. ... given money to an environmental group?
c. ... taken part in a protest or demonstration about an environmental issue?

2.22 Please tick one box below to show which statement comes closest to expressing what you believe about God.
PLEASE TICK ONE BOX ONLY

I don't believe in God ☐
I don't know whether there is a God and I don't believe there is any way to find out ☐
I don't believe in a personal God, but I do believe in a Higher Power of some kind ☐
I find myself believing in God some of the time, but not at others ☐
While I have doubts, I feel that I do believe in God ☐
I know God really exists and I have no doubts about it ☐
Can't choose ☐

2.23 Would you describe the place where you live as....
PLEASE TICK ONE BOX ONLY

... a big city, ☐
the suburbs or outskirts of a big city, ☐
a small city or town, ☐
a country village, ☐
or, a farm or home in the country? ☐

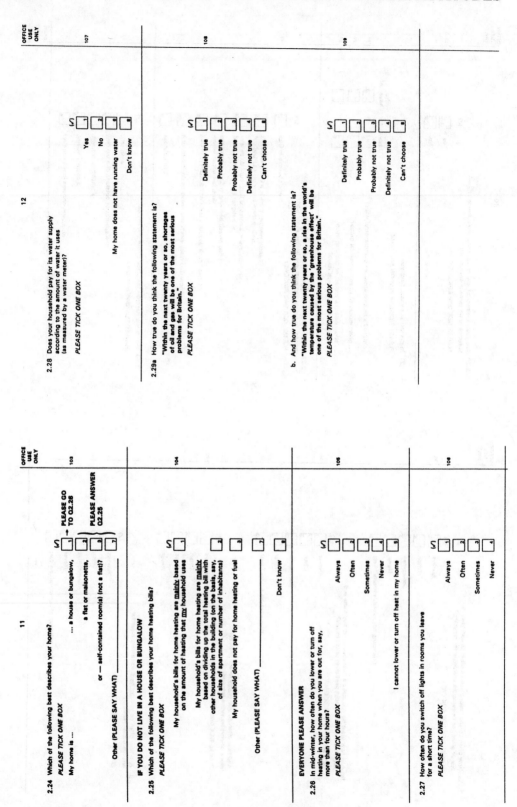

11

2.24 Which of the following best describes your home?

PLEASE TICK ONE BOX

My home is ...

... a house or bungalow, → PLEASE GO TO Q2.26

a flat or maisonette, PLEASE ANSWER Q2.25

or — self-contained room(s) (not a flat)?

Other (PLEASE SAY WHAT) _____

103

IF YOU DO NOT LIVE IN A HOUSE OR BUNGALOW

2.25 Which of the following best describes your home heating bills?

PLEASE TICK ONE BOX

My household's bills for home heating are mainly based on the amount of heating that my household uses

My household's bills for home heating are mainly based on dividing up the total heating bill with other households in the building (on the basis, say, of size of apartment or number of inhabitants)

My household does not pay for home heating or fuel

Other (PLEASE SAY WHAT) _____

Don't know

104

EVERYONE PLEASE ANSWER

2.26 In mid-winter, how often do you lower or turn off heating in your home when you are out for, say, more than four hours?

PLEASE TICK ONE BOX

Always

Often

Sometimes

Never

I cannot lower or turn off heat in my home

105

2.27 How often do you switch off lights in rooms you leave for a short time?

PLEASE TICK ONE BOX

Always

Often

Sometimes

Never

106

12

2.28 Does your household pay for its water supply according to the amount of water it uses (as measured by a water meter)?

PLEASE TICK ONE BOX

Yes

No

Don't know

My home does not have running water

107

2.29a How true do you think the following statement is?

"Within the next twenty years or so, shortages of oil and gas will be one of the most serious problems for Britain."

PLEASE TICK ONE BOX

Definitely true

Probably true

Probably not true

Definitely not true

Can't choose

108

b. And how true do you think the following statement is?

"Within the next twenty years or so, a rise in the world's temperature caused by the 'greenhouse effect' will be one of the most serious problems for Britain."

PLEASE TICK ONE BOX

Definitely true

Probably true

Probably not true

Definitely not true

Can't choose

109

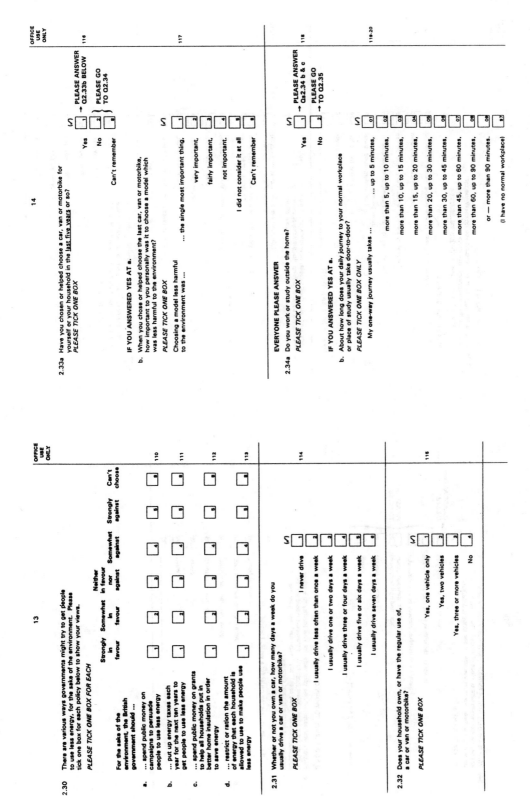

13

2.30 There are various ways governments might try to get people to use less energy, for the sake of the environment. Please tick one box for each policy below to show your views.

PLEASE TICK ONE BOX FOR EACH

For the sake of the environment, the British government should ...	Strongly in favour	Somewhat in favour	Neither in favour nor against	Somewhat against	Strongly against	Can't choose
a. ... spend public money on campaigns to persuade people to use less energy	☐	☐	☐	☐	☐	☐ 110
b. ... put up energy taxes each year for the next ten years to get people to use less energy	☐	☐	☐	☐	☐	☐ 111
c. ... spend public money on grants to help all households put in better home insulation in order to save energy	☐	☐	☐	☐	☐	☐ 112
d. ... restrict or ration the amount of energy that each household is allowed to use to make people use less energy	☐	☐	☐	☐	☐	☐ 113

2.31 Whether or not you own a car, how many days a week do you usually drive a car or van or motorbike?

PLEASE TICK ONE BOX

I never drive ☐ 1
I usually drive less often than once a week ☐ 2
I usually drive one or two days a week ☐ 3
I usually drive three or four days a week ☐ 4
I usually drive five or six days a week ☐ 5
I usually drive seven days a week ☐ 6   114

2.32 Does your household own, or have the regular use of, a car or van or motorbike?

PLEASE TICK ONE BOX

Yes, one vehicle only ☐ 1
Yes, two vehicles ☐ 2
Yes, three or more vehicles ☐ 3
No ☐ 4   115

14

2.33a Have you chosen or helped choose a car, van or motorbike for yourself or your household in the <u>last five years</u> or so?

PLEASE TICK ONE BOX

Yes ☐ 1 → PLEASE ANSWER Q2.33b BELOW
No ☐ 2 ⎫ PLEASE GO
Can't remember ☐ 8 ⎭ TO Q2.34   116

IF YOU ANSWERED YES AT a.

b. When you chose or helped choose the last car, van or motorbike, how important to you personally was it to choose a model which was less harmful to the environment?

PLEASE TICK ONE BOX

Choosing a model less harmful to the environment was ... ... the single most important thing, ☐ 1
very important, ☐ 2
fairly important, ☐ 3
not important. ☐ 4
I did not consider it at all ☐ 5
Can't remember ☐ 8   117

2.34a EVERYONE PLEASE ANSWER
Do you work or study outside the home?

PLEASE TICK ONE BOX

Yes ☐ 1 → PLEASE ANSWER Q2.34 b & c
No ☐ 2 → PLEASE GO TO Q2.35   118

IF YOU ANSWERED YES AT a.

b. About how long does your daily journey to your normal workplace or place of study usually take door-to-door?

PLEASE TICK ONE BOX ONLY

My one-way journey usually takes ... ... up to 5 minutes, ☐ 01
more than 5, up to 10 minutes, ☐ 02
more than 10, up to 15 minutes, ☐ 03
more than 15, up to 20 minutes, ☐ 04
more than 20, up to 30 minutes, ☐ 05
more than 30, up to 45 minutes, ☐ 06
more than 45, up to 60 minutes, ☐ 07
more than 60, up to 90 minutes, ☐ 08
or — more than 90 minutes. ☐ 09
(I have no normal workplace) ☐ 97   119-20

OFFICE USE ONLY

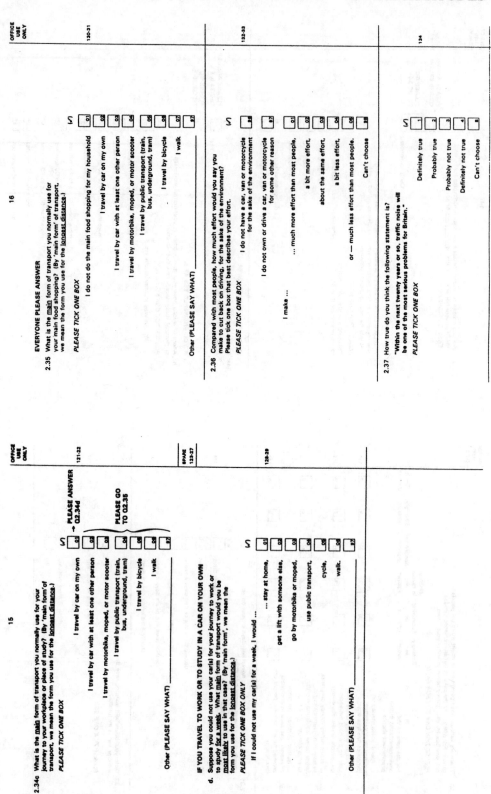

15

2.34c What is the <u>main</u> form of transport you normally use for your journey to your workplace or place of study? (By 'main form' of transport, we mean the form you use for the <u>longest distance</u>.)

PLEASE TICK ONE BOX

- I travel by car on my own → **PLEASE ANSWER Q2.34d**
- I travel by car with at least one other person
- I travel by motorbike, moped, or motor scooter
- I travel by public transport (train, bus, underground, tram) → **PLEASE GO TO Q2.35**
- I travel by bicycle
- I walk

Other (PLEASE SAY WHAT) _____

IF YOU TRAVEL TO WORK OR TO STUDY IN A CAR ON YOUR OWN

d. Suppose you could not use your car/s for your journey to work or to study <u>for a week</u>. What <u>main</u> form of transport would you be <u>most likely</u> to use in that case? (By 'main form', we mean the form you use for the <u>longest distance</u>.)

PLEASE TICK ONE BOX ONLY

If I could not use my car(s) for a week, I would ...

- ... stay at home,
- get a lift with someone else,
- go by motorbike or moped,
- use public transport,
- cycle,
- walk.

Other (PLEASE SAY WHAT) _____

16

EVERYONE PLEASE ANSWER

2.35 What is the <u>main</u> form of transport you normally use for your main food shopping? (By 'main form' of transport, we mean the form you use for the <u>longest distance</u>.)

PLEASE TICK ONE BOX

- I do not do the main food shopping for my household
- I travel by car on my own
- I travel by car with at least one other person
- I travel by motorbike, moped, or motor scooter
- I travel by public transport (train, bus, underground, tram)
- I travel by bicycle
- I walk

Other (PLEASE SAY WHAT) _____

2.36 Compared with most people, how much effort would you say you make to cut back on driving, for the sake of the environment? Please tick one box that best describes your effort.

PLEASE TICK ONE BOX

- I do not have a car, van or motorcycle
- I do not own or drive a car, van or motorcycle for some other reason
- I make ... much more effort than most people,
- ... a bit more effort,
- about the same effort,
- a bit less effort,
- or — much less effort than most people.
- Can't choose

2.37 How true do you think the following statement is?

"Within the next twenty years or so, traffic noise will be one of the most serious problems for Britain."

PLEASE TICK ONE BOX

- Definitely true
- Probably true
- Probably not true
- Definitely not true
- Can't choose

17

2.38 There are various ways governments might try to get people to cut back on driving, for the sake of the environment. Please tick one box for each policy below to show your views.

PLEASE TICK ONE BOX FOR EACH

For the sake of the environment, the British government should ...	Strongly in favour	Somewhat in favour	Neither in favour nor against	Somewhat against	Strongly against	Can't choose	
a. ... spend public money on campaigns to persuade people to cut back on driving	1	2	3	4	5	8	135
b. ... put up taxes on petrol each year for the next ten years to get people to cut back on driving	1	2	3	4	5	8	136
c. ... put a special environment tax on private cars and use the money to improve public transport.	1	2	3	4	5	8	137
d. ... restrict or ration the amount of petrol or diesel that people are allowed to buy to make them cut back on driving	1	2	3	4	5	8	138

2.39 When you are shopping, how often do you pay attention to the amount of wrapping or packaging used on products before you decide to buy something?

PLEASE TICK ONE BOX

Always	1	139
Often	2	
Sometimes	3	
Never	4	

2.40 In the last month or so, did you actually NOT buy something because you felt it used too much packaging or wrapping?

PLEASE TICK ONE BOX

Yes, did NOT buy something because of the amount of packaging or wrapping	1	140
No	2	
Don't know/can't remember	8	

18

2.41 Some household waste can be recycled (for instance, glass, paper, tins and plastics).

In your area, are there regular collections from your home of any materials for recycling?

PLEASE TICK ONE BOX

Yes	1	141
No	2	
Don't know	8	

2.42 How true do you think the following statement is?

"Within the next twenty years or so, finding official sites to dump or burn household waste will be one of the most serious problems for Britain."

PLEASE TICK ONE BOX

Definitely true	1	142
Probably true	2	
Probably not true	3	
Definitely not true	4	
Can't choose	8	

2.43 There are various ways governments might try to get people to produce less household waste, for the sake of the environment. Please tick one box for each policy below to show your views.

PLEASE TICK ONE BOX FOR EACH

For the sake of the environment, the British government should ...	Strongly in favour	Somewhat in favour	Neither in favour nor against	Somewhat against	Strongly against	Can't choose	
a. ... spend public money on campaigns to persuade people to produce less household waste	1	2	3	4	5	8	143
b. ... make each household pay for its rubbish collection according to the amount of rubbish it leaves out, to get people to produce less household waste	1	2	3	4	5	8	144
c. ... control the amount and type of packaging on products, even if it leads to higher prices or less convenience for the customer	1	2	3	4	5	8	145

19

Now a few questions about environmental labelling, that is, information about how a product or its packaging may affect the environment.

2.44 When you are choosing a product, how often do you pay attention to any environmental labelling before deciding to buy?

PLEASE TICK ONE BOX

Always
Often
Sometimes
Never

2.45 And if you look at environmental labelling on products, how often do you trust it?

PLEASE TICK ONE BOX

(Never look at environmental labelling)
Always
Often
Sometimes
Never

2.46 There are various ways governments might try to get people to do less harm to the environment. Please tick one box for each policy below to show your views.

PLEASE TICK ONE BOX FOR EACH

For the sake of the environment, the British government should ...	Strongly in favour	Somewhat in favour	Neither in favour nor against	Somewhat against	Strongly against	Can't choose
a. ... spend public money on campaigns to persuade people not to harm the environment						
b. ... put up taxes on things which harm the environment each year for the next ten years, to get people not to buy or use them						
c. ... pass strict environmental laws in order to stop people causing harm to the environment						

20

2.47 Thinking now of all the possible things that people can do: compared with most people, how much effort would you say you make, in general, to do what is right for the environment?

PLEASE TICK ONE BOX

In general, I make ... ... much more effort than most people,
a bit more effort,
about the same effort,
a bit less effort,
or — much less effort than most people.
Can't choose

2.48 Who do you think should have the final say when it comes to passing laws to protect the environment...

PLEASE TICK ONE BOX

... the British Parliament,
OR ... the European Community?
Can't choose

2.49 Compared to other countries in the European Community, how much do you think Britain does to protect the environment?

PLEASE TICK ONE BOX

Britain does ... ... much more than other EC countries to protect the environment,
a bit more,
about the same amount,
a bit less,
or — a lot less than other EC countries to protect the environment?
Can't choose

2.50 Do you agree or disagree:

"Britain should pass special laws to protect the environment *only* if all the other European Community countries do the same."

PLEASE TICK ONE BOX

Strongly agree
Somewhat agree
Neither agree nor disagree
Somewhat disagree
Strongly disagree
Can't choose

INTERNATIONAL SOCIAL SURVEY PROGRAMME

1994 MODULE

FAMILY AND CHANGING GENDER ROLES II

(ENGLISH LANGUAGE VERSION)

C2.01 To begin, we have some questions about women. Do you agree or disagree ...?

PLEASE TICK ONE BOX ON EACH LINE

	Strongly agree	Agree	Neither agree nor disagree	Disagree	Strongly disagree	Can't choose	OFFICE USE ONLY
a. A working mother can establish just as warm and secure a relationship with her children as a mother who does not work.	☐	☐	☐	☐	☐	☐	2235
b. A pre-school child is likely to suffer if his or her mother works	☐	☐	☐	☐	☐	☐	2236
c. All in all, family life suffers when the woman has a full-time job	☐	☐	☐	☐	☐	☐	2237
d. A job is all right, but what most women really want is a home and children	☐	☐	☐	☐	☐	☐	2238
e. Being a housewife is just as fulfilling as working for pay	☐	☐	☐	☐	☐	☐	2239
f. Having a job is the best way for a woman to be an independent person	☐	☐	☐	☐	☐	☐	2240
g. Most women have to work these days to support their families	☐	☐	☐	☐	☐	☐	2241

C2.02 And, do you agree or disagree ...?

PLEASE TICK ONE BOX ON EACH LINE

	Strongly agree	Agree	Neither agree nor disagree	Disagree	Strongly disagree	Can't choose	OFFICE USE ONLY
a. Both the man and woman should contribute to the household income	☐	☐	☐	☐	☐	☐	2242
b. A man's job is to earn money; a woman's job is to look after the home and family	☐	☐	☐	☐	☐	☐	2243
c. It is not good if the man stays at home and cares for the children and the woman goes out to work	☐	☐	☐	☐	☐	☐	2244
d. Family life often suffers because men concentrate too much on their work	☐	☐	☐	☐	☐	☐	2245

C2.03 Do you think that women should work outside the home full-time, part-time or not at all under these circumstances?

PLEASE TICK ONE BOX ON EACH LINE

	Work full-time	Work part-time	Stay at home	Can't choose	OFFICE USE ONLY
a. After marrying and before there are children	☐	☐	☐	☐	2246
b. When there is a child under school age	☐	☐	☐	☐	2247
c. After the youngest child starts school	☐	☐	☐	☐	2248
d. After the children leave home	☐	☐	☐	☐	2249

C2.04 Do you agree or disagree ...?

PLEASE TICK ONE BOX ON EACH LINE

	Strongly agree	Agree	Neither agree nor disagree	Disagree	Strongly disagree	Can't choose	OFFICE USE ONLY
a. Married people are generally happier than unmarried people	☐	☐	☐	☐	☐	☐	2250
b. The main advantage of marriage is that it gives financial security	☐	☐	☐	☐	☐	☐	2251
c. The main purpose of marriage these days is to have children	☐	☐	☐	☐	☐	☐	2252
d. It is better to have a bad marriage than no marriage at all	☐	☐	☐	☐	☐	☐	2253
e. People who want children ought to get married	☐	☐	☐	☐	☐	☐	2254
f. One parent can bring up a child as well as two parents together	☐	☐	☐	☐	☐	☐	2255
g. It is all right for a couple to live together without intending to get married	☐	☐	☐	☐	☐	☐	2256
h. It is a good idea for a couple who intend to get married to live together first	☐	☐	☐	☐	☐	☐	2257
i. Divorce is usually the best solution when a couple can't seem to work out their marriage problems	☐	☐	☐	☐	☐	☐	2258

C2.05 All in all, what do you think is the ideal number of children for a family to have?

PLEASE WRITE THE NUMBER IN THE BOX → ☐   2259-60

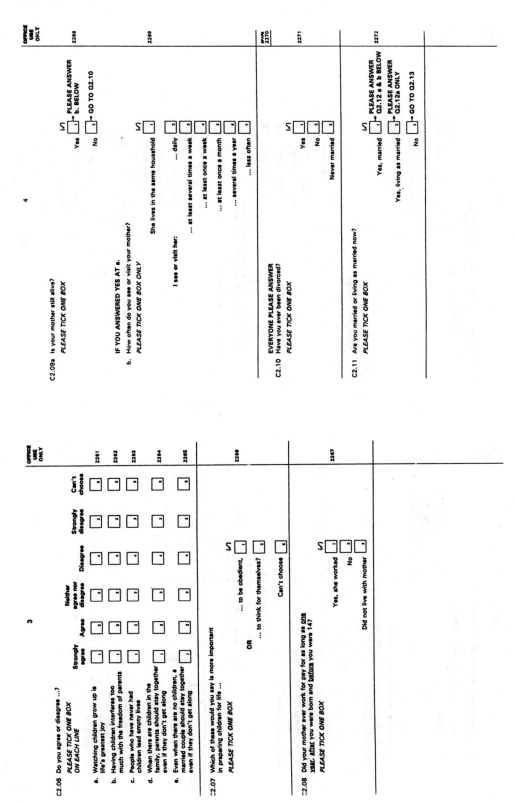

C2.06 Do you agree or disagree ...?
PLEASE TICK ONE BOX
ON EACH LINE

	Strongly agree	Agree	Neither agree nor disagree	Disagree	Strongly disagree	Can't choose	
a. Watching children grow up is life's greatest joy							2261
b. Having children interferes too much with the freedom of parents							2262
c. People who have never had children lead empty lives							2263
d. When there are children in the family, parents should stay together even if they don't get along							2264
e. Even when there are no children, a married couple should stay together even if they don't get along							2265

C2.07 Which of these would you say is more important in preparing children for life ...
PLEASE TICK ONE BOX

... to be obedient,

OR

... to think for themselves?

Can't choose

2266

C2.08 Did your mother ever work for pay for as long as one year, after you were born and before you were 14?
PLEASE TICK ONE BOX

Yes, she worked

No

Did not live with mother

2267

C2.09a Is your mother still alive?
PLEASE TICK ONE BOX

Yes — PLEASE ANSWER b. BELOW

No — GO TO Q2.10

2268

IF YOU ANSWERED YES AT a.

b. How often do you see or visit your mother?
PLEASE TICK ONE BOX ONLY

She lives in the same household

I see or visit her:

... daily

... at least several times a week

... at least once a week

... at least once a month

... several times a year

... less often

2269

SPARE 2270

C2.10 EVERYONE PLEASE ANSWER
Have you ever been divorced?
PLEASE TICK ONE BOX

Yes

No

Never married

2271

C2.11 Are you married or living as married now?
PLEASE TICK ONE BOX

Yes, married — PLEASE ANSWER Q2.12 a & b BELOW

Yes, living as married — PLEASE ANSWER Q2.12a ONLY

No — GO TO Q2.13

2272

OFFICE USE ONLY

3

4

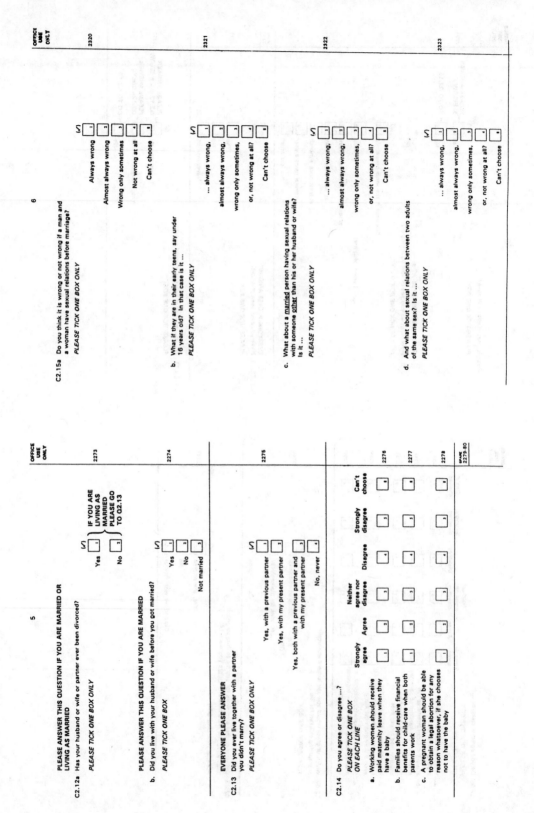

5

PLEASE ANSWER THIS QUESTION IF YOU ARE MARRIED OR LIVING AS MARRIED

C2.12a Has your husband or wife or partner ever been divorced?

PLEASE TICK ONE BOX ONLY

Yes
No

IF YOU ARE LIVING AS MARRIED PLEASE GO TO Q2.13

2273

PLEASE ANSWER THIS QUESTION IF YOU ARE MARRIED

b. Did you live with your husband or wife before you got married?

PLEASE TICK ONE BOX

Yes
No
Not married

2274

EVERYONE PLEASE ANSWER

C2.13 Did you ever live together with a partner you didn't marry?

PLEASE TICK ONE BOX ONLY

Yes, with a previous partner
Yes, with my present partner
Yes, both with a previous partner and with my present partner
No, never

2275

C2.14 Do you agree or disagree ...?
PLEASE TICK ONE BOX ON EACH LINE

	Strongly agree	Agree	Neither agree nor disagree	Disagree	Strongly disagree	Can't choose	
a. Working women should receive paid maternity leave when they have a baby							2276
b. Families should receive financial benefits for child-care when both parents work							2277
c. A pregnant woman should be able to obtain a legal abortion for any reason whatsoever, if she chooses not to have the baby							2278

SPACE 2279-80

6

C2.15a Do you think it is wrong or not wrong if a man and a woman have sexual relations before marriage?

PLEASE TICK ONE BOX ONLY

Always wrong
Almost always wrong
Wrong only sometimes
Not wrong at all
Can't choose

2320

b. What if they are in their early teens, say under 16 years old? In that case is it ...

PLEASE TICK ONE BOX ONLY

... always wrong,
almost always wrong,
wrong only sometimes,
or, not wrong at all?
Can't choose

2321

c. What about a <u>married</u> person having sexual relations with someone <u>other</u> than his or her husband or wife? Is it ...

PLEASE TICK ONE BOX ONLY

... always wrong,
almost always wrong,
wrong only sometimes,
or, not wrong at all?
Can't choose

2322

d. And what about sexual relations between two adults of the same sex? Is it ...

PLEASE TICK ONE BOX ONLY

... always wrong,
almost always wrong,
wrong only sometimes,
or, not wrong at all?
Can't choose

2323

7

C2.16 Sometimes at work people find themselves the object of sexual advances, propositions, or unwanted sexual discussions from co-workers or supervisors. The advances sometimes involve physical contact and sometimes just involve sexual conversations. Has this ever happened to you?

PLEASE TICK ONE BOX

Yes ☐
No ☐
Never have worked ☐

2324

PLEASE ANSWER Q2.17 TO Q2.19 IF YOU ARE MARRIED OR LIVING AS MARRIED. IF NOT MARRIED OR NOT LIVING AS MARRIED, PLEASE GO TO Q2.20.

C2.17 How do you and your spouse/partner organise the income that one or both of you receive? Please choose the option that comes closest.

PLEASE TICK BOX ONE BOX ONLY

I manage all the money and give my partner his or her share ☐
My partner manages all the money and gives me my share ☐
We pool all the money and each take out what we need ☐
We pool some of the money and keep the rest separate ☐
We each keep our own money separate ☐
Not married or living as married ☐

2325

C2.18 **PLEASE ANSWER IF YOU ARE MARRIED OR LIVING AS MARRIED**
In your household, who does the following things?

PLEASE TICK ONE BOX ON EACH LINE

	Always the woman	Usually the woman	About equal or both together	Usually the man	Always the man	Is done by a third person	Can't choose	
a. The washing and ironing	☐	☐	☐	☐	☐	☐	☐	2326
b. Small repairs around the house	☐	☐	☐	☐	☐	☐	☐	2327
c. Looking after sick family members	☐	☐	☐	☐	☐	☐	☐	2328
d. Shopping for groceries	☐	☐	☐	☐	☐	☐	☐	2329
e. Deciding what to have for dinner	☐	☐	☐	☐	☐	☐	☐	2330

8

PLEASE ANSWER IF YOU ARE MARRIED OR LIVING AS MARRIED

C2.19a Do you and your husband or wife or partner both have paid work at the moment?

PLEASE TICK ONE BOX

Yes ☐ → PLEASE ANSWER Q2.19b
No ☐ → PLEASE GO TO Q2.20

2331

b. Who earns more money?

PLEASE TICK ONE BOX ONLY

The man earns much more ☐
The man earns a bit more ☐
We earn about the same amount ☐
The woman earns a bit more ☐
The woman earns much more ☐

2332

PLEASE ANSWER Q2.20 AND Q2.21 IF YOU HAVE EVER HAD CHILDREN. IF YOU HAVE NEVER HAD CHILDREN, PLEASE GO TO Q2.22.

C2.20 Did you work outside the home full-time, part-time or not at all ...

PLEASE TICK ONE BOX ON EACH LINE

	Worked full-time	Worked part-time	Stayed at home	Does not apply	
a. After marrying and before you had children?	☐	☐	☐	☐	2333
b. And what about when a child was under school age?	☐	☐	☐	☐	2334
c. After the youngest child started school?	☐	☐	☐	☐	2335
d. And how about after the children left home?	☐	☐	☐	☐	2336

C2.21 What about your spouse/partner at that time - did he/she work outside the home full-time, part-time or not at all ...

PLEASE TICK ONE BOX ON EACH LINE

	Worked full-time	Worked part-time	Stayed at home	Does not apply	
a. After marrying and before you had children?	☐	☐	☐	☐	2337
b. And what about when a child was under school age?	☐	☐	☐	☐	2338
c. After the youngest child started school?	☐	☐	☐	☐	2339
d. And how about after the children left home?	☐	☐	☐	☐	2340

SPARE 2341-45

INTERNATIONAL SOCIAL SURVEY PROGRAMME

1995 MODULE

NATIONAL IDENTITY

(ENGLISH LANGUAGE VERSION)

OFFICE USE ONLY

1

To begin, we have some questions about <u>where</u> you live: your neighbourhood or village; your town or city, your (county), and so on. (By "neighbourhood" we mean the part of the town/city you live in. If you live in a village, we take this as your "neighbourhood".

1. How close do you feel to ...

PLEASE TICK ONE BOX ON EACH LINE

	Very close	Close	Not very close	Not close at all	Can't choose
a. your neighbourhood (or village)					
b. your town or city					
c. your county					
d. Britain					
e. Europe					

2. If you could improve your work or living conditions, how willing or unwilling would you be to ...

PLEASE TICK ONE BOX ON EACH LINE

	Very willing	Fairly willing	Neither willing nor unwilling	Fairly unwilling	Very unwilling	Can't choose
a. move to another neighbourhood (or village)						
b. move to a(nother) town or city within this county						
c. move to another county						
d. move outside Britain						
e. move outside Europe						

3. Which of these two statements comes closer to your own view?

PLEASE TICK ONE BOX ONLY

It is essential that the United Kingdom remains one nation ☐

OR Parts of the United Kingdom should be allowed to become fully separate nations if they choose to ☐

Can't choose ☐

OFFICE USE ONLY

2

4. Some people say the following things are important for being truly British. Others say they are not important. How important do you think each of the following is ...

PLEASE TICK ONE BOX ON EACH LINE

	Very Important	Fairly Important	Not very Important	Not important at all	Can't choose
a. to have been born in Britain					
b. to have British citizenship					
c. to have lived in Britain for most of one's life					
d. to be able to speak English					
e. to be a Christian					
f. to respect Britain's political institutions and laws					
g. to feel British					

5. How much do you agree or disagree with the following statements?

PLEASE TICK ONE BOX ON EACH LINE

	Agree strongly	Agree	Neither agree nor disagree	Disagree	Disagree strongly	Can't choose
a. I would rather be a citizen of Britain than of any other country in the world						
b. There are some things about Britain today that make me feel ashamed of Britain						
c. The world would be a better place if people from other countries were more like the British						
d. Generally speaking Britain is a better country than most other countries						
e. People should support their country even if the country is in the wrong						
f. When my country does well in international sports, it makes me proud to be British						

3

6. How proud are you of Britain in each of the following?

PLEASE TICK ONE BOX ON EACH LINE

	Very proud	Somewhat proud	Not very proud	Not proud at all	Can't choose
a. The way democracy works					
b. Its political influence in the world					
c. Britain's economic achievements					
d. Its social security system					
e. Its scientific and technological achievements					
f. Its achievements in sports					
g. Its achievements in the arts and literature					
h. Britain's armed forces					
i. Its history					
j. Its fair and equal treatment of all groups in society					

Now we would like to ask a few questions about relations between Britain and other countries.

7. How much do you agree or disagree with the following statements?

PLEASE TICK ONE BOX ON EACH LINE

	Agree strongly	Agree	Neither agree nor disagree	Disagree	Disagree strongly	Can't choose
a. Britain should limit the import of foreign products in order to protect its national economy						
b. For certain problems, like environmental pollution, international bodies should have the right to enforce solutions						
c. British schools should make much more effort to teach foreign languages properly						
d. Britain should follow its own interests, even if this leads to conflicts with other nations						
e. Foreigners should not be allowed to buy land in Britain						
f. British television should give preference to British films and programmes						

4

Now we would like to ask a few questions about minorities in Britain.

8. How much do you agree or disagree with the following statements?

PLEASE TICK ONE BOX ON EACH LINE

	Agree strongly	Agree	Neither agree nor disagree	Disagree	Disagree strongly	Can't choose
a. It is impossible for people who do not share British customs and traditions to become fully British						
b. Ethnic minorities should be given government assistance to preserve their customs and traditions						

9. Some people say that it is better for a country if different racial and ethnic groups maintain their distinct customs and traditions. Others say that it is better if these groups adapt and blend into the larger society. Which of these views comes closer to your own?

PLEASE TICK ONE BOX ONLY

It is better for society if groups maintain their distinct customs and traditions □

It is better if groups adapt and blend into the larger society □

Don't know □

10. There are different opinions about immigrants from other countries living in Britain. (By "immigrants" we mean people who come to settle in Britain.)

How much do you agree or disagree with each of the following statements?

PLEASE TICK ONE BOX ON EACH LINE

	Agree strongly	Agree	Neither agree nor disagree	Disagree	Disagree strongly	Can't choose
a. Immigrants increase crime rates						
b. Immigrants are generally good for Britain's economy						
c. Immigrants make Britain more open to new ideas and cultures						

OFFICE USE ONLY

6

15. About how long altogether have you lived in other countries?

PLEASE TICK ONE BOX ONLY

Never lived in other countries
Less than 1 year in all
1 to 4 years in all
5 years or longer

16a. What language(s) do you speak at home?

PLEASE FILL IN

At home I speak: ....

b. What language(s) do you speak well?

PLEASE FILL IN ....

17a. Are you a citizen of Britain?

Yes
No

b. At the time of your birth, were both, one or neither of your parents citizens of Britain?

PLEASE TICK ONE BOX ONLY

Both were citizens of Britain
Only father was a citizen of Britain
Only mother was a citizen of Britain
Neither parent was a citizen of Britain

18. How much have you heard or read about the European Union?

PLEASE TICK ONE BOX ONLY

A lot
Quite a bit
Not much
Nothing at all

OFFICE USE ONLY

5

11. Do you think the number of immigrants to Britain nowadays should be ...

PLEASE TICK ONE BOX ONLY

... increased a lot,
increased a little,
remain the same as it is,
reduced a little,
or reduced a lot?
Can't choose

12. How much do you agree or disagree that refugees who have suffered political repression in their own country should be allowed to stay in Britain?

PLEASE TICK ONE BOX ONLY

Agree strongly
Agree
Neither agree nor disagree
Disagree
Disagree strongly
Can't choose

13. Where did you spend most of your childhood, that is, until you turned 17?

PLEASE TICK ONE BOX ONLY

In this town (city, village)
In a different town (city, village), but in this county
In a different county in Britain
Outside Britain

14. How long have you lived in the town (city, village), where you live now?

PLEASE FILL IN NUMBER OF YEARS OR TICK BOX IF LESS THAN ONE YEAR

Less than 1 year
_____ years

7

19. Generally speaking, would you say that Britain benefits or
does not benefit from being a member of the European Union?

PLEASE TICK *ONE BOX ONLY*

Benefits

Does not benefit

Don't know

Have never heard of the European Union

20. Which of the following statements comes closer to your own view?

PLEASE TICK *ONE BOX ONLY*

Britain should do all it can to unite fully
with the European Union

OR

Britain should do all it can to protect its
independence from the European Union

Don't know

21. How much do you agree or disagree with the following statement?

Britain should take stronger measures to exclude illegal immigrants.

PLEASE TICK *ONE BOX ONLY*

Agree strongly

Agree

Neither agree nor disagree

Disagree

Disagree strongly

Can't choose

INTERNATIONAL SOCIAL SURVEY PROGRAMME

1996 MODULE

ROLE OF GOVERNMENT III

(ENGLISH LANGUAGE VERSION)

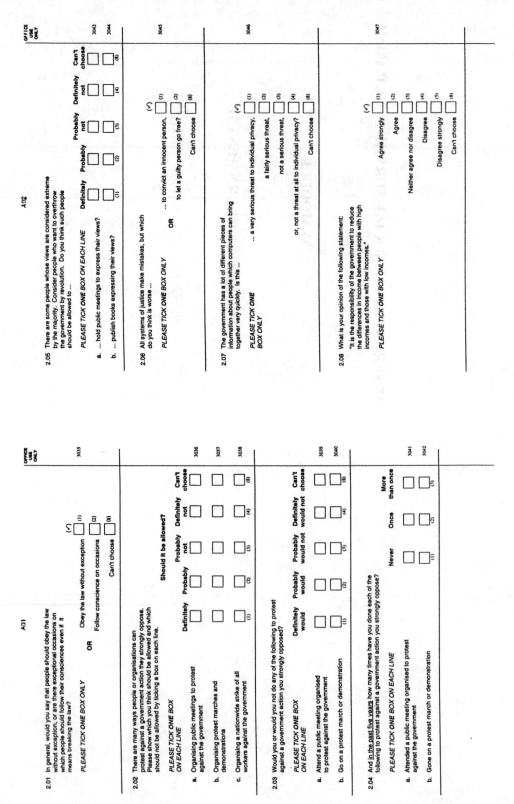

A.01

OFFICE USE ONLY

2.01 In general, would you say that people should obey the law without exception, or are there exceptional occasions on which people should follow their consciences even if it means breaking the law?

PLEASE TICK ONE BOX ONLY

Obey the law without exception (1)

OR Follow conscience on occasions (2)

Can't choose (8)

3035

2.02 There are many ways people or organisations can protest against a government action they strongly oppose. Please show which you think should be allowed and which should not be allowed by ticking a box on each line.

PLEASE TICK ONE BOX ON EACH LINE

Should it be allowed?

	Definitely probably	Probably	Probably not	Definitely not	Can't choose
	(1)	(2)	(3)	(4)	(8)

a. Organising public meetings to protest against the government — 3036

b. Organising protest marches and demonstrations — 3037

c. Organising a nationwide strike of all workers against the government — 3038

2.03 Would you or would you not do any of the following to protest against a government action you strongly opposed?

PLEASE TICK ONE BOX ON EACH LINE

	Definitely would	Probably would	Probably would not	Definitely would not	Can't choose
	(1)	(2)	(3)	(4)	(8)

a. Attend a public meeting organised to protest against the government — 3039

b. Go on a protest march or demonstration — 3040

2.04 And in the past five years how many times have you done each of the following to protest against a government action you strongly oppose?

PLEASE TICK ONE BOX ON EACH LINE

	Never	Once	More than once
	(1)	(2)	(3)

a. Attended a public meeting organised to protest against the government — 3041

b. Gone on a protest march or demonstration — 3042

A.02

OFFICE USE ONLY

2.05 There are some people whose views are considered extreme by the majority. Consider people who want to overthrow the government by revolution. Do you think such people should be allowed to ...

PLEASE TICK ONE BOX ON EACH LINE

	Definitely	Probably	Probably not	Definitely not	Can't choose
	(1)	(2)	(3)	(4)	(8)

a. ... hold public meetings to express their views? — 3043

b. ... publish books expressing their views? — 3044

2.06 All systems of justice make mistakes, but which do you think is worse ...

PLEASE TICK ONE BOX ONLY

... to convict an innocent person, (1)

OR to let a guilty person go free? (2)

Can't choose (8)

3045

2.07 The government has a lot of different pieces of information about people which computers can bring together very quickly. Is this ...

PLEASE TICK ONE BOX ONLY

... a very serious threat to individual privacy, (1)

a fairly serious threat, (2)

not a serious threat, (3)

or, not a threat at all to individual privacy? (4)

Can't choose (8)

3046

2.08 What is your opinion of the following statement:

"It is the responsibility of the government to reduce the differences in income between people with high incomes and those with low incomes."

PLEASE TICK ONE BOX ONLY

Agree strongly (1)

Agree (2)

Neither agree nor disagree (3)

Disagree (4)

Disagree strongly (5)

Can't choose (8)

3047

A03

2.09 Here are some things the government might do for the economy. Please show which actions you are in favour of and which you are against.

PLEASE TICK ONE BOX ON EACH LINE

	Strongly in favour of (1)	In favour of (2)	Neither in favour of nor against (3)	Against (4)	Strongly against (5)	OFFICE USE ONLY
a. Control of wages by law	☐	☐	☐	☐	☐	3048
b. Control of prices by law	☐	☐	☐	☐	☐	3049
c. Cuts in government spending	☐	☐	☐	☐	☐	3050
d. Government financing of projects to create new jobs	☐	☐	☐	☐	☐	3051
e. Less government regulation of business	☐	☐	☐	☐	☐	3052
f. Support for industry to develop new products and technology	☐	☐	☐	☐	☐	3053
g. Support for declining industries to protect jobs	☐	☐	☐	☐	☐	3054
h. Reducing the working week to create more jobs	☐	☐	☐	☐	☐	3055

2.10 Listed below are various areas of government spending. Please show whether you would like to see more or less government spending in each area. Remember that if you say "much more", it might require a tax increase to pay for it.

PLEASE TICK ONE BOX ON EACH LINE

	Spend much more (1)	Spend more (2)	Spend the same as now (3)	Spend less (4)	Spend much less (5)	Can't choose (8)	OFFICE USE ONLY
a. The environment	☐	☐	☐	☐	☐	☐	3056
b. Health	☐	☐	☐	☐	☐	☐	3057
c. The police and law enforcement	☐	☐	☐	☐	☐	☐	3058
d. Education	☐	☐	☐	☐	☐	☐	3059
e. The military and defence	☐	☐	☐	☐	☐	☐	3060
f. Old age pensions	☐	☐	☐	☐	☐	☐	3061
g. Unemployment benefits	☐	☐	☐	☐	☐	☐	3062
h. Culture and the arts	☐	☐	☐	☐	☐	☐	3063

A04

2.11a Do you think that trade unions in this country have too much power or too little power?

PLEASE TICK ONE BOX ONLY

Far too much power ☐ (1)
Too much power ☐ (2)
About the right amount of power ☐ (3)
Too little power ☐ (4)
Far too little power ☐ (5)
Can't choose ☐ (8)

OFFICE USE ONLY 3064

b. How about business and industry? Do they have too much power or too little power?

PLEASE TICK ONE BOX ONLY

Far too much power ☐ (1)
Too much power ☐ (2)
About the right amount of power ☐ (3)
Too little power ☐ (4)
Far too little power ☐ (5)
Can't choose ☐ (8)

3065

c. And what about the government, does it have too much power or too little power?

PLEASE TICK ONE BOX ONLY

Far too much power ☐ (1)
Too much power ☐ (2)
About the right amount of power ☐ (3)
Too little power ☐ (4)
Far too little power ☐ (5)
Can't choose ☐ (8)

3066

SPARE 3067-3080

A05

2.12 On the whole, do you think it should or should not be the government's responsibility to ...

PLEASE TICK ONE BOX ON EACH LINE

	Definitely should be (1)	Probably should be (2)	Probably should not be (3)	Definitely should not be (4)	Can't choose (8)	OFFICE USE ONLY
a. ... provide a job for everyone who wants one	☐	☐	☐	☐	☐	3120
b. ... keep prices under control	☐	☐	☐	☐	☐	3121
c. ... provide health care for the sick	☐	☐	☐	☐	☐	3122
d. ... provide a decent standard of living for the old	☐	☐	☐	☐	☐	3123
e. ... provide industry with the help it needs to grow	☐	☐	☐	☐	☐	3124
f. ... provide a decent standard of living for the unemployed	☐	☐	☐	☐	☐	3125
g. ... reduce income differences between the rich and the poor	☐	☐	☐	☐	☐	3126
h. ... give financial help to university students from low-income families	☐	☐	☐	☐	☐	3127
i. ... provide decent housing for those who can't afford it	☐	☐	☐	☐	☐	3128
j. ... impose strict laws to make industry do less damage to the environment	☐	☐	☐	☐	☐	3129

Now some questions about politics.

2.13 How interested would you say you personally are in politics?

PLEASE TICK ONE BOX ONLY

Very interested ☐ (1)
Fairly interested ☐ (2)
Somewhat interested ☐ (3)
Not very interested ☐ (4)
Not at all interested ☐ (5)
Can't choose ☐ (8)

OFFICE USE ONLY 3130

A06

2.14 Please tick one box on each line to show how much you agree or disagree with each of the following statements.

PLEASE TICK ONE BOX ON EACH LINE

	Strongly agree (1)	Agree (2)	Neither agree nor disagree (3)	Disagree (4)	Strongly disagree (5)	Can't choose (8)	OFFICE USE ONLY
a. People like me don't have any say about what the government does	☐	☐	☐	☐	☐	☐	3131
b. The average citizen has considerable influence on politics	☐	☐	☐	☐	☐	☐	3132
c. Even the best politician cannot have much impact because of the way government works	☐	☐	☐	☐	☐	☐	3133
d. I feel that I have a pretty good understanding of the important political issues facing our country	☐	☐	☐	☐	☐	☐	3134
e. Elections are a good way of making governments pay attention to what the people think	☐	☐	☐	☐	☐	☐	3135
f. I think most people are better informed about politics and government than I am	☐	☐	☐	☐	☐	☐	3136
g. People we elect as MPs try to keep the promises they have made during the election	☐	☐	☐	☐	☐	☐	3137
h. Most civil servants can be trusted to do what is best for the country	☐	☐	☐	☐	☐	☐	3138

2.15 All in all, how well or badly do you think the system of democracy in Britain works these days?

PLEASE TICK ONE BOX ONLY

It works well and needs no changes ☐ (1)
It works well but needs some changes ☐ (2)
It does not work well and needs a lot of changes ☐ (3)
It does not work well and needs to be completely changed ☐ (4)
Can't choose ☐ (8)

OFFICE USE ONLY 3139

And now some questions about taxes.

2.16 If the government had a choice between reducing taxes or spending more on social services which do you think it should do? (We mean all taxes together, including Income Tax, National Insurance, VAT and all the rest.)

PLEASE TICK ONE BOX ONLY

Reduce taxes, even if this means spending less on social services ☐ (1)

OR

Spend more on social services, even if this means higher taxes? ☐ (2)

Can't choose ☐ (8)

OFFICE USE ONLY 3140

A07

OFFICE USE ONLY

2.17a Generally, how would you describe taxes in Britain today?
First, for those with <u>high</u> incomes, are taxes ...

PLEASE TICK ONE BOX ONLY

(✓)	
... much too high,	(1)
too high,	(2)
about right,	(3)
too low,	(4)
or, are they much too low?	(5)
Can't choose	(8)

3142

b. Next, for those with <u>middle</u> incomes, are taxes ...

PLEASE TICK ONE BOX ONLY

(✓)	
... much too high,	(1)
too high,	(2)
about right,	(3)
too low,	(4)
or, are they much too low?	(5)
Can't choose	(8)

3142

c. Lastly, for those with <u>low</u> incomes, are taxes ...

PLEASE TICK ONE BOX ONLY

(✓)	
... much too high,	(1)
too high,	(2)
about right,	(3)
too low,	(4)
or, are they much too low?	(5)
Can't choose	(8)

3143

INTERNATIONAL SOCIAL SURVEY PROGRAMME

1997 MODULE

WORK ORIENTATIONS II

(ENGLISH LANGUAGE VERSION)

1

1. Suppose you could change the way you spend your time, spending more time on some things and less time on others.

Which of the things on the following list would you like to spend _more_ time on, which would you like to spend _less_ time on and which would you like to spend the _same_ amount of time on as now?

PLEASE TICK ONE BOX ON EACH LINE

	Much more time	A bit more time	Same time as now	A bit less time	Much less time	Can't choose/ Doesn't apply	
	(1)	(2)	(3)	(4)	(5)	(8)	
a. Time in a paid job?	☐	☐	☐	☐	☐	☐	2035
b. Time doing household work?	☐	☐	☐	☐	☐	☐	2036
c. Time with your family?	☐	☐	☐	☐	☐	☐	2037
d. Time with your friends?	☐	☐	☐	☐	☐	☐	2038
e. Time in leisure activities?	☐	☐	☐	☐	☐	☐	2039

2. Please tick one box for _each_ statement below to show how much you agree or disagree with it, thinking of work in general.

PLEASE TICK ONE BOX ON EACH LINE

	Strongly agree	Agree	Neither agree nor disagree	Disagree	Strongly disagree	Can't choose	
	(1)	(2)	(3)	(4)	(5)	(8)	
a. A job is just a way of earning money - no more	☐	☐	☐	☐	☐	☐	2040
b. I would enjoy having a paid job even if I did not need the money	☐	☐	☐	☐	☐	☐	2041
c. Work is a person's most important activity	☐	☐	☐	☐	☐	☐	2042

3. Are _you_ the person responsible for doing the general domestic duties - like cleaning, cooking, washing and so on - in your household?

PLEASE TICK ONE BOX ONLY

Yes, I am _mainly_ responsible ☐ (1)

Yes, I am _equally_ responsible with someone else ☐ (2)

No, _someone else_ is _mainly_ responsible ☐ (3)

2043

2

4. From the following list, please tick one box for _each_ item to show how important _you personally_ think it is in a job.

PLEASE TICK ONE BOX ON EACH LINE

How important is ...	Very important	Important	Neither important nor unimportant	Not important	Not important at all	Can't choose	
	(1)	(2)	(3)	(4)	(5)	(8)	
a. ... job security?	☐	☐	☐	☐	☐	☐	2044
b. ... high income?	☐	☐	☐	☐	☐	☐	2045
c. ... good opportunities for advancement?	☐	☐	☐	☐	☐	☐	2046
d. ... an interesting job?	☐	☐	☐	☐	☐	☐	2047
e. ... a job that allows someone to work independently?	☐	☐	☐	☐	☐	☐	2048
f. ... a job that allows someone to help other people?	☐	☐	☐	☐	☐	☐	2049
g. ... a job that is useful to society?	☐	☐	☐	☐	☐	☐	2050
h. ... a job that allows someone to decide their times or days of work?	☐	☐	☐	☐	☐	☐	2051

5. In deciding on pay for two people doing the same kind of work, how important _should_ be ...

PLEASE TICK ONE BOX ON EACH LINE

	Essential	Very important	Fairly important	Not very important	Not important at all	Can't choose	
	(1)	(2)	(3)	(4)	(5)	(8)	
a. ... how well the person does the job?	☐	☐	☐	☐	☐	☐	2052
b. ... the person's family responsibilities?	☐	☐	☐	☐	☐	☐	2053
c. ... the person's education and formal qualifications?	☐	☐	☐	☐	☐	☐	2054
d. ... how long the person has been with the firm?	☐	☐	☐	☐	☐	☐	2055

6. New kinds of technology are being introduced more and more in Britain: computers, robots, and so on. Do you think these new technologies will over the next few years ...

PLEASE TICK ONE BOX ONLY

... greatly increase the number of jobs, ☐ (1)

... slightly increase the number of jobs, ☐ (2)

... make no difference to the number of jobs, ☐ (3)

... slightly reduce the number of jobs, ☐ (4)

or, greatly reduce the number of jobs? ☐ (5)

Can't choose ☐ (8)

2056

4

10. If you were looking actively, how easy or difficult do you think it would be for you to find an acceptable job?

PLEASE TICK ONE BOX ONLY

Very easy	(1)
Fairly easy	(2)
Neither easy nor difficult	(3)
Fairly difficult	(4)
Very difficult	(5)
Can't choose	(8)

2062

11. Are you currently working for pay?

PLEASE TICK ONE BOX ONLY

Yes	(1)	→ Please answer Q12
No	(2)	→ Please go to Q27

2063

PLEASE ANSWER Q12 - Q26 ABOUT YOUR MAIN JOB

12. Which of the following statements best describes your feelings about your job?

PLEASE TICK ONE BOX ONLY

In my job ...

... I only work as hard as I have to	(1)
... I work hard, but not so that it interferes with the rest of my life	(2)
... I make a point of doing the best work I can, even if it sometimes does interfere with the rest of my life	(3)
Can't choose	(8)

2064

13. Think of the number of hours you work, and the money you earn in your main job, including any regular overtime.

If you had only one of these three choices, which of the following would you prefer?

PLEASE TICK ONE BOX ONLY

Work longer hours and earn more money	(1)
Work the same number of hours and earn the same money	(2)
Work fewer hours and earn less money	(3)
Can't choose	(8)

2065

SPARE 2066-80

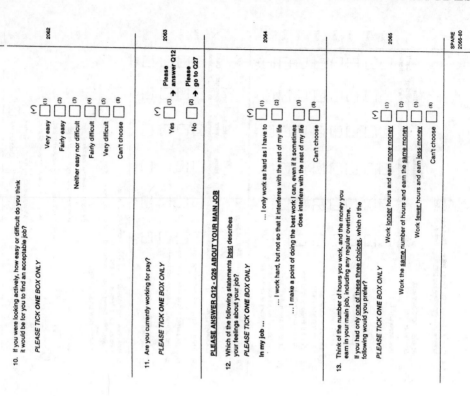

3

7. Do you think that the introduction of new technologies in Britain over the next few years will make work ...

PLEASE TICK ONE BOX ONLY

... much more interesting,	(1)
a little more interesting,	(2)
neither more nor less interesting,	(3)
a little less interesting,	(4)
much less interesting?	(5)
Can't choose	(8)

2057

8. Suppose you were working and could choose between different kinds of job. Which of the following would you personally choose?

a. I would choose ...

PLEASE TICK ONE BOX ONLY

... being an employee	(1)
... being self-employed	(2)
Can't choose	(8)

2058

b. I would choose ...

PLEASE TICK ONE BOX ONLY

... working in a small firm	(1)
... working in a large firm	(2)
Can't choose	(8)

2059

c. I would choose ...

PLEASE TICK ONE BOX ONLY

... working in a private business	(1)
... working for the government or civil service	(2)
Can't choose	(8)

2060

9. Suppose you could decide on your work situation at present. Which of the following would you prefer?

PLEASE TICK ONE BOX ONLY

A full-time job [30 hours or more per week]	(1)
A part-time job [10-29 hours per week]	(2)
A job with less than 10 hours a week	(3)
No paid job at all	(4)

2061

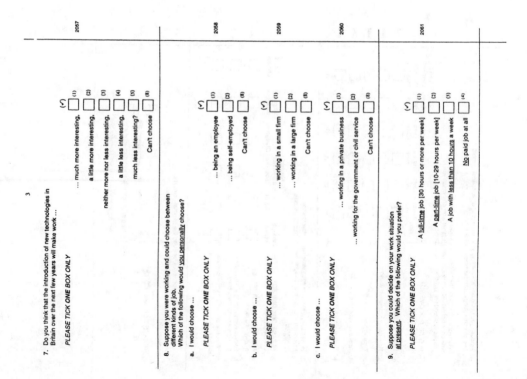

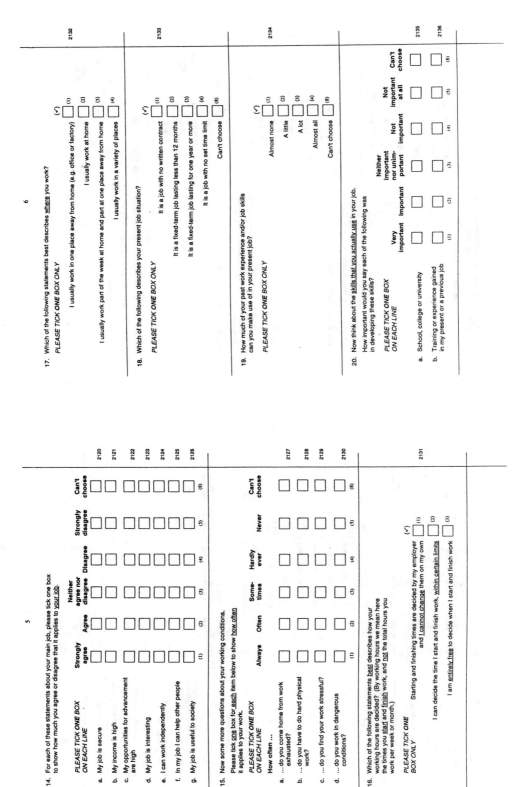

5

14. For each of these statements about your main job, please tick one box to show how much you agree or disagree that it applies to your job.

PLEASE TICK ONE BOX ON EACH LINE

	Strongly agree (1)	Agree (2)	Neither agree nor disagree (3)	Disagree (4)	Strongly disagree (5)	Can't choose (8)
a. My job is secure							2120
b. My income is high							2121
c. My opportunities for advancement are high							2122
d. My job is interesting							2123
e. I can work independently							2124
f. In my job I can help other people							2125
g. My job is useful to society							2126

15. Now some more questions about your working conditions. Please tick one box for each item below to show how often it applies to your work.

PLEASE TICK ONE BOX ON EACH LINE

How often ...

	Always (1)	Often (2)	Some-times (3)	Hardly ever (4)	Never (5)	Can't choose (8)
a. ...do you come home from work exhausted?							2127
b. ...do you have to do hard physical work?							2128
c. ...do you find your work stressful?							2129
d. ...do you work in dangerous conditions?							2130

16. Which of the following statements best describes how your working hours are decided? (By working hours we mean here the times you start and finish work, and not the total hours you work per week or month.)

PLEASE TICK ONE BOX ONLY

- Starting and finishing times are decided by my employer and I cannot change them on my own (1)
- I can decide the time I start and finish work, within certain limits (2)
- I am entirely free to decide when I start and finish work (3)

2131

6

17. Which of the following statements best describes where you work?

PLEASE TICK ONE BOX ONLY

- I usually work in one place away from home (e.g. office or factory) (1)
- I usually work at home (2)
- I usually work part of the week at home and part at one place away from home (3)
- I usually work in a variety of places (4)

2132

18. Which of the following describes your present job situation?

PLEASE TICK ONE BOX ONLY

- It is a job with no written contract (1)
- It is a fixed-term job lasting less than 12 months (2)
- It is a fixed-term job lasting for one year or more (3)
- It is a job with no set time limit (4)
- Can't choose (8)

2133

19. How much of your past work experience and/or job skills can you make use of in your present job?

PLEASE TICK ONE BOX ONLY

- Almost none (1)
- A little (2)
- A lot (3)
- Almost all (4)
- Can't choose (8)

2134

20. Now think about the skills that you actually use in your job. How important would you say each of the following was in developing these skills?

PLEASE TICK ONE BOX ON EACH LINE

	Very Important (1)	Important (2)	Neither important nor unimportant (3)	Not important (4)	Not important at all (5)	Can't choose (8)
a. School, college or university							2135
b. Training or experience gained in my present or a previous job							2136

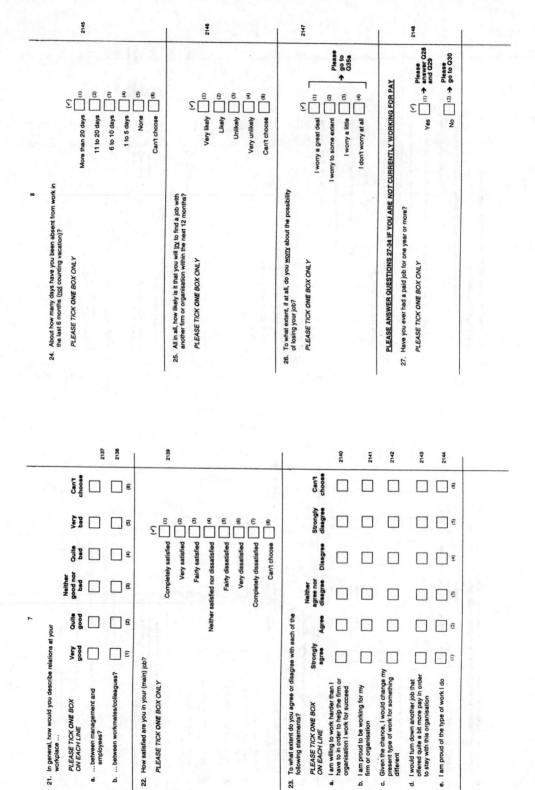

7

21. In general, how would you describe relations at your workplace ...

PLEASE TICK ONE BOX ON EACH LINE

	Very good	Quite good	Neither good nor bad	Quite bad	Very bad	Can't choose	
	(1)	(2)	(3)	(4)	(5)	(8)	
a. ...between management and employees?	☐	☐	☐	☐	☐	☐	2137
b. ...between workmates/colleagues?	☐	☐	☐	☐	☐	☐	2138

22. How satisfied are you in your (main) job?

PLEASE TICK ONE BOX ONLY

- Completely satisfied (1) ☐
- Very satisfied (2) ☐
- Fairly satisfied (3) ☐
- Neither satisfied nor dissatisfied (4) ☐
- Fairly dissatisfied (5) ☐
- Very dissatisfied (6) ☐
- Completely dissatisfied (7) ☐
- Can't choose (8) ☐

2139

23. To what extent do you agree or disagree with each of the following statements?

PLEASE TICK ONE BOX ON EACH LINE

	Strongly agree	Agree	Neither agree nor disagree	Disagree	Strongly disagree	Can't choose	
	(1)	(2)	(3)	(4)	(5)	(8)	
a. I am willing to work harder than I have to in order to help the firm or organisation I work for succeed	☐	☐	☐	☐	☐	☐	2140
b. I am proud to be working for my firm or organisation	☐	☐	☐	☐	☐	☐	2141
c. Given the chance, I would change my present type of work for something different	☐	☐	☐	☐	☐	☐	2142
d. I would turn down another job that offered quite a bit more pay in order to stay with this organisation	☐	☐	☐	☐	☐	☐	2143
e. I am proud of the type of work I do	☐	☐	☐	☐	☐	☐	2144

8

24. About how many days have you been absent from work in the last 6 months (not counting vacation)?

PLEASE TICK ONE BOX ONLY

- More than 20 days (1) ☐
- 11 to 20 days (2) ☐
- 6 to 10 days (3) ☐
- 1 to 5 days (4) ☐
- None (5) ☐
- Can't choose (8) ☐

2145

25. All in all, how likely is it that you will try to find a job with another firm or organisation within the next 12 months?

PLEASE TICK ONE BOX ONLY

- Very likely (1) ☐
- Likely (2) ☐
- Unlikely (3) ☐
- Very unlikely (4) ☐
- Can't choose (8) ☐

2146

26. To what extent, if at all, do you worry about the possibility of losing your job?

PLEASE TICK ONE BOX ONLY

- I worry a great deal (1) ☐
- I worry to some extent (2) ☐
- I worry a little (3) ☐ — Please go to Q35a
- I don't worry at all (4) ☐

2147

PLEASE ANSWER QUESTIONS 27-34 IF YOU ARE NOT CURRENTLY WORKING FOR PAY

27. Have you ever had a paid job for one year or more?

PLEASE TICK ONE BOX ONLY

- Yes (1) → Please answer Q28 and Q29
- No (2) → Please go to Q30

2148

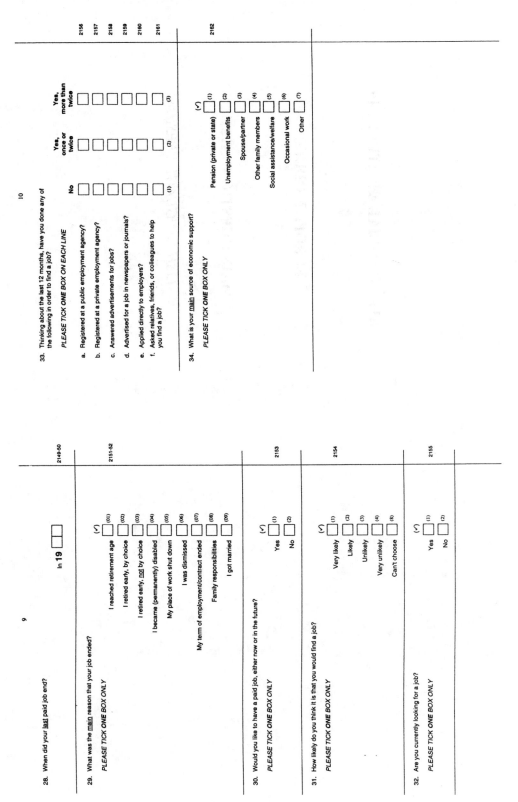

10

33. Thinking about the last 12 months, have you done any of the following in order to find a job?

PLEASE TICK ONE BOX ON EACH LINE

	No	Yes, once or twice	Yes, more than twice	
	(1)	(2)	(3)	
a. Registered at a public employment agency?	□	□	□	2156
b. Registered at a private employment agency?	□	□	□	2157
c. Answered advertisements for jobs?	□	□	□	2158
d. Advertised for a job in newspapers or journals?	□	□	□	2159
e. Applied directly to employers?	□	□	□	2160
f. Asked relatives, friends, or colleagues to help you find a job?	□	□	□	2161

34. What is your main source of economic support?

PLEASE TICK ONE BOX ONLY

Pension (private or state) □ (1)
Unemployment benefits □ (2)
Spouse/partner □ (3)
Other family members □ (4)
Social assistance/welfare □ (5)
Occasional work □ (6)
Other □ (7)

2162

9

28. When did your last job end?

In 19 ☐☐   2149-50

29. What was the main reason that your job ended?

PLEASE TICK ONE BOX ONLY

I reached retirement age □ (01)
I retired early, by choice □ (02)
I retired early, not by choice □ (03)
I became (permanently) disabled □ (04)
My place of work shut down □ (05)
I was dismissed □ (06)
My term of employment/contract ended □ (07)
Family responsibilities □ (08)
I got married □ (09)

2151-52

30. Would you like to have a paid job, either now or in the future?

PLEASE TICK ONE BOX ONLY

Yes □ (1)
No □ (2)

2153

31. How likely do you think it is that you would find a job?

PLEASE TICK ONE BOX ONLY

Very likely □ (1)
Likely □ (2)
Unlikely □ (3)
Very unlikely □ (4)
Can't choose □ (5)

2154

32. Are you currently looking for a job?

PLEASE TICK ONE BOX ONLY

Yes □ (1)
No □ (2)

2155

BRITISH SOCIAL ATTITUDES 1997

EUROPE MODULE

MAIN QUESTIONNAIRE

(ENGLISH LANGUAGE VERSION)

British Social Attitudes 1997
Europe Module

IF READS A DAILY NEWSPAPER AT LEAST THREE TIMES A WEEK

Q305 *[EUPaper]*
I'd now like to turn to some questions about the European Union (sometimes still called the European Community).
How much do you think **you yourself** get to know about Britain's relations with the European Union from *(paper given)*. Do you get to know ... **READ OUT** ...

1 a lot about Britain's relations with the EU,
2 quite a bit,
3 very little,
4 or, nothing at all?
8 (Don't Know)
9 (Refusal/NA)

IF 'a lot', 'quite a bit' OR 'very little' AT [EUPaper]

Q306 *[EUPapSde]*
Say there is an argument between Britain and the European Union.
On the whole, do you think that *(paper given)* .. **READ OUT** ...

1 usually sides with Britain,
2 usually sides with the rest of Europe,
3 or, usually gives equal weight to both sides?
8 (Don't Know)
9 (Refusal/NA)

ASK ALL

Q307 *[EEC]*
Do you think Britain should continue to be a member of the European Union or should it withdraw?

1 Continue
2 Withdraw
8 (Don't Know)
9 (Refusal/NA)

Q308 *[EUTenYrs]*
Regardless of what you think should happen, do you think that Britain will actually ... **READ OUT** ...

1 leave the EU within the next ten years or so,
2 or, stay in the EU?
8 (Don't Know)
9 (Refusal/NA)

Q309 *[EULinks]*
Regardless of whether Britain leaves or stays in, do you think that the other European Union members .. **READ OUT** ...

1 will gradually strengthen their links within the EU,
2 will stay more or less as they are,
3 or, will gradually weaken their links within the EU?
7 Other **(WRITE IN)**
8 (Don't Know)
9 (Refusal/NA)

Q311 *[ECLnkInf]*
Do you think that closer links with the European Union would give Britain .. **READ OUT** ...

1 **more** influence in the world,
2 **less** influence in the world,
3 or, would it make no difference?
8 (Don't Know)
9 (Refusal/NA)

Q312 *[ECLnkStr]*
And would closer links with the European Union make Britain .. **READ OUT** ...

1 **stronger** economically,
2 **weaker** economically,
3 or, would it make no difference?
8 (Don't Know)
9 (Refusal/NA)

Q313 *[ECPolicy]*
CARD
Do you think Britain's long-term policy should be to .. **READ OUT** ...

1 leave the European Union,
2 stay in the EU and try to **reduce** the EU's powers,
3 leave things as they are,
4 stay in the EU and try to **increase** the EU's powers,
5 or, work for the formation of a single European government?
8 (Don't Know)
9 (Refusal/NA)

Q314 [EUFeder]

IF RESPONSE AT [ECPolicy] (I.E. NOT DK/Refusal)
CARD
Which of the two statements on this card comes closer to your own view about Britain's future in the European Union.
On the whole, do you think that ... READ OUT AND SHOW CARD ...

1 Britain should help the EU turn into a closer political and economic union,
2 or, Britain should help the EU turn into a trading bloc alone?
3 (Neither)
4 (Britain should leave the EU)
7 Other (WRITE IN)
8 (Don't Know)
9 (Refusal/NA)

ASK ALL
Q316 [ECUView]
CARD
Here are three statements about the future of the pound in the European Union. Which done comes closest to your view?

1 Replace the pound by a single currency
2 Use both the pound and a new European currency in Britain
3 Keep the pound as the only currency for Britain
8 (Don't Know)
9 (Refusal/NA)

Q317 [ECUFut]
CARD
Regardless of what you would like to happen, what do you think will happen within the next five years or so?

1 The pound will be replaced by a single currency
2 Both the pound and a new European currency will be used in Britain
3 The pound will be kept as the only currency for Britain
8 (Don't Know)
9 (Refusal/NA)

Q318 [EuroUnem] *
CARD
Just suppose there were to be a single currency, with all member nations replacing their own currency with the new 'Euro'. Please choose a phrase from this card to say how much you agree or disagree that, if the pound were replaced by the new 'Euro' ...
unemployment in Britain would become higher?

Q319 [EuroMort] *
CARD AGAIN
(How much do you agree or disagree that, if the pound were replaced with the new 'Euro',)
mortgage rates in Britain would become lower?

Q320 [EuroTax] *
CARD AGAIN
(How much do you agree or disagree that, if the pound were replaced with the new 'Euro',)
Britain would lose its ability to decide its own tax and spending plans?

Q321 [EuroTrde] *
CARD AGAIN
(How much do you agree or disagree that, if the pound were replaced with the new 'Euro',)
Britain would be able to trade in Europe more successfully?

* [EuroUnem] to [EuroTrde]
1 Agree strongly
2 Agree
3 Neither agree nor disagree
4 Disagree
5 Disagree strongly
8 (Don't Know)
9 (Refusal/NA)

Q322 [EUQuiz1] *
Now a quick quiz about Europe.
For each thing I say, please say whether you think it is true or false. If you don't know, just say so and we will skip to the next one. Remember, true, false, or don't know.
The European Union now has 15 member countries

Q323 [EUQuiz2] *
(True, false, or don't know?)
Hungary has applied to join the European Union

Q324 [EUQuiz3] *
(True, false, or don't know?)
Britain's income tax rates are decided in Brussels

Q325 [EUQuiz4] *
(True, false, or don't know?)
Elections to the European Parliament are held every 5 years

Q326 [EUQuiz5] *
(True, false, or don't know?)
Norway is a member of the European Union

Q327 [EUQuiz6] *
(True, false, or don't know?)
Britain doesn't have any European Commissioners at the moment

[EUQuiz1] to [EUQuiz6]
* True
1 False
8 (Don't Know)
9 (Refusal/NA)

Q328 [EUPtyWin]
CARD AGAIN
Please use this card to say how much you agree or disagree with this statement.
It doesn't really matter which party wins the next general election, Britain's relations with the EU will stay much the same.
1 Agree strongly
2 Agree
3 Neither agree nor disagree
4 Disagree
5 Disagree strongly
8 (Don't Know)
9 (Refusal/NA)

Q329 [EUConPol] *
As far as you know, is Conservative Party policy in favour of ... READ OUT ...

Q330 [EULabPol] *
And Labour Party policy? As far as you know, is it in favour of...READ OUT ...

Q331 [EULibPol] *
And Liberal Democrat Party policy? As far as you know, is it in favour of ... READ OUT ...

[EUConPol] to [EULibPol]
*
1 closer links with the EU than now,
2 less close links,
3 or, of keeping things much the same as they are now?
8 (Don't Know)
9 (Refusal/NA)

BRITISH SOCIAL ATTITUDES 1997

EUROPE MODULE

SELF-COMPLETION QUESTIONNAIRE

(ENGLISH LANGUAGE VERSION)

41. Please tick one box for each of these statements about the European Union to show how much you agree or disagree.

PLEASE TICK ONE BOX
ON EACH LINE

	Agree strongly	Agree	Neither agree nor disagree	Disagree	Disagree strongly	Can't choose
a. All passport controls between countries in the EU should be removed	☐	☐	☐	☐	☐	☐
b. The competition from the other EU countries is making Britain more modern and efficient	☐	☐	☐	☐	☐	☐
c. One of the good things about belonging to the EU is that it makes Britain more open to new ideas and cultures	☐	☐	☐	☐	☐	☐
	(1)	(2)	(3)	(4)	(5)	(8)

42. Some say that more decisions should be made by the European Union. Others say that more decisions should be made by individual governments. For each of the following, do you think that decisions should mostly be made by the European Union or mostly by individual governments?

PLEASE TICK ONE BOX
ON EACH LINE

	Mostly made by the European Union	Mostly made by individual governments	Made by both equally	Can't choose
a. Decisions about taxes?	☐	☐	☐	☐
b. And what about decisions about controlling pollution?	☐	☐	☐	☐
c. Decisions about defence?	☐	☐	☐	☐
d. Decisions about the rights of people at work?	☐	☐	☐	☐
e. Decisions about immigration?	☐	☐	☐	☐
f. Funding scientific research?	☐	☐	☐	☐
g. How much farmers should produce?	☐	☐	☐	☐
h. How to stop drug trafficking?	☐	☐	☐	☐
	(1)	(2)	(3)	(8)

43. Some big decisions could be made either by the MPs we elect to parliament, or by everyone having a say in a special vote or referendum.
For example, who should make the decision about whether or not Britain should replace the pound by a single European currency? Should the decision be made ...

PLEASE TICK ONE BOX ONLY

... by elected MPs in parliament, ☐ (1)
OR
by everyone in a referendum? ☐ (2)

Can't choose ☐ (8)

44. When Britain asks to be treated differently from the rest of the EU, in your view does this generally ...

PLEASE TICK ONE BOX ONLY

... help Britain's long-term interests in the EU, ☐ (1)
harm Britain's long-term interests in the EU, ☐ (2)
or, doesn't it make much difference? ☐ (3)
Can't choose ☐ (8)

45. How important or unimportant do you think it is for people in Britain that ...

PLEASE TICK ONE BOX
ON EACH LINE

	Very important	Fairly important	Not very important	Not at all important	Can't choose
a. ... they are free to get jobs in any other EU countries?	☐	☐	☐	☐	☐
b. ... they are able to take their cases to the European Court of Justice, which can override decisions of British courts?	☐	☐	☐	☐	☐
c. ... Britain is able to sell its goods anywhere else in the EU without paying customs duties?	☐	☐	☐	☐	☐
	(1)	(2)	(3)	(4)	(5)

46. Which of these two statements comes closer to your views?

PLEASE TICK ONE BOX ONLY

Workers in Britain should have the same protection as other EU workers against being made to work very long hours ☐ (1)
OR
The EU has no business deciding how many hours a week workers in Britain should work ☐ (2)

Can't choose ☐ (8)

47. Which of these two statements comes closer to your views?

PLEASE TICK ONE BOX ONLY

The British government should sign up to the Social Chapter so that British workers have the same rights at work as everyone else in Europe ☐ (1)
OR
It should always be up to the British government, not the European Union, to decide what rights British workers should have ☐ (2)

Can't choose ☐ (8)

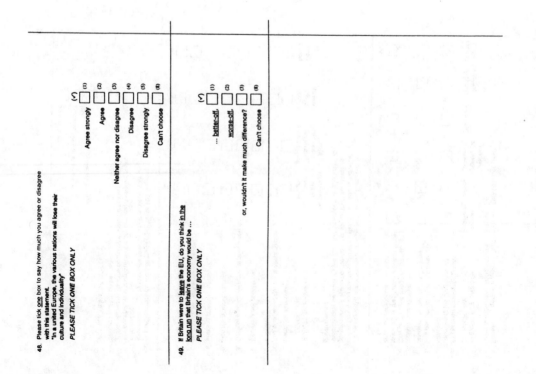

48. Please tick one box to say how much you agree or disagree with this statement.

"In a united Europe, the various nations will lose their culture and individuality"

PLEASE TICK ONE BOX ONLY

(✓)

Agree strongly ☐ (1)

Agree ☐ (2)

Neither agree nor disagree ☐ (3)

Disagree ☐ (4)

Disagree strongly ☐ (5)

Can't choose ☐ (8)

49. If Britain were to leave the EU, do you think in the long run that Britain's economy would be ...

PLEASE TICK ONE BOX ONLY

(✓)

... better-off, ☐ (1)

worse-off, ☐ (2)

or, wouldn't it make much difference? ☐ (3)

Can't choose ☐ (8)

Subject index